MAKING THINGS AND DRAWING BOUNDARIES

DEBATES IN THE DIGITAL HUMANITIES

*Matthew K. Gold and Lauren F. Klein, Series Editors*

# MAKING THINGS *and* DRAWING BOUNDARIES

## EXPERIMENTS IN THE DIGITAL HUMANITIES

**Jentery Sayers**
**EDITOR**

DEBATES IN THE DIGITAL HUMANITIES

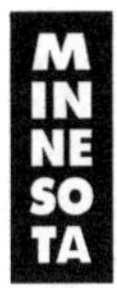


*University of Minnesota Press*
*Minneapolis*
*London*

Published by the University of Minnesota Press
111 Third Avenue South, Suite 290
Minneapolis, MN 55401-2520
http://www.upress.umn.edu

ISSN: 2380-5935
ISBN 978-1-5179-0284-1 (hc)
ISBN 978-1-5179-0285-8 (pb)

Printed in the United States of America on acid-free paper



24 23 22 21 20 19 18 17 10 9 8 7 6 5 4 3 2 1

*This book is dedicated to everyone who worked with me at the MLab to prototype the past: Nina Belojevic, Teddie Brock, Tiffany Chan, Patrick Close, Nicole Clouston, Laura Dosky, Katherine Goertz, Jonathan O. Johnson, Fiona Keenan, Maasa Lebus, Evan Locke, Shaun Macpherson, Kaitlynn McQueston, Danielle Morgan, Victoria Murawski, Nadia Timperio, Zaqir Virani, and Karly Wilson. It was all a kludge in the best possible way. I'm sorry we never made those lab coats.*

*Contents*

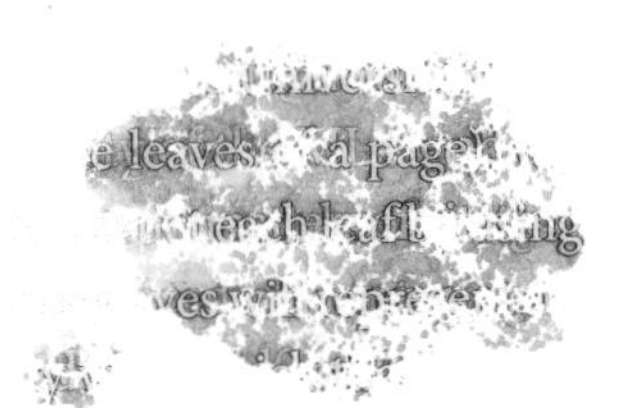

*Introduction*

# "I Don't Know All the Circuitry"

JENTERY SAYERS

"Well, I don't know all the circuitry, but I can do first aid," said artist Laurie Anderson in October 1981. She was responding to Rob La Frenais, who asked her a few questions about hardware (in La Frenais 140). By 1981, Anderson had worked extensively with technologies as art forms. In 1977, she built a tape bow violin with Bob Bielecki. Substituting magnetic tape for horsehair and a tape head for a bridge, she bowed audio, distorting it by playing canned sounds forward and backward across a range of speeds (Collins 50). Her approach transformed a recording and playback technology into a creative expression, and her style resonated with turntable experiments by Kool Herc, Grand Wizzard Theodore, and Grandmaster Flash. Later, just before her interview with La Frenais, Anderson also released the popular single, "O Superman" (1981), a minimalist composition driven by a harmonizer and vocoder. She used the vocoder to synthesize her voice and the harmonizer to loop the syllable "ha" throughout the eight-minute track. Combining these two technologies, she performed alone yet polyvocally, as a chorus of one.

Today, Anderson is widely recognized for her innovative media systems; hence the modest irony of "I can do first aid." Despite her expansive familiarity with technologies, she makes no claims to understand them all the way down. She starts in the middle, experiments, and anticipates inevitable moments of surprise.[1] "If I'm on tour and a machine breaks down," she said, "I have to know something about that machine so I can fix it" (in La Frenais 139). For Anderson, technology becomes extremely alienating if you cannot repair it.[2] Of course, there is an artist's spin here. Anderson keeps the machine running—keeps it breathing "ha ha ha ha"—but is reluctant to identify as a technician. While she resists delegating significant choices to technologies, professing to know all the circuitry risks a certain purism. She worries, too, about programming her performances for push-button delivery across settings, even if some prerecorded components repeat in a loop: "ha ha ha ha . . ."[3] Anderson lets technologies run in the background, and she does not. Her systems are neither fully automated nor devoid of hiccups, demonstrating how what we might call matter—machine, instrument, circuitry, hardware, vocoder, harmonizer, tape, bow—we might also call a *negotiation,* always in the making.

Anderson's treatment of technologies as negotiations is palpable when we account for the context of "O Superman." The song and its title are a commentary on Operation Eagle Claw (April 1980), when U.S. Armed Forces attempted to release staff from the U.S. embassy in Tehran. In November 1979, the embassy was occupied by the Muslim Student Followers of the Imam's Line, a group who wanted to prevent the United States from restoring Shah Mohammad Reza Pahlavi to his throne (Rieffer-Flanagan 149). In 2016, Anderson said the following to music critic Dave Simpson:

> In 1979, Iranian students stormed the US embassy in Tehran. America went blazing in with helicopters to get the hostages out. But it backfired majorly. A helicopter and a plane crashed in the desert. We were left with dead bodies, a pile of burning debris and the hostages nowhere to be seen. So I thought I'd write a song about all that and the failure of technology (in Simpson).

Here, failure is not simply a technical matter. Technology also fails when exerted as a force: in this instance, the jingoist aggression of the United States blazing to rescue its own, with its own, from others. "Here come the planes," sings Anderson. "They're American planes. Made in America." Such force is symbolic, represented by aircraft and eagle's claws. It is real, leaving behind dead bodies and debris. And it is affective; in "O Superman," it is an embrace that feels more like toxicity than care. Anderson said, "The lyrics are a one-sided conversation" (in Simpson), and they conclude with, "So hold me, Mom, in your long arms, your petrochemical arms, your military arms, in your electronic arms." With this closing gesture, she highlights how U.S. aggression is personified, gendered, and maternalized to code patriarchal force as protection, or to make a one-way conversation feel as if someone loving is listening. "I can do first aid" thus assumes a new valence: "O Superman" intervenes in the failure of force with creative critique. Instead of reducing technologies to their technical particulars, vulgar symbolism, or instrumental effects, Anderson shows how entwined technologies are with lives and living—with matters of aid and shared concern.[4]

For a series such as *Debates in the Digital Humanities* (of which this volume is a part), Anderson's art and commentary are important because they remind us that technologies are not "withdrawn" from interactions even if they are frequently fetishized as noumenal objects outside phenomena.[5] To say, "I can do first aid," is to underscore our *entanglement* with circuitry.[6] And to say, "I don't know all the circuitry," at least implies the impossibility of such knowledge. That is, we can reject the autonomy or privacy of technologies without supposing we know them completely. Although we may understand how something works, we may not apprehend how or under what conditions it was made.[7] It and interactions with it will change across settings, and together they will influence matters of perception and epistemology over time. Still, knowledge of circuitry is often conflated with (superheroic) command over people, situations, and things. In present-day "maker" cultures, consider the ubiquity of remarks such as "getting under the hood" or "knowing the nuts and bolts," which tend to fuse logic with mastery, control with masculinity, engineering with rationality, and programming with revealing.[8] This volume works against these norms and assumptions.

## *The Conceptual Matter of This Volume*

As a negotiation, technology is about desire and power first and foremost,[9] even when we play, tinker, experiment, or make.[10] Like the archives we study, technologies are never neutral or transparent. They, too, are replete with hiccups and ambiguities. Yet these indeterminacies are active, not inert, in the making of things.[11] They are features of a given system or infrastructure, and they are material as well. They are what, throughout this introduction, I call *conceptual matter*, and—most relevant to the aims of this volume—they comprise the core of creative and critical responsibility: what may not be obvious or visible to some but demands reference and communication. In that October 1981 interview with La Frenais, Anderson said, "My work is about what happens when you pick up the phone and try to get through" (139).[12] From this position, technology is but an *attempt* at communication, brimming with chance mediation and filters, or rife with indeterminacies most likely ignored in the interests of time, efficiency, or scope. Putting two points in touch may also require a patch or fix, and Anderson is deeply aware of how much labor such maintenance demands.[13]

For example, in 1989 she released "The Dream Before," dedicated to Walter Benjamin. The song's second half is drawn almost verbatim from Benjamin's ninth thesis "On the Concept of History" (1940). The angel of history is blown backward into the future by a storm called progress, with a pile of debris growing before him.[14] His impulse is to return and mend—to "make whole what has been smashed" into catastrophe (Benjamin 392).[15] But the parts will never be made whole. History, or the work of history, will never be complete. The circuitry of the past will never be known all the way down, and its context will never be fully recovered from the stuff at hand.[16] In both "The Dream Before" and the ninth thesis, there is nevertheless a desire to arrest the fragments of history from the predictable trajectories of "once upon a time" tales to examine them fastidiously against their inscription in narratives of progress.[17] Perhaps ironically, stewarding materials into the present—transmitting a thesis from 1940 through a phone call in 1981, for instance—is the closest we may come to such an arrest, even if some context is lost in the recontextualization. Although tangible materials may outlast the ephemerality of lived reality, they still address us and require constant care—restoration, remediation, reformatting, upgrading, and migration—to persist.[18] During these rather quotidian processes, they enter into new relations over and over again. Put this way, interpretation with and through technologies may be closer to maintenance or "remaking" than romantic invention, individual genius, or even critical distance.[19] Not only does it happen in the middle, with influence from the interpreter; at its most persuasive, it also refuses to impose a chain of events on what came before it or what may come after. Compelling interpretations thus *sustain conversations* with collections of materials against prescription or push-button delivery, letting those materials surprise us without controlling them or isolating them from interaction.

True, this approach to interpretation and technology may be too elliptical for many digital humanities practitioners, especially those who are deeply invested in making things "on the ground" or "where the rubber meets the road." It does not sound as epic as innovation, as grand as big data, as impactful as disruption, or as concrete as tool-building, either. However, it may most accurately describe both our everyday engagements with technologies and the physical reality of our materials: *not made from scratch but in media res; not transparent platforms but patchworks of memory and practice.* From third-party dependencies and plug-ins to emulations and repurposed hardware, starting in the middle is not some abstract idea cooked up by critics and artists on high. Negotiation and maintenance constitute the conceptual matter that makes up making.

In fact, conceptual matter weaves together the chapters collected here. It represents the inability to unmoor materials from how we interpret materials. It is what Karen Barad (2007) calls an "apparatus" that entwines subjects with objects (19–20, 114–115), or what McKenzie Wark (2015) calls a "realist media theory" that "engag[es] closely with practices and their particular points of view" (158). In this case, it is not about broken worlds, ideal worlds, or the withdrawn worlds of objects.[20] It is about the desire for continuity and persistence amidst storms of progress and states of constant change: the circuitry of values and patterns, perhaps difficult to perceive or apprehend, that converts fragments into a narrative, or parts into a whole.

Conceptual matter may be considered an "invisible" space between parts: a "gap" that may invite a patch. "I have to know something about that machine so I can fix it," said Anderson (in La Frenais 139). However, conceptual matter is more accurately described as a boundary-making process (e.g., between old and new, broken and repaired, or this and that).[21] Like the activity of blank spaces in Stéphane Mallarmé's *A Throw of the Dice Will Never Abolish Chance* (1897), conceptual matter is a gerund: designing, shaping, sculpting, stitching, or inscribing lines. Although it may feel abstract, it is quite material and no doubt embodied. Although it strikes us as a noun, it is ultimately about dynamics. It is, for instance, the apparatus of exploded view diagrams, which visualize how components relate and form a whole.[22] Before I proceed, allow me to elaborate for a moment.

Dating back to at least the fourteenth century, exploded view diagrams are documentations of how we start in the middle. They are consulted during processes of assembly: putting together IKEA furniture or a LEGO set, for example. They are

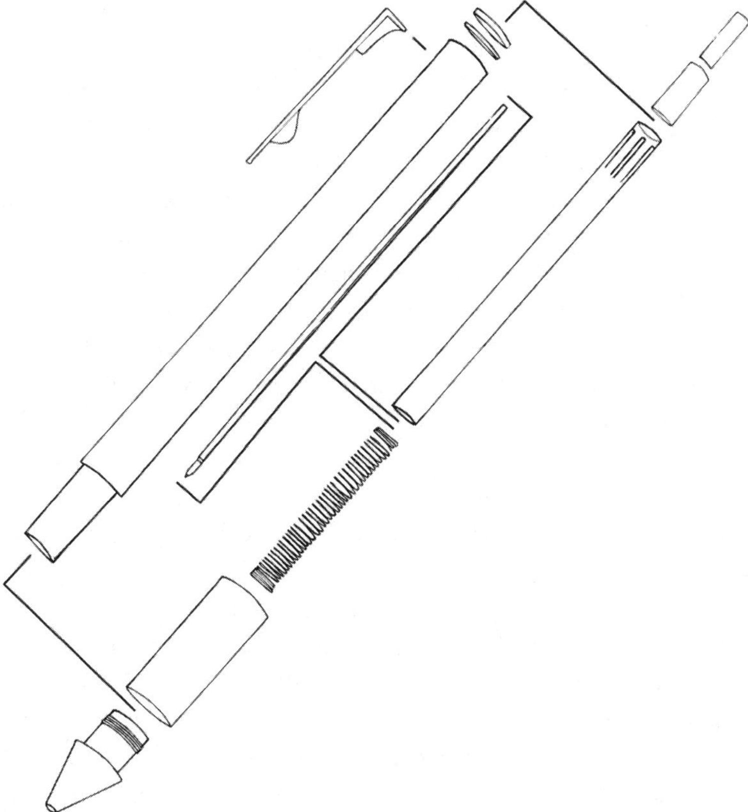

**Figure I.1.** Exploded view diagram of a pen. Illustration by Danielle Morgan

also consulted during moments of maintenance, when we do not know the circuitry but need to keep the machine running. Instances abound in disciplines such as engineering and architecture, but here is an example (Figure I.1), illustrated by artist Danielle Morgan.

One problem with exploded view diagrams is that they are usually premised on "kit-of-parts" construction, where—much like the storm of progress—an ideal form prescribes the assembly of "discrete components that function as modular parts within a coherent system" (Perner-Wilson 6). In her critique of this approach, Hannah Perner-Wilson (2011) adds, "These parts have been optimized for speed, efficiency, and repeatability of assembly" (6).[23] They are creativity in a box: prescribed workflows and prefabbed systems disseminated for uniform use. What is needed, then, are opportunities to re-signify the conceptual matter of assembly and maintenance as an indeterminacy, not a given. This way, both assembly and maintenance are interpretive practices or negotiations instead of how-to scripts. Along these lines, consider an exploded view from the arts.

In a gallery, Cornelia Parker's *Cold Dark Matter: An Exploded View* (1991) suspends the contents of a mundane garden shed blown up by the British Army. Audiences may examine the surface details of the fire-damaged fragments, including charred pieces of the shed's frame as well as the warped tools, toys, and other quotidian objects around it.[24] Yet the conceptual matter of Parker's work is far more suggestive, as it holds the fragments in suspended animation. Distinctions between exterior and interior are replaced by a hovering constellation of pieces, as spaces point to spectral moments in a past event, now arrested in time in a gallery.[25] How did the shed explode? With what sort of force? After it all occurred, why were the pieces arranged this way? Rather than confirming the cause or meaning of Parker's installation, these questions encourage the indeterminacies, and the exploded view becomes a time-stamped collection of ambiguous relations, not a diagram of how the system or form got this way. Many chapters in this volume engage how to make things with such ambiguities in mind, or how to convey scholarship (across software, hardware, interfaces, installations, and essays) as conceptual matter for ongoing change and intervention.

Yet, while the "dark matter" in Parker's title refers simultaneously to fire-damaged fragments and the conceptual matter across them, it carries different meanings elsewhere. In *Dark Matters: On the Surveillance of Blackness,* Simone Browne (2015) notes that dark matter is a theoretical or conceptual term usually articulated in a "planetary sense": "its distribution cannot be measured; its properties cannot be determined; and so it remains undetectable" (9). But dark matter is also a way to approach race (9). Browne refers to the work of Howard Winant (2012), who observes that "race remains *dark matter,* the invisible substance that in many ways structures the universe of modernity" (Winant 605). She then responds to Winant's observation with, "invisible to whom? If [dark matter / race] is often invisible, then how is it sensed, experienced, and lived? Is it really invisible, or is it rather unseen and unperceived by many?" (9). In the context of today's technologies, for example, race and dark matter structure supply chains, as children of color in the Democratic Republic of the Congo mine for cobalt, which is a core element of lithium-ion batteries used to power mobile phones (Amnesty 4–6, 28–31). This labor is willfully ignored or "unseen" by consumers around the world, even though it supports countless routine communications.

Echoing Browne's terminology, such ignorance is enabled by "prototypical whiteness" (26, 92, 113–14), which "sees whiteness, or lightness, as privileged in enrollment, measurement, and recognition processes, and . . . is reliant upon dark matter for its own meaning" (162). Prototypical whiteness may manifest technically in infrastructure (e.g., how computer vision algorithms for face detection validate whiteness in relation to blackness),[26] but also in how technologies are interpreted and embedded in contexts, with whiteness as the default setting for cultural reproduction. Across technical and cultural materials—through machines, actions, and ideologies—prototypical whiteness is complicit with structural racism. It profoundly shapes interpretation, and it operates as the basis upon which most technologies are sourced and maintained. From this perspective, not knowing all the circuitry reflects white privilege and supremacy: for instance, the habitual act of ignoring how dark matter is entangled with the elements of everyday devices;[27] of not considering the differences between who gets to make, who must mine, or who has to care; of not seeing labor in the exploded view; of saying "all lives matter" to dismiss the lived realities of racism entwined with our technologies. In the epilogue of her book, Browne underscores the subversive potential of how "dark matter troubles algorithms" and surveillance technologies (163). Following her research, humanities projects could unlearn and deprogram prototypical whiteness by transforming praxis as an *apparatus*—by changing the language, habits, relations, technologies, infrastructures, and spaces for making. Instead of focusing such changes on white guilt, which may only further white supremacy, practitioners could yield the floor to the social justice, decolonization, and intersectional methodologies at work in the circuits of collectives such as *#TransformDH, AbTeC, FemTechNet,* and *HASTAC* as well as projects like *Diaspora Hypertext* (by Jessica Marie Johnson), not to mention various chapters in this volume.

Such interventions are increasingly important, as the creative and critical methods of Browne, Parker, Benjamin, and Anderson are not common in the maker cultures or makerspaces of our present moment. In this sense, the conceptual matter of the following chapters does not align with, say, Chris Anderson's *Makers* (2012) or Mark Hatch's *The Maker Movement Manifesto* (2014).[28] This volume not only critiques the normative assumptions and effects of popular maker cultures—usually white, cisgender, straight, male, and able-bodied—but also conveys different histories and paradigms of making, including those associated with the arts, writing, design, fashion, history, libraries, museums, cultural studies, archaeology, experimental media, feminism, and activism, none of which especially concerns the evangelist entrepreneurialism of Anderson and Hatch. One result of these critiques and alternatives is some healthy skepticism about how maker cultures manifest both on and off academic campuses. Another is research demonstrating how making is or can be critical: how, for instance, it may examine questions of labor, justice, ethics, and participation. And yet another is an emphasis on social relations against the reduction of technologies and culture to technical matters. A significant portion of this work stresses the spaces and interfaces for material experimentation, including makerspaces and projects that do not adhere to the maker norm. Across the chapters, there is also a pervasive sense that *not knowing all the circuitry may actually spark persuasive interventions from the periphery,* altering people's expectations of making in and beyond the humanities. We see, for instance, creative and critical research involving circuit bending, tinkering, prototyping, and participatory design, each of which relies on trial-and-error experimentation and multiple forms of feedback. When these approaches are combined with more established methods in the humanities (e.g., deconstruction, historiography, bibliography, translation, and fieldwork), the results produce evocative interactions with the indeterminacies and conceptual matters that humanists tend to study.

While not all of the authors in this volume agree on a definition of "making" (or even care much for the term), and although the methods and domains shift from chapter to chapter, each contribution shares a tendency toward speculation or unlearning rather than proving or "wrangling" things with technologies. If technology is a negotiation, then it is also inquiry for these authors. Even when the chapters get technical, they are most invested in the granularity of interpretation. But perhaps most important, the research presented here exhibits an intricate awareness of how making and scholarship start in the middle. With each chapter, *we witness partial knowledge and situated relations with materials,*[29] the sort of approach that keeps conversations going against the hubris of mastery and the force of progress. We also witness how conceptual matter—or the inability to unmoor materials from how we interpret materials—demarcates this from that and thus puts them into relation. "*It's all a matter of where we place the cut,*" writes Barad (348). Below are six such demarcations of potential interest to readers of this volume.

### *Demarcations in This Volume*

In the following pages, we see boundaries drawn and cuts made with the logic of visibility—between what is seen or superficial and what is unseen or hidden: "front end" and "back end," containers and processors, content and metadata, interfaces and source code. Even if these components are fused and networked together in messy ways, they are usually parsed for reasons of intelligibility and tangibility. Yet many chapters in this volume are interested precisely in the mess and what it tells us about the epistemologies and phenomenologies of material experimentation. Within the context of experimentation, we also see distinctions between communities of practice: artists, architects, designers, content experts, writers, editors, librarians, curators, teachers, programmers, developers, managers, and so on. In reality, people tend to perform multiple identities within these communities, or—as many of the following chapters show—they collaborate across them. Still, lines are repeatedly drawn in and beyond the academy, with a bias toward individual qualifications and experience over collective expertise.

Such lines manifest, too, as demarcations between disciplines: the arts, humanities, social sciences, engineering, and sciences, for example. While this volume represents work from each discipline as well as non-/para-academic work (often with transdisciplinary and trans-sector concerns in mind), most of its contributors occupy a specific discipline or occupation with particular expectations anchored in recognizable practices and points of view. Here, how work counts, or how it is validated, depends in part on the cuts made between media or formats: from software, hardware, installations, interfaces, data, film, audio, images, and paper to PDF, DOCX, XML, MP3, HTML, TXT, JPG, OBJ, STL, PY, JS, and 16mm. In the following chapters, materials are expressed across this list; nonetheless, the legibility of a given project frequently depends on community preferences for specific media and formats. Of course, legibility is intricately linked to audience. How and for whom is work communicated? In what context? Through which definitions of community or public? As these chapters suggest, research involving technologies almost always speaks to multiple audiences, with shifts in modes and means depending on settings and expectations. Who or what matters will shift, too, as material experimentation heightens practitioner awareness of the entanglements between circuitry and meaning.

Finally, this volume is replete with boundaries drawn by labor: between thinking and doing, hacking and yacking, writing and building, scholarship and service, creating and critiquing, breaking and repairing, innovation and maintenance, and making and not making. Such boundaries mark how and where value is attributed and accrued. They also correspond with ideologies and environments for who gets to make, who can maintain, and who must source. As readers may expect, each of the following chapters complicates these boundaries while pointing to why and whether they should exist. In the last instance, I believe this work—from the labor point of view—is most pressing for both digital humanities and "making" at the moment. Such work examines the circuits and conditions we may not fully apprehend but with which we are no doubt complicit. They also give us much-needed conceptual matter for action, and I encourage other digital humanities practitioners to read them carefully and respond where possible.

## *Outline of This Volume*

I arranged this volume's 38 chapters into five sections. The sections include original essays, several pieces republished with revisions, and a number of "project snapshots": one-page chapters about particular projects to prompt further study and dialogue about making and experimental methods in the humanities. The differences between the sections and chapters matter, and the contributions are most engaging when read collectively, as a series of negotiations with shared terms and problems.

The first section, "Making and the Humanities," addresses foundational issues about how boundaries are drawn between thinking and doing (Klein) as well as how creative work manifests in humanities contexts, and vice versa (Staley). Entwined with these issues are key matters of literacy (Endres), or how much making, writing, building, coding, digitizing, and fabricating intersect despite common cuts between them. Equally important to this section are the embodied acts of translation and framing we perform in our research and how those acts are imbricated with maintenance across technical and non-technical work (Sneha). The projects featured in this first section also represent compelling collaborations between artists, humanists, and designers (Rajko et al.), where acts of making are collective (not individuated) and give us a tangible sense of how cultural criticism is enacted through experiments with circuits and interfaces (Burgess).

"Made by Whom? For Whom?" is the second section, which stresses what is routinely taken for granted in popular maker cultures: who is working, for whom, and under what assumptions about labor and power. Here we have questions about how collaboration and agency are articulated across ranks in the academy (Jenstad and Takeda), together with inquiries into how the academy is made and reproduced, often through affective labor that parses scholarship from service (Shirazi). Service and scholarship are interwoven even further when we consider how digital materials are maintained post-production (Gardner et al.), not to mention how research environments are built, with what resources, and through which dependencies (Smithies). Of course, we must also ask how "makers" get defined in the first place (Hunter et al.; O'Gorman), and in what relation to normalcy and ability (Hendren). Projects in this section parody popular maker cultures (Hertz) as they expose the long-standing alliance of technologies with force and surveillance (Burtch and Rosenthal). Ultimately, this section resists celebratory or romantic models of making to instead examine how technologies—as negotiations—correspond with agency and vulnerability.

Next, "Making as Inquiry" stresses making as an action, which involves developing, prototyping, testing, and sharing conceptual matter. Central to such inquiry is the communicability of experimental research as both process and product to audiences other than academics (Resch et al.), how we might prototype across print and electronic materials (Hancock et al.), and how hacking and reverse engineering technologies (Boeva et al.; Teboul) immerse us in indeterminacies against kit-of-parts construction. In this section, we see numerous creative/critical approaches to technologies, both new and old. Curation becomes a creative act (Bernardi and Dimmock), circuit bending becomes a technique for interface and console design (Belojevic), poems become 3-D models (Tucker et al.), and poetry readings become disembodied audio and then re-embodied performances (Flamenco et al.). Each of these inquiries stewards materials across settings and contexts and prompts us to consider how matter and mediation influence our conversations with the past (Garfinkel). While we can get carried away by the wow factor of gadgets, this section reminds us to pause and, if only in vain, try to arrest the fragments of history against the predictability of positivism.

The fourth section, "Making Spaces and Interfaces," shares several perspectives on how what appears ephemeral or immaterial is framed and designed. It also stresses the settings and values of making. Foregrounding the straight, white, cisgender masculinity pervading maker cultures and makerspaces, we see arguments for feminist hackerspaces (Burek et al.) and interdisciplinary makerspaces informed by queer feminisms (Rogers), combined with feminist approaches to wearable technologies and public humanities research (Knight et al.). We also encounter mobile projects invested in the politics of technologies and social relations (Hsu et al.; Martin et al.) as well as in the values of intelligent devices and smart cities (DiSalvo et al.). These projects underscore how important design and interaction are to persuasive work with technologies. Experience design, participatory design, applied cultural criticism, public interactives, and networked acts of witnessing all play a fundamental role in this section (Ruecker and Roberts-Smith; Balsamo et al.; Cooley and Buell; Knochel and Papaelias). These shared investments show how interfaces are not merely tools for re-presentation or copying; they are interpretations, and indeterminacy may very well be their primary ingredient (Sullivan et al.). Even when interfaces are steeped in machine knowledge and computer processing, their significance exceeds the circuits through which they are transmitted, and the conceptual matter that emerges with them is far more interesting than their tech specs.

This volume of *Debates in the Digital Humanities* concludes with "Making, Justice, Ethics" and focuses on issues of labor, equity, intersectionality, and material conditions that run throughout it. We are prompted to move beyond the "gendered, capitalist benefits of being a person who makes products" and "celebrate and foster education, maintenance, analysis, critique, and, above all, caregiving—all of the undervalued, underappreciated, ongoing work of making other people's lives better" (Chachra). We are also given several examples of how social justice may inform project design and development in humanities labs (Boggs et al.). And we conclude with a thought-provoking consideration of how we define "we" through material practice (Anderson and Campbell). So crucial to a digital humanities of the present moment, this final section offers us some language as well as a few paradigms for work that is aware of the boundaries it draws.

Read together, I hope these five sections demonstrate how creative and critical activity may be combined to engage—in media res—cultural issues. We may not be technicians, and we may not know all the circuitry. However, the chapters collected here direct our attention to what matters most: the entanglements of our work with labor. As they evoke interactions, they index where we make demarcations in our research. And they highlight why we are responsible for the boundaries drawn. From this perspective, technologies are comparable to the stuff of art, history, language, and culture: not something we control or master but rather a relationship we negotiate with some skepticism and surprise. Let us maintain the conversation.

## NOTES

1. On starting from the middle, see Deleuze and Guattari: "Let someone attempt to seize a blade of grass and hold fast to it when it begins to grow only from the middle. . . . It's not easy to see things in the middle, rather than looking down on them from above or up at them from below, or from left to right or right to left: try it, you'll see that everything changes. It's not easy to see the grass in things and in words" (25). Also see Galloway.

2. On alienation and repair, Anderson says, "Now, in terms of technology affecting people's lives on a daily basis, this is what my work is really centered on. How does a person really cope with being in an electronic world? You turn on a TV and it doesn't work, and unless you're a technician or an engineer, you probably can't fix it. You're living in a world that's extremely alienating" (in La Frenais, 139). In some ways, Anderson's perspective resonates with Bruno Latour's "black box" theory of technological development in *Science in Action*.

3. On automation and design, Anderson says, "[T]ools will teach you things. I want to control the technology I use. And not just set them on automatic . . . then it's just some kind of show you've designed and you're the technician" (in La Frenais, 139).

4. "Matters of concern" is a common term in science and technology studies. For more, see Latour, "Why Has Critique Run out of Steam?" For more on matters of concern and material experimentation, see Ratto. For more on ethics and entanglement, see Barad. For more on the importance of material or technical particulars, see Kirschenbaum.

5. For more on withdrawn objects, see Bryant and Shaviro. In short, I agree with Shaviro, who writes, "A thing is perfectly publicly accessible to other things; but at the same time it retains a certain privacy." And I disagree with Bryant, who writes, "Objects are thus withdrawn in a dual sense. On the one hand, objects are withdrawn from other objects in that they never directly encounter these other objects, but rather transform these perturbations into information according to their own organization. On the other hand, objects are withdrawn even from themselves as the distinction through which operations are possible, the endo-structure of objects, withdraw into the background, as it were, in the course of operations."

6. For instance, see Chun and Keenan. Chun suggests that their edited collection "concentrates on the actualities of the media itself—its hardware, its software, its user interface—and on the experience of using it, of being *entangled* within it" (9, emphasis added). This volume of *Debates* shares a similar impulse, with an emphasis on the actualities of technologies/media and the experience of making or remaking them.

7. In the second class of "Reading Marx's Capital," David Harvey says, "First off, we can't possibly know about the conditions of labor of all of the people who worked to put breakfast on our table. We can't possibly know it. . . . Millions and millions and millions of people are involved in putting breakfast upon our table. And the big question then arises: 'Well, where does our breakfast come from?' "

8. For more on technology and rationality, see Marcuse. For more on mastery and technology as masculine culture, see Wajcman. She shows how "[g]ender is not just about difference but about power: . . . technical expertise is a source of men's actual or potential power over women. It is also an important part of woman's experience of being less than, and dependent on, men. However, it should be remembered that the construction of masculinity is a complex process. There is not one monolithic masculinity and not all men are competent with technology. Rather, technical competence is central to the dominant cultural ideal of masculinity, and its absence a key feature of stereotyped femininity" (159). As many chapters in this volume show, this cultural ideal remains common in many technology spaces, including hackerspaces, makerspaces, and laboratories.

9. On technology, desire, and power, see Stone.

10. In the first volume of *Debates in the Digital Humanities,* Tom Scheinfeldt argues, "At the very least, we need to make room for both kinds of digital humanities, the kind that seeks to make arguments and answer questions now and the kind that builds tools and resources with questions in mind, but only in the back of its mind and only for later. We need time to experiment and even, as Bill Turkel and Kevin Kee have argued, time to play" (57–58). In several ways, this volume troubles the argument/experiment binary in Scheinfeldt's claim. Building technologies and resources *is* a form of argumentation. Also, various chapters collected here raise important questions about who gets to play and who is expected to either answer questions or keep the machine running. In other words, play and experimentation are not free from questions of desire, power, and ideology, which have no "sunset" (Scheinfeldt, "Sunset for Ideology").

11. For one of the most compelling treatments of absence and indeterminacy in digital humanities, see Klein.

12. In many ways, Anderson's description of her work ("what happens when you pick up the phone and try to get through") resonates with John Cage's approach to indeterminacy.

13. For Anderson, such care and labor involve human and non-human elements (including machines). As Wark suggests, "Labor is the mingling of many things, most of them not human" (217).

14. In the ninth thesis, Benjamin writes, "There is a picture by Klee called *Angelus Novus.* It shows an angel who seems about to move away from something he stares at. His eyes are wide, his mouth is open, his wings are spread. This is how the angel of history must look. His face is turned toward the past. Where a chain of events appears before *us, he* sees one single catastrophe, which keeps piling wreckage upon wreckage and hurls it as his feet. The angel would like to stay, awaken the dead, and make whole what has been smashed. But a storm is blowing from Paradise and has got caught in his wings; it is so strong that the angel can no longer close them. This storm drives him irresistibly into the future, to which his back is turned, while the pile of debris before him grows toward the sky. What we call progress is *this* storm" (392). Benjamin was a German Jewish critic writing in 1940, during World War II, which deeply informs the "wreckage" and "progress" in this excerpt. In a compelling interpretation of the ninth thesis, Robert S. Lehman suggests that, "The *Angelus* sees history . . . without reading it. . . . [H]e is . . . the perfect materialist historian" (247).

15. For a reading of the ninth thesis in the context of repair, see Jackson.

16. On the topic of Benjamin and historical materialism, Lehman writes, "For both the historical materialist and the allegorist, the object is preserved, but torn from its lived context. Indeed, the object survives while the context is irremediably lost . . . To tear a moment from history, then, is to be left with a collection of fragments; or, since history is only ever cited . . . it is to be left with [what Benjamin, in *The Origin of German Tragic Drama,* called] 'stirring writing'" (246).

17. Benjamin refers to "once upon a time" narratives in the sixteenth thesis, "On the Concept of History" (396), and Anderson's "The Dream Before" begins with the Hansel and Gretel fairy tale.

18. On remediation, see Bolter and Grusin. On formatting, see Sterne.

19. In "Prototyping the Past" (2015), I elaborate on the concept of remaking, which assumes we can never inhabit historical experiences or create exact reproductions of historical processes and materials.

20. See Jackson on broken world thinking, which "asks what happens when we take erosion, breakdown, and decay, rather than novelty, growth, and progress, as our starting points in thinking through the nature, use, and effects of information technology and new media" (221). In this introduction, I am more interested in how breakdown is linked with growth or progress via actions such as maintenance and stewardship. Put differently, conceptual matter is akin to Barad's "agential realism" (26, 132–86). It is also informed by Kirschenbaum's formal materiality, which, at one point in *Mechanisms,* he describes parenthetically, thus: "Formal materiality is perhaps also the lingering perception of some genuine material residue—however misplaced—which presents, like sensation in a phantom limb, when one cannot quite accept the exclusively formal nature of a digital process; for example, the vague sense of unease that attends me after leaving my desktop music player application on Pause for hours on end, something that would harm a physical tape system because of the tension on the reels" (13). I am particularly struck by Kirschenbaum's emphasis on the relational nature of formal materiality, or how it depends on interactions with materials. I am also interested in formal materiality as a space of both maintenance and intervention.

21. For more on boundary-making practices, see Bowker and Star.

22. I would like to thank Kari Kraus for pointing me to the history of exploded view diagrams.

23. Perner-Wilson devised an alternative to kit-of-parts optimization: a "kit-of-no-parts" motivated by "intimate knowledge of materials" and the need for "more diverse and intelligible results" from material experimentation (6).

24. The Tate's webpage for *Cold Dark Matter* elaborates on how both the shed was exploded and the resulting fragments were gathered: "Parker contacted the army to see if they would be prepared to help her, and to her surprise they were very co-operative. She was invited to the Army School of Ammunition where they demonstrated various types of explosives, and what these explosives could do, by blowing up a range of objects including a table and a car. . . . After the explosion the bits of shed and dispersed objects, twisted and blackened from the force of the explosives[,] were carefully gathered together. Some objects were never found—either blown far away and missed or totally destroyed."

25. For more on pointing and indexical relations, see Peirce, who describes an index as a "true symptom, just as a weather-cock indicates the direction of the wind or a thermometer the temperature" (373). Here, I would suggest that an index directs people in the traversal of conceptual matter—across the material spaces between tangible parts.

26. In *Dark Matters,* see Browne's epilogue, which focuses on Desi Cryer and Wanda Zamen's video, "HP Computers Are Racist."

27. For more on elemental media, see Peters.

28. This gesture is not meant to dismiss entirely publications by groups such as Maker Media. For example, see Borenstein, Hartman, Igoe, and Morris, which combine critical and creative approaches to technologies in the format of "how to" books.

29. For more on partial knowledge, situated relations, and technology, see Haraway.

### BIBLIOGRAPHY


*#TransformDH*. http://transformdh.org/.

AbTeC (Aboriginal Territories in Cyberspace). http://abtec.org/.

Amnesty International. "'This Is What We Die For': Human Rights Abuses in the Democratic Republic of the Congo Power the Global Trade in Cobalt." London: Amnesty International, 2016. https://www.amnesty.org/en/documents/afr62/3183/2016/en/.

Anderson, Chris. *Makers: The New Industrial Revolution*. New York: Random House, 2012.

Anderson, Laurie. "The Dream Before." In *Strange Angels*. New York: Warner, 1989.

———. "O Superman / Walk the Dog." New York: Warner, 1981.

Barad, Karen. *Meeting the Universe Halfway: Quantum Physics and the Entanglement of Matter and Meaning*. Durham, N.C.: Duke University Press, 2007.

Benjamin, Walter. "On the Concept of History," trans. Harry Zohn. In *Selected Writings*, vol. 4, 1938–1940, ed. Howard Eiland and Michael W. Jennings, 389–400. Cambridge, Mass.: Belknap Press of Harvard University Press, 2003.

Bolter, J. David, and Richard Grusin. *Remediation: Understanding New Media*. Cambridge, Mass.: MIT Press, 1999.

Borenstein, Greg. *Making Things See: 3D Vision with Kinect, Processing, Arduino, and MakerBot*. Sebastopol, Calif.: Maker Media, 2012.

Bowker, Geoffrey C., and Susan Leigh Star. *Sorting Things Out: Classification and Its Consequences*. Cambridge, Mass.: MIT Press, 1999.

Browne, Simone. *Dark Matters: On the Surveillance of Blackness*. Durham, N.C.: Duke University Press, 2015.

Bryant, Levi R. *The Democracy of Objects*. Open Humanities Press, 2011. http://quod.lib.umich.edu/o/ohp/9750134.0001.001/1:8/—democracy-of-objects?rgn=div1;view=toc.

Chun, Wendy Hui Kyong. "Introduction: Did Somebody Say New Media?" In *New Media, Old Media: A History and Theory Reader*, ed. Wendy Hui Kyong Chun and Thomas Keenan, 1–10. New York: Routledge, 2006.

Collins, Nicolas. *Handmade Electronic Music: The Art of Hardware Hacking*. New York: Routledge, 2006.

Deleuze, Gilles, and Félix Guattari. *A Thousand Plateaus: Capitalism and Schizophrenia*, trans. Brian Massumi. New York: Continuum, 2004.

*FemTechNet*. http://femtechnet.org/.

Galloway, Alexander R. "Love of the Middle." In *Excommunication: Three Inquiries in Media and Mediation*, by Alexander R. Galloway, Eugene Thacker, and McKenzie Wark, 25–76. Chicago, Ill.: University of Chicago Press, 2014.

Haraway, Donna J. *Modest_Witness@Second_Millennium.FemaleMan_Meets_OncoMouse: Feminism and Technoscience*. New York: Routledge, 1997.

Hartman, Kate. *Wearable Electronics: Design, Prototype, and Wear Your Own Interactive Garments*. Sebastopol, Calif.: Maker Media, 2014.

Harvey, David. "Class 02 Reading Marx's Capital, Vol I with David Harvey." YouTube, 2011. https://www.youtube.com/watch?v=zwuMrd_Hgww.

HASTAC (Humanities, Arts, Science, and Technology Alliance and Collaboratory). https://www.hastac.org/.

Hatch, Mark. *The Maker Movement Manifesto: Rules for Innovation in the New World of Crafters, Hackers, and Tinkerers*. New York: McGraw Hill, 2014.

Igoe, Tom. *Making Things Talk: Practical Methods for Connecting Physical Objects*. Sebastopol, Calif.: Maker Media, 2007.

Jackson, Steven J. "Rethinking Repair." In *Media Technologies: Essays on Communication, Materiality, and Society*, ed. Tarleton Gillespie, Pablo J. Boczkowski, and Kirsten A. Foot, 221–40. Cambridge, Mass.: MIT Press, 2014.

Johnson, Jessica Marie. *Diaspora Hypertext*. https://diasporahypertext.com/.

Kirschenbaum, Matthew. *Mechanisms: New Media and the Forensic Imagination*. Cambridge, Mass.: MIT Press, 2008.

Klein, Lauren. "The Image of Absence: Archival Silence, Data Visualization, and James Hemings." *American Literature* 85, no. 4 (2013): 661–88.

La Frenais, Rob. "An Interview with Laurie Anderson." In *The Art of Performance: A Critical Anthology*, ed. Gregory Battcock and Robert Nickas. Ubu Edition, ed. Lucia della Paolera, 135–42. UbuWeb, 2010. http://www.ubu.com/historical/battcock/Battcock_The-Art-of-Performance_1984.pdf.

Latour, Bruno. *Science in Action: How to Follow Scientists and Engineers through Society*. Cambridge, Mass.: Harvard University Press, 1987.

———. "Why Has Critique Run out of Steam? From Matters of Fact to Matters of Concern." *Critical Inquiry* 30, no. 2 (Winter 2004): 225–48.

Lehman, Robert S. "Allegories of Rending: Killing Time with Walter Benjamin." *New Literary History* 39, no. 2 (2008): 233–50.

Mallarmé, Stéphane. "Un Coup de Dés Jamais N'abolira le Hasard." Paris: Revue Internationale, 1897.

———. "A Dice Throw at Any Time Never Will Abolish Chance." In *Stéphane Mallarmé: Collected Poems and Other Verse*, trans. E. H. and A. M. Blackmore, 161–81. Oxford: Oxford University Press, 2006.

Marcuse, Herbert. "Some Social Implications of Modern Technology." In *The Essential Frankfurt School Reader*, ed. Andrew Arato and Eike Gebhardt. New York: Continuum, 1982. 138–62.

Morris, Kief. *Infrastructure as Code: Managing Servers in the Cloud*. Sebastopol, Calif.: Maker Media, 2016.

Parker, Cornelia. *Cold Dark Matter: An Exploded View*. London: Tate Modern, 1991. http://www.tate.org.uk/learn/online-resources/cold-dark-matter.

Peirce, Charles Sanders. *Collected Papers of Charles Sanders Peirce,* vols. 7 and 8, ed. Arthur W. Burks. Cambridge, Mass.: Belknap Press of Harvard University Press, 1966.

Perner-Wilson, Hannah. "A Kit-of-No-Parts: Recipes for Materially Diverse, Functionally Transparent and Expressive Electronics." Thesis. Massachusetts Institute of Technology, 2011.

Peters, John Durham. *The Marvelous Clouds: Toward a Philosophy of Elemental Media.* Chicago, Ill.: University of Chicago Press, 2015.

Ratto, Matt. "Critical Making: Conceptual and Material Studies in Technology and Social Life." *The Information Society* 27, no. 4 (2011): 252–60.

Rieffer-Flanagan, Barbara Ann. *Evolving Iran: An Introduction to Politics and Problems in the Islamic Republic.* Washington, D.C.: Georgetown University Press, 2013.

Rosner, Daniela K., and Morgan Ames. "Designing for Repair?: Infrastructures and Materialities of Breakdown." In *Proceedings of the 17th ACM Conference on Computer Supported Cooperative Work and Social Computing,* 319–31. New York: ACM, 2014.

Sayers, Jentery. "Prototyping the Past." *Visible Language* 49, no. 3 (2015): 157–77.

Scheinfeldt, Tom. "Sunset for Ideology, Sunrise for Methodology?" In *Debates in the Digital Humanities,* ed. Matthew K. Gold, 124–26. Minneapolis: University of Minnesota Press, 2012.

———. "Where's the Beef? Does Digital Humanities Have to Answer Questions?" In *Debates in the Digital Humanities,* ed. Matthew K. Gold, 56–58. Minneapolis: University of Minnesota Press, 2012.

Shaviro, Steven. "Panpsychism, Whitehead, and OOO." *The Pinocchio Theory.* November 25, 2010. http://www.shaviro.com/Blog/?p=935.

Simpson, Dave. "How We Made Laurie Anderson's 'O Superman.'" *The Guardian,* April 19, 2016. https://www.theguardian.com/culture/2016/apr/19/how-we-made-laurie-anderson-o-superman.

Sterne, Jonathan. *MP3: The Meaning of a Format.* Durham, N.C.: Duke University Press, 2012.

Stone, Allucquère Rosanne. *The War of Desire and Technology at the Close of the Mechanical Age.* Cambridge, Mass.: MIT Press, 1995.

Wajcman, Judy. *Feminism Confronts Technology.* Oxford: Polity, 1991.

Wark, McKenzie. *Molecular Red: Theory for the Anthropocene.* Brooklyn, N.Y.: Verso, 2015.

Winant, Howard. "The Dark Matter." *Ethnic and Racial Studies* 35, no. 4 (2012): 600–607.

# PART I

# MAKING AND THE HUMANITIES

# The Boundary Work of Making in Digital Humanities

JULIE THOMPSON KLEIN

Debates on digital humanities are sites of boundary work in a history of arguments about the nature of the field. Boundary work is a composite label for the claims, activities, and structures by which individuals and groups create, maintain, break down, and reformulate boundaries between knowledge units (Fisher 13–14; Klein, *Crossing* 1–2). Thomas Gieryn coined the term in 1983 in a study of demarcating science from non-science. It is an ideological style that constructs boundaries rhetorically in three ways: by expanding authority or expertise into domains claimed by other professions or occupations, by monopolizing authority and resources, and by protecting autonomy over professional activities (781, 791–92). The advent of digital technologies in humanities was the catalyst for two major forms of boundary work: protecting traditional scholarship and teaching from the encroachment of new methods that bridge the traditional separation of humanities from technology and asserting the authority of some practices over others in an emergent field.

Practices range widely, from computational linguistics and electronic text editing associated with the early label "humanities computing" to expanding connotations of "digital humanities" (DH) in new modes of data visualization, digital-born scholarship, and subfields such as code studies, software studies, and game studies, to name but a few examples. Priorities vary, in turn, depending on whether emphasis falls on technical production or the cultural impact of new information technologies and media. This chapter tracks the practice of making in arguments and activities that have reconceptualized building tools from reductive mechanical work to an intellectual endeavor in its own right. It begins by aligning making with the historical boundary between thinking and doing, then tracks refiguration of their relationship framed by Patrik Svensson's five modes of engagement. It continues by identifying intellectual warrants in the concept of thinking-through-practice and an epistemology, aesthetics, and rhetoric of building, including work associated with critical making and the materiality of things. The status of these warrants differs across disciplines, interdisciplinary fields, and occupational professions, but making has also become a shared thematic across DH communities of practice.

### *Making Digital Humanities*

The boundary work of making is framed historically by distinctions in Greek philosophy between *epistēmē,* understood as knowledge, and *technē,* understood as a craft, skill, or art. In *The Republic* and other philosophical dialogues, Plato argues that knowledge is found, not made, distinguishing discovery of *true* knowledge from actions producing *practical* knowledge. Aristotle, in turn, writing in the *Nicomachean Ethics* and *Metaphysics,* demarcates *theoretical science* for its own sake from the *practical science* of conduct and goodness in action and the *productive science* of creating beautiful or useful objects. Over the following centuries demarcation of intellectual activity from theory and practical and productive work was reinforced in parallel distinctions between *liberal* versus *mechanical arts* and *fine* versus *useful arts.* The English word "making," which derives from the Old English "macung," also distinguished thinking from doing by constructing something.[1] As a result, the relationship of humanities and new technologies was confronted from the beginning by the higher status of interpretation, analysis, and abstraction over fabrication, application, and production. Introduction of the name "digital humanities" was a significant intervention in this hierarchy of valuing.

The emergence of digital humanities is dated conventionally to the search for machines capable of automating linguistic analysis of written texts. The year 1949 is enshrined in most origin stories, benchmarked by Father Roberto Busa's efforts to create an automated *index variorum* of words in the works of Thomas Aquinas and related authors. Alternative histories, though, situate origin elsewhere: in, for example, early information theory and computer science, the rise of the Internet, new forms of media and communication platforms, and the expanding role of computation in culture. The names given to developments are not neutral. Names, Cathy Davidson (2010) explains, are historical reference points that mark converging energies at particular moments, demarcating what is considered tangential, intersectional, or orthogonal to a field (207). The earliest labels—"humanities computing" and "computational humanities"—grounded definition in production of concordances and thesauri, textual informatics, language processing, vocabulary studies, stylometrics, and analysis of encoded textual material (Hockey 3, 7–10). Stephen Ramsay (2011) and John Unsworth (in Fitzpatrick 2011) claim the term "digital humanities" was introduced in order to shift the perceived status of technology. Ramsay traced the origin to the late 1990s at the University of Virginia's Institute for Advanced Technology in the Humanities (IATH). The new name countered narrow equations of "humanities computing" with low-prestige computing in favor of an intellectual endeavor with its own practices, standards, and theories (quoted in Hayles 24). Unsworth dated its introduction somewhat later, to discussions about a title for the first anthology in the field, Blackwell's 2004 *A Companion to Digital Humanities*. The name moved beyond connotations of "simple digitization" in the original proposed title (Fitzpatrick). In both cases, though, the boundary work of naming was similar, establishing authority for work lacking legitimacy in the hierarchy of humanities at the time.

As the field grew, its boundaries were redrawn multiple times in order to position an expanding array of practices. Svensson's (2010) typology of paradigmatic modes of engagement provides a framework for gauging the relationship of humanities and technology as a tool, a study object, an expressive medium, an experimental laboratory, and an activist venue. All five modes entail making but in different ways and to different degrees. The first mode—as a tool—highlights the instrumentality of production and related processes. It has been especially strong in text analysis, text encoding, and markup systems in corpus stylistics, digitization, preservation, and curation. In the second mode—as a study object—the digital is an object of analysis, aligning the field more closely with cultural studies and critique. The third mode—as an expressive medium—benchmarks new modes of communication, including born-digital and multimodal forms of expression ranging from long-form blogging to interactive hybrids of text, image, and sound engaging authors and designers in collaborative production. The fourth mode—as an experimental laboratory—has become a major site of exploring ideas, testing tools, and modifying data sets and complex objects. In contrast, the fifth mode—as an activist venue—aligns digital humanities with change, prioritizing inclusion, accessibility, and the democratic imperative of social justice.

Although driven by differing epistemic commitments, the five categories are not airtight. Svensson describes them as both borders of difference and junctures of overlapping interest. Mode two—as a study object—aligns technology with sociopolitical change in critiques of the dominant structure of knowledge and information technologies. Mode five—as an activist venue—also blurs boundaries of genre. Sharon Daniel's *Public Secrets* (2007), for instance, is an activist production in a hybrid form of scholarship on prison abolition and women in prison; designed in collaboration with Erik Loyer, it is simultaneously an artistic installation, cultural critique, and intervention (cited in Balsamo 87–88). Other examples in this category include the Electronic Disturbance Theater, b.a.n.g. lab at the California Institute for Telecommunications and Information Technology, Electronic Democracy Network's research on online practices of political participation, and acts of "political coding" and "performative hacking" by new-media dissidents (Losh 168–69, 171). The boundaries of modes one, two, and five also blur in *Postcolonial Digital Humanities*, *#TransformDH's* explorations of DH and race, and the Fembot Collective. These initiatives, to echo David Berry (2013), build on earlier work on critical cultural studies of race, ethnicity, gender, sexuality, and class in contexts of design, programming, and coding.

With its orientation to tools, mode one perpetuates the belief that digital humanities is primarily about technical production and methods, rendering it a handmaiden to humanities. Authors of *The Digital Humanities Manifesto 2.0,* Jeffrey Schnapp and Todd Presner, cite common dismissals: "It's *just* a tool; it's *just* a repository; it's *just* pedagogy" (10). These judgments perpetuate a hierarchy of value that regards resource production as less worthy than interpretation, archival work in libraries as secondary to scholarship, and teaching of lesser value than research. The underlying "knowledge jukebox" conception of humanities work, Willard McCarty (2005) lamented, renders technology makers "mere assistants or delivery boys to scholarship," tools little more than "vending machines for knowledge," and the machine an efficient "servant" (6). Yet, in introducing Blackwell's *A Companion to Digital Humanities,* co-editors Susan Schreibman, Ray Siemens, and John Unsworth contend that tools and interpretation are not oppositional: "application is as important as theory," and tasks typically associated with "humanities computing" put digital representation of archival materials "on a par with analysis of critical inquiry and theories of analysis or critical inquiry originating in the study of those materials" (xxv). In some instances, Svensson's fifth mode of activism also takes the form of critical thinking about design and use. *Preemptive Media*, for instance, is a project for discussing emerging policies and technologies through beta tests, trial runs, and impact assessments.

New practices also cross institutional boundaries by creating transactional spaces. The location of academic work is framed by two sets of metaphors in the discourse of knowledge fields. Spatial images of boundaries, borders, turf, and territory accentuate controlling practices. In contrast, organic metaphors of cross-fertilization, mutations, and intersections liken development of new practices to ecological processes and the evolution of new species. Yet, Michael Winter suggests, partial and organic metaphors may be combined to form a third type that highlights interactions between social groups and environments. The Greek word "ecology" (*oikeo*) means household or settlement. The root idea is to make and reinforce jurisdictional claims and exploit resources to produce new forms and settlements (343–46). In defining the dynamics of learning in a digital age, Anne Balsamo (2011) invokes a similar concept: Michael de Certeau's (1984) distinction between place and space. A "place," such as a school, has stable boundaries and a fixed location. Space is "a practiced place," created through actions and practices including the learning that happens when inhabiting it (Balsamo 143; de Certeau 117).

Digital humanities labs, which host Svensson's mode four, exemplify spatializing practices. Many, such as the Stanford Humanities Lab and the Maker Lab at the University of Victoria, are located within existing academic institutions. Yet, Jon Saklofske, Estelle Clements, and Richard Cunningham (2012) liken them to "experimental sandboxes" (325), and Bethany Nowviskie (2013) compares them to small "skunkworks" teams of research and development engineers at the Lockheed Martin aeronautics corporation in the 1940s. Nowviskie describes library-based digital humanities skunkworks as semi-independent "prototyping and makerspace labs" where librarians take on new roles as "scholar-practitioners." The Scholars' Lab at the University of Virginia Library, for instance, has produced not only tools but also innovative digital scholarship as well as technical and social frameworks needed for support and sustainability (Nowviskie 53, 56, 61). One of the sites Svensson visited, the ACTLab (Advanced Communication Technology) at the University of Texas, was established as a combined studio, performance, and seminar space. Svensson likens it to an art school or media production studio more than a humanities department. Moreover, Sandy Stone explains, theory flows from the act of making "stuff" in the lab. Its members believed that tinkering with tools engaged thinking as well as a means of expression and activism (quoted in Svensson 57–66).

### *Formulating an Epistemology, Aesthetics, and Rhetoric of Building*

Crossing the boundaries of thinking and doing has also resulted in new theorizations of what Anne Burdick (2012) and colleagues call "thinking-through-practice." It brings the creative practice of design to the center of research, favoring process over product as well as versioning and extensibility over definitive editions and research silos. It also underscores the iterative and incremental contours of making activated in new contexts, openness to new contributions and extensions, and dialogue and debate (vii, 13, 22, 132). In a parallel distinction, Geoffrey Rockwell and Andrew Mactavish (2004) differentiate "thinking about" from "thinking with" technology. Thinking *about* produces definitions, histories, examples, and theoretical problems disseminated in textbooks, articles, and lectures. Thinking *with* is a craft with its own tradition of discourse, forms of organization, tools, and outcomes (117). It goes beyond a narrow conception of tools to epistemological reflection and critical thinking about their capacities and limits. Working with technology, Ramsay and Rockwell (2012) further contend, has a hermeneutic power that generates an "epistemology of building." Prototypes may be considered theories, not in the standard sense of observations capable of predicting future observations but a humanities connotation of deeper understanding and a form of argumentation with explanatory power. Viewing digital artifacts as hermeneutic instruments also opens the possibility of a "materialist epistemology" for interpreting phenomena through technologies (77–79).

Balsamo's integration of hermeneutics and reverse engineering demonstrates what a materialist epistemology looks like. "Reverse engineering" is a process of working backwards from construction of an existing technology to gain information for a new instance. The concept of "hermeneutic reverse engineering" couples insights from interpretive theory with practices of engineers, computer scientists, and creative tinkerers. Its iterative nature erases boundaries between stages of design through rapid prototyping, user testing, and assessment in situ. It also factors in social and cultural contexts of innovations, as well as reflection and critique. And, it reaches beyond narrow ranges of collaboration among computer scientists and engineers to broad interdisciplinary bridging of science and humanities, technology and arts. Technical expertise and skills are combined with methods of understanding meaning, including parsing linguistics and grammar, decoding visual symbols or representation, and analyzing dynamics of artistic performance. Social scientists also contribute understanding of social impacts, and physical scientists offer new theoretical possibilities and methods of evaluation. For example, *Women of the World Talk Back,* Balsamo's multimedia project with Mary Hocks, combined communicative, graphic, and transactional practices to produce an interactive application for an NGO Forum in China in 1995. Designers built layers of meaning from people, devices, objects, and events, including relationships between women and digital technologies cast as feminist cultural activism.

Thinking-through-practice also entails an aesthetics of making at the heart of Johanna Drucker's (2009) distinction between "speculative computing" and "digital humanities."[2] Many who call themselves digital humanists would argue they are doing speculative computing. Yet, Drucker's distinction highlights a shift from conceptions of materiality as mechanistic readings of formal properties to generative provocations. Drucker associates digital humanities with a philosophy of *Mathesis* that privileges objectivity, formal logic, and instrumental applications. In contrast, she aligns speculative computing with a philosophy of *Aesthesis* that privileges subjectivity, aesthetics, interpretation, and emergent phenomena. *Aesthesis* also recognizes cultural and historical characteristics of visual forms and their rhetorical assumptions. Drucker based her distinction on projects in the Speculative Computing Laboratory (SpecLab) at the University of Virginia's Institute for Advanced Technology in the Humanities, including temporal modeling and a game based on Walter Scott's novel *Ivanhoe*. The game was a flexible space for engaging with characters and generating alternative versions, experimenting with digital media as a means of facilitating critical modes of reading in literary studies. As a thinking process, Drucker adds, making things is both formative and transformative.

The shift from "things" as technical mechanics to arguments based on processes, flows, and signals has also generated a rhetoric of building that is especially strong in new subfields such as critical code studies, software studies, and platform studies. Computational procedures, James J. Brown, Jr. (2015) explains, are not just tools. They can be deployed as an expressive and rhetorical medium (27, 29). Ian Bogost's (2012) concept of "procedural rhetoric" propelled new studies of how computational rules in software and game design make arguments, and the concept of a "carpentry" of building asks "how things make their world" (85). Recalling the foundational work of Matthew Kirschenbaum (2008), Steven E. Jones (2014) identifies two strands of definition: a *forensic materiality* of silicon, wire, and magnetic impulses inscribed on hard drives; and a *formal materiality* of symbols, code, and logical and procedural structures (Jones 81; Kirschenbaum 9-15). The "New Materialism," David Gruber (2015) sums up, elevates materialist analysis of environments and local practices over the older paradigm of discursivity grounded in text and past conceptualizations of the material environment as a passive entity (296–97, 301, 304). Yet, as Karen Barad (2007) shows, matter is still entangled with meaning and materiality with discourse.

The concept of "critical making" has also gained traction in digital humanities discourse. It is associated with developments in the public and private sectors, especially the maker movement, DIY culture, prosumer markets, and the resurgence of handicraft and tinkering (Balsamo 177). Ratto and Boler (2014) link the term "DIY," in particular, with the counterculture of the late 1960s, and subsequent practices, such as zines and communities of "critical makers" spanning fandom, tactical media, and collective indie radio activism as well as community gardens and other civic engagements, challenge conventional authority and power. At the same time, Ratto and Boler add, "critical" has another connotation linking making things with "critically-infused reflection" on process and practice (3). Despite the case for making as a scholarly practice, though, gatekeeping mechanisms continue to reinforce the boundary of what "counts" as legitimate professional activity—and what does not. The fine arts offer a model of outcomes beyond traditional publication, yet humanities practitioners still encounter resistance in the tenure and promotion process when their work does not resemble conventional forms of scholarship. Moreover, as Stone observed from the ACTLab experience, experimental spaces confront the tension of being "outside" rather than "inside" boundaries of traditional academic structure.

## *Coda: Moving beyond Dichotomy*

More than sixty-five years of research, design, and education have established, fortified, interrogated, and refigured the boundaries of digital humanities. The historical shift from "humanities computing" to "digital humanities" is not the only benchmark. Interventions asserting greater priority for media studies, cultural critique, activism, public engagement, and making have heightened the contest of definition and control of the field. The emergence of making, in particular, has several implications. It dismantles the dichotomies of doing versus thinking, production versus interpretation, and application versus theory. The evolving community of practice centered on shared questions and problems also builds authority for a new understanding of the complexity of making both within digital humanities and beyond, anchored by a growing body of literature and projects. And warrants for epistemology, aesthetics, and rhetoric of building establish intellectual legitimacy on humanities ground, without the need for imported methods and concepts premised on technical or scientific validity. Older pragmatics of digitizing and archiving are not jettisoned, however. They are resituated. The pragmatics of digitizing, archiving, designing, coding, analyzing, and publishing digital objects, Jones argues, are more than narrow utility. They embody investigation and creativity. Indicative of the growing visibility of the discourse of making in current conceptions of the field, Claire Warwick's chapter on the relationship of theory and making is the closing statement in *A New Companion to Digital Humanities* (2016). Mindful of binary opposition reinforced by the slogan, "more hack, less yack," Warwick asks whether such tensions are part of the evolution of a new field. The history of interdisciplinary fields provides ample evidence of ongoing differences in their construction in response to both ongoing and new imperatives.

Jones also notes that newer forms of practical and instrumental digital humanities were produced by younger scholars, some of whom worked as programmers or designers in technology industries and "alt-ac" positions (31). When bringing their experience into academic centers and projects, they legitimated a turn to hands-on practice. This development, he suggests, may be seen as a countermove to the idealism associated with cyberculture studies in the 1990s. New activities did not avoid theory or strive for scientific instrumentalism; they embodied critiques of the ideology of cyberspace as it manifested through reductive conceptions such as screen essentialism and the immateriality of digital texts.[3] New work, Jones adds, has fostered more complex understanding of the materialities of digital platforms and physical objects, exemplified by digital forensics, critical code studies, platform studies, and game studies, as well as work with linguistic data and large corpora of texts, data visualization, and new content management systems. In his classic study of boundary work, Thomas Gieryn acknowledges the power of monopoly, but he also concludes that boundaries are "ambiguous, flexible, historically changing, contextually variable, internally inconsistent, and sometimes disputed" (792). Digital humanities is no exception. It calls into question how boundaries of disciplines, interdisciplinary fields, occupational professions, and institutional structures have been drawn, prompting us to rethink, in Brown's words, the "state lines" they fix, protect, and sustain (29).

## NOTES

I thank three internal reviewers of an earlier draft for helpful suggestions: the volume editor Jentery Sayers and CommentPress reviewers, William J. Turkel and David Wright. Kim Lacey of Saginaw Valley State University also read the draft and raised excellent questions for revision.

1. *Oxford English Dictionary*, "making," n.1.
2. See also Drucker and Nowviskie.
3. For more on screen essentialism and the ostensible immateriality of digital texts, see Kirschenbaum.

## BIBLIOGRAPHY

*#TransformDH*. http://transformdh.org/.
ACTLab (Advanced Communication Technology). https://actlab.us/.

Balsamo, Anne. *Designing Culture: The Technological Imagination at Work*. Durham, N.C.: Duke University Press, 2011.

Barad, Karen. *Meeting the Universe Halfway: Quantum Physics and the Entanglement of Matter and Meaning*. Durham, N.C.: Duke University Press, 2007.

Berry, David M. "Critical Digital Humanities." Author's blog. http://stunlaw.blogspot.com/2013/01/critical-digital-humanities.html.

———. "Introduction: Understanding the Digital Humanities." In *Understanding Digital Humanities,* ed. David M. Berry, 1–20. Hampshire, U.K.: Palgrave Macmillan, 2012.

Bogost, Ian. *Alien Phenomenology; or, What It's Like to Be a Thing*. Minneapolis: University of Minnesota Press, 2012.

Brown, James, Jr. "Crossing State Lines: Rhetoric and Software Studies." In *Rhetoric and the Digital Humanities,* ed. Jim Ridolfo and William Hart-Davidson, 20–32. Chicago, Ill.: University of Chicago Press, 2015.

Burdick, Anne, Johanna Drucker, Peter Lunenfeld, Todd Presner, and Jeffrey Schnapp. *Digital_Humanities*. Cambridge, Mass.: MIT Press, 2012.

Daniel, Sharon, and Erik Loyer. "Public Secrets." *Vectors 2,* no. 2 (2007). http://vectors.usc.edu/projects/index.php?project=57.

Davidson, Cathy. "Humanities and Technology in the Information Age." In *The Oxford Handbook of Interdisciplinarity,* ed. Robert Frodeman, Julie Thompson Klein, and Carl Mitcham, 206–19. Oxford: Oxford University Press, 2010.

de Certeau, Michel. *The Practice of Everyday Life*. Translated by Steven Randall. Berkeley, Calif.: University of California Press, 1984.

Drucker, Johanna. *SPECLAB: Digital Aesthetics and Projects in Speculative Computing*. Chicago, Ill.: University of Chicago Press, 2009.

Drucker, Johanna, and Bethany Nowviskie. "Speculative Computing: Aesthetic Provocations in Humanities Computing." In *A Companion to Digital Humanities,* ed. Susan Schreibman, Ray Siemens, and John Unsworth, 431–37. Oxford: Blackwell, 2004.

Fembot Collective. http://fembotcollective.org/.

Fisher, Donald. *Fundamental Development of the Social Sciences: Rockefeller Philanthropy and the United States Social Science Research Council*. Ann Arbor, Mich.: University of Michigan Press, 1993.

Fitzpatrick, Kathleen. "The Humanities Done Digitally." *The Chronicle of Higher Education,* May 8, 2011. http://chronicle.com/article/The-Humanities-Done-Digitally/127382.

Gieryn, Thomas P. "Boundary-Work and the Demarcation of Science from Non-Science: Strains and Interests in Professional Ideologies of Scientists." *American Sociological Review* 48 (1983): 781–95.

Gruber, David. "New Materialism and a Rhetoric of Scientific Practice in the Digital Humanities." In *Rhetoric and the Digital Humanities,* ed. Jim Ridolfo and William Hart-Davidson, 296–306. Chicago, Ill.: University of Chicago Press, 2015.

Harris, Katherine. "Explaining Digital Humanities in Promotion Documents." *The Journal of Digital Humanities* 1, no. 4 (2012). http://journalofdigitalhumanities.org/1-4/explaining-digital-humanities-in-promotion-documents-by-katherine-harris.

Hayles, N. Katherine. *How We Think: Digital Media and Contemporary Technogenesis*. Chicago, Ill.: University of Chicago Press, 2012.

Hockey, Susan. "The History of Humanities Computing." In *A Companion to Digital Humanities*, ed. Susan Schreibman, Raymond Siemens, and John Unsworth, 3–19. Oxford: Blackwell, 2004.

"Interchange: The Promise of Digital History." *The Journal of American History* 95, no. 2 (2008): 452–91.

*Ivanhoe*. http://www.ivanhoegame.org/.

Jones, Steven E. *The Emergence of the Digital Humanities*. New York: Routledge, 2014.

Kirschenbaum, Matthew. *Mechanisms: New Media and the Forensic Imagination*. Cambridge, Mass.: MIT Press, 2008.

Klein, Julie Thompson. *Crossing Boundaries: Knowledge, Disciplinarities, and Interdisciplinarities*. Charlottesville, Va.: University of Virginia Press, 1996.

———. *Interdisciplining Digital Humanities: Boundary Work in an Emerging Field*. Ann Arbor, Mich.: University of Michigan Press, 2015.

Losh, Elizabeth. "Hacktivism and the Humanities: Programming Protest in the Era of the Digital University." In *Debates in the Digital Humanities*, ed. Matthew K. Gold, 161–86. Minneapolis: University of Minnesota Press, 2012.

Maker Lab in the Humanities. http://maker.uvic.ca/.

McCarty, Willard. *Humanities Computing*. London: Palgrave Macmillan, 2005.

Nowviskie, Bethany. "Skunks in the Library: A Path to Production for Scholarly R&D." *Journal of Library Administration* 53 (2013): 53–66.

*Preemptive Media*. http://www.preemptivemedia.net.

Ramsay, Stephen. *Reading Machines: Towards an Algorithmic Criticism*. Urbana, Ill.: University of Illinois Press, 2011.

Ramsay, Stephen, and Geoffrey Rockwell. "Developing Things: Notes toward an Epistemology of Building in the Digital Humanities." In *Debates in the Digital Humanities*, ed. Matthew K. Gold, 75–84. Minneapolis: University of Minnesota Press, 2012.

Ratto, Matt, and Megan Boler. "Introduction." In *DIY Citizenship: Critical Making and Social Media*, ed. Matt Ratto and Megan Boler, 1–22. Cambridge, Mass.: MIT Press, 2014.

Rockwell, Geoffrey, and Andrew Mactavish. "Multimedia." In *A Companion to Digital Humanities*, ed. Susan Schreibman, Raymond Siemens, and John Unsworth, 108–20. Oxford: Blackwell, 2004.

Saklofske, Jon, Estelle Clements, and Richard Cunningham. "On the Digital Future of Humanities." *In Digital Humanities Pedagogy: Practices, Principles and Policies*, ed. Brett D. Hirsch, 311–30. Cambridge, U.K.: Open Book Publishers, 2012.

Sample, Mark. "Tenure as a Risk-Taking Venture." *The Journal of Digital Humanities* 1, no. 4 (2012). http://journalofdigitalhumanities.org/1-4/tenure-as-a-risk-taking-venture-by-mark-sample.

Scholars' Lab. http://scholarslab.org/.

Schnapp, Jeffrey, and Todd Presner. *The Digital Humanities Manifesto 2.0.* http://www.humanitiesblast.com/manifesto/Manifesto_V2.pdf. Peter Lunenfeld and Johanna Drucker are also credited with making contributions to the document.

Schreibman, Susan, Raymond Siemens, and John Unsworth. "The Digital Humanities and Humanities Computing: An Introduction." In *A Companion to Digital Humanities,* ed. Susan Schreibman, Raymond Siemens, and John Unsworth, xxiii–xxvii. Oxford: Blackwell, 2004.

Stanford Humanities Lab. http://shc.stanford.edu/digital-humanities.

Sternfeld, Joshua. "Pedagogical Principles of Digital Historiography." In *Digital Humanities Pedagogy: Practices, Principles and Policies*, ed. Brett D. Hirsch, 255–90. Cambridge, U.K.: Open Book Publishers, 2012.

Svensson, Patrik. "The Landscape of Digital Humanities." *Digital Humanities Quarterly* 4, no. 1 (2010). http://digitalhumanities.org/dhq/vol/4/1/000080/000080.html.

Warwick, Claire. "Building Theories or Theories of Building? A Tension at the Heart of Digital Humanities." In *A New Companion to Digital Humanities,* ed. Susan Schreibman, Ray Siemens, and John Unsworth, 538–52. Hoboken, N.J.: Wiley, 2016.

Winter, Michael. "Specialization, Territoriality, and Jurisdiction in Librarianship." *Library Trends* 45, no. 2 (1996): 343–63.

*Women of the World Talk Back.* http://www.annebalsamo.net/production/journalistic-projects/women-of-the-world-talk-back/.

PART I ][ *Chapter 2*

# On the "Maker Turn" in the Humanities

DAVID STALEY

The move to read big data in the humanities necessitates new forms of reading, new types of interpretation. As we consider macro-level readings of large corpora, visualization is especially helpful. The most effective way to draw meaning from large data sets is through visual forms and patterns. Stephen Ramsay (2011) makes a claim for "the primacy of pattern as the basic hermeneutical function" (xi), meaning the display of visual patterns is a form of interpretation. Rather than "translating" those patterns into textual form, humanists can retain them as evidence of reading. Ramsay maintains that visual forms do indeed constitute a reading since "any reading of a text that is not a recapitulation of that text relies on a heuristic of radical transformation. The critic who endeavors to put forth a 'reading' puts forth not the text, but a new text in which the data has been paraphrased, elaborated, selected, truncated, and transduced" (16)—converted into another form.

Now that the maker movement has come to the humanities, and digital fabrication tools and computer numerical control (CNC) machines are potential parts of the humanist's tool kit, what sorts of things will humanists make? In this chapter, I argue that these tools provide humanists with the means to fashion and trace new forms of evidence of their readings. The kinds of material forms I am imagining are similar to the visual patterns identified by Ramsay, not as two-dimensional diagrams on a printed page, but as three-dimensional physical objects. Humanists may sculpt into material form the visual patterns of humanistic texts. If the goal of interpretation is to unlock meaning, then one approach to making in the humanities is creating physical objects as an interpretive act. These things are not simply aesthetic objects or "pretty pictures." As art historian Esther Pasztory (2005) observes, "Thinking of things as having cognitive rather than purely visual value is to release them from the low position in which technologies such as writing have placed them" (24). The experience of things often involves pre-linguistic or pre-discursive forms of knowing, where meaning is derived from thinking with

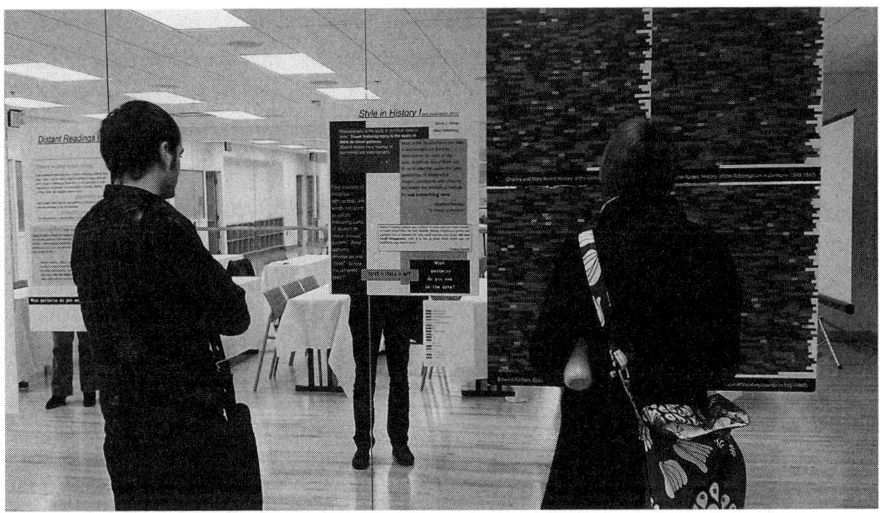


Figure 2.1. *Style in History*, a data visualization of several classic works of history, exhibited at the "Digital Media in a Social World" conference at Ohio State University in 2011. Making interpretive objects like this often means novel types of venues for publication. Author's photograph.

objects. As I demonstrate in this chapter, making, designing, and experiencing these visual, tactile, and material objects are hermeneutic acts, which afford the kind of inquiry expected in the humanities. Or, to state it another way, creativity *is* a form of scholarship.

Figure 2.1 depicts *Style in History*, an example of radical transformation. My team in the Harvey Goldberg Center at Ohio State University developed a tool that would identify the parts of speech from any text and color-code that word based on whether it was a noun, verb, adjective, etc. The length of each block is the length of the word in the text. (We literally replaced words with colored blocks.) For this display, we looked at a randomly chosen section of one thousand words from a dozen classic works of history and displayed them side-by-side.

Before I displayed this work at a conference, I shared it with my colleagues in the Department of History to get their reactions and feedback. Many described the work as "creative," which they meant, and I took, as a compliment. But hiding beneath that compliment was the judgment, voiced by some, that this work was not "scholarship." In describing it as creative, my colleagues understood this work to be art, perhaps. However, it was not scholarly because it did not conform to prescribed models, defined by writing, by prose, by words on the printed page. I should not have been surprised by this reaction. Indeed, *Style in History* does appear more like an artwork than humanities scholarship: it is non-textual and was designed to be viewed and exhibited rather than read. Yet it also serves as an example of one approach to making in the humanities. While the result resembles an art object, what my team and I created is a humanistic object.

*Style in History* is the product of my particular approach to digital humanities, a term with ambiguous definition and scope. My belief is that to effectively answer the question, "What are the digital humanities?" people must first answer the question, "What are the humanities?" And that question is not so easily answered. Even with lists of departments and specializations that comprise the humanities, humanists are less certain as to what makes the humanities cohere. "Unlike academic departments," notes Geoffrey Galt Harpham (2011), "the category of the humanities seems even to humanists themselves a mere administrative convenience, a kind of phantom entity rather than a real principle of identity; and like all things administrative, it is resisted with indifference. The humanities are something like 'North America,' a level of organization with neither the urgency of the local nor the grand significance of the global" (21).

The humanities study the human, although one could argue that the social sciences study the human, too. Is there, then, a common method that unifies the humanities such that they are distinguished from other disciplines? Harpham offers a simple and elegant definition: "The scholarly study of documents and artifacts produced by human beings in the past enables us to see the world from different points of view so that we may better understand ourselves" (23). I will amend Harpham's definition here to state that humanists interpret texts, and the evidence of that reading is a written performance. Humanists, of course, take an expansive view of what is meant by a text, widening that definition and expanding the range of objects to read, all to their benefit.

On the other hand, their performances, their evidence of that reading, remain limited to only a few forms. James Anderson Winn (1998) observes that the humanities "have identified themselves excessively with analytical processes based narrowly on language, thus disassociating themselves from performance in most of its guises" (3). Winn describes the object of humanistic inquiry as a written textual performance. "Our conception of the humanities," he concludes, "remains largely confined to [as Alexander Pope noted] 'the pale of Words'" (74). Extending Winn's observation, the practice of the humanities is also defined by textual performances. Humanists produce written monographs, articles, and papers as their principal forms of scholarly performance, and the representation of their readings and interpretations is almost always written.

The digital humanities are disruptive precisely because evidence of a reading is often displayed in forms other than text and written prose. Consider the use of databases, maps, graphs, and diagrams, for instance.[1] Digital humanists are, in my formulation, those who read and interpret texts with the aid of digital tools; and, importantly, the evidence of their reading is a digitally mediated performance. The screen expands the possibilities for how humanists demonstrate evidence and proves especially valuable as a space for visual representations and visualizations. The screen also affords new options for what humanists can make, beyond what is possible with print.

In 2009, George Mason University invited me to design a work that employed their newly created VideoWall, a 4×4 panel of screens. I designed *syncretism:mashup,* a large-scale collage of text and images. I was interested in exploring the idea of syncretism as a cultural phenomenon and chose images for the display that physically embodied the syncretism of two or more cultural forms. The display was based on the principle of associative linking. I arranged and reconfigured the images in random patterns such that a viewer would encounter different juxtapositions at any given moment. Associative linking involves seeing patterns of similarity in the midst of apparent differences. The visual argument of the piece, therefore, was that seemingly disparate items—from Pokémon and Dangermouse's *Grey Album* to a McDonald's menu in India and Australians playing cricket in an Indian league—are conceptually linked. My reading of these texts derives from the associative and analogical connections a viewer draws from their unique experience.

Although the conference organizers devoted a session to this site-specific installation, my idea was to let the display run throughout the conference, allowing participants to view it at their leisure. In displaying *syncretism:mashup* in this fashion, I was commenting on the rhetoric and culture of conference presentations: viewing the piece like an artwork expanded how humanists might share work with colleagues beyond whatever messages that work contains. *syncretism:mashup* was also a statement about how humanists might manufacture alternative, interpretive "things."

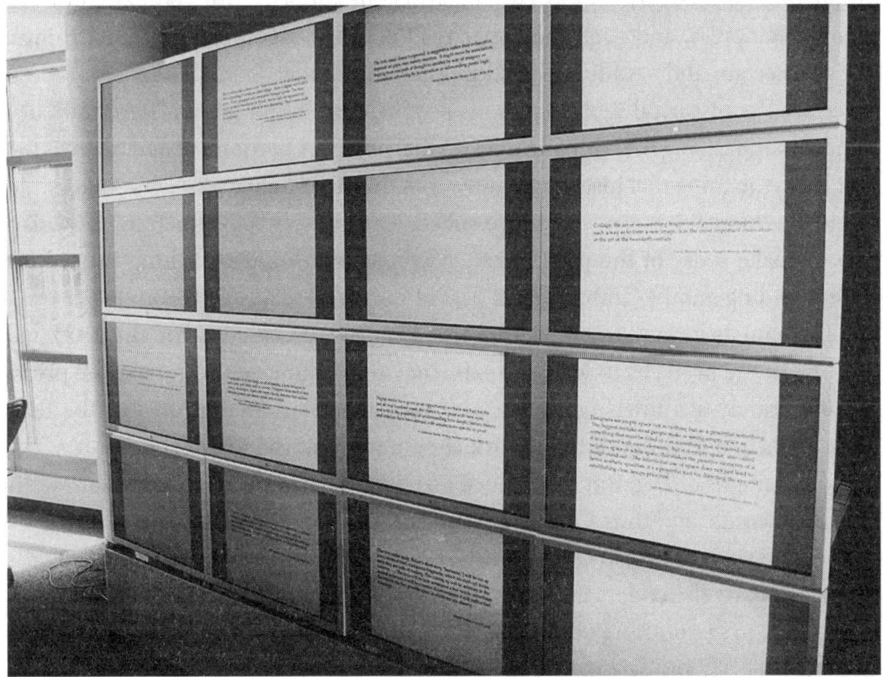

**Figure 2.2.** *Writing Space,* a site-specific digital installation exhibited at THATCamp 2010. Author's photograph.

The next year, I was invited back to George Mason to once again design something using the VideoWall (see Figure 2.2). Rather than juxtaposing images, I wanted to explore the idea of the VideoWall as a writing space. One of my interests as a digital humanist is to explore the affordances of the screen beyond what is possible with the printed page. *Writing Space* was a large-scale text collage that was displayed throughout the conference. I was interested in the idea of "reading" as a humanist in public and at a large scale, unencumbered by the limitations of the page or book. The piece consisted of quotations, each concerning the use of grids (like the display itself), commonplace books, text fragments, negative space, collage, or the screen as a writing space. The text fragments appeared and disappeared in a random pattern of juxtaposition, including interesting asymmetrical patterns of negative space. The quotations and their juxtaposition were also self-referential, drawing attention to the installation itself as an interpretive object. The meaning of the piece was thus a feature of the particular moment as well as the particular juxtapositions a viewer might encounter.

Humanists do not have a name (other than "art" or "performance") for an interpretation or reading that is not written. Thus, pieces such as *Style in History, syncretism:mashup,* or *Writing Space* might appear as works of art or design, but they belong in humanities departments. The idea that humanists might use tools to make things may sound counterintuitive; however, humanists already make things: textual things. These things are not usually identified as such, and their material production goes largely unnoticed. The article in a journal, the monograph from a university press, and even the paper read aloud at a conference are all things, just of a certain and very limited kind.[2] The philosopher Frank Ankersmit (2001) describes the historical representations produced by historians as "narrative substance," emphasizing the "thingness" of textual objects. On the one hand, there is the past itself, the thing that historians study. "On the other hand," observes Ankersmit, "there are linguistic things (narrative substances), in terms of which the historian tries to make sense of the past. In other words, one (linguistic) thing is used for understanding another thing (that is part of historical reality)" (138).

Humanists rarely acknowledge the material production of their textual objects. In the prefaces to written texts, they may thank the editors at the press, but they rarely acknowledge those who produce the material form of the text. Humanists like to think of their work as solitary, that the text is the result of the work of a single author. But to produce textual objects requires a team: I am writing these words, and thus I am doing my part in creating this textual object. The editors and reviewers also construct the object, as do those who set up the words for printing, or the coders and programmers who will design the digital version of this text, to say nothing of those who make the paper, who bind the pages, who ship the objects, and so on. The texts humanists produce as evidence of reading are manufactured objects; as Ankersmit concludes, "The narrative substance is a linguistic object that satisfies all the ontological requirements of objectness"

(137). In this formulation, a written text—as evidence of a reading—is an interpretive object.

A humanist using a 3-D printer to fashion a material object reflects a difference in degree rather than a difference in kind. In pointing to an example such as *Style in History,* I seek to expand the definition and practice of interpretive objects. The objects I create as evidence of my reading are non-textual and perhaps even non-discursive objects. When humanists fill pages with words (a design act), they fill them according to conventions.[3] Textual objects are frequently based on templates, and the humanist's act of making text rarely has an interpretive dimension.[4] That is, the act of making text plays only a small role in the hermeneutic act of evidencing a reading, in that the materials are already known and the form is already given. The "maker turn" expands the range of objects humanists might construct. Since there are few standardized templates, each object—each evidence of a reading—must be imagined anew. Once freed from the printed page, the design of an interpretive object foregrounds the act of making as an important feature of the interpretive act. Design is thus a crucial part of interpretation and making in the humanities.

When humanists expand their definition of the objects they can make, they assume characteristics of designers, where design means "giving form." Humanists might produce objects like those from the Witness Tree Project at the Rhode Island School of Design (RISD). Using fallen trees provided by the National Park Service, design students study the history that the tree would have "witnessed" and make objects from the wood of the tree that represent the history so witnessed (Somerson and Hermano 61). There are no templates for the designer to follow when making these interpretive objects. Interpretive meaning is instead derived from context and the material itself. "A successful scholarly paper," observes Daniel Cavicchi, who teaches the Witness Tree Project studio course, "follows a clear sequence to make a persuasive argument. By contrast, a successful studio object often abides by very different principles of layering, suggestion, association, and provocation. John Dewey explained this as the difference between a statement, which one deciphers, and expression, which one experiences" (68–69). The objects produced by the RISD students are derived from humanist form-giving and viewer experience. Cavicchi concludes that "object-making seems at least as well-suited for the practice of history as writing does. The relationship between objects and the past, after all, is a deep one; in history seminars . . . we make history by 'reading' the past in old artifacts. In the Witness Tree Project studio, students make history too, only they do so by 'writing' the past into new objects. If anything, the Witness Tree Project aligns, to mutual benefit, the realms of creativity and scholarship" (69).

When thinking of non-textual objects as evidence of reading, the first act is to design the form of the object. This act is a little like designing a game board before a game is played. Visualizing form is an important interpretive practice, which is uncommon in humanities teaching, learning, and research. But, for an example from the humanities, consider *FHQIII.* A team I led from Ohio State University and the

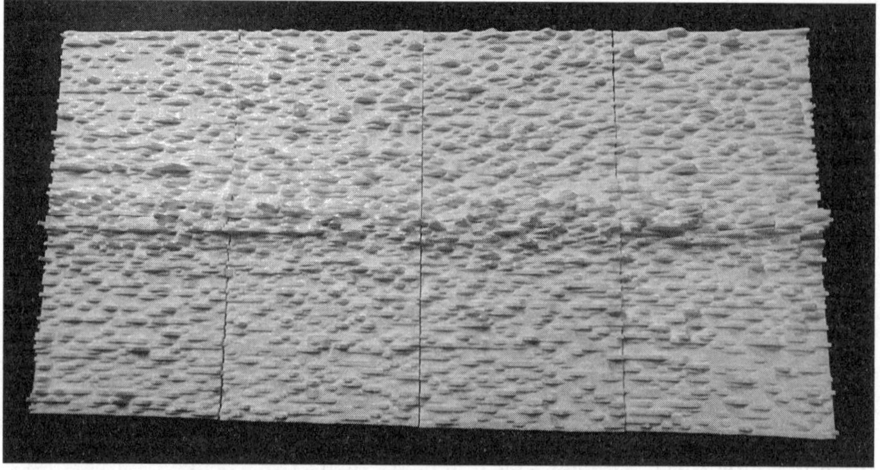

**Figure 2.3.** *FHQ III,* a 3-D printed data sculpture depicting the top 100 key terms across the entire history of the journal, *The Florida Historical Quarterly.* Exhibited at the Lumos Gallery in Columbus, December 2014. Author's photograph.

University of Central Florida designed a 3-D–printed model of the entire run of the *Florida Historical Quarterly* (*FHQ*) in visual, material, sculptural, and haptic form (see Figure 2.3).[5]

Using the term frequency–inverse document frequency (TF-IDF) statistical method provided by JSTOR's Data for Research application, we machine-read over 1,500 articles, identified the top hundred key terms, and then determined the number of times those key terms appeared per year. This analysis produced a representation of subjects and topics of interest to historians of Florida: Native American culture, the Seminole Wars, and eighteenth- and nineteenth-century history, for instance. However, the analysis did not share what those historians say about particular topics or how they say it. Using a 3-D printer, we created a "sculptural model" of this data set.[6] This sculpture was displayed at two academic conferences, but was also exhibited at the Lumos Gallery in Columbus, as part of a show on 3-D–printed art.

Arranging the *FHQ* data proved to be a complex issue. We debated how we would represent the key terms. We experimented with grouping or clustering them based on shared characteristics, but we found that some terms might align with more than one group while others might defy clustering with other topics. In the end, we settled on a pattern where the y-axis contained key words in order of frequency, and we numbered those terms by placing the largest key term in the middle of the axis, the second above, the third below the first, the fourth above the second, etc. These were arrayed initially as a two-dimensional graphical plot, revealing a concentrated cluster across the middle of the display that appeared to "fan out" after the 1960s. (We attributed this phenomenon to an editorial shift from a concentration on relatively few topics to an expanded range of topics.) When 3-D–printed, the numbers of key terms per year were shown on the z-axis as "peaks" of varying height, producing a ridge-like structure that some viewers thought of as a mountain range. Giving form to these data was an interpretive act. How we chose to frame the data was a physical expression of our reading practices. We were, at the same time, revealing and constructing a pattern.

A viewer's physical orientation to *FHQIII* plays a role in how the data are viewed and understood. The presence of the body and its position relative to the data are integral parts of the experience and interpretation. I have long had a fascination with the idea of placing a viewer in physical proximity to a visualization. What would be the result if a viewer were able to "climb inside" a visualization? Indeed, an early version of *FHQIII* was a 3-D digital model that a viewer could rotate and spin in any direction. Were they to choose, a viewer could also "climb inside" the data and experience it from within. I was interested to watch how viewers interacted with the printed sculpture in comparison with the digital model. Their first impulse (when it was displayed flat on a table) was to crouch down and look at the peaks and valleys from a horizontal perspective. Unlike a flat, two-dimensional graph, a viewer was able to examine the data from a variety of perspectives. Their second impulse, usually expressed with hesitant reservation, was to ask, "Can I touch it?" This gesture made embodiment a clear part of the interpretive experience. With textual objects, embodiment is mostly limited to the movement of the eyes across the page; with *FHQIII,* the desire to touch the data and to shift physical positions relative to it suggests an expanded role for a viewer's body in the interpretive act.[7]

Using the same statistical techniques as we did with *FHQIII,* the team and I have machine-read the *American Historical Review*. We will similarly display the top 50 key terms across the entire history of the journal, only this object will be a multi-story installation. Our working title is *Leaves of History*, which we are designing for the interior of a rotunda in a building at Ohio State University. We will represent the key terms as rectangular squares (like the leaves of a page), which will hang down from the top of the rotunda. We will construct each leaf by using a CNC router to cut key terms from gator board. A string of leaves will represent a year; the size of the individual leaf will reflect the frequency with which that term appeared in a given year. Taken together, the 3,700 leaves will appear like a tree.

While a viewer will not be able to move inside *Leaves of History*, the size of the installation will nevertheless envelop their body. They will be able to see the data from a variety of perspectives: underneath it when entering the rotunda on the ground floor and looking up, around it as they encircle the display, and at various levels as they walk up the stairs to one of three floors. As with *FHQIII, syncretism:mashup,* and *Writing Space,* movement and embodiment will be an integral part of how meaning is made.

Creating humanistic objects means rethinking venues for the display of performances in the humanities. Textual objects have established sites for their presentation and preservation: conferences, journals, and libraries. Where will other types of physical objects be displayed and preserved? Many of my objects have been displayed at academic conferences, which may continue to be important venues. However, humanities conferences may need to alter the definition of a "session" and value display more than they currently do. For example, think of poster sessions, which do not have the prestige of papers or talks. Perhaps humanistic objects will be displayed, like public art, in more public venues. The library might serve this role as well, as both site for display and agent for preservation. Art museums and galleries might also extend their infrastructures to humanist makers.

Whatever the location may be, humanists should carve out a space for interpretive objects. In the same way they have expanded not only the definition of a text but also the range of texts to read, humanists may approach the maker turn as an occasion to expand their definition of reading and interpretation by treating creativity as a scholarly act.

## NOTES

1. For instance, see Moretti.

2. Kant, for instance, talks about books as things, as an *opus* (Latin for "object"). See Wellmon, 127.

3. I note how Nick Sousanius in *Unflattening* challenges this idea—how the comic form subverts the conventions of the printed page. Indeed, he contends that the design of the page represents the shape of our thoughts.

4. Of course, there have been experiments with form; consider the journal *Rethinking History*. But, while the types of narrative historians write might evolve, the conventions of print continue to exert such an influence.

5. See Staley, French, and Ferster.

6. See Staley.

7. See this 3-D visualization from the *New York Times*: http://www.nytimes.com/interactive/2015/03/19/upshot/3d-yield-curve-economic-growth.html. While not a physical sculpture, a viewer's orientation to the data is important for how those data are to be interpreted.

## BIBLIOGRAPHY

Ankersmit, Frank. *Historical Representation*. Stanford, Calif.: Stanford University Press, 2001.

Finger, Anke, and Danielle Follett, eds. *The Aesthetics of the Total Artwork: On Borders and Fragments*. Baltimore, Md.: Johns Hopkins University Press, 2010.

Harpham, Geoffrey Galt. *The Humanities and the Dream of America*. Chicago, Ill.: University of Chicago Press, 2011.

Moretti, Franco. *Graphs, Maps, Trees: Abstract Models for a Literary History*. New York: Verso, 2005.

Pasztory, Esther. *Thinking with Things: Toward a New Vision of Art*. Austin, Tex.: University of Texas Press, 2005.

Ramsay, Stephen. *Reading Machines: Toward an Algorithmic Criticism*. Champaign, Ill.: University of Illinois Press, 2011.

Somerson, Rosanne, and Mara Hermano, eds. *The Art of Critical Making: Rhode Island School of Design on Creative Practice*. Hoboken, N.J.: Wiley, 2013.

Sousanius, Nick. *Unflattening*. Cambridge, Mass.: Harvard University Press, 2015.

Staley, David J. "Visual Historiography: Toward an Object-Oriented Hermeneutics." *The American Historian*. http://tah.oah.org/content/visual-historiography/.

Staley, David J., Scot A. French, and Bill Ferster. "Visual Historiography: Visualizing 'The Literature of a Field,'" *Journal of Digital Humanities* 3, no. 1 (Spring 2014). http://journalofdigitalhumanities.org/3-1/visual-historiography-visualizing-the-literature-of-a-field/.

Wellmon, Chad. *Organizing Enlightenment: Information Overload and the Invention of the Modern Research University*. Baltimore, Md.: Johns Hopkins University Press, 2015.

Winn, James Anderson. *The Pale of Words: Reflections on the Humanities and Performance*. New Haven, Conn.: Yale University Press, 1998.

Witness Tree Project. http://www.witnesstreeproject.org/.

# Vibrant Lives Presents *The Living Net*

JESSICA RAJKO, JACQUELINE WERNIMONT, EILEEN STANDLEY, STJEPAN RAJKO, AND MICHAEL KRZYZANIAK

*The Living Net* is one of several techno-textile projects created by the Vibrant Lives team. Using our Vibrant Lives app, we transform the network activity—or "data shed"—of event participants into a sound file that then plays through subsonic subwoofers, thereby causing the Living Net to vibrate at a variable rate depending on the amount of data being shed.

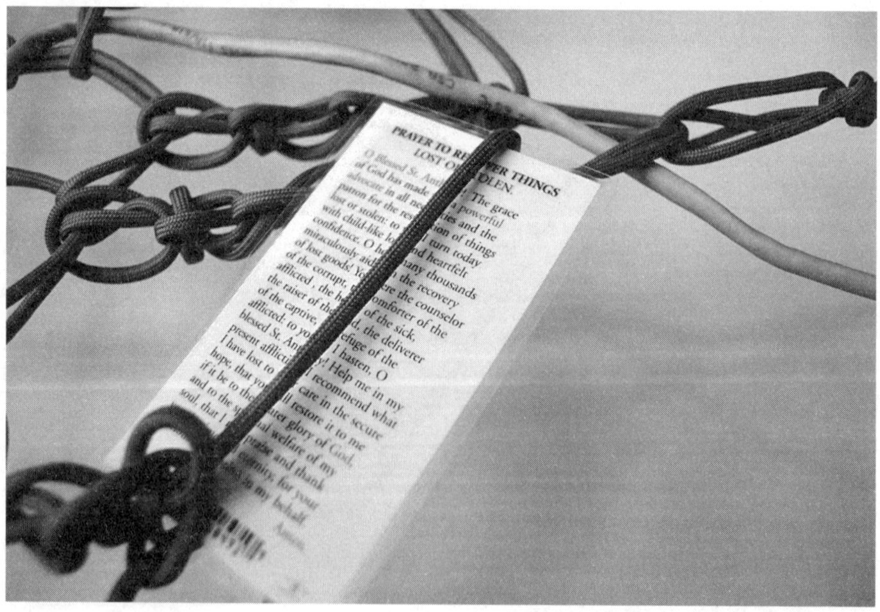

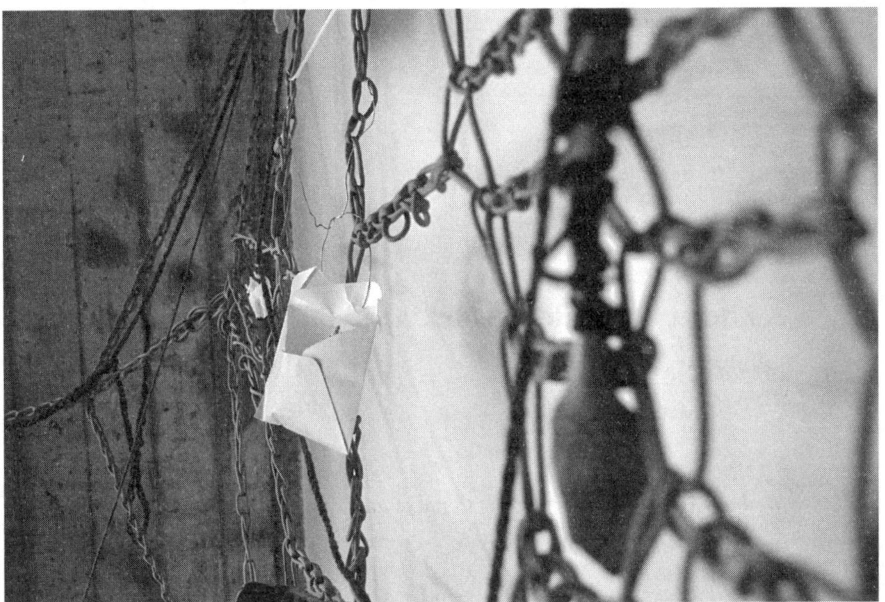

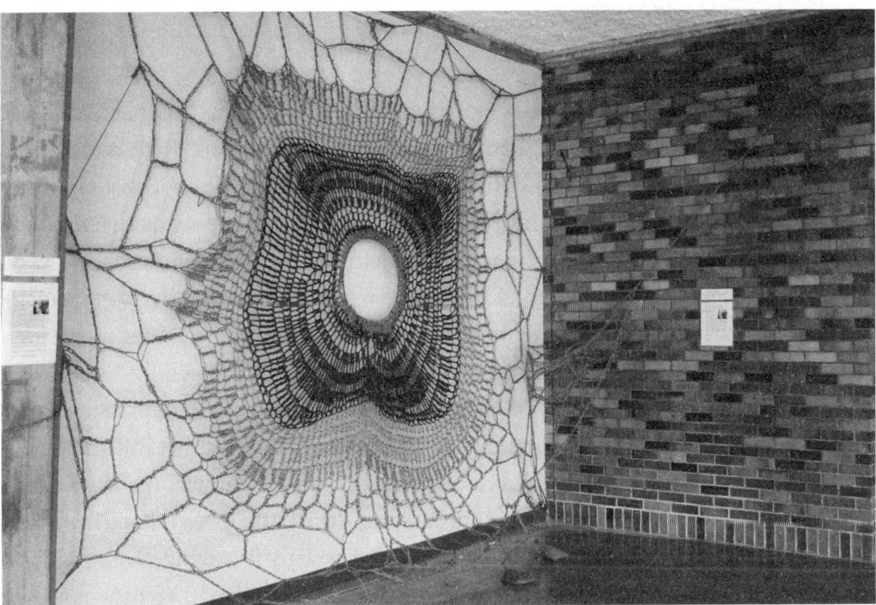

**Figure 3.1.** Vibrant Lives presents *The Living Net*. Format: Mixed media interactive piece. Materials: Finger-crocheted paracord and yarn with Woojers and custom sonification app. Additional mixed media from our scholarly networks woven into the net-work as part of the performance. Research by Jessica Rajko, Jacqueline Wernimont, and Eileen Standley. Textile work by Jessica Rajko with Jacqueline Wernimont. Software design by Stjepan Rajko and Michael Krzyzaniak. Photograph courtesy of Jessica Rajko.

PART I ][ *Chapter 4*

# A Literacy of Building: Making in the Digital Humanities

BILL ENDRES

*We have rights rooted in words to make and remake the world.*

—Guillaume Apollinaire

*Every CSV is an expression of power, every API is an argument.*

—Tim Sherratt

In 2011, Steven Ramsay caused controversy when he gave his provocative talk at the Modern Language Association: "Who's In and Who's Out." Ramsay claimed, "Digital Humanities is about building things." While scholars criticized Ramsay for being exclusionary, they ironically ignored the fact that building has been generally excluded from tenure and promotion guidelines in the humanities.

Building faces the challenge of not being writing. However, the commonalities between writing and building far exceed their differences. The present circumstances that exclude building from institutional rewards, especially tenure and promotion, have more to do with the institutionalization of scholarship. As Kenneth Burke (1984) explains, institutionalized practices regularly promote inflexible perspectives, what Burke calls bureaucratization of the imagination: "the vexing things that happen when men try to translate some pure aim or vision into terms of its corresponding material embodiment, thus necessarily involving elements alien to the original, 'spiritual' ('imaginative') motive" ("Introduction"). Writing is one of many possible material embodiments of "pure aim or vision." Its status as the gold standard for measuring scholarly production is an accident of available technologies. Scholarly activity can be measured in many ways.[1]

Building is also often viewed reductively, as a set of isolated, technical skills. When Stephen Ramsay speaks about building and the importance of digital humanities (DH) scholars knowing how to code, he is talking about coding as a complex intellectual activity ("Who's In"). He recognizes it as practical know-how and an ability to intercede in the world, but he also recognizes its importance in how digital scholars choose to intercede and have impact. Such impact depends upon knowledge of coding (not necessarily coding itself) for envisioning and assessing current possibilities, analyzing and critiquing digital structures, understanding digitally generated ontologies, and apprehending the epistemic principles enmeshed in layers of code (from algorithms to application programming interfaces to scripts to network protocols). Code underpins digital scholarship and affects what can be known, its reliability, and what can be envisioned as possible.

To move beyond superficial differences between writing and building, I employ literacy as a metaphor to examine the complex intellectual activity that building entails and the complexities it shares with writing. I draw from the insights of scholars who revolutionized the study of literacy by viewing it as ideologically constructed rather than a set of autonomous skills. For supporting examples, I turn to my own digital building. This work includes representing the materiality of an eighth-century illuminated manuscript (St. Chad Gospels) through the likes of interactive 3-D renderings and Reflectance Transformation Imaging (RTI).[2] My scholarship is ideologically constructed in the tradition of humanistic inquiry. It functions as a critique of 2-D photography as well as an assessment of and argument for specific uses of emerging technologies and the knowledge they generate.

### *Literacy as Ideologically Constructed*

In the 1980s, scholars began to understand literacy as ideologically constructed. Until this time, literacy was generally viewed as a series of successively learned skills, starting with the recognition and formation of letters and progressing to assembling letters into words and words into sentences. In *Literacy in Theory and Practice* (1985), Brian Street named this approach the "autonomous method" and a second, more theoretically dynamic approach the "ideological method." The main difference between the two is that the ideological method views literate practices as embedded in culture. As Street explains, "In talking about literacy we are referring to the ideology and concrete social forms and institutions that give meaning to any particular practice of reading and writing" (121). When values and beliefs that give meaning to a culture's practices go unexamined—as happens with an autonomous model of literacy—the resulting understanding is fundamentally flawed, understating the dynamics and intellectual complexities of the practices.

Moreover, a year prior to Street's book, Shirley Brice Heath published *Ways with Words: Language, Life and Work in Communities and Classrooms* (1983), a groundbreaking ethnographic study. Heath's book made any return to an autonomous method seem intellectually naïve. Her work documents the disparate struggles faced by children from two communities in a small mill town as they attempt to learn the literacies of school. As Heath explains, children from these communities adopted different literate practices and came to divergent understandings of literacy, structured by their community's ideology: "Their socially determined habits and values have created for them an ideology in which all that they do [including reading and writing] makes sense to their current identity and their preparation for the achievements which will frame their futures" (368). Heath goes on to explain how ideology learned at home and structured by a community makes nonconforming literate practices seem unintelligible or lacking in common sense, creating various types of conflicts around identity and social preparation.

The ideological model of literacy opened possibilities and encouraged scholars to view literacy as a dynamic cultural engagement. It invited questions about how individual communities invent or transform literate practices, integrating these practices into a communal identity. Nowhere is this integration more evident than in international studies of literacy.[3] These studies tend to focus on literacy initiatives that teach literate practices to communities that previously depended upon oral traditions. Researchers regularly note how such communities transform the practices taught to them, not simply adopting them.

Important to my concerns, an ideological model likewise reveals building as ideologically constructed. It provides explanatory power for the dynamic and complex social, scholarly, and intellectual activity that building entails.

### *Building as Literacy*

For the purpose of this essay, building is constructing something digitally, through which a scholarly discourse community can generate knowledge. It can be an archive, piece of software, model constructed in a virtual realm, or interactive feature of a website, such as my digitized and overlaid 125 years of historical photographs for the St. Chad Gospels.

Viewing such building through the lens of literacy calls attention to its ideological construction. It discourages the temptation to view building reductively as mere technical skill. Moreover, literacy provides a model for understanding claims made by DH scholars about building as a scholarly activity. For instance, scholars have proposed building as theoretical modeling (McCarty 2004), prototype as theory (Manovich in Ramsay and Rockwell 2012), prototype as argument (Galey and Rucker 2010), API as argument (Sherratt 2015), design as argument (Galey and Ruecker 2010; Eyman and Ball 2015), visualization tools as hermeneutical theory (Rockwell 2001), digital artifacts as theoretical lenses or "telescopes for the mind" (McCarty 2012), building as scholarly intervention (Ramsay and Rockwell 2012), and tinkering as a process of scholarly reverie, where theory and making collide (Prescott 2012).

Andrew Prescott's view is particularly intriguing because it echoes claims about writing found in much scholarship in the field of rhetoric and composition. This scholarship examines writing as a process of engagement, thinking, discovery, arranging, testing, rethinking, rearranging, and learning. With roots in Aristotelian rhetoric, this perspective has long been valued in the humanities (Ramsay and

Rockwell 82). One of the most influential articles about writing as an intellectual activity, "Writing as a Mode of Learning" by Janet Emig (1977), supports building as a scholarly activity. It claims that writing only has its preeminence over other modes for teaching and intellectual expression, such as dance, architecture, painting, and film, because it represents "the most available medium for composing" (122). Emig adds that such availability "can probably not be overstressed" (122). While digital technologies were not prevalent during the time of Emig's writing, digital building contains all of the qualities that Emig celebrates.

These qualities, however, do not necessarily belong to either writing or building. Rather, they are located in the communities that adopt and adapt them as practices. Communities and their ideologies drive practice. In DH, the ideological construction of building is predicated on answering specific questions posed by scholars in specific fields. It is guided by disciplinary knowledge, participation in a scholarly discourse community, training in the tradition of humanistic inquiry, and pursuit of knowledge previously beyond a single field. DH scholars recognize that the digital brings something new to the table and can contribute to answering questions that could not be answered prior to the computer. While computer scientists and archivists contribute to digital building, the tradition of humanistic inquiry and pursuit of humanistic knowledge consciously constructs a DH project as ideology at its inception.

Disciplinary knowledge, perspectives, and questions inform my own digital building. One important question concerns the materiality of manuscripts and its significance for meaning and interpretation. Part of my training is as a visual rhetorician. Rhetoric, like most fields in the humanities, experienced a "material" turn.[4] This turn was felt in manuscript studies through theorists such as D. F. McKenzie.[5] McKenzie (1999) argues that comprehending a text requires more than interpreting its symbolic meaning. Following Marshall McLuhan's "the medium is the message," McKenzie demonstrates that a scholar cannot exclude "the relations between form, function, and symbolic meaning" (10). For a manuscript, especially an illuminated one, size, layout, and grandeur are part of its expression, part of the complex layering of embodied knowledge. Grandeur, for instance, structures spiritual expression by tapping into the human capacity for wonder.

When studying manuscripts, 3-D digital methods promote McKenzie's call for attending to their materiality. To represent the materiality of the St. Chad Gospels, I employ 3-D flyovers, interactive 3-D renderings, and RTI. Because the humanities have a long-standing orientation toward text, ingrained textual practices tend to emphasize linguistic meaning. This emphasis makes it easy to forget that text on a page is a three-dimensional phenomenon. 3-D renders the contours of a page and restores an awareness of text as three-dimensional. I use 3-D flyovers to provide the experience of looking over a page, offering various perspectives and a sense of a page's grandeur (see Figure 4.1).[6] For exploration, I provide interactive, high-resolution 3-D renderings. These renderings resist the left-to-right and top-to-bottom heuristics

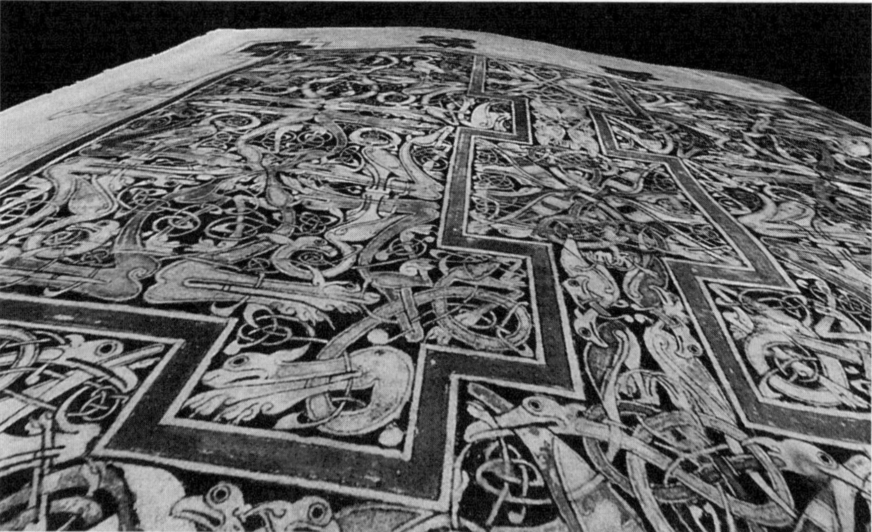

**Figure 4.1.** This 3-D rendering of the Cross-Carpet page of the St. Chad Gospels allows viewers to experience the dimensionality of the page, such as its contours and vanishing point. It enables a different way of studying the page, escaping the up/down and left-to-right dictates of scrollbars. Photographed in 2010 by a team led by Bill Endres; reproduced by kind permission of the Chapter of Lichfield Cathedral.

that favor most forms of reading as well as sole attention to linguistic meaning. They also eliminate the need for and dictates of horizontal/vertical scrollbars common for 2-D images. With 3-D renderings, I include helpful tools, such as a measurement tool and means for making and storing annotations.[7]

Furthermore, 3-D poses significant epistemological questions for humanistic inquiry: What are the implications for knowing when a digital artifact has a vanishing point? How do 3-D renderings affect our relationship to a manuscript, and therefore, how we explore it, remember it, think about it, and know it? Building engages these questions theoretically and experientially. It enriches scholarly expression, enabling theorized positions to have manifest form that can be tested, experienced, critiqued, and examined over time.

Yet using a collection of imaging technologies also meets the demands of scholarly rigor. Rigor constantly requires more from images and imaging technologies. 3-D might capture contours, but it does not necessarily do well in capturing and representing surface details. Fortunately, a new technology, RTI, does. RTI requires a series of photographs taken with different directional lighting. Its software combines these photographs into a composite file that enables control over the angle of light and mathematical enhancements for viewing surface details.[8] For manuscripts, RTI captures the texture of vellum (calfskin), condition of pigments (such as where they are lifting from the page), and notoriously difficult to see features (such as dry-point glosses) (see Figures 4.2 and 4.3). Dry-point glosses

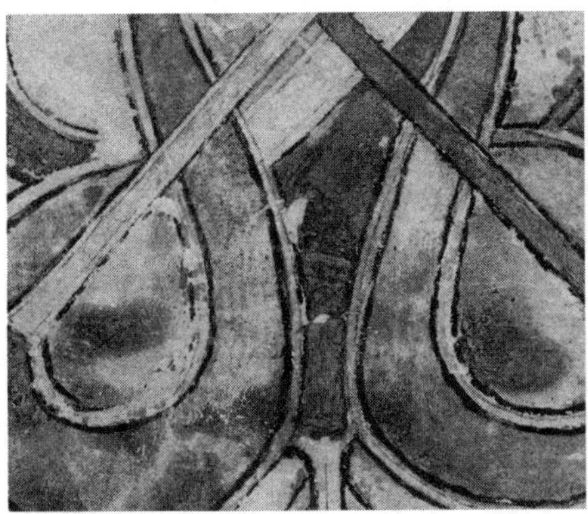
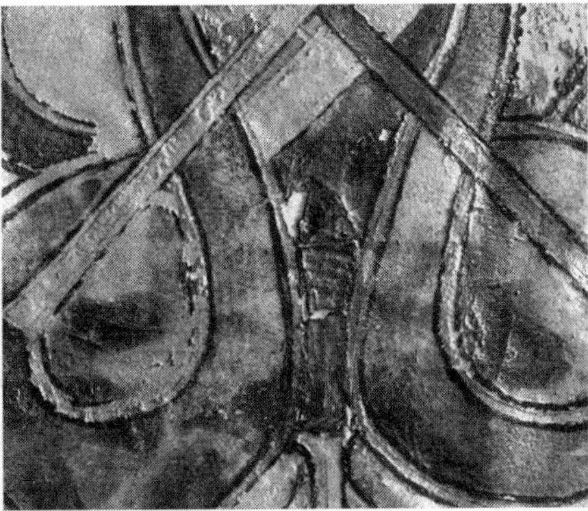

**Figure 4.2.** On the left is a regular 2-D photograph of Luke's robe in the St. Chad Gospels. On the right is an RTI rendering. The RTI renderings show surface details, such as the thickness of pigments and where pigments are lifting from the page. Photographed in 2010 by a team led by Bill Endres; reproduced by kind permission of the Chapter of Lichfield Cathedral.

**Figure 4.3.** This RTI rendering shows a dry-point gloss on page 226 of the St. Chad Gospels. Dry-point glosses are etched with a stylus but no ink and meant to go unnoticed. This gloss is an Anglo-Saxon woman's name, likely a scribe. Photographed in 2014 by a team led by Bill Endres; reproduced by kind permission of the Chapter of Lichfield Cathedral.

are especially intriguing, etched with a stylus but no ink and meant to go unnoticed. Without scholarly rigor informing digital imaging, visual information such as that for dry-point glosses will be overlooked, underappreciated, and lost to history.

### *Digital Objects Are Rhetorical Objects*

While I do not have space to pursue this notion completely, I want to emphasize that digital objects are rhetorical objects. Recognizing their rhetorical nature increases understanding of their limits in generating knowledge and kinship with scholarly text. In the humanities, digital data is often viewed as scientific (or scientifically verified) rather than rhetorical. This causes problems, such as when digital images are considered data. Belief in 2-D photographs as faithful representations of manuscripts has tempted some institutions and scholars to define them, microfilm, and microfiche as primary sources.[9] Such a stance ignores the arguments that McKenzie makes about materiality and raises doubts about manuscript studies based on 2-D photographs. It suggests a lack of critical perspective about media, interpretation, and photography.

I include all digital objects as rhetorical objects, whether images, virtual environments, visualizations, databases, or software. Such recognition emphasizes the weave of beliefs, values, assumptions, epistemologies, theories, and interpretive strategies that underwrite their construction and use. Digital objects are made to participate in an ideologically charged scholarly discourse community and to generate, transmit, and debate its knowledge. The nature of digital objects is rhetorical. Here, the pre-Socratic Greek philosopher Protagoras is worth quoting: "Of all things, man is the measure; of things that are, that they are; and of the things that are not, that they are not" (Kent 4). A definition of 2-D photographs as primary sources eliminates materiality from interpretation and features such as dry-point glosses from historical contribution. Furthermore, the collection of digital objects I mentioned, from software to databases, functions similarly. A database, for instance, stores data by categories determined by a human being. A simple database, such as menus of restaurants, might seem straightforward and yet can run into difficulties when defining what counts as an entrée or side, especially if a few of the sides cannot be ordered separately and only come with certain entrées. Recognizing the rhetorical and relational nature of digital objects makes scholars wiser in constructing and using them. But important for this chapter, it acknowledges the kinship of digital objects to other rhetorical objects, such as scholarly essays and monographs.

### *Yes, There Will Be Differences*

How scholars ideologically construct writing and building will generate differences. However, building faces the challenge of overcoming or at least addressing the ideological features of academic prose. Alan Liu (2014) identifies two such features that I find of particular importance. First, Liu calls attention to how objects of study in the humanities have encouraged scholars to adopt a high style for their language practices: "higher value is ascribed to scholarly writings that at least to some degree are as crafted, nuanced, or elegant as complex literary language; as classically or biblically periodic as famous historical speeches; or otherwise as linguistically tour-de-force as some variant of the above." Liu's characterization of the high style of humanistic writing sets up an immediate tension between academic prose and building. When examined, code or a digital archive does not provide the same order of linguistic phenomena that is expected of humanistic discourse. A well-designed archive is normally efficient in its navigation and content. Code functions behind the screen, and when it is examined, it is not "classically or biblically periodic." The tour-de-force of language is missing. This tour-de-force is an assumed marker of intellectual engagement, scholarly insight, complexity of thought, and academic accomplishment. Digital building, whether code or archive, is not typically wrapped in the "high-pitch verbatim performance" of language and does not feel like scholarly activity.

Second, Liu points out that the data supporting humanistic scholarship is regularly implicit. It results from what he calls "entrained" practices, such as close reading, with only pieces of evidence woven into the narrative of arguments. For finding and retrieving data, humanities scholars rely upon a massive infrastructure of libraries and publishers. The empirical sciences have a different model. They tend to separate the generation of data into its own scholarly activity. Meanwhile, humanities discourse generally does not have the epistemic pressure, as Liu puts it, "for making all its data explicit, shareable, and open to critical examination." Therefore, generating data that other scholars can use is ideologically undervalued in the humanities.

Following Liu, the question of data and how it constructs knowledge is likewise related to medium.[10] While I view ideological construction as the most salient attribute of building, I do not want to neglect differences in media that contribute to knowledge production. For digital technologies, one major contribution is overlay. Overlay is impossible with prose, its linearity requiring juxtaposition.[11] Juxtaposition manifests itself in academic writing in the likes of the dramatic reversal. Such reversals are common and readily observed in significant places, such as setting up a problem in the introduction of an academic essay with the word "however" (Williams and Bizup 101–4). The digital does not need to present information sequentially. In my building, I have taken advantage of digital opportunities for overlay. I built an overlay viewer and use it to organize the thirteen multispectral images I took of each page for the St. Chad Gospels. It allows visitors to stack and compare any two images from a drop-down list, adjusting the transparency of the top image through a slidebar. However, I also use overlay to reveal a significant aspect of the materiality of the St. Chad Gospels: how it is aging. I have digitized images from 1887, 1911, 1929, 1956, 1962, and 2003. Overlaying them reveals changes in the St. Chad Gospels, particularly where small chips of pigment have broken free.[12] Such chips normally measure a fraction of a millimeter, making overlay essential.

### *Closing Proposition*

Pitting writing against building is counterproductive. It circumvents understanding the intellectual complexity and ideological construction that building and writing share. In the introduction, I mention Ramsay's claim, "Digital Humanities is about building things." Instead of proposing coding as a distinguishing characteristic for DH scholars, I propose something based on the shared commonalties between writing and building, and I recognize that my epigraph by Apollinaire could as easily refer to building things—that likewise rooted in images and tools (such as the fifteenth-century printing press) is the power to remake the world. Therefore, I propose that scholars do not need to build to be considered part of DH. Instead, if a scholar supports building as part of tenure and promotion guidelines, then the scholar is part of DH. If scholars recognize the complex intellectual task of building, its scholarly ideological construction, and its kinship with linguistic production, then they are in. Such a proposition opens possibilities for the humanities to meet the needs of current historical circumstances and also support digital building through sponsorship, promotion, and tenure. Such a change will enrich scholarship and perhaps even help to remake the humanities.

## NOTES

1. See Fitzpatrick and the Fall 2012 issue of the *Journal of the Digital Humanities*.

2. For my building, I collaborate with talented programmer Noah Adler.

3. See Street.

4. For a history of the material turn in the humanities, see Miller. For the material turn in the field of rhetoric, see McGee; Greene; and Seltzer and Crowley.

5. Jerome McGann has also been highly influential in these scholarly debates.

6. For 3-D flyovers, see my video: "The St. Chad Gospels: Potentials for 3D in the Study of Manuscripts": https://youtu.be/ebr0HNnNNrs.

7. See my 3-D gallery: https://lichfield.ou.edu/models/gallery.

8. See my RTI gallery: https://lichfield.ou.edu/st-chad-gospels/rti.

9. See statement on primary sources at Yale University: http://www.yale.edu/collections_collaborative/primarysources/primarysources.html. A number of liberal arts colleges make similar claims. How well this position has been thought through is difficult to know. Colleges are marketing their undergraduate programs by claiming that students will work with primary research materials.

10. Numerous scholars have worked on this issue since Marshall McLuhan's well-known statement, "The medium is the message." However, scholars are beginning to uncover problems with scholarship's reliance on writing. For instance, in *Virtually Anglo-Saxon*, Martin Foys demonstrates misconceptions about medieval artifacts originating from text and textual practices.

11. I share an affinity on this point with Kevin Kiernan, who discussed the power of overlay for his *Electronic Beowulf* at the NEDIMAH Workshop: New Methods of Manuscript Imaging and Analysis, National Library of Wales, 2015.

12. For a discussion and an animated GIF of comparing historical photographs, see https://lichfield.ou.edu/historical-images.

**BIBLIOGRAPHY**

Apollinaire, Guillaume. *Selected Writings*. Trans. Roger Shattuck. New York: New Direction Books, 1971.

Burke, Kenneth. *Attitudes toward History*. Berkeley, Calif.: University of California Press, 1984.

Eyman, Douglas, and Cheryl Ball. "Digital Humanities Scholarship and Electronic Publication." In *Rhetoric and the Digital Humanities*, ed. Jim Ridolfo and William Hart-Davidson, 65–79. Chicago, Ill.: University of Chicago Press, 2015.

Fitzpatrick, Kathleen. *Planned Obsolescence: Publishing, Technology, and the Future of the Academy*. New York: New York University Press, 2011.

Foys, Martin. *Virtually Anglo-Saxon: Old Media, New Media, and Early Medieval Studies in the Late Age of Print*. Gainesville, Fla.: University Press of Florida, 2007.

Galey, Alan, Stan Rucker, and the INKE team. "How a Prototype Argues." *Literary and Linguistic Computing* 25, no. 4 (2010): 405–24.

Greene, Ronald. "Another Materialist Rhetoric." *Critical Studies in Mass Communication* 15, no. 1 (1998): 21–41.

Heath, Shirley Brice. *Ways with Words: Language, Life and Work in Communities and Classrooms*. Cambridge: Cambridge University Press, 1983.

Kent, Rosamond, ed. *The Older Sophists*. Indianapolis, Ind.: Hackett Publishing, 1972.

Liu, Alan. "Theses on the Epistemology of the Digital: Advice for the Cambridge Centre for Digital Knowledge." Author's blog, August 14, 2014. http://liu.english.ucsb.edu/theses-on-the-epistemology-of-the-digital-page.

McCarty, Willard. "Modeling: A Study in Words and Meanings." In A Companion to Digital Humanities, ed. Susan Schreibman, Ray Siemens, John Unsworth. Oxford: Blackwell, 2004. http://www.digitalhumanities.org/companion/.

———. "A Telescope for the Mind?" In *Debates in the Digital Humanities*, ed. Matthew Gold, 113-123. Minneapolis: University of Minnesota Press, 2012.

McGee, Michael Calvin. "A Materialist's Conception of Rhetoric." In *Explorations in Rhetoric: Studies in Honor of Douglas Ehninger*, ed. Ray McKerrow, 23–48. Glenview, Ill.: Scott, Foresman, 1982.

McKenzie, D. F. *Bibliography and the Sociology of Text*. Cambridge: Cambridge University Press, 1999.

Miller, Peter. "Introduction." In *Cultural Histories of the Material World*, ed. Peter Miller. Ann Arbor, Mich.: University of Michigan Press, 2013.

Prescott, Andrew. "Made in Sheffield: Industrial Perspectives on the Digital Humanities." In *Proceedings of the Digital Humanities Congress 2012*, ed. Clare Mills, Michael Pidd, and Esther Ward. http://www.hrionline.ac.uk/openbook/chapter/dhc2012-prescott.

Ramsay, Stephen. "On Building." Author's blog, January 11, 2011. http://stephenramsay.us/text/2011/01/11/on-building.

———. "Who's In and Who's Out." Author's blog, January 8, 2011. http://stephenramsay.us/text/2011/01/08/whos-in-and-whos-out.

Ramsay, Stephen, and Geoffrey Rockwell. "Developing Things: Notes toward an Epistemology of Building in the Digital Humanities." In *Debates in the Digital Humanities*, ed. Matthew Gold, 75–84. Minneapolis: University of Minnesota Press, 2012.

Rockwell, Geoffrey. "The Visual Concordance: The Design of Eye-ConTact." *Technology* 10, no. 1 (2001): 73–86.

Seltzer, Jack, and Sharon Crowley, eds. *Rhetorical Bodies*. Madison, Wis.: University of Wisconsin Press, 1999.

Sherratt, Tim. "Unremembering the Forgotten." Keynote, DH2015. July 3, 2015. http://discontents.com.au/unremembering-the-forgotten.

Street, Brian, ed. *Literacy and Development: Ethnographic Perspectives*. New York: Routledge, 2001.

———. *Literacy in Theory and Practice*. Cambridge: Cambridge University Press, 1985.

Williams, Joseph M., and Joseph Bizup. *Style: Lessons in Clarity and Grace*. 11th ed. Upper Saddle River, N.J.: Pearson, 2013.

PART I ][ *Chapter 5*

# MashBOT

HELEN J. BURGESS

MashBOT consists of a small thermal receipt printer connected to Twitter via an Arduino microcontroller. Love notes are generated using Markov chains from a corpus consisting of 90 lines from Roland Barthes's *A Lover's Discourse: Fragments* and ten from Bruno Latour's *Aramis, or the Love of Technology*. They are then published to the @mashomatic Twitter account and printed as "receipts" for display. MashBOT asks us to think about the ways in which the written declaration of love (the "mash note") is a document at once transactional and unfathomable.

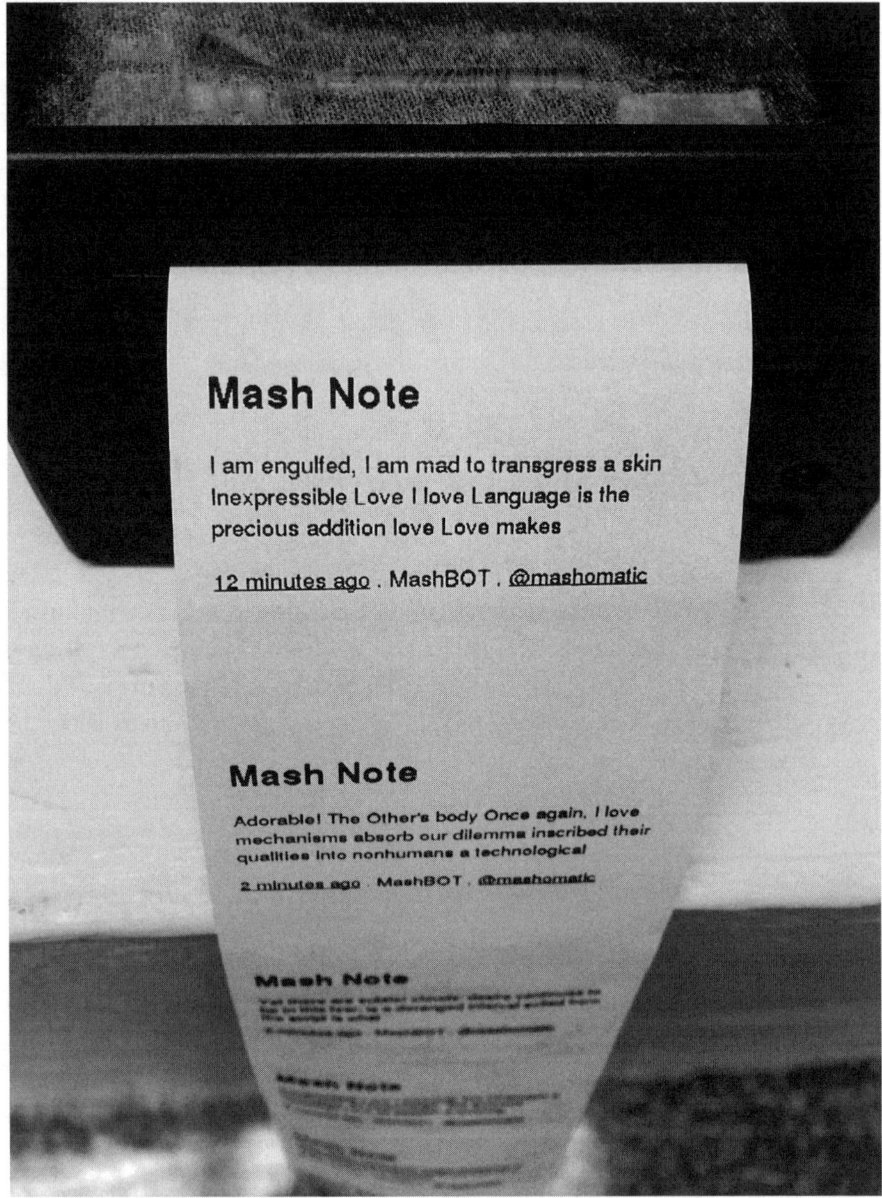


**Figure 5.1.** Love notes emerging from MashBOT's thermal printer. Format: Love notes. Materials: Arduino, ethernet, thermal printer, breadboard components, and Twitter. Rutgers University-Camden Digital Studies Center, August 2015. Helen J. Burgess. Photograph by the artist.

# Making Humanities in the Digital: Embodiment and Framing in *Bichitra* and *Indiancine.ma*

P. P. SNEHA

The humanities are traditionally text-based disciplines, domains of interpreting and representing human experience in its many forms and facets. The object of humanities inquiry is the cultural artifact, of which text is almost always a primary component. In the last decade or so, however, with the growth of predominantly digital environments in which the humanities now function, these objects and the approaches used to study them have changed significantly. Apart from texts (in the form of written material), images and audiovisual archival objects have added new dimensions to humanities research, creating potential for unique modes of inquiry while also imposing different demands and disciplinary challenges in terms of methods, concepts, and scope.

The "digital object" is a rather slippery notion, as it raises significant questions about the materiality and ontology of technologies present around us. Kallinikos, Aaltonen, and Marton (2010) describe digital objects as:

> editable, interactive, open or reprogrammable and distributed. Rather than being simply the contingent outcome of design, these attributes derive from the constitutional texture of digital technologies, most notably the modular and granular make-up of digital objects and their numerical nature. Taken together the attributes of digital objects and the operations by which they are sustained mingle with social practices redefining the scope, the object of work and the modes of conduct underlying them.

Elsewhere, Lev Manovich (1999) describes how numerical representation, modular organization, variability, and automation distinguish new media from old media, particularly in terms of the former's programmability, which he attributes to the advent of a post-industrial society, where digital objects are customized to suit the choices of individual users.

The rather evasive, variable nature of digital objects also makes the processes of creating them difficult to capture, as such labor is often invisible. What, then, comprises "making" in the context of digital objects, and more broadly in the humanities today? Is making a catchall term that includes everything from digitization and remediation to programming and design, or can we narrow it down to a specific form of engagement? Just as it may be difficult to treat digital objects as finished cultural products of some kind, it is important to think of making as an open, flexible process, which includes within its ambit a constantly evolving, changing interaction—a mode of meaning-making with objects. In the humanities, this flexibility not only complicates how certain disciplines are understood, but also creates new challenges for the study of objects.

Perhaps the most evocative articulation of making in the humanities is Stephen Ramsay's (2011) call for "moving from reading and critiquing to building and making" as the radical shift achieved by fields such as digital humanities. This idea of a transition or movement from a scholarly, critical process to one that is tacit and embodied should be resisted, as the prevalent understanding is that the processes are mutually exclusive, akin to other binaries such as conceptual and material, or theory and praxis. These binaries have been questioned in areas of work such as critical making, which, according to Matt Ratto (2011), seeks to "use material forms of engagement with technologies to supplement and extend critical reflection, and, in doing so, to reconnect our lived experiences with technologies to social and conceptual critique" (8). This research is increasingly being done through creative and critical work that utilizes digital or multimedia formats, which, as pointed out by several new media scholars, often contest the primacy of traditional humanities scholarship that continues to privilege content over form, intellectual labor over physical labor, and print over digital media, apart from retaining strict binaries such as old and new media (Burgess and Hamming 2011).

Practices of building and making may not be new in the humanities or especially in the arts, where the boundaries of concept, medium, material, and tools are much more fluid, and to which the production of cultural artifacts is so intimately connected. As illustrated by Roger Whitson (2013) with examples from the works of William Blake, William Morris, Charles Babbage, and Ada Lovelace, there are several possible precursors of critical making, cutting across the arts, humanities, design, and technology. "Making" thus emerges as an important trope to understand and question academic tendencies to emphasize critical, scholarly analysis at the expense of tacit, embodied practices. It is a multipronged, nuanced word that brings together apparently divergent processes and strands of meaning, and it functions as a creative and critical category across thought and practice. Making digital objects in the humanities complicates academic binaries and poses new challenges of form, evaluation, and use in academic contexts.

By drawing on recent work in text and film archival initiatives in India, this chapter discusses some of the issues that arise when digital objects are "made" and made available for humanities research and practice. It explores an online film archive, *Indiancine.ma,* as well as a digital variorum of Rabindranath Tagore's works called *Bichitra,* developed at Jadavpur University, Calcutta. Through an exploration of these two projects, the chapter extends the above thoughts on making by suggesting that: (a) the processes of making digital objects are creative, analytical, affective, and embodied, and (b) the digital itself, in a perpetual state of change, collapses different processes of making into one, namely that of "framing" information. The chapter draws mainly from interviews with researchers and practitioners working with these and similar initiatives, conducted as part of a study by the Centre for Internet and Society, Bangalore, on mapping the field of digital humanities in India. What do these projects tell us about making and the humanities in India, and what are their implications for research, pedagogy, and practice? While these projects may not claim to fall within the ambit of digital humanities (largely due to a lack of consensus in India about what exactly constitutes the field), the concerns they raise resonate with those of others engaged in similar explorations in other parts of the world.

## *Making Textual Objects*

In literary studies, a variorum is perhaps the best example of encapsulating the ways in which a literary work evolves through various forms over a period of time to become the classic that is read and circulated for years. *Bichitra* is an online variorum of the works of the Indian writer, Rabindranath Tagore. Developed by the School of Cultural Texts and Records at Jadavpur University, Calcutta, it contains most versions of Tagore's works—poetry, drama, fiction, and nonfiction—but excludes letters, speeches, textbooks, and translations, except those done by Tagore himself.[1] Sukanta Chaudhuri[2] notes that apparently simple matters of digitization are in fact rather long-drawn processes of sourcing material, photographing/scanning, rendering copies searchable with optical character recognition (OCR), and uploading. As Chaudhuri observes, the innovative aspects of *Bichitra* are ultimately functions of cross-referencing and integration. In fact, he calls it an "integrated knowledge site."

The bibliography is a hyperlinked structure, which connects to all the different digital versions of a particular text (the most being 20 versions of a single poem). The search engine integrates these resources: searching for a word or phrase leads to all its occurrences in the entire corpus of Tagore's works. The team also developed a unique collation software, titled "Prabhed" (meaning "difference" in Bengali), that helps to assemble text at three levels—chapter, paragraph, and words—and compare occurrences across editions and versions of the work to note matches and differences. As Chaudhuri further outlines, working with Indic scripts is a key challenge for digital initiatives in India. In Bengali, some work has been done in the form of scientifically designed keyboard software called Avro, which stores all the conjunct letters and preserves their separate characteristics. However, developing OCR for scanned material in Indian languages has been a persistent problem for most digitization and archival initiatives in India. Apart from this challenge, there are issues like vowel markers appearing before consonants as well as spellings that change over the years.

Backroom file management, whether of actual paper files or digital files, remains a big but largely invisible task on such a platform. The total number of files generated from *Bichitra* is tens of millions or even hundreds of millions, and many of these are offline files not even published on the website. The process of making text available as hypertext is invisible labor, rarely or never available to the end user. The text in the digital variorum is therefore the result of several interrelated tasks, and it facilitates new modes of reading and engaging with it. This kind of reading, which is simultaneously close and distant, can track changes and migrations across the corpus of the writer's works over a period of time, facilitating new approaches to textual analysis. The object of the inquiry itself goes through numerous changes to become available for study on a digital platform, where it is amenable to intense searching and querying of a different kind altogether. It is now possible to search across a large corpus of Tagore's texts for minute changes in words or sentences and then ask questions about their usage, instances, and contexts of occurrence.

The digital object is made through all of these processes: digitization, encoding, cross-referencing, querying, collation, reading, and narrating—all of which involve conceptual and material aspects of thinking and doing. The variorum, unlike an archive, is supposed to be a finished cultural product, a comprehensive collection of textual material. But the digital text, by virtue of its medium being an extended network of meanings, is never complete. It is being "made" constantly through a multitude of processes. By extension, electronic text helps scholars better theorize the notion of a fluid text[3]—the fact that a text is never complete, only bound between the covers of a book at a given point involving several processes that are technological as well as social (Johns 3; Bryant 17). Electronic text also raises important questions of how humanists understand technology in a certain fashion, with the move toward language and representation as an important way to articulate these concepts. Is technology a tool for textual analysis, or is it inherent to our understanding of text? Is the development of digital or computational methods shaped by certain disciplinary requirements, and does it create new conflicts for traditional methods? The growth in the study of different media objects, such as video and cinema, and the advent of areas such as oral history and media archaeology have prompted further concerns about digital objects in these disciplines.

### *Making Video Objects*

*Indiancine.ma* is an expansive online archive of Indian films that are presently out of copyright. Like its predecessor, *Pad.ma*, it is built using Pan.do/ra,[4] a desktop-class web application for organizing, managing, annotating, analyzing, and remixing large archives of video materials. The software includes an editing tool that enables a user to pause, cut, and annotate a particular sequence in the film according to a time code. Content can be searched for and organized through different filters, such as color and object recognition. These features open up fresh possibilities for interpreting films as well as methods that could not be applied until recently.

Ashish Rajadhyaksha,[5] a film and cultural studies scholar who has worked with the team behind *Pad.ma* and *Indiancine.ma*, says the most unique aspect of this archive is that it creates a new kind of research object, which is structured through different layers of meaning: time, date, maps, annotations, images, and so on. A film becomes a placeholder around which various kinds of data are mobilized, affording a unique intensity. Rajadhyaksha gives an interesting example: the Hindi film, *Dharti Ke Lal* (1946), which has a few street scenes shot surreptitiously in Calcutta when the city was under military occupation. The director, K. A. Abbas, writes of this experience later in his autobiography, where he mentions how the scenes are noticeable due to the presence of American GIs and British Tommies. These scenes can now be searched for and found, and the director's narrative, along with excerpts from other writing on the film and events from that period (notably the Bengal Famine), have been layered onto *Dharti Ke Lal* through the annotation tool.[6] This kind of contextualization and layering is possible precisely because of digital objects. An archive such as *Indiancine.ma* also illustrates how humanities methods and scholarship are shaped by technological possibilities. Now both textual and film studies are being urged to rethink their methods due to the challenges and potential offered by technologies when organizing source material.

Moinak Biswas,[7] faculty member at Jadavpur University, Calcutta, speaks of the changes that digital technologies have brought to video in general and films in particular. According to him, the creative practice of "image-making" comes together with analytical and scholarly practices in the digital, especially on a platform such as *Indiancine.ma*. This combination, which is both distributed and collaborative, changes how scholars create and engage with texts. In the study of digital film objects, acts of creation are visible, tangible, and made possible through a digital environment that thrives on shared methods of learning. Madhuja Mukherjee,[8] faculty member at Jadavpur University, Calcutta, talks of how the film object itself changed greatly with the shift from celluloid to digital as well as the ubiquitous presence of the Internet in everyday life, where people can shoot, upload, and circulate video much more easily than in the past. *Indiancine.ma, Pad.ma,* and *Bichitra* illustrate these changes in terms of how cultural materials enter networks of circulation and meaning once they are in digital form.

Jan Gerber and Sebastian Lutgert,[9] the artists and software programmers who developed Pan.do/ra (on which both *Indiancine.ma* and *Pad.ma* are based), talk about the different ways in which people have imagined the projects—as online archives, software projects, and pedagogical tools and resources. The opacity of video as a digital object, due to its mathematical "compositing" (Rodowick 165–66) through different elements that cannot be captured finitely or seamlessly, further complicates any attempt to define the projects and their materiality. The Pan.do/ra platform has developed many ways or entry points into the material, through color, shape, and so forth, to allow more varied and evocative access to films. The annotations let the user enter the archive at different points and explore films through inscriptions left there by other users. This capability renders film objects even more fluid than they already are. Additional variability is created through context, interpretation, and further use, leaving both the films and the archive always incomplete—always "in the making."

Digitization therefore changes the artifact significantly, often demanding a new method to approach the object of study. For example, Padmini Ray Murray,[10] faculty member at Srishti School of Art, Design, and Technology, Bangalore, suggests that the digital is one way to mediate material objects, particularly those that are not textual, since certain kinds of experiential access can only be provided by digital means. The Internet as a space is also useful because it helps to find and create niches for the audience who uses and adds to online archives, contributing further to knowledge about the object. However, a significant divide exists between the people who conceptualize these projects and those who design and build the infrastructure for them. It is difficult to find people who can do both, a reflection of the rigid separation of skills as well as methods into categories of thinking and doing. The lack of a common language to speak across disciplinary barriers is quite problematic, and more collaborative methods for project development need to be encouraged. This lack also points to the difficulty of working with digital objects and describing their material aspects. The transformation of cultural artifacts—including both textual and audiovisual archival materials—into digital form is an interesting entry point to understanding digitality itself and the role that making plays in engendering, maintaining, and furthering the state of digital objects.

In his work on "technesis," Mark Hansen (2000) describes this conundrum effectively when he talks about the difficulty of adequately capturing the materiality of technology in discourse. Hansen describes technesis as "the putting-into-discourse of technology" (4), a reductive strategy of assimilating technology into thought. He extends this argument further by drawing from Bergson's theory of perception,[11] which places a crucial emphasis on the body as "a center of indetermination within an acentered universe" (in *New Philosophy for New Media* 98). The body itself becomes an image among others and acts as a filter, selecting from other images around it, depending on its capacities and relevance. Hansen also draws from Gilles Deleuze's work on cinema,[12] particularly Deleuze's notion of "framing." In particular, Hansen renders Deleuze's "movement-image" and "time-image" analogous to the framing a body undertakes when making sense of information. Critiquing Deleuze's more formal understanding of cinematic framing, Hansen argues for an embodied form of enframing where affect[13] and memory are important in sensorimotor perception. He says this turn is specific to the digital, where there is a convergence of all media forms (xiv–xxvii).

This characterization of the digital image can be extrapolated to other kinds of digital objects as well, in that they are essentially dynamic, manipulable, and modifiable, whether they are texts in a variorum or films in an online archive. By this very nature, they are also unfinished, as they are constantly being remade and unmade. Making, here, becomes *a process that is creative, analytical, and affective,* always inscribed by traces of technology, memory, and perception. It thus serves the purpose of trying to capture this unfinished aspect of materiality, as it facilitates an embodied enframing of information, which is also constantly changing. For the humanities, then, making poses several interesting questions and challenges for the study of digital objects.

### *Making Humanities in the Digital*

As is apparent in their functionality, digital objects are constituted by the processes of their making—through edits, annotation, compression, transcription, and so forth. As Hansen suggests in *New Philosophy for New Media* (2004), "The digital image is processual" (5), and the processes of its making help uncover the manner of its constitution by incorporating affect within studies of materiality. The focus on process in most contemporary accounts of making, such as critical making, is a focus on this dynamic nature of the digital. Such a focus urges the humanities to move from a mode of inquiry dealing largely with representation to engage with objects in a manner that is more embodied. This suggestion is contentious, for it proposes an inquiry that is perhaps quite physical and clinical, even if it is also intellectual, rather than one invested primarily in discourse and context, which are historically central to the humanities. Does the study of digital objects then blur the lines between methods in the humanities and sciences? As opposed to studying finished cultural texts, would the humanities contribute to their making?

The practice and discourse around critical making in a way reiterates the classic two cultures debate.[14] What C. P. Snow saw as a widening schism between the sciences and humanities, and an emphasis on humanities at the expense of scientific advancement, has implications for both disciplines today. In a neat division of labor, relegating the humanities to a discipline of abstract relevance, while endowing the sciences with the empiricism necessary to understand and improve the human condition, the two cultures divide gives the sciences the task of effecting change in a real, material way. One manifestation of this divide suggests that certain skills in building, coding, or making are the province of a particular section of people, further deepening the chasm between disciplines and domains. Critical making questions this boundary, specifically between material and conceptual practices, in our engagement with the world. It is an attempt to better understand the material aspects of technologies around us, through the "processes of their making" and their lived experience, rather than treating them as finished products. The objective is therefore to bring together two approaches or modes of engagement with technology.

As the projects above illustrate, a combination of diverse skills helps create digital platforms, but some aspects of labor become more visible, or are made more visible, as a result of which existing categories or silos—making/writing, theory/praxis—are reinforced. As Gerber and Lutgert recount their experience of not only creating *Pad.ma* and *Indiancine.ma* but also working with a diverse set of people in India and Germany, there is a need to translate ideas across domains of expertise. While such translation is difficult, this gap between "tech and non-tech" people is something they find very problematic; their own areas of training range from philosophy to software programming. Although they have developed the platforms for *Pad.ma* and *Indiancine.ma,* they feel their contributions have been more conceptual. Perhaps, then, there is also a need to foster more spaces where making encourages conversations across different domains of practice, research, and learning.

Pushing this notion further, we may also ask whether writing and making are necessarily divided and mutually exclusive processes as such. Perhaps they are different expressions of the same framing. The notion of framing, as Hansen describes it, is drawn from cinema and carries within it a critique of ocularcentrism. Here, a frame is not an external or literal frame but rather the process by which formless information is made apprehensible to the body through consciousness. Hansen argues that this act of enframing information must be seen as the source of all technical, external frames (even if they appear to be primary) to the extent that they are designed to make information perceivable by the body—that is, "to transform it into the form of the image" (*New Philosophy for New Media* 10). Framing is a process by which consciousness creates information by allowing meaning to inhere in the images it produces (162–64). It thus becomes a crucial process of embodied perception, and separating it from the visual register to trace its connection to consciousness also makes it an effective way to understand making itself as an embodied, affective, and critical process.

As such, *making, writing, playing, and building can be understood as ways to frame information.* To "make" in the humanities may well mean to "read" or "write" and therefore no longer appears to be a contentious proposition. Brushing against neat divisions of labor, perhaps making is also creative, physical, clinical, and intellectual. With the digital turn, the advent of new modes of making helps us not only better understand existing forms of humanities practice but also comprehend the conflicts inherent in the roles technology plays in these processes. This turn contests and in many ways transforms traditional humanities scholarship (including print-based work). It also opens up various avenues to think of multimedia and digital scholarship, research, and practice today. As illustrated in the examples above, the digital text in the variorum or the film in the online archive is an amalgamation of practices that are simultaneously creative and analytical, physical and intellectual.

In many cases, the intersections are seamless. For example, as mentioned by film studies scholars interviewed here, annotations in the form of marginalia, errata, and paraphernalia (e.g., notes, pamphlets, tickets, and lobby cards) for films are actually new objects, and textual or discourse analysis may be inadequate methods to interpret a film clip that has been layered with these objects. Approaching them through only one mode of engagement may no longer be a persuasive way to fully understand them, or it may not reveal the scope and limitations of its own methods. While digital objects make demands on the skills and competences of researchers, they also push the boundaries and framing of research, practice, and scholarship in interesting directions.

To reiterate Hansen's argument about framing, affect is a modality of the body, produced through the processes of embodiment, and in turn functions as a medium that helps us understand the relationship between bodies and information. In mediating between the two, it also allows the body to "collaborate with information" in the production of new experiences and perspectives. More important, it raises questions about the ontology and materiality of digital objects—whether the text in the variorum or the film in the archive—thereby opening the digital itself to a space where objects are constantly being made, remade, and unmade. An exploration of digital objects reveals perennial binaries such as digital/physical, material/conceptual, and creative/critical, also unraveling in the process new conflicts and definitions of what it means to inhabit the digital. In the Indian context, this work is also a varied, multilayered space, which is in transition from analog to digital. With an entry into the processual, making in the humanities thus offers a new perspective and approach to understanding the condition and very idea of the digital as something more than a binary, formal, or static representation. Through an exploration of the material and conceptual processes of digital objects—a form of close reading, in a way—making affords a nuanced understanding of the humanities' many possibilities.

## NOTES

The author would like to thank all the people interviewed for their generosity in sharing their views and the details of their work, and Sumandro Chattapadhyay, Lawrence Liang, and Nishant Shah for their valuable input in writing this chapter.

1. See http://bichitra.jdvu.ac.in/index.php.

2. Professor Emeritus in the Department of English and School of Cultural Texts and Records at Jadavpur University, Calcutta. Interview on Skype with author, July 30, 2015.

3. John Bryant describes the fluid text as "any written work that exists in multiple material versions due to revisions (authorial, editorial, cultural) upon which we may construct an interpretation" (17). He argues for the need to make the "process of revisions" and evolution of textual versions more visible and central to the process of interpretation.

4. Pan.do/ra is a Free/Libre and Open Source Software (FLOSS). See https://pan.do/ra.

5. Interview with author, Centre for Internet and Society, Bangalore, February 19, 2015.

6. For the film clip and annotations, see http://indiancine.ma/EIC/player/ANK.

7. Professor in the Department of Film Studies and founder of the Media Lab at Jadavpur University, Calcutta. See http://www.medialabju.org. Interview with author, Jadavpur University, December 17, 2013.

8. Associate Professor in the Department of Film Studies and Joint Director of the Media Lab at Jadavpur University, Calcutta. Interview with author, Jadavpur University, December 18, 2013.

9. Interview with author, Centre for Internet and Society, Bangalore, February 24, 2015.

10. Interview with author, Centre for Public History, February 18, 2015.

11. See Bergson, *Creative Evolution*.

12. See Deleuze, *Cinema 1* and *Cinema 2*.

13. See Hansen, "Affect as Medium or the 'Digital-Facial-Image.'" Drawing from Henri Bergson's and Gilbert Simondon's work on affect, Hansen explores the digitized facial image, or what he terms the digital-facial-image (DFI), as a "new paradigm to understand the human interface with digital data" (207). The DFI helps "catalyze the production of affect as *an interface between the domain of information (the digital) and embodied human experience*" (209). He therefore describes "affectivity" as this crucial relation between body and image: "Insofar as the confrontation with the DFI functions by triggering affectivity as, precisely, a faculty of embodied heterogenesis, it operates a transfer of affective power *from* the image to the body. Instead of a static dimension or element intrinsic to the image, affectivity thereby becomes the very medium of interface with the image" (208). Affect and affective are used here in this specific register.

14. See Snow, "The Two Cultures."

## BIBLIOGRAPHY

Bergson, Henri. *Creative Evolution.* Translated by Arthur Mitchell. New York: Henry Holt, 1911.

Bryant, John. "Witness and Access: Uses of the Fluid Text." *Textual Cultures* 2, no.1 (2007): 17–18.

Burgess, Helen J., and Jeanne Hamming. "New Media in the Academy: Labor and the Production of Knowledge in Scholarly Multimedia." *Digital Humanities Quarterly* 5, no. 3 (2011): 2–3.

Deleuze, Gilles. *Cinema 1: The Movement Image.* Translated by Hugh Tomlinson and Barbara Habberjam. Minneapolis: University of Minnesota Press, 1986.

———. *Cinema 2: The Time Image.* Translated by Hugh Tomlinson and Barbara Habberjam. Minneapolis: University of Minnesota Press, 1989.

Hansen, Mark B. N. "Affect as Medium or the 'Digital-Facial-Image.'" *Journal of Visual Culture* 2, no. 2 (2003): 205–28.

———. *Embodying Technesis: Technology Beyond Writing*. Ann Arbor, Mich: University of Michigan Press, 2000.

———. *New Philosophy for New Media*, ed. Timothy Lenoir. Cambridge, Mass.: MIT Press, 2004.

Johns, Adrian. *The Nature of the Book: Print and Knowledge in the Making*. Chicago, Ill.: University of Chicago Press, 1998.

Kallinikos, Jannis, Aleksi Aaltonen, and Attila Marton. "A Theory of Digital Objects." *First Monday* 15, no. 6 (2010). http://firstmonday.org/ojs/index.php/fm/article/view/3033/2564 - author.

Manovich, Lev. "New Media—A User's Guide." Author's website, 1999. http://manovich.net/content/04-projects/026-new-media-a-user-s-guide/23_article_1999.pdf.

Ramsay, Stephen. "On Building." Author's blog, January 11, 2011. http://stephenramsay.us/text/2011/01/11/on-building.

Ratto, Matt. "Critical Making: Conceptual and Material Studies in Technology and Social Life." *The Information Society* 27, no. 4 (2011): 252–60.

Rodowick, D. N. *The Virtual Life of Film*. Cambridge, Mass.: Harvard University Press, 2007.

Snow, C. P. "The Two Cultures." *Leonardo* 23, no. 2/3 (1990): 169–73.

Whitson, Roger. "Critical Making in Digital Humanities: A MLA 2014 Special Session Proposal." Author's blog, March 31, 2013. http://www.rogerwhitson.net/?p=2026.

# PART II

# MADE BY WHOM? FOR WHOM?

# Making the RA Matter: Pedagogy, Interface, and Practices

JANELLE JENSTAD AND JOSEPH TAKEDA

*We are the makers of manners.*

—William Shakespeare, *Henry V*

For many years at *The Map of Early Modern London* (*MoEML*, a Canada-based literary mapping project), our project mantra has been "we are the makers of manners." It began in a teachable moment, when a research assistant (RA) questioned our non-compliance with MLA citation guidelines. Jenstad spontaneously quoted "We are the makers of manners" from the final scene of Shakespeare's *Henry V*, where Henry tells his manners-conscious bride-to-be that they are not to be "confined within . . . a country's fashion."[1] In other words, Henry and Katherine, by breaking the old rules, *make* the new fashions of the country; others will follow their lead. This potentially presumptuous mantra has allowed the project director (Jenstad) to deconstruct the authority of the MLA and other academic rulebooks so that our project could be innovative in matters of citation, credit, and collaboration. Perhaps inevitably, the remaking of academic manners led to the remaking of project hierarchies. If the project's leaders could challenge the authority of even the venerable *MLA Handbook*, then perhaps the RAs could challenge the project directors and lead programmer.[2] Our project ideal has thus become our training ideal, with the consequence that *MoEML* RAs are themselves "makers of manners." Just as our project challenges disciplinary authorities, the RAs challenge the directors' and programmers' authority in ways that change the "manners" of our project. They become full collaborators, complementing and sometimes superseding the project leaders' expertise. They take responsibility for key areas of the project, identify opportunities, propose solutions, set the standards, and document project practices. In this process, we make the RA matter.

"We" is the key word in that last sentence.[3] Jenstad does not build the digital humanist, any more than she alone is responsible for building *MoEML*. This chapter is co-authored by Jenstad (a tenured faculty member) and Takeda (an undergraduate student who began as an RA and has since become *MoEML*'s first Junior Programmer), because making the RA matter is a collaborative venture. The RA has a role in her[4] own "becoming" or "sense-making" (Chachra).[5] In keeping with *MoEML*'s training obligations as a federally funded project, the director provides training and learning opportunities. In order that the project's goals are met, the director requires the RAs to learn from the training; in fact, a precondition of hiring is "teachability," an expectation we formalize in our RA contract.[6] However, "making" requires not just "the will to know" but also "the will to become" (hooks 19). This distinction comes from bell hooks's vision of liberatory pedagogy in *Teaching to Transgress* (1994). She suggests that students want "knowledge that is meaningful" and connected to their "overall life experiences," with the important caveat that students "will not always accept our [teachers'] guidance" (19). In this model of teaching, students "assume responsibility for their own choices" (19). Is it possible to implement a liberatory pedagogy (a model developed for the classroom) in a project environment where the granting agency demands benchmarks, fiscal accountability, and final reports? We argue that it is not only possible but also ultimately beneficial to the project to create a space for RAs to challenge the project leaders and take responsibility for their choices.

Our contribution to this volume articulates the potential for a liberatory model of training and describes the process of making[7] the RA. Our argument takes place in three movements. First, we address *MoEML*'s training history, arguing that *MoEML*, like any other institution, had and still has the potential to be hierarchical, inverted, flat, or transgressive. Second, we reflect on what it means to "make" the RA. We mobilize the recent work in interface theory, namely Wendy Chun's (2011) historicization of human interfaces and Johanna Drucker's (2013) work on interfaces as border zones, to argue that positioning the RA as an interface allows us to realize hooks's transgressive model of liberatory pedagogy. Third, we look at the manners—the practices, habits of mind, and guiding principles—that are required and called into being by this new model of training. In this chapter we seek not to prescribe another set of rules for building digital humanities (DH) project teams or write another set of learning outcomes for granting agencies, but rather to emphasize the pedagogical potential of allowing the team to make itself in ways that work for the project and personnel.

## *Institutional History*

What is *MoEML*? The quick answer is that it is a grant-funded, open-access suite of digital resources and tools for the study of Shakespeare's London. The longer answer positions us somewhere between a DH center, maker lab, program, and classroom at the University of Victoria (UVic); we are not any one of those things, but we have certain practices and values in common with each of those models. *MoEML* is not a center with its own physical space, but we do book work stations in the shared space of the Humanities Computing and Media Centre (HCMC), where we rub shoulders and refine ideas with personnel from other DH projects.[8] Other places we gather include Jenstad's departmental office, a project office in the same building, the Special Collections and University Archives classroom, the computer teaching labs, and occasionally the campus pub. We conduct much of our business via virtual workspaces: e-mail, Google Drive, a Subversion repository, GitHub, and web-based project management tools (Asana). *MoEML* is not a makerspace, at least insofar as we are not engaged in physical computing or fabrication. However, our work toggles between the digital and the material on a daily basis: our new map of London was made partly with paper, tape, and artists' pens; our site menus were first built with yellow sticky notes on long sheets of Kraft paper; rare books sit beside our mouse pads. We have made a number of digital things: a map interface, a gazetteer, mapping tools, and a CodeSharing tool. And we have remade, or remediated, a number of rare books and maps by digitizing, transcribing, and encoding them. Nor is *MoEML* a program; we operate in some ways like the Praxis Program,[9] but we tend to hire undergraduate and MA students rather than PhD students, and our students join an ongoing project rather than collaboratively conceiving and completing the new project that the Praxis program requires. Although it is a grant-funded project hosted on UVic servers, it is no longer a single-researcher-directed project; we now have a leadership team and are answerable to our editorial board, contributors, peer reviewers, and pedagogical partners. Despite our training mandate, *MoEML* is not a classroom, either. We do not offer for-credit courses, although we often provide opportunities for students undertaking research scholarships,[10] theses, DHUM or DHSI projects,[11] or work placements in Professional Communication. Even now, as a peer-reviewed, indexed project, we honor our classroom roots in our current pedagogical partnerships.[12] In short, we inhabit multiple campus spaces, retain the do-it-yourself (DIY) ethos of making, follow the ethics of the Praxis program, and find ourselves teaching others and each other all the time.

Given that our project history and current structure are both well documented (see Jenstad, "Restoring Place to the Digital Archive"; Jenstad, "Using Early Modern Maps in Literary Studies"; Jenstad, "History of MoEML"), we focus here on our identity as a pedagogical "institution" with a training mandate derived from the Social Sciences and Humanities Research Council (SSHRC), the federal funding agency that has supported *MoEML* through two research grants. A key part of any SSHRC application is the "Research Training Plan." According to SSHRC's "Guidelines for Effective Research Training," the plan must describe how the supervisor or grant applicant will *train* students and *build* their competencies so that students *acquire* "valuable skills" and *gain* "new perspectives and knowledge." Ultimately, SSHRC thinks of the RA as a product of the academic world for the benefit of the non-academic world: such students will carry their humanities skills into post-academic life and "make strong contributions in Canada and globally."

The SSHRC model presupposes that grant-funded projects inherit the structures of traditional learning institutions. Cathy N. Davidson and David Theo Goldberg

(2010) note that "[i]n conventional learning institutions, the lines of authorship and authority are clearly delineated, and the place of teacher, student, and technology are known" (7). Our first "RA Contract," based on Jenstad's 2011 "Research Training Plan," expected that, by the end of their tenure, RAs should have "internalized *MoEML*'s standards" after gaining "more autonomy in individual tasks." Following SSHRC's language, the contract sets out an apprenticeship model anticipating that the student will gain mastery of trade secrets in the process of making increasingly complex digital things under the direction of a master-practitioner (Jenstad, "Training and Work Practices Contract"). The contract's transferable learning outcomes describe what skills the RA will have and the tasks the RA will be able to do by the end of the *MoEML* work period. The verbs—deploy, digest, write, understand, troubleshoot, document, record, work with—lend themselves to repetition on the students' resumes; those learning outcomes also align with one or more of the tasks required for *MoEML* to achieve its goals, suggesting there is a close relationship between the making of the project and the making of the RA's competencies. The RA makes the project according to the supervisor's specifications; simultaneously, the supervisor, fulfilling the funding agency's mandate, makes the RA. Jenstad has always seen project leadership as an extension of her classroom-based pedagogical practice. *MoEML* team members are accustomed to regular pauses in the work where we seize teachable moments. Jenstad and the other project leaders (Kim McLean-Fiander and Martin Holmes) regularly take the time to explain the ideological and scholarly issues that drive the project, as well as to share their knowledge of historical, technological, bibliographical, and cultural matters.

But, as Davidson and Goldberg suggest, with "*digital* learning, these conventional modes of authority break down" (7, our emphasis). Jenstad has long appreciated the way the project inverts the roles of teacher and student. The teachable moments have never been uni-directional at *MoEML*. Since 1999, when *MoEML* began as a project for three students who needed a "client" (i.e., Jenstad) and a challenge ("Well, I've got this old map . . .") in a second-year "Writing Hypertext" course at the University of Windsor, *MoEML* has often been indebted to student initiative and expertise. Initially, Jenstad, who did not train as a digital humanist, relied on students to teach her. She paid students from that "Writing Hypertext" course to teach her HTML; other students later tutored her in the Text Encoding Initiative (TEI), Extensible Markup Language (XML), and Extensible Stylesheet Language Transformations (XSLT). As work-study RAs, students working for academic credit, and grant-funded RAs came and went, the project developed a pattern whereby Jenstad taught each new team member everything she knew; the RA's final responsibility was to teach Jenstad everything she had learned on the job. Eventually, the team became big enough to warrant formal training sessions that covered analytical bibliography, text encoding, research hygiene, and project praxis; by staggering RAs' terms, Jenstad was able to delegate much of the training to outgoing and experienced RAs. Role-switching helps everyone learn, but the inversion of roles ultimately reifies the one-way model of training. This carnivalesque inversion of teacher and student implies that someone must always be the teacher and someone else the student and ultimately reinforces the hierarchical nature of traditional training.

As we rethink our training plan for another SSHRC application, we have the opportunity to reflect on and revise the model Jenstad derived in 2011 from the rhetoric of SSHRC. Jenstad did not articulate in that initial grant application what she already knew to be true: that the project director is also a trainee and, furthermore, that inviting the RAs to be teachers is a key component of their "training." During the lifetime of that grant (2012–16), *MoEML* developed its model of student training still further and came to believe that the hierarchical and occasionally inverted model of teacher and student is not the best model for the project, the students, or the project leaders. In our 2015 grant application, we articulated more clearly that our RAs are "contributors with a stake in the project." In fact, outgoing RAs Takeda and Tye Landels *wrote* that section of the grant. When asked to "copyedit" what Jenstad had drafted, they argued that they were the people best qualified to articulate what and how *MoEML* RAs learn during their tenure with the project. The collaborative work on the grant is itself a sign of how a hierarchical model can give way to a more dynamic team model in which diversely talented people challenge and complement each other daily. *MoEML* is in fact more like the "mobilizing network" that Davidson and Goldberg propose as the future of learning institutions (127). Instead of being hierarchical, *MoEML* tries to "aggregate, coordinate, disperse, balance, and adjudicate complex flows of resources" (129). McKenzie Wark (2013) observes that "collaborative labor is an *and-also*" kind of play (our emphasis). We try to avoid "thinking that X is by origins higher in rank than Y." Each *MoEML* team member brings unique qualifications and natural talents to the project; during the course of the work, each team member develops particular domain expertise and even a sense of ownership over aspects of the project, thereby dispersing and balancing resources. We need both X *and* Y to move their domains forward independently. We develop new domains when X *also* helps Y and *vice versa.*

Our shift towards a liberatory or transgressive model of training occurred in step with other new models, especially those articulated by the Scholars' Lab Charter and the Collaborators' Bill of Rights. The Scholars' Lab (SLab) is a collaborative digital scholarship center and makerspace that fosters teaching, learning, and mentoring through consultation with other projects. The SLab Charter appeals to the pathos of working for a digital project by focusing on the "whole person"; at SLab, where they "build up people, not tools," you are "more than your job, your field, your role." The Charter does not spell out what collaborators might become; rather, it values collaborators' agency and encourages everyone "to develop new ideas and grow as scholars and practitioners" (The Scholars' Lab). Although *MoEML* is a project, not a place for supporting projects, we can learn from SLab's focus on the whole person. The collaboratively written Collaborators' Bill of Rights (CBR)[13] articulates the ethical problems of and solutions for acknowledging collaboration. Formed as a response to the single-author-credit paradigm of the humanities wherein the first writer is often the only individual acknowledged, the CBR argues for proper accreditation of labor within DH projects: credit must be given where credit is due, collaborators should be "empowered to take credit for their work," and attribution for labor should be listed publicly on the project website. Like many other projects, *MoEML* has adopted the CBR's principles of crediting all contributors and recognizing their right to articulate the nature of their contributions.

While these documents articulate exemplary models of collaboration between graduate students, postdocs, early career scholars, and senior faculty, they do not provide guidance for collaborations with the *undergraduate* students who comprise the majority of *MoEML*'s team. The Student Collaborators' Bill of Rights (SCBR) extends the CBR by acknowledging the centrality of undergraduate contributions to many digital projects. The SCBR spells out the numerous ways a student may contribute to a digital project: as a hired research assistant, via a directed reading or capstone project, or through an assignment within a course structure. Students must be acknowledged for all "non-mechanical" labor that furthers the site in some way, whether financially compensated or not. The SCBR provides an "additional safeguard for students" by recognizing the hierarchies within DH projects and institutions (Di Pressi et al.). Undergraduate students find themselves working with graduate students, early career scholars, programmers, and tenured faculty members. The SCBR does not fully address the complexities of acknowledging content created by students as students (for credit), by students as employees (for remuneration), or by and *with* undergraduate students at the *intersection* of their roles as student, advisee, expert, and employee. However, from the SCBR, we learn to acknowledge the hierarchies that pertain on projects where contributors occupy multiple roles in the larger institution.

### *Where Making Happens: The RA as Interface*

How do we create the preconditions for the RA to mobilize the will to become? We believe that the way to create a liberatory training plan is to position the RA as the interface. Given the history of interfaces, our desire to position the RA as interface could sound regressive. Interfaces have not traditionally been liberatory. Human interfaces, like the "women of the ENIAC," have been invisible, underpaid, and unacknowledged. Yet recent work on these early human interfaces between machines and output shows that they "did not simply operate the machine, they helped shape it and make it functional" (Chun 31). We do not want students to be the new (derogatorily named) "ENIAC girls"—essential but unacknowledged. Our strategy is to invite the RA to take on and adapt some of the director's interface functions.

Normally, the director is the interface in that she is the "place of interaction between two systems,"[14] the two systems being a scholarly-professional system on the one hand, and a pedagogical system on the other. In the SSHRC model, the director is the hub of the project, where she serves as the interface between the RA and the research problems. In order to solve the research problems or achieve the agenda that she has set out in the grant application, the director directs and bridges the different personnel on the project: the co-applicants, the programmers, the contributors, and the RAs. The RAs accomplish specific tasks that allow the director to achieve her agenda and address the research questions. In performing those tasks, the RAs achieve certain learning outcomes that serve their own professional development. Eventually, the RA is the vehicle by which competencies and skills are transferred "to a variety of settings" outside academia.

In that model, the RAs might function as the historically regressive kind of interface that invisibly enables "techno-human mediations" (Drucker 213). Transforming data in the service of larger research questions to which they may not be privy, RAs could be the "invisible hands" that transcribe, collate, transmediate, encode, or correct. This type of work might easily be categorized as the "mechanical" labor that does not need to be acknowledged even under the generous terms of the SCBR. SSHRC's training mandate does not require acknowledgment of the RAs' labor: their remuneration is fiscal and intellectual. In our experience, however, even so-called "mechanical" labor demands critical decisions and domain knowledge. Not only does *MoEML* leave a trace on the RA, but the RA leaves a critical trace on the project. In keeping with the SCBR, we need to render that trace visible through credits and acknowledgment. Such a practice ensures that the RA is not an invisible mediator between the digital data and the project director. However, it does not liberate RAs or, to borrow from hooks, invite them to become. Giving credit does not, by itself, necessitate the transgression of traditional project hierarchies.

*MoEML* has a long history of positioning RAs between domains. Our preferred training mechanism is, in fact, to position the RA, rather than the project leaders, as the "place of interaction between systems." We can draw on various meanings of interface to theorize the roles of the *MoEML* RA. The RA can be useful as a mediator between the technologist and the humanist. Jenstad has often needed RAs with computer training to "translate" between her and the project's programmers; in that work, the RA functions as a kind of HPI, a humanist-programmer interface or what Drucker deems a "place of interaction between two systems" (213). But how do we ensure that the RA is not simply a membrane between systems? We want the RA to inhabit Drucker's "space of individual and collective formation" (217). At *MoEML*, we move the director out of the way and make the RA the interface between the project and the research questions. That place is not only a "border zone between cultural systems, with all the complexity and emergent relations that suggests" (216) but also an "autonomous zone . . . of activity" (Galloway vii).

When RAs as human interfaces have agency and autonomy, they "are not simply objects or boundary points" (vii). The RA is an agent "in constant formation" (Drucker 216), inhabiting a zone where new skillsets and relationships emerge. For example, Takeda came to *MoEML* as an English major with an interest in computer science, making him a logical candidate for liaising with lead programmer Martin Holmes. Takeda's expertise in the site infrastructure and development code is now far superior to Jenstad's, and on occasion we have experienced the hierarchical inversion of Takeda assuming the role of teacher. But what is really valuable is the *labor process* that invites Takeda to "map the thinking from one labor process onto another experimentally" (Wark). He wields both the programmer's hammer and the humanist's idea of a hammer; he can see both the nail and the idea of the nail at the same time. Takeda's position as interface between systems invited him to become something new: a humanist programmer or programming humanist. By occupying that ecological border zone between humanities and programming, Takeda willed himself to become our junior programmer, a role he chose to inhabit and a title he claimed for himself in the project's credits.

### *Making New Manners*

What does it mean in practice to position the RA as interface? We are not suggesting that a liberatory model of training simply invites RAs to define new roles for themselves. On the contrary, there are a number of practices, habits of mind, and guiding principles that are required and called into being by this new model of training.

Recognizing that a truly flat team structure is probably impossible in a hierarchically organized institution, we strive in our small corner of the institution to keep our team dynamic and flexible; the institutional gaps between professor and student are thereby "compressed" so that we can achieve what we might call a "flatter" team structure. For example, anyone can add items to the agenda for team meetings. Agenda items are solicited by the project manager, and the final list is given out at the team meeting; Jenstad does not pre-approve the agenda, and her items have no more or less weight than those of any other team member. Team members will often prepare presentations to contextualize a problem or justify a recommendation. Using the task management software, anyone can assign tasks to anyone else, and everyone can track all the tasks in our shared workspace. Occasionally, Jenstad will exercise "directorial privilege" in a self-conscious way, invoking her experience and longer view of the big picture. However, anyone on the team can, at any time, call us back to our guiding principles (such as "Tell the truth in encoding"), and everyone is free to disagree and make a case for a different way of proceeding. The flatter model invites the transgressive challenges that often push the project where it needs to go next. The transgressive model is not simply a "world-upside-down" model where we occasionally reverse the hierarchy; on the contrary, it disperses and localizes authority by recognizing that the person best qualified to make a specific judgment call is not necessarily the project director.

In a flatter structure, individuals' knowledge of the project can be recognized as a domain expertise. We actually see Jenstad's "big-picture thinking," grant-writing skills, and project memory as particular kinds of domain expertise and not as overarching expertise. While Jenstad has large objectives, she invites team members to gravitate toward the work that attends to their own research interests and skills. The RA can choose tasks out of the pool of tasks, create new tasks in keeping with larger project goals, and suggest new ways of achieving those goals. A key part of team culture is mutual recognition of each other's nascent and maturing domains. We call regularly on each other's experience and specialized knowledge, saying things like "Tye is our Praxis expert," "Ask Joey to show you how to make tables," and "Katie is tackling the mayoral shows." Our project culture therefore "mobilizes collective activity and activates inspiring and productive resources and social relations" in the way that Davidson and Goldberg suggest (138). Across our distinct domains, we take ownership for our own work, but we also feel a sense of shared ownership for the project. Inclusive language is a natural extension of our working practices: our working pronouns are "we," "our," and "us."

The overarching principle of our project is "Tell the Truth." The phrase comes from our programmer, Martin Holmes, who insists at every turn that our encoding of texts be truthful. Markup must be faithful to the text we are encoding and to our own project guidelines. The concept has percolated through other aspects of the project. We show our XML—four versions of our XML, in fact[15]—to make our treatment of the text fully visible to (and reusable by) other scholars. In doing so, we become accountable for every change to the text and every comment we leave in the XML file. Holmes developed the aforementioned CodeSharing tool and an Application Programming Interface (API) that allows users to search every element, attribute, and value used in our project.[16] Having committed to the principle of telling the truth about our encoding, we have done all our work in the knowledge that every aspect of it is public-facing. All of the project documentation and encoding instructions are captured in the Praxis section of our site, which is itself indexed in multiple ways.[17]

## ENCODING OUR PRACTICES

We are now guided by the imperative to tell the truth about *who* did *what when* on our project, an imperative that has had radical implications for how we acknowledge collaborative work and student work in particular. Like Davidson and Goldberg, we have observed that "the more collaborative the project, the more we must think about individual credit" (9). Our encoding practices are meant to encode our practices as a team and recognize individuals. The metadata for each document (captured in the <teiHeader>) includes multiple responsibility statements, each captured inside the <respStmt> element, which "supplies a statement of responsibility for the intellectual content of a text, edition, . . . where the specialized elements for authors, editors, etc. do not suffice or do not apply" (TEI Consortium). Any contributor can have more than one responsibility statement, which allows us to describe various roles that any one person might have played at various points with respect to a particular document. Consider one of Sarah Milligan's responsibility statements in the metadata for our forthcoming edition of John Stow's 1598 *Survey of London:*

```
<respStmt>
  <resp ref="molresp:mrk">
    Date, Forme Work, and Foreign Words Encoder
    <date from="2012" to="2014"/>
  </resp>
  <name ref="mol:MILL2">Sarah Milligan</name>
</respStmt>
```

The role is described in the <resp> element, which uses the @ref attribute to point to *MoEML*'s taxonomy of responsibilities.[18] The <date> element allows us to map the period over which the work was performed. These <respStmt> elements are rendered as credits that appear on the left-hand side of each *MoEML* document. In keeping with the SCBR, we invite RAs to characterize their contribution precisely in their own words. The content of the <resp> element is a free-text field, which allows contributors to customize the description of their role(s). Milligan corrected the original TEI-XML in the transcription of Stow's *Survey* that we obtained from the *Early English Books Online Text Creation Partnership* (*EEBO-TCP*). While the standard code "mrk" ensures that Milligan is listed with all the other markup editors who have contributed to *MoEML,* her self-description as "Date, Forme Work, and Foreign Words Encoder" captures the precise nature of her work.

To tell the full truth about our project, we would have to give credit even to so-called "mechanical labor." In fact, we believe that very little labor is actually purely mechanical; therefore, we have developed a taxonomy to describe the many ways in which RAs contribute to the project. In order to expand our vocabulary beyond the ubiquitous and limiting "author" and "editor" categories, we turned to the marcRelators used by the Library of Congress (LoC) cataloguing system to express "the relationship between a name and a resource . . . in bibliographic records." From this list, we have adopted and adapted many roles, including some that are often considered too "mechanical" to be acknowledged. For example, we give credit to the proofreader of a document. *MoEML* uses the LoC marcRelator "pfr" "to designate a contributor who checks a transcription against an original document, or a person who corrects formatting and typographical errors in a born-digital article." We also credit the person who proofreads the TEI tagging (in *MoEML* terminology, the "markup editor") in a unique <respStmt>. The 37 named roles that we credit include annotator, conceptor, consultant, data manager, researcher, and transcriber. We have supplemented the LoC marcRelators with our own molRelators, which include copy editor, toponymist, vetter, cross-vetter, Cascading Style Sheets (CSS) editor, and guest editor. We have even corresponded with the LoC and successfully suggested new roles for their list of marcRelators.

These roles are not wedded to the particular RA or contributor in their entry in *MoEML's* personography. We hired Milligan as a novice encoder, but her role changed considerably over her two years with *MoEML*. She now works as the Publishing Manager for British History Online but continues to contribute to *MoEML* as a research associate. We understand that people inhabit different roles at different times. In keeping with the SLab Charter, we see the person, not the role, as paramount. The granularity and multiplicity of the responsibility statements allow us to capture the person's work in great detail without identifying the person with any one of those roles or limiting the RA to the nebulous identity of "RA." All of these roles are linked to the contributor's biography page, which offers a curated narrative and bio-bibliographical note about the person as well as a dynamically generated list of all the person's contributions and roles.

## REMAKING PRACTICE

Our most innovative work comes about when we aggregate and coordinate our resources and expertise. In our praxis of telling the truth, we often find ourselves challenging established standards, thus asking new sets of research questions. One such instance is *MoEML's* ongoing engagement with historical dates. *MoEML's* temporal scope puts it in the period of maximum calendar confusion for England, which did not adopt the Gregorian calendar until 1752, nearly two centuries after most other European countries. In the process of encoding Stow's list of regnal years in the 1598 *Survey of London,* Milligan had to determine best practices for parsing and representing historical dates. Due to the complexities of early modern dating and the conversion from the Julian calendar to the proleptic Gregorian, historians have come to accept early modern dates as an insoluble problem of the field. But Milligan came to this problem using *MoEML's* principle of honesty and consulted with Jenstad and Holmes to find a way to encode Julian dates truthfully.[19]

We believe the solution spurred by Milligan's research and questioning, crafted by Jenstad and Holmes, and documented by another RA, Tye Landels, came into being through positioning the RA as interface. Milligan developed the research question and approached the various project personnel with complementary domain expertise. *MoEML's* initial solution for encoding dates remained in use for two years but was recently questioned by Takeda. He came across a new problem with early modern calendars during a directed reading course on the weekly and yearly publications of the London Bills of Mortality. Takeda discovered that Milligan, Jenstad, and Holmes's previous solution was not precise enough to record the various idiosyncratic scholarly attempts to regularize dates.[20] Just as Milligan had done some years prior, Takeda approached Holmes in hopes of finding a solution at the level of tagging; Takeda and Holmes then consulted with Landels and the three of them met, discussed, deliberated, and corresponded until they achieved consensus on a new practice for encoding and processing dates. They then approached Jenstad and the rest of the *MoEML* team with their recommendations; in this case, Jenstad was the *last* person to know of both the problem and Holmes, Takeda, and Landels's solution. At the time of writing this present chapter, Takeda and Holmes are co-writing new code to handle a variety of dates in use in the early modern period while Landels crafts the rendering schemes and the explanatory Praxis documentation.

We discuss our long struggle with historical dates to show the effects of positioning the RA as interface. Indeed, forging the liberatory space for the RA to express their will to become has lasting consequences; acknowledging the RA's autonomy betters not just the project and the RA's experience but also the scholarship produced. Milligan's project of recording regnal dates, which began as mechanical labor—transcribing the dates as recorded in Cheney, Holinshed, and Stow—grew to become an important research question that has the potential to rewrite the scholarly protocols for recording and regularizing early modern dates.

### *Conclusion*

*MoEML* RAs now leave the project having rewritten the manners that were supposed to guide their work. In the process of telling the truth, we have also transgressed the manners of academic rule books, the practices of other digital projects, and disciplinary standards. Forming these new standards was never an action item on our grant applications; they came into being through our project practices, habits of mind, and guiding principles. For us, telling the truth about our work means acknowledging the need to decenter the project director and reconceiving the project as a space of "collective and individual formation." We may articulate specific goals and outcomes in our grant application, but necessary and productive deviations take place. What the RA makes and what the RA will become are not foreseeable by the director when she writes the Research Training Plan for the grant proposal, which specifies the necessary steps to make the RA. In fact, what Takeda and Landels wrote in the Training Plan came as a gratifying surprise to Jenstad. She was not—and could not be—aware of the full extent of their learning, precisely because liberatory pedagogy demands that the teacher not control the lessons. Indeed, just as the most interesting use of our data will not be what we think it is (Poston), the most interesting outcomes of the RA are not predetermined. Their ownership of the project means that they become collaborating agents, in charge of not just domains of expertise but also their own willingness to become. Takeda and Jenstad wrote this chapter in much the same way that the project itself is made: drawing on our respective expertise, experience, and critical inclinations; teaching each other; shifting tasks (research, visioning, writing, editing, and documenting) depending on who was best suited for the task in that moment; and working together to create something that neither of us could have made without the other's input. Opening up the team structure and positioning the RA as the interface between the director and the research questions invites the "transgressive" moments that change and challenge the way we work. Here, we believe, hooks's "vision of liberatory education" becomes possible, where allowing RAs agency connects the "will to know" to the "will to become" (18–19). In the process, the RAs become makers—the makers of new *MoEML* manners.

## NOTES

*The Map of Early Modern London* has been supported by a Social Sciences and Humanities Research Council of Canada (SSHRC) Standard Research Grant (2003–08), a SSHRC Insight Grant (2012–16), and three UVic General Research Grants (2010, 2011, and 2016). *MoEML* enjoys ongoing support from the UVic Faculty of Humanities via the programmers and staff of the Humanities Computing and Media Centre.

1. William Shakespeare, *Henry V* 5.2 TLN 3260, http://internetshakespeare.uvic.ca/Library/Texts/H5/FM/scene/5.2 - tln-3260.

2. The project leaders are Janelle Jenstad (Director), Kim McLean-Fiander (Associate Project Director, 2013–2015), and Martin Holmes (Lead Programmer, 2012–Present).

3. Takeda joined *MoEML* in 2014 as an undergraduate research assistant and encoder. He is now junior programmer for *MoEML* under the supervision of Martin Holmes and Jenstad.

4. We use the pronoun "she" throughout this essay when referring to an RA in general; we use the appropriate pronoun when referring to specific RAs.

5. We agree with Chachra that the student (and here, the RA) cannot be made—instead makers (project directors or educators) must work to make the *space* in which an RA/student can thrive.

6. Our contract is encoded on *MoEML*. See http://mapoflondon.uvic.ca/RA_contract.htm.

7. We use the terms "building" and "making" interchangeably in this chapter.

8. The Humanities Computing and Media Centre (HCMC) is a computing space for research in the humanities. They have dedicated programming staff (Stewart Arneil, Martin Holmes, Greg Newton, and Pat Szpak) who provide technical support and guidance for a number of projects at the University of Victoria. For more information, see http://hcmc.uvic.ca.

9. The Praxis Program, founded in 2011 at the Scholars' Lab at the University of Virginia, represents itself as an apprentice program *and* as "as an opportunity to experiment with an action-oriented curriculum *live and in public*." See http://praxis.scholarslab.org/about. *MoEML* also sees itself partly as an apprenticeship and partly as a living, public experiment in co-created knowledge.

10. *MoEML* has benefitted from a number of undergraduate scholars since the inception of the Jamie Cassels Undergraduate Research Award (JCURA) in 2009. Students are awarded a $1500 scholarship to conduct and give a presentation on an independent research

project. A number of *MoEML*'s pages are the result of these scholarships; the most recent addition is a complete list of maps of London to 1700 (see *MoEML*'s "Mappography," http://mapoflondon.uvic.ca/MAPS1.htm).

11. Independent study Digital Humanities (DHUM) courses conducted in conjunction with *MoEML* are projects that stem from the data or the infrastructure of the site. The two most recent have been (current RA) Tye Landel's "Georeferencing London Books," which was taken in conjunction with the Digital Humanities Summer Institute (DHSI) at the University of Victoria, and Takeda's "Remediating Bills of Mortality" (see http://mapoflondon.uvic.ca/DHUM491_2014 and http://mapoflondon.uvic.ca/DHUM491_2015, respectively).

12. *MoEML*'s pedagogical partnership is an initiative whereby professors and students collaboratively write and edit contributions for *MoEML*'s encyclopedia. For more information and past and present partners, see http://mapoflondon.uvic.ca/pedagogical_partners.htm.

13. The CBR is a collaboratively authored document composed as a result of the *Off the Tracks: Laying New Lines for Digital Humanities Scholars* report (2011). The collaborators are Tanya Clement, Brian Croxall, Julia Flanders, Neil Fraistat, Steve Jones, Matthew Kirschenbaum, Suzanne Lodato, Laura Mandell, Paul Marty, David Miller, Bethany Nowviskie, Stephen Olsen, Doug Reside, Tom Scheinfeldt, David Seaman, Mark Tebeau, John Unsworth, and Kay Walter.

14. *Oxford English Dictionary,* "interface," n.2.a.

15. From our XML, we produce four different XML outputs that include and exclude various components as necessary; for more information see, Martin Holmes's "XML Outputs," http://mapoflondon.uvic.ca/xml_outputs.htm.

16. For more information on Holmes's CodeSharing API, see http://mapoflondon.uvic.ca/BLOG10.htm.

17. See the index for Praxis, http://mapoflondon.uvic.ca/praxis_index.htm.

18. See "Responsibility Taxonomy," http://mapoflondon.uvic.ca/responsibility_taxonomy.htm.

19. For a detailed explanation of the *MoEML*'s date encoding practices, see http://mapoflondon.uvic.ca/encoding_dates.htm.

20. As Cheney notes, "The practice of historians, both in England and on the Continent, has varied in the past, and the result is confusion" (xiii).

## BIBLIOGRAPHY

Chachra, Debbie. "Why I Am Not a Maker." *The Atlantic,* January 23, 2015.

Cheney, C. R., ed. *A Handbook of Dates for Students of British History,* 2nd ed., revised by Michael Jones. Cambridge: Cambridge University Press, 2004.

Chun, Wendy Hui Kyong. *Programmed Visions: Software and Memory*. Cambridge, Mass.: MIT Press, 2011.

Davidson, Cathy N., and David Theo Goldberg. *The Future of Thinking: Learning Institutions in a Digital Age*. Cambridge, Mass.: MIT Press, 2010.

Di Pressi, Haley, Stephanie Gorman, Miriam Posner, Raphael Sasayama, and Tori Schmitt (with Roderic Crooks, Megan Driscoll, Amy Earhart, Spencer Keralis, Tiffany Naiman, and Todd Presner). "The Student Collaborators' Bill of Rights." In *UCLA Digital Humanities*. http://www.cdh.ucla.edu/news-events/a-student-collaborators-bill-of-rights.

Drucker, Johanna. "Reading Interface." *PMLA* 128, no. 1 (2013): 213–20.

Galloway, Alexander R. *The Interface Effect*. Cambridge, U.K.: Polity, 2012.

hooks, bell. *Teaching to Transgress*. New York: Routledge, 1994.

Jenstad, Janelle. "History of MoEML." *The Map of Early Modern London*. http://mapoflondon.uvic.ca/history.htm.

———. "Restoring Place to the Digital Archive." In *Teaching Early Modern English Literature from the Archives*, ed. Heidi Brayman Hackel and Ian Frederick Moulton, 101–12. New York: Modern Language Association, 2015.

———. "Training and Work Practices Contract." *The Map of Early Modern London*. http://mapoflondon.uvic.ca/moeml_contract.htm.

———. "Using Early Modern Maps in Literary Studies: Views and Caveats from London." In *Geohumanities: Art, History, Text at the Edge of Place*, ed. Michael Dear, Jim Ketchum, Sarah Luria, and Douglas Richardson, 112–19. London: Routledge, 2011.

Library of Congress. "Marc Code List for Relators." www.loc.gov/marc/relators/index.html.

*Map of Early Modern London* (*MoEML*). https://mapoflondon.uvic.ca/.

Poston, Michael. "The Most Interesting Use of Our Data Will Not Be What We Think It Is." *The Collation: A Gathering of Scholarship from the Folger Shakespeare Library*. December 5, 2011. http://collation.folger.edu/2011/12/the-most-interesting-use-of-our-data-will-not-be-what-we-think-it-is.

Scholars' Lab, The. "Charter." *The Scholars' Lab*. http://scholarslab.org/about/charter.

Shakespeare, William. *Henry V*, ed. James Mardock (Internet Shakespeare Editions). http://internetshakespeare.uvic.ca/Library/Texts/H5/FM/scene/5.2 - tln-3260.

TEI Consortium, eds. "respStmt." *TEI P5: Guidelines for Electronic Text Encoding and Interchange*. TEI Consortium. http://www.tei-c.org/release/doc/tei-p5-doc/en/html/ref-respStmt.

Wark, McKenzie. "Against Social Determinism." *Public Seminar* 1, no. 1 (2013).

PART II ][ *Chapter 8*

# Reproducing the Academy: Librarians and the Question of Service in the Digital Humanities

ROXANNE SHIRAZI

One of the central questions that arise whenever we talk about digital humanities (DH) and librarianship is the question of service in academic libraries. Do libraries support DH scholarship, or are they producers of it? Is DH just another suite of services to be offered by the library? Recent contributions from Trevor Muñoz,[1] Bethany Nowviskie,[2] Miriam Posner,[3] Dot Porter,[4] and Barbara Rockenbach,[5] among others, have examined the role that libraries play in supporting or partnering with digital humanists. Much of this discussion assumes a great deal of overlap between libraries and the digital humanities, a connection that scholars such as Glen Worthey[6] and Chris Alen Sula[7] are laudably exploring.

But this chapter is about librarians, not libraries.

I will stitch together some of the threads that have informed my thinking about these issues and attempt to contextualize this question of service in the history of librarianship as a feminized profession. I will go over what the term "service" means, and by the end of this chapter I hope to have you questioning assumptions about service, scholarship, work, and power.

## *Feminization*

The term feminization has made the rounds recently as economists and sociologists talk about the shift from the manufacturing economy to a service-sector economy. As jobs move from an industrial, often unionized factory setting to service provision, we are seeing more low-paid, contingent, part-time positions that may require workers to engage in what has been termed *affective labor.* Instead of producing a good that is then sold for profit, affective labor produces satisfied clients and positive brand associations that contribute to a company's financial value. Thus, feminization can alternately mean an influx of women into the workforce (or a profession) and the ascription of "feminine" characteristics to that work. Discussions of the labor conditions of this "new economy" are frequently centered on the idea that we *all* do women's work now.

Ahem. As librarians, we have always been feminized.

## *Professions*

What does it mean to be a feminized profession?

It is important to distinguish between professions and occupations.[8] Professions, like law and medicine, generally require specialized knowledge and expertise, which bring along a certain amount of professional autonomy. Such autonomy may require accreditation or certification by professional associations. Professions also generally adhere to a code of ethics, so that the practitioner maintains allegiance to a higher calling than personal gain. The question of whether librarianship is a *true* profession has been debated for some time now, and it is beyond the scope of this chapter. I will just say that librarianship is often considered a semi-profession by sociologists (Etzioni 1969). Coincidentally or not, the prototypical semi-professions (social work, teaching, and nursing) also happen to be feminized professions. More recently, they have been called empowering professions (Maack 1997).

The idea of a feminized profession is part of the larger idea of a sexual division of labor, an occupational stratification based on one's gender presentation. Historians have studied how occupations come to be dominated by women by looking at the histories of social workers (Walkowitz 1990), clerical workers (Strom 1989), nurses (Melosh 1982), waitresses (Cobble 1991), flight attendants (Barry 2007), and even librarians (Garrison 1972–73). For example, clerical and secretarial work was once dominated by men, as a sort of apprenticeship for the nineteenth-century business world. Many historians attribute the introduction of the typewriter and its deliberate association with the feminine activity of piano playing (such as in an 1872 Scholes and Glidden typewriter ad[9]) to the feminization of office work.

In 1979, Dee Garrison's book, *Apostles of Culture: The Public Librarian and American Society, 1876–1920,* inspired a fair amount of controversy among feminist librarians who felt that the portrayal of negative aspects of this feminized profession neglected the achievements of individual women in library history (Pritchard 2004). Yet the section of the book titled, "The Tender Technicians," tells a story very similar to other studies of feminized professions and occupations: to gain entry to the workforce, women must emphasize the work's feminine qualities (real or imagined) to minimize any perceived social transgression in working outside of the home. When women succeed and begin to make up close to 50 percent of the workforce, men no longer pursue the work because it is seen as "women's work." The work is then devalued. Put differently:

service => women's work
women working => service

That is, *who* is doing the work determines *what* is valued as work.

### *Emotion Work*

Sociologist Arlie Russell Hochschild coined the term "emotion work" in her 1983 study of flight attendants, *The Managed Heart*. Hochschild was interested in the personal costs for workers who were paid to provide "service with a smile" and how those costs affected workers' off-duty emotional lives. Emotion work and related terms (emotional labor, affective labor, and immaterial labor) have resurfaced with the post-manufacturing economy (both feminized and financialized). In the digital sphere, service work is conducted by community facilitators, comment moderators, or social media managers who field the complaints, comments, and harassment that is endemic to online spaces.

Emotion work and, more specifically, affective labor, are often brought into conversation with care work or domestic labor. However, we can associate them with any occupation that not only has few tangible productivity measures but also requires workers to appear as though they love their job. All of these terms are related to digital labor[10] in the sense that they are immaterial and, taken together, convey the many challenges that service work brings for those who must perform it.

### *Reproductive Labor*

Reproductive labor is the domestic work of the home, the labor that *reproduces the workforce* and therefore contributes to the labor value of the waged worker and indirectly creates financial value for corporations. You might be familiar with the Wages for Housework[11] campaign in the 1970s, led by Marxist feminists such as Selma James and Silvia Federici, among others. It called attention to how unwaged labor is exploited in a capitalist system. Federici's 2004 book, *Caliban and the Witch,* further examines how women's subjugation as well as the devaluation of their reproductive labor are part and parcel of capitalism.

A related concept is Ivan Illich's (1981) idea of shadow labor, which refers to the unpaid work that accompanies people's roles as wage workers. Activities such as grocery shopping, maintaining a vehicle or residence, and housework are all examples of uncompensated labor that facilitates participation in the wage system.

Both of these concepts articulate the labor of support that should be very familiar to academic librarians. We perform labor that *reproduces the academy,* from teaching information literacy, research skills, and citation formats to students to selecting, cataloging, and preserving materials for current and future use. This work is vital, and it is intellectual labor. But, because it does not conform to the "publish or perish" model at the top of the academic hierarchy, it is reduced to (and devalued as) "service."

## *Service versus Scholarship*

Perhaps what we resent when we discuss service in libraries is—as Hochschild discovered in her study of flight attendants—"the appearance of working at a low level of skills" (84). As William Goode (1961) explains in his study of the library profession, the domain expertise of academic librarians is often rendered invisible to our academic colleagues:

> The academic expert will usually know much better than the librarian how to find the material in his *own* field, and he is also likely to evaluate the *additional* knowledge possessed by the librarian in other areas as somewhat irrelevant or unimportant. The academic expert does not see the basic *library* skills in action, in part because he rarely has the experience of working with the librarian to find out what help he might obtain. (314)

This invisibility can lead to a lack of respect in the shared space of scholarship: "If the library is the laboratory of the humanist, the librarian is all too often the bottle-washer in that lab" (Hildenbrand 6). Following Goode, do librarians work *in service of scholarship*, or are they *servile to scholars*? I want to explore further the idea of service in the academy writ large and connect it to the work that librarians are doing. So I am going to tell a story about Zotero.

Zotero[12] is an open-source citation manager developed at the Roy Rosenzweig Center for History and New Media at George Mason University. Recently, Sean Takats (the Rosenzweig Center's Director of Research Projects) shared publicly some comments from his tenure case, which included substantial sections devoted to his digital work. One of the members of the review committee commented:

> Some on the committee questioned to what degree Dr. Takats' [sic] involvement in these activities constitutes actual research (as opposed to project management). Hence, some determined that projects like Zotero et al., while highly valuable, should be considered as major service activity instead. (in Takats)

Dr. Takats crafted his portfolio with a carefully balanced mix of traditional scholarship (his monograph on French history) and digital work, knowing that he might face pushback despite having broad guidelines at his university. Still, he was perturbed.

> To recap: Conceive projects? Service. Develop prototype software? Service. Write successful grant proposals? Service. Write code? Service. Lead developers and designers? Service. Disseminate the results of the project? Service. (Takats)

Sound familiar? We might ask, as Mark Sample (2013) does, "When does service become scholarship?" We might also ask to what extent Zotero's resemblance to library work affected perceptions of Takats's work as a service activity. Regardless, there is a clear need for skilled project managers in digital humanities, and librarians have embraced these roles in part because we already have experience with them. But what does that embrace mean for collaborative scholarship between librarians and faculty when project management and other "major service activity" is so clearly secondary to "actual research"?

Jennifer Guiliano, former Assistant Director of the Maryland Institute of Technology in the Humanities (MITH), followed Takats's tale with a blog post (2013) explaining that this perception of service is why she prefers the term Project Developer over Project Manager. She shared her experience in meetings with "people looking for labor to get them to where they want to go; not collaborators who are seeking true partnerships where all members of the team are elevated to be better researchers, teachers, and scholars." She writes, "They want someone to make their website, schedule their meetings, and write their grant applications; not argue about the meaning, scope, scale, and conclusions that get included in the project." She then reminds them that she is Dr. Guiliano: "I shouldn't need a degree to be recognized for my thoughts. But let's be real, it definitely eases the way."

### *The Status Shield*

Hochschild refers to the "status shield" that marginalized service workers lack in relation to their white, male counterparts engaged in similar work. That is, customers (or clients, users, patrons, and even colleagues) are more likely to unload criticisms and rudeness to women and people of color because women and people of color lack the social status that affords respect. Librarians, then—and by this I mean MLS-holding librarians without a PhD—face the dual hurdle of breaking through these gendered and racialized assumptions and dealing with the deep credentialism found within the academy. And this is a profession that remains 88 percent white.[13] The discrimination gets worse as we move through the matrix of oppression. So when we call for librarians to approach collaborative digital work as partners and not service providers, I would like to see some acknowledgment of the fact that there are different power relations at play in these collaborative relationships—power relations that are embedded in the hierarchies that make up academia, in both the social stratification of varying job ranks and the hierarchical classification of service and scholarship. Let us have a more nuanced conversation about how librarians position ourselves as collaborators in the digital humanities and accede that some of us might need to embrace the label of service or might not be able to escape it.

Perhaps the problem is not service itself, but exploitation:

> In any system, exploitation depends on the actual distribution of many kinds of profits—money, authority, status, honor, well-being. It is not emotional labor itself, therefore, but the *underlying system of recompense* that raises the question of what the cost of it is. (Hochschild 12, my emphasis)

### *We Are Not Alone*

While I welcome calls, such as the one issued recently by Trevor Muñoz (2014) at the Data Driven conference, to make visible the intellectual labor of librarians, I do not want to further isolate and denigrate the important yet often intangible support work that *needs to be done and is done by librarians.* Let us focus instead on expanding our conception of what work is valued in the academy: "So much real intellectual work is considered 'service' and you can't get tenure for 'service' . . . Support diversity of work" (Mandell in Walker). Let us join our colleagues who are struggling with the narrow system of rewards that favors individual research over (collaborative) service work—the same system in which women, people of color, and queer scholars disproportionately shoulder the burden of committee work, community building, and service work that reproduces the academy.

We are not alone. Teaching faculty may encounter the "ivory ceiling of service work," in which gendered service duties edge out other tenure requirements. Joya Misra et al. (2011) conducted research demonstrating that:

> Women associate professors taught an hour more each week than men, mentored an additional two hours a week, and spent nearly five hours more a week on service. This translates to women spending roughly 220 more hours on teaching, mentoring, and service over two semesters than men at that rank.

We need to account for the ways in which institutions benefit from our labor while devaluing our contributions and recognize, again, that we are not alone. Sekile Nzinga-Johnson (2013) observes that:

> Institutions can no longer ignore the invisible abundance of care labor that black, women of color and queer faculty perform on behalf of institutions. That work often takes the form of engaged pedagogy and teaching, diversity initiatives, student recruitment and retention, community engagement and intellectual contributions and *financially benefits institutions.* These marginalized faculty are often the standard bearers of their institutions' mission and vision statements. (interviewed by Gumbs, my emphasis)

The question of service in librarianship and the digital humanities raises concerns that go beyond our small corner of academia. How can we bring an ethic of care and collaboration to our scholarly work when the academic system of rewards is structured to devalue our labor?

### *Reproducing the Academy?*

In sum, librarians perform "shadow labor" that may be considered the reproductive labor of the academy. We need a "status shield" to enable fruitful partnerships that bring mutual respect to collaborative digital work. We need to talk about working conditions (e.g., dedicated research time[14]) *and* structures (e.g., status shields) when we talk about librarians as true collaborators in the production of digital humanities scholarship. We need to talk about the *library profession* and its "underlying system of recompense": money, authority, status, honor, and well-being.

#### NOTES

This chapter is a revised version of the talk I gave as part of a panel at the 2014 American Library Association conference, sponsored by the Women and Gender Studies Section of the Association of College & Research Libraries and organized by Heather Tompkins (Carleton College). The title of the panel was "Digital Humanities and Libraries: Power and Privilege, Practice and Theory" and also included Jane Nichols, Elvia Arroyo-Ramirez, and Megan Wacha.

1. See Muñoz, "In Service?"
2. See Nowviskie, "Skunks in the Library."
3. See Posner, "No Half Measures."
4. See Porter, "What If We Do, in Fact, Know Best?"
5. See Rockenbach, "Digital Humanities in Libraries."
6. See Worthy, "Literary Texts and the Library in the Digital Age, or, How Library DH Is Made."
7. See Sula, "Digital Humanities and Libraries: A Conceptual Model."
8. There are varying sociological theories of what makes a profession, and this discussion will necessarily paint broad strokes.
9. See https://en.wikipedia.org/wiki/Sholes_and_Glidden_typewriter.
10. See the Digital Labor Reference Library, part of the Digital Labor Working Group at CUNY Graduate Center.
11. See Federici, "Wages against Housework."
12. See https://www.zotero.org.
13. See Bourg, "Lack of Diversity by the Numbers in Librarianship and in Book Stuff."
14. See Nowviskie, "Skunks in the Library."

**BIBLIOGRAPHY**

Barry, Kathleen M. *Femininity in Flight: A History of Flight Attendants*. Durham, N.C.: Duke University Press, 2007.

Bourg, Chris. "Lack of Diversity by the Numbers in Librarianship and in Book Stuff." Feral Librarian. February 22, 2014. https://chrisbourg.wordpress.com/2014/02/22/lack-of-diversity-by-the-numbers-in-librarianship-and-in-book-stuff.

Cobble, Dorothy Sue. *Dishing It Out: Waitresses and Their Unions in the Twentieth Century*. Urbana, Ill.: University of Illinois Press, 1991.

Digital Labor Reference Library. Digital Labor Working Group. CUNY Graduate Center. https://digitallabor.commons.gc.cuny.edu/digital-labor-reference-library/.

Etzioni, Amitai. *The Semi-Professions and Their Organization: Teachers, Nurses, Social Workers*. New York: Free Press, 1969.

Federici, Silvia. *Caliban and the Witch*. New York: Autonomedia, 2004.

———. "Wages against Housework." Bristol, Eng.: Power of Women Collective and Falling Wall Press, 1975.

Garrison, Dee. "The Tender Technicians: The Feminization of Public Librarianship, 1876–1905." *Journal of Social History* 6, no. 2 (1972–73): 131–59.

Goode, W. J. "The Librarian: From Occupation to Profession?" *The Library Quarterly* 31, no. 4 (1961): 306–20.

Guiliano, Jennifer. "Don't Call Me." Author's blog. February 8, 2013. http://jguiliano.com/blog/2013/02/08/dont-call-me.

Gumbs, Alexis Pauline. "Laboring Positions: Black Women, Mothering, and the Academy (A conversation with editor Sekile Nzinga-Johnson)." *The Feminist Wire*. October 15, 2013. http://thefeministwire.com/2013/10/laboring-positions-black-women-mothering-and-the-academy-a-conversation-with-editor-sekile-nzinga-johnson.

Hildenbrand, S. *Reclaiming the American Library Past: Writing the Women In*. Norwood, N.J.: Ablex Publishing, 1996.

Hochschild, Arlie Russell. *The Managed Heart: Commercialization of Human Feeling*. Berkeley, Calif.: University of California Press, 1983.

Illich, Ivan. *Shadow Work*. Boston, Mass.: M. Boyars, 1981.

Maack, Mary Niles. "Toward a New Model of the Information Professions: Embracing Empowerment." *Journal of Education for Library and Information Science* 38, no. 4 (1997): 283–302.

Melosh, Barbara. *"The Physician's Hand": Work Culture and Conflict in American Nursing*. Philadelphia, Pa.: Temple University Press, 1982.

Misra, Joy, Jennifer Hickes Lundquist, Elissa Holmes, and Stephanie Agiomavritis. "The Ivory Ceiling of Service Work." *Academe*, January–February 2011. http://aaup.org/article/ivory-ceiling-service-work - .U8TSV41B_EJ.

Muñoz, Trevor. "Data Driven . . . But How Do We Steer This Thing?" Presentation slides from *Data Driven: Digital Humanities in the Library Conference*. Charleston, S.C.

June 20–22, 2014. https://speakerdeck.com/trevormunoz/data-driven-but-how-do-we-steer-this-thing.

———. "In Service? A Further Provocation on Digital Humanities Research in Libraries." *dh + lib*. June 19, 2013. http://acrl.ala.org/dh/2013/06/19/in-service-a-further-provocation-on-digital-humanities-research-in-libraries.

Nowviskie, Bethany. "Skunks in the Library: A Path to Production for Scholarly R&D." *Journal of Library Administration* 53, no. 1 (2013): 53–66. http://libra.virginia.edu/catalog/libra-oa:2745.

Porter, Dot. "What If We Do, in Fact, Know Best? A Response to the OCLC Report on DH and Research Libraries." *dh + lib*. February 12, 2014. http://acrl.ala.org/dh/2014/02/12/what-if-we-do-in-fact-know-best-a-response-to-the-oclc-report-on-dh-and-research-libraries.

Posner, Miriam. "No Half Measures: Overcoming Common Challenges to Doing Digital Humanities in the Library." *Journal of Library Administration* 53, no. 1 (2013): 43–52. http://escholarship.org/uc/item/6q2625np#page-1.

Pritchard, Sarah M. "Reviewed Work: *Apostles of Culture: The Public Librarian and American Society, 1876–1920,* by Dee Garrison and Christine Pawley." *The Library Quarterly: Information, Community, Policy* 74, No. 4 (2004): 477–86.

Rockenbach, Barbara A. Introduction. "Digital Humanities in Libraries: New Models for Scholarly Engagement." *Journal of Library Administration* 53, no. 1 (2013): 1–9. https://academiccommons.columbia.edu/catalog/ac:156033.

Sample, Mark. "When Does Service Become Scholarship?" Author's blog. February 8, 2013. http://www.samplereality.com/2013/02/08/when-does-service-become-scholarship.

Strom, Sharon Hartman. "'Light Manufacturing': The Feminization of American Office Work, 1900–1930." *Industrial and Labor Relations Review* 43, no. 1 (1989): 53–71.

Sula, Chris Alen. "Digital Humanities and Libraries: A Conceptual Model." *Journal of Library Administration* 53, no. 1 (2013): 10–26. http://chrisalensula.org/digital-humanities-and-libraries-a-conceptual-model/.

Takats, Sean. "A Digital Humanities Tenure Case, Part 2: Letters and Committees." Author's blog. February 8, 2013. http://quintessenceofham.org/2013/02/07/a-digital-humanities-tenure-case-part-2-letters-and-committees.

Walker, Leila (leilathebrave). "'So much real intellectual work is considered 'service' & you can't get tenure for service' @mandellc Support diversity of work #dhsi2014." June 4, 2014, 1:35 p.m. tweet.

Walkowitz, Daniel J. "The Making of a Feminine Professional Identity: Social Workers in the 1920s." *The American Historical Review* 95, no. 4 (1990): 1051–75.

Worthy, Glen. "Literary Texts and the Library in the Digital Age, or, How Library DH is Made." *Stanford | Digital Humanities*. March 4, 2014. https://digitalhumanities.stanford.edu/literary-texts-and-library-digital-age-or-how-library-dh-made.

Zotero. https://www.zotero.org/.

# Looks Like We Made It, But Are We Sustaining Digital Scholarship?

CHELSEA A. M. GARDNER, GWYNAETH McINTYRE,
KAITLYN SOLBERG, AND LISA TWETEN

The increasing amount of digital projects relating to the field of antiquity is especially promising for the future of traditionally archaic academic fields, including Ancient History, Classics, and Classical Archaeology. An enormous number of fragile, irreplaceable artifacts have survived from antiquity, but only a small number are accessible to the public. The vast majority are housed in storage rooms or isolated collections in museums and universities, as well as private collections around the world. For decades, this global scattering of antiquity resulted in widespread inaccessibility to ancient artifacts for both teaching and research. Through the process of digitization and the increased presence of online databases, these materials are finally becoming available to a wider audience.[1]

How, then, does digitization relate precisely to making? In our case, our small scale digitization project *From Stone to Screen* (*FSTS*) has challenged the expected raison d'être of Classics by shifting research from literary critiques and historical analysis to the creation of several websites and digital versions of over a thousand artifacts. We strive to deliver fragments of history through the digital reconstruction of these artifacts. We encourage interaction through teaching modules designed for our digitized collections, and we are "making" by creating spaces where students can interact with ancient objects without fear of damaging irreplaceable artifacts.

Universities are exerting increasing pressure on individual scholars to become involved in digital endeavors;[2] however, such work should meet the same standards of relevance and applicability as any other academic work. As a case study, this chapter presents how *FSTS* approaches the "Three Rs" for creating sustainable digital humanities (DH) projects: Research, Relevance, and Replicability, a framework we created for practicality and mnemonic convenience, but also because we firmly believe these three principles should underpin any DH project.

### *Making a Digital Collection: Digitization and Accessibility*

*FSTS* is a multidisciplinary, collaborative, open-access digitization project that hosts high-quality, 2-D scans and images of ancient artifacts from the collections of the University of British Columbia (UBC) in Vancouver, Canada. At present, the project has digitized and published five collections:

1. The project's inaugural collection, The Malcolm McGregor Squeeze Collection, a corpus of Greek epigraphic squeezes (filter paper impressions of ancient Greek stone inscriptions), was given to the Department of Classical, Near Eastern and Religious Studies (CNERS) in 1975. This collection represents the culmination of McGregor's life work and is the inspiration for the project's title.
2. The George Fuller Collection, featuring 27 artifacts collected from Cairo, Jerusalem, and Baghdad during the 1930s, was donated to CNERS by George Fuller Jr. in 2009.
3. The O. J. Todd Coin Collection, a selection of predominantly Roman coins dating from the fourth century B.C.E. to the fourth century C.E., was bequeathed to CNERS by emeritus professor O. J. Todd in 1999.
4. The Harvey F. Blackmore Collection comprises 196 artifacts from Bahrain and was donated to the UBC's Laboratory of Archaeology in 2014.
5. The Ancient Artefacts Collection, currently housed at the Rare Books and Special Collections department of the UBC Library, contains two ancient papyri from Roman Egypt and seven cuneiform tablets.

To bridge the gap between DH research and DH pedagogy, our project strives for a continued presence in the classroom, both in university courses and high school curricula.[3] Objects from the collections are transported to various classrooms for hands-on exposure to the ancient world. Following this initial introduction, students are encouraged to further pursue their interests in antiquity through the digital resources available on our website.[4] For language classes, the digitized squeezes are used to broaden student appreciation for the importance of primary source materials and are the basis for interactive assignments that allow students to engage directly with documents from antiquity. We encourage student contributions that, to date, include bibliographic research on the artifacts in the Fuller collection, cataloguing the Blackmore and Todd artifacts, translations of Greek texts into English, interactive maps of communities mentioned in the Athenian Tribute Lists, and open-access teaching modules.[5] All research done on the materials in the *FSTS* collections is made available online for future study and curriculum use; therefore, the *FSTS* material grows continuously as a resource for teaching and research. Ancient Greek language, epigraphy, archaeology, history, and other specialized courses all stand to benefit from the incorporation of primary materials into research and teaching, and they also demonstrate to students how one can interact with and study ancient material. Ultimately, we hope that our current database will continue to be expanded and developed through direct, hands-on learning by students of all levels.

Furthermore, *FSTS* maintains a popular blog with regular posts of interest to scholars and the general public alike. Blogs are quickly becoming a standard tool for academics to disseminate their research, publications, and projects without enduring an arduous publishing process. Broadcasting our research, outreach, and other projects online not only helps to advertise the project but also creates invaluable contacts in the DH community.[6]

In addition to the "Three R's," *FSTS*'s strength lies in its threefold goals for longevity:

1. Ensuring a sustainable project afterlife through the open-access, 2-D image database hosted by the UBC library; [7]
2. Full disclosure and encouragement of replicability of all imaging and digitization methods;[8] and
3. Making pedagogical resources (classroom-ready modules) freely available to a global community.

## *Research, Relevance, and Replicability: Ensuring Sustainability*

### RESEARCH

Graduate students conceived of, initiated, and currently direct *FSTS*. It is designed to facilitate scholarly research and collaboration between all levels of the academy. In our case, undergraduate, graduate, post-doctoral, early-career scholars, and tenured professors work together on various aspects of the project. Our ultimate goal is for scholars around the world to collaborate with us and use our digital resources in their own research and teaching. The McGregor Squeeze Collection in particular includes copies of some of the most important documents from the zenith (mid-fifth century B.C.E.) of the Athenian Empire: the so-called Athenian Tribute Lists (ATLs). These lists provide crucial information regarding the political makeup of the Athenian Empire and the Greek alliances that existed in the fifth century B.C.E. The ATLs themselves are extremely fragmentary and comprise several hundred marble blocks of varying size, most of which are housed today in the Athens Epigraphical Museum. By creating digital resources for these squeezes alongside images of the stone fragments themselves, scholars are able to contribute to ATL research from all corners of the globe. One of our future project goals is to locate the remaining squeezes (those that McGregor did not possess and that number in the thousands) to create a complete online compendium of these political documents.

### RELEVANCE

We believe *FSTS* maintains relevance because its design is closely connected to the academic interests and goals of its founding members and its intended (scholarly) audience—goals that are appropriate in terms of our budget and time constraints as early-career scholars and graduate students. Moreover, *FSTS* provides access to squeezes and artifacts that would otherwise sit unstudied and largely inaccessible in various storerooms and private collections. The fragility of some of these artifacts makes empirical study even more difficult as regular handling further contributes to their degradation. The process of digitization thus helps to protect the physical objects themselves, while enabling many more individuals to access artifacts and documents from antiquity.[9]

### REPLICABILITY

Finally, our technique for digitizing the squeezes produces high quality, 2-D digital images, and it is fully replicable and accessible to any interested party. Since developing our imaging process in 2013, we have shared our technique at conferences and in publications,[10] and we invite and encourage academics with similar collections to replicate our process. Likewise, we welcome interested parties to use our pedagogical materials in their own teaching and learning environments. These materials are open-access, ensuring that our project remains available to a global community.

With regard to replicability in particular, we want to make a point about "making" and, more specifically, our decision to situate collections in a 2-D digital realm (rather than concentrating on 3-D modeling and fabrication). A fetish for the tactile is now quite common in academic research; it manifests through an obsession with the conversion from tactile object to digital record to tactile object once again.[11] While we acknowledge the importance of 3-D objects to humanities inquiry—and, in fact, practice tactile interaction with our objects in various classrooms—2-D digitization and 3-D fabrication are not mutually exclusive. They are complementary processes, particularly in the field of archaeology. Although the intimate experience of holding an object in hand may be difficult to replace, it is directly associated with issues of safety, cost, and preservation. 3-D models of our artifacts would solve problems regarding the security and transport of ancient objects, but would also be accompanied by their own expenses. (3-D modeling is a time-, resource-, and labor-intensive process.) Moreover, the fact remains that a 3-D print and a 2-D/3-D digital model of an ancient artifact share one crucial characteristic: neither *is* the ancient artifact. Therefore, we resist the popular assumption that 2-D digitization is somehow *inferior to fabrication*. Again, they are complementary processes. And in the case of *FSTS*, 2-D replicas are less expensive, safer for the primary materials, and more accessible to a wider audience.

The authenticity of digitized items is at the forefront of modern archaeology. As the wholesale destruction of sites, museums, and antiquities plays out in the Middle East, for instance, the current generation of archaeologists must seriously consider the value of replicated objects—both on screen and in hand. These replicas are becoming our only means to study select ancient objects in the face of rampant destruction and disregard for material culture and history. Studying replicas in place of originals is not ideal. However, this problem is not new to Ancient History, Classics, or Classical Archaeology. Many of the ancient Roman marble statues surviving from antiquity are themselves copies of Greek bronze statues long since lost and known only by these Roman replicas. While the option of digital or printed replicas is technologically new and represents a far different set of skills than painstakingly hand-carving marble, the fundamental questions of authenticity and loss of access to originals are not substantially different. When faced with the complete destruction of the original artifact, replicas of any sort become invaluable, not just as tools for academic study but as the only means by which we can preserve cultural materials. Debates about whether replicas should be digitally or physically produced will ultimately be determined by the resources available to the parties undertaking the work on a case-by-case basis.

The response to recent instances of cultural destruction makes it clear that archaeologists are embracing any and all means at their disposal to preserve threatened cultural materials. However, the advent of 3-D printing will create new challenges for the field and for museums that once held a monopoly on the preservation and presentation of artifacts. Will people still pay to go to a museum when they can download and 3-D–print copies of ancient urns, vases, statues, and artworks for their own homes? Will a recreated object have the same value for display as the ancient original? Will a future generation of scholars and enthusiasts reject the "easy" replication of 3-D printing in favor of casting their own bronzes, throwing their own pottery, or carving their own marble statues? We may arguably learn far more about ancient objects by attempting to replicate their processes of creation than by re-creating them digitally. Future debates may therefore center on questions of authenticity of material and process rather than on comparisons between digital and physical products. Archaeologists will continue to negotiate the value of technological advances in the preservation and replication of damaged, inaccessible, and destroyed artifacts, including those destroyed by deliberate means or merely through the slow and inevitable degradation of time. All of us involved in *From Stone to Screen* aim to digitize and preserve a small fragment of antiquity, and we are grateful to have the opportunity to provide the upcoming generation of scholars and archaeologists with some of the necessary tools they will need for the reality of scholarship in our modern world.

**NOTES**

1. Many museums, art galleries, and universities are making their collections available online. Examples include the Smithsonian's Freer Gallery of Art and the Arthur M. Sackler Gallery Archives (http://www.asia.si.edu/research/squeezeproject/), Indiana University's Art Museum online galleries (http://www.iub.edu/~iuam/online_modules/coptic/cophome.html), and the American Numismatic Society's MANTIS database (http://www.numismatics.org/search/).

2. This pressure is, of course, frustrating due to the ongoing difficulty of making DH projects "count" in terms of traditional scholarship (Brier 390).

3. For opposing views on DH in research and pedagogy, respectively, see Kirschenbaum, "What Is Digital Humanities and What's It Doing in English Departments?" and Brier, "Where's the Pedagogy?"

4. See www.fromstonetoscreen.com, www.fstsartifacts.fromstonetoscreen.com, and http://digitalcollections.library.ubc.ca/cdm/landingpage/collection/squeezes.

5. See www.fromstonetoscreen.com/references-and-links/teaching-modules/. All pedagogical resources created by students will be made available on our website as they are completed.

6. See Spiro for a summary of these debates and the various approaches and attempts to define digital humanities (16–17). See also Gold, "The Digital Humanities Moment;" and Ramsay, "On Building."

7. Our collaboration with UBC's Digital Initiatives ensures the sustainability of this project through their commitment to building and preserving "sustainable digital collections to support and enrich the educational, cultural, and economic endeavors of the University, the people of British Columbia, and communities beyond" (http://digitize.library.ubc.ca; "About Us"). Challenges with managing and maintaining a digital project (largely ignored in DH scholarship) are addressed in Reed, "Managing an Established Digital Humanities Project."

8. See www.fromstonetoscreen.com/references-and-links/teaching-modules/hour-long-course-lectures.

9. Exhibits help increase the "browsability" of collections. Issues associated with digital databases and the problematic reliance on the search box are discussed in Whitelaw, "Generous Interfaces for Digital Cultural Collections."

10. See Tweten, McIntyre, and Gardner; "From Stone to Screen: Digitally Recapturing Antiquity" (Digital Classicist New England Seminar Series, Boston, March 2015); "From Stone to Screen: Squeezing into the World of Digital Archaeology" (SAA Annual Meeting, San Francisco, April 2015); "From Stone to Screen: Putting the Squeeze on Digital Epigraphy" (AIA Annual Meeting, New Orleans, January 2015); and "From Stone to Screen: Digitizing Epigraphic Squeezes" (EAGLE Europeana International Conference, Paris, October 2014). For a complete list of conference presentations and publications, see http://fromstonetoscreen.com/curriculum-vitae/.

11. See Jones, *The Emergence of the Digital Humanities.*

## BIBLIOGRAPHY

Brier, Stephen. "Where's the Pedagogy? The Role of Teaching and Learning in the Digital Humanities." In *Debates in the Digital Humanities,* ed. Matthew K. Gold, 390–401. Minneapolis: University of Minnesota Press, 2012.

*From Stone to Screen.* http://fromstonetoscreen.com/.

Gold, Matthew K. "The Digital Humanities Moment." In *Debates in the Digital Humanities,* ed. Matthew K. Gold, ix–xvi. Minneapolis: University of Minnesota Press, 2012.

Jones, Steven E. *The Emergence of the Digital Humanities.* New York: Routledge, 2013.

Kirschenbaum, Matthew. "What Is Digital Humanities and What's It Doing in English Departments?" *ADE Bulletin* 150 (2010): 55–61.

———. "What is 'Digital Humanities,' and Why Are They Saying Such Terrible Things about It?" *differences* 25, no. 1 (2014): 46–63.

Ramsay, Stephen. "On Building." In *Defining Digital Humanities: A Reader,* ed. Edward Vanhoutte, 243–47. Farnham, U. K.: Ashgate Publishing, 2013.

Reed, Ashley. "Managing an Established Digital Humanities Project: Principles and Practices from the Twentieth Year of the William Blake Archive." *Digital Humanities Quarterly* 8, no. 1 (2014). http://digitalhumanities.org/dhq/vol/8/1/000174/000174.html.

Spiro, Lisa. "'This Is Why We Fight': Defining the Values of the Digital Humanities." In *Debates in the Digital Humanities,* ed. Matthew K Gold, 16–36. Minneapolis: University of Minnesota Press, 2012.

Tweten, Lisa, Gwynaeth McIntyre, and Chelsea Gardner. "From Stone to Screen: Digital Revitalization of Ancient Epigraphy." *Digital Humanities Quarterly* 10, no. 1 (2016). www.digitalhumanities.org/dhq/vol/10/1/000236/000236.html.

Whitelaw, Mitchell. "Generous Interfaces for Digital Cultural Collections." *Digital Humanities Quarterly* 9, no. 1 (2015). www.digitalhumanities.org/dhq/vol/9/1/000205/000205.html.

# Full Stack DH: Building a Virtual Research Environment on a Raspberry Pi

JAMES SMITHIES

Ian Hodder (2014) recently pointed to a "return to things" in the humanities and social sciences—a mode of analysis that explores the relationships between people and the objects we use to construct and make sense of the world (19). In digital humanities (DH), we see this turn in Matthew Kirschenbaum's (2007) forensic analysis of computer hard disks; platform studies that investigate the relationship between computing culture, consoles, and other hardware (Monfort and Bogost 2009); and maker cultures that explore the humanities through practical experimentation (Dieter and Lovink 2014). A return to things suggests a desire to pay attention to and interact with the material world, rather than retreat to a purely digital one. Some commentators go beyond this position. They propose that entanglement with material objects represents a ground of being for humans and their societies—a postphenomenological "dialectic of dependence and dependency between humans and things" worthy of deep contemplation (Hodder 19). We rely on the things we have created to such a degree that our identity has become inseparable from them. In Donald Ihde's (2009) original conception, such reliance amounts to a "recognition that 'consciousness' is an abstraction, that experience in its deeper and broader sense entails its embeddedness in both the physical or material world and its cultural-social dimensions" (19). As literary historian Bill Brown (2001, 2003) suggests, knowledge, art, religion, and science are entangled, in turn, with books, oil paint, churches, and laboratories: "thing theory" grounds epistemology in the myriad interactions between the physical and non-physical world (Preda 347–66).

My "Full Stack DH" project explored these ideas by engaging in a practical experiment: migrating my personal website—jamessmithies.org—from Wordpress.org (a free, fully hosted service) to a home server running on a Raspberry Pi minimal computer. In doing so, it extended the site from a limited blog to a Virtual Research Environment (VRE) capable of further development, and it also challenged me to consider the myriad connections between my scholarly identity, technical ability, and wider technological culture. The intention was not necessarily to create a monolithic product, but to take control of all aspects of the computing architecture to gain a better understanding of my scholarly infrastructure needs, from hardware and maintenance of the Internet domain name to the content management system and firewalls that secure it. Unexpectedly, the project also confronted me with ethical decisions about corporate information technology (IT) and the security challenges posed by bots. My colleagues can be forgiven for finding the purpose of the project opaque. It does not use archival sources or critique a text. It does not describe a historical event or argue a philosophical position. I do not recommend it as a model for widespread adoption. Rather, the project functions as a prototype, performance, and experiment: it asks to be read as scholarly objet d'art, instantiated in hardware and code.

In using a minimal computer, the project adopts an oppositional stance toward large-scale infrastructure, but it is intended as more than a statement in critical theory and by no means rejects large-scale infrastructure out of hand. Quite the opposite: it embraces digital infrastructure as an exciting new site for humanistic inquiry and calls for experimentation to "integrate theory and practice," as Tara McPherson (2014) puts it, and take into account the "full stack" of our computational tools, from circuitry to software (177–88).

It does so by reporting on the development of a personal VRE. VREs come in a range of different configurations and are notoriously difficult to define, but they represent a central trope in the discourse of cyber-infrastructure. Although they sound like concrete things (and therefore present likely candidates for funding), in many ways they are undertheorized and misunderstood (e.g., "vaporware," a software product that sounds like something everyone needs but is never delivered). To their detractors, VREs symbolize retrograde policy positions that assume humanists should use tools that will increase our productivity, legitimize our work in relation to the STEM disciplines, and give us fingertip access to everything the digital world promises. This project takes those concerns seriously. It uses prototyping to reconsider what a VRE might mean in a humanities context free of the issues large-scale VRE projects involve. The goal is to use a minimal computer and free software to create a prototype environment that is under my control, without the constraints and expectations of a large project, and (crucially) capable of ongoing extension and elaboration by a lone scholar.

Design and development of humanities VREs are made difficult by the plethora of tools, websites, resources, and methods available to researchers as well as the range of techniques used across the different humanities disciplines. A VRE to enable prosopographical research like the *Lands of the Normans* project about elite medieval landholders (Mackenzie et al. 127–42) will have quite different requirements than one designed to enable research into late-twentieth-century New Zealand poetry. Because of these differences, many countries are putting resources into aggregation and discovery projects (e.g., HuNI in Australia, DigitalNZ in New

Zealand, and the DPLA in the United States) that form large distributed databases capable (in theory) of enabling computationally intensive research. These services offer public search interfaces but also Application Programming Interfaces (API) that can be used to provide source documents for a new generation of research tools; they represent an essential step toward the development of future VREs. Australian historian Tim Sherratt's *QueryPic* website, which provides a search interface for the national libraries of Australia and New Zealand's digitized newspaper collections, is an example of grassroots use of cultural heritage sector APIs. At the Digital Humanities 2014 conference in Lausanne, Adam Farquhar and James Baker from the British Library suggested a similarly flexible approach to the development of VREs based on five principles: keep it simple, lower the bar, bring your own tools, be creative, and enable users to start small and grow big (Farquhar and Baker).

We are clearly at a stage where small-scale tinkering needs to occur in parallel to large-scale data integration. This attitude is valuable when approaching the problem of humanities cyber-infrastructure. Why should we assume, after all, that humanists will need the kind of high performance computing (HPC) environments used in the hard sciences, or (more accurately) that investment in digital humanities should be directed toward such projects before other options that privilege education and services over physical systems? Similarly, how can we develop strong arguments that we need to invest in different kinds of tools and methods if we do not have examples of what we *do* need? In a simpler sense, how can we contribute to conversations involving the allocation of cyber-infrastructure funding if we do not understand the practical difference between megabytes and petaflops? I am involved in large-scale infrastructure projects, including the CEISMIC Canterbury Earthquakes Digital Archive and, more recently, Digital Research Infrastructure for the Arts and Humanities (DARIAH), but I recognize that we have a responsibility to attend to the small as well as the large.

Having said that, and although minimal computers offer a way to explore potential designs for VREs without the overhead that comes with large cyber-infrastructure projects, they cannot offer a canvas free of cultural or political bias. We should be wary of the culture surrounding them as much as we are of national and transnational cyber-infrastructure efforts.

Minimal or physical computing uses extremely small, low-powered, and cheap computers (often embedded on a single circuit board) to create anything from interactive art installations to mini weather stations and electronic sensors. The movement began in the art and design community as a way to integrate contemporary technologies into their practices. It moved into schools, libraries, art galleries, and museums when people decided that hacking (cobbling together working prototypes using cheap and easily available components) might offer a way to engage students with the material affordances of contemporary technology (Przybylla and Romeike 241–54). Many engineering and computer science teachers feel that students have lost an understanding of hardware that came naturally to earlier generations who had to struggle to get the most out of limited devices. These practices exist in the context of a broader "maker culture," which extends Do-It-Yourself (DIY) principles from traditional arts and craft practices (e.g., needlework, stained glass making, etc.) to all manner of technology (e.g., minimal computing, 3-D printing, amateur robotics, etc.). They can be easily aligned to some areas of humanities theory, in a superficial sense at least. If we concentrate on the contents of our screens rather than investigating hardware and circuitry, for example, then we succumb to what Matthew Kirschenbaum calls a "medial ideology" (36): the mistaken belief that digital reality is "infinitely fungible" and unconstrained by physical limitations. Experimenting with physical hardware reminds us that the digital world is grounded in physical reality.

This is well and good, and more effort should go into exploring the intersections between maker culture and humanities theory, but it is equally important to avoid hitching the humanities to questionable trends in technology. In 1991 Mark Weiser, a computer scientist at the famed PARC research center, predicted that computers would "disappear" in the twenty-first century as production processes allowed them to be made ever smaller (94–104). This notion of ubiquitous computing (Greenfield), pervasive computing, or ambient computing (McCullough, *Digital Ground*; *Ambient Commons*)—each term holds a slightly different meaning—is viewed by many commentators as the inevitable next step in technological development. Large multinational corporations, including IBM, Google, and Microsoft, are making significant investments in the field. Rather than being mere toys, minimal computers such as the Raspberry Pi used in this project are now used in a wide variety of settings, including factory automation and systems monitoring, and they are central to the developing rhetoric of "ubicomp" (Dourish and Bell 23). The goal is to leverage miniaturization and falling costs of production to produce computers so small that they become "wearables," embedded in walls, and eventually implanted in human bodies.

The aim is to connect billions of these devices over an Internet of Things, enabling radically useful new software tools. The business community is enthralled by the possibilities:

> The vision of a future filled with smart and interacting everyday objects offers a whole range of fascinating possibilities. For example, parents will no longer lose track of their children, even in the busiest of crowds, when location sensors and communications modules are sewn into their clothes. Similar devices attached to timetables and signposts could guide blind people in unknown environments by "talking" to them via a wireless headset. Tiny communicating computers could also play a valuable role in protecting the environment; for example, sensors the size of dust particles that detect the dispersion of oil spills or forest fires. Another interesting possibility is that of linking any sort of information to everyday objects, allowing future washing machines to query our dirty clothes for washing instructions. (Raisinghani)

Needless to say, such a vision has worryingly Orwellian echoes to humanities researchers sensitive to issues of online privacy, surveillance, and a "digital panopticon" (Terras 257–69).

Rita Raley (2014) argues that an awareness of contemporary technology requires "more critical reflection upon, and ironic self-awareness about, the embedded place of digital humanities in the contemporary knowledge economy" ("Digital Humanities for the Next Five Minutes" 35). According to Raley, the way to achieve this awareness is to use technology to circumvent sociocultural systems oriented toward instrumentalist modes of reason or operational efficiency; "reverse engineering, hacktivism, denial-of-service attacks, the digital hijack, contestational robotics, collaborative software, and open-access technology labs" are all cited as potential vectors to critique digital culture from within, instead of merely criticizing from without (*Tactical Media* 6). In other words, it is not so much a case of the tools you use, but the philosophical perspectives and level of critical awareness you evince in their deployment. The claim is that (rather than attempting to regain an antediluvian, pre-digital past) digital technology should be hijacked for creative, ethical, and critically informed goals, in an effort to construct new forms of subjectivity that can support less compromised forms of political engagement. This kind of "tactical" activity asks to be understood in terms of "performance" as much as the postphenomenological entanglement that inspired jamessmithies.org (9). It privileges the artistic act over instrumentalism and seeks to prompt thought and further exploration rather than (necessarily) resulting in outcomes that can be measured or operationalized.

Michael Deiter and Geert Lovink suggest similar approaches in their "Theses on Making in the Digital Age." They propose that humanists develop prototypes designed to function as a "model" or "ideal type" at the interface "between the workshop and the factory." So-called "critical making" can improve our understanding of technology in academic contexts and broaden its potential for teaching and research. Despite traditional resistance to manual, laboratory-like activity in the core humanities disciplines, resources are becoming available to support maker culture and minimal computing within them (Fuller 78). These resources range from this volume of essays to advice offered at major institutions such as the Smithsonian Institution[1] to university-based laboratories and centers dedicated to experimenting with emerging tools and methods. Theoretical approaches to critical making "are intended to bridge the gap between creative physical and conceptual exploration" (Ratto 252–60) and guide researchers interested in exploring the relationship between technology and sociocultural life. Frameworks such as design thinking are being used to guide the design process (Plattner, Meinel, and Leifer).

As Matt Ratto (2011) points out, "devices themselves are not the ultimate goal" of critical making (253). Rather, the idea is to produce prototypes and basic models in the service of wider intellectual goals, blending "practice-based engagement with pragmatic and theoretical issues" (253). He suggests that the approach can be particularly useful in the context of so-called "wicked problems" (253), defined by architectural scholar Horst Rittel in the 1960s and 1970s (Rittel and Webber 160). This class of problem is characterized by the existence of "many clients and decision makers with conflicting values, and where the ramifications in the whole system are thoroughly confusing" (Churchman B141). Rittel was interested in problems associated with large-scale planning projects. Significantly, he claimed there is a *moral* element to such problems, in that it is *immoral* to solve only one component of a wicked problem when such an approach will leave the larger issue unresolved. Prototyping and critical making can thus be positioned not as inadequate tinkering but as a mode of activity well-suited to the resolution of very complex problems. In this way we come to an intersection of tactical media, critical making, cyber-infrastructure, and the humanities.

My website, jamessmithies.org, is hosted on a Raspberry Pi 2 Model B, a minimal computer built in the United Kingdom at Sony's manufacturing plant in Pencoed in South Wales and supported by a registered charity, the Raspberry Pi Foundation. The computer measures 85.60 mm by 56 mm by 21 mm (or roughly 3.37" by 2.21" by 0.83"), has 1 GB of Random Access Memory (RAM), and is powered by a 900-MHz quad-core ARM Cortex-A7 Central Processing Unit (CPU). ARM processors were developed by a British company, ARM Holdings, and are designed for low-power mobile devices. According to Wikipedia, the Pi is the fastest selling British personal computer in history, with over five million units sold as of February 2015. The computer uses "system on a chip" architecture, meaning the RAM, CPU, and video capabilities are all embedded on a single integrated circuit. Long-term storage is provided by a removable mini SD card, which can be bought in sizes from 8 GB to 128 GB.

The Pi can be connected to a keyboard, mouse, and monitor as well as the Internet (via an ethernet connection or wifi). It has four USB ports, an audio jack, and a High-Definition Multimedia Interface (HDMI) video/audio port. Power is supplied using a micro connection, the kind of power pack used to charge mobile phones. Minimal computers like the Pi often run "headless" without keyboard and monitor. In that case, as with this project, maintenance of the Pi is undertaken remotely using another computer connected to the Internet or a local network. This approach allows all available resources to be directed to specific goals (such as running a web server) instead of running processes required for a monitor and other peripheral devices. Lack of computational power is a feature, not a design flaw, of the Raspberry Pi. Aside from keeping unit costs down, it forces people to think carefully about use and performance.

This thinking increases computational literacy by forcing people to interact with the computer as a thing-in-itself: merely an engineered device with affordances and constraints. The question of over-engineering and its relationship to economics arises, too. Computer manufacturers and software developers make money by selling new devices to consumers in a marketing cycle that transfers personal and organizational funds into the accounts of multinational corporations. While new features are exciting and often useful, most modern computers have significantly more functionality than their users need. This excess is not a problem if someone simply wants to experience the added benefits of the latest iPhone or Galaxy S, but it is a problem if investments are being made in computing devices at the expense of, say, books and faculty. Most humanists only ever use word processors, web browsers, and e-mail applications, but are supplied with computers that far exceed those requirements. While a 1-GB minimal computer is too low-powered for everyday professional use, it is closer to the minimum requirements than its NZD $65 price tag might suggest.

Like most minimal computing devices, Raspberry Pi runs versions of the open-source Linux operating system (OS) (Raymond). Linux was heavily influenced by Unix operating systems developed at AT&T's Bell Laboratories in the 1970s, so it has deep connections to computing history (Toomey 74–82). Although not widely used for desktop PCs, Linux and Unix-like operating systems are used for over 67 percent of the world's web servers,[2] along with a wide variety of mundane devices from televisions to traffic lights. Although the community's culture is not without its problems (its initiator and figurehead, Linus Torvalds, is recognized as a "benign dictator for life," and there are periodic claims of bullying and overly aggressive behavior), over twelve thousand programmers have contributed to the Linux project since 2005. Yochai Benkler (2002) describes it as a system of peer production and "sociological phenomenon" that changed software development norms and raised questions about the dominant paradigms underlying economists' definition of productivity (373). Linux is licensed so freely that over six hundred different "distributions" or "distros" of its kernel have been created by people and organizations in need of bespoke operating systems, including systems for minimal computers such as the Raspberry Pi. At the time of writing, at least ten Linux operating systems, from "Debian Wheezy" (suitable for general users and recommended for school projects) to "Pidora" (based on Fedora, a popular operating system for web servers and the OS chosen for this project), were available to install on Raspberry Pi. The vast majority are free to download and use and also offered under the GNU General Public License (GPLv2) that allows modification and redistribution.

The Raspberry Pi computer and Linux operating system thus provide the foundations of jamessmithies.org: a credit-card-sized computer stored inside a cheap plastic box, plugged into a standard home modem, and nestled under a desk in a home office. The Pi and OS can perhaps be viewed as the filing cabinet and folders of the VRE, accessible only to their owner and configured according to their personal requirements. The application architecture that sits on top of this device enables the core functions and creates the opportunity for further development (see Figure 10.1).

I built the VRE application using Django, a Python-based web framework designed for newspaper websites but now deployed in a wide variety of scenarios. Social media service Pinterest is one of the largest services to use Django, with over

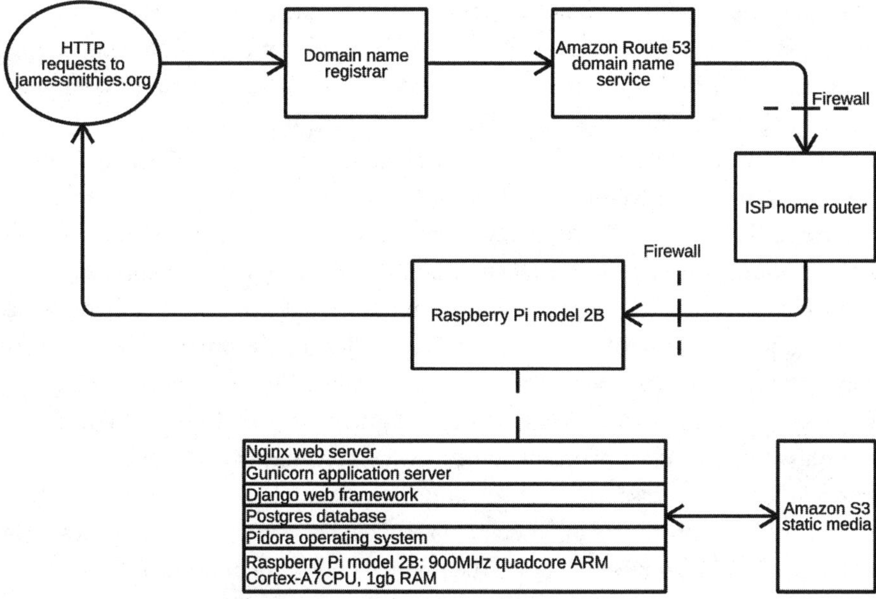


**Figure 10.1.** Technical architecture of http://www.jamessmithies.org.

forty-six million unique visitors between 2011 and 2015 (Statista). The framework is highly adaptable and could be used to develop almost any functionality a humanities researcher might need. Jamessmithies.org is served by the Gunicorn application server and lightweight Nginx web server. The latter was developed by Russian programmer Igor Sysoev in 2002 but is now maintained in San Francisco; it is used by NASA and dozens of other high-profile sites. Content is saved in Postgres, one of the more advanced database systems available. All of these products are available free through the open-source community. They require a reasonable level of technical proficiency to install and configure, but many tutorials are available online and their user communities openly share knowledge. Although a massive gap exists between jamessmithies.org and well-funded cyber-infrastructure projects, the nature of the open-source software movement means only a small gap (if any) exists in terms of scalability and potential functionality.

One of the most powerful things about the project—in both technical and tactical terms—is the level of control conferred by the architecture of the "stack." Not only is the Pi itself accessible and configurable, but its operating system can also be changed, and Gunicorn and Nginx can be configured at both an administrative level and through their core code base. Django can be programmed to support an extremely wide range of functionality. To extend the metaphor of control toward the incomprehensibly large infrastructures used by multinational digital corporations (and to escape criticism that the Pi is a fundamentally limited device, or a mere toy), static files like Cascading Style Sheets (CSS) and images are hosted in the Amazon Web Services (AWS) cloud, too, integrating the Pi with a truly enormous global data infrastructure. These files could have been hosted on the Pi, but developer communities consider it best practice to deliver files separately for Django projects. Essentially, much of the heavy lifting is outsourced to a high-performance computer, allowing almost limitless options for expansion of the site.

The fact that Amazon is a multinational giant responsible for changes in publishing and the wider culture industry that challenges the humanities is both ironic and somewhat perverse, of course. Resisting Amazon's low-cost services and massive economy of scale is difficult, even when starting with a little computer that is relatively free of the more negative associations of corporate IT. Let there be no doubt: any facade of purity (technological or intellectual) is compromised and perhaps entirely lost despite radical gains in functionality. The services offered include, remarkably enough, easy development of a Content Delivery Network (CDN) like those used by corporate giants to spread site content across multiple edge servers around the world in cases of extraordinarily high demand, reducing the latency that results when bits are forced to flow across vast distances. Storage for these files costs less than NZD $1 per month, despite the fact that they share the same infrastructure as commercial sites such as Netflix and Reddit. I also used AWS to connect the VRE to the Internet. Instead of third-party services that hide details of Internet Protocol (IP) redirection, I used accessible hosting tables and the AWS Route 53 service to route the domain name jamessmithies.org to the Pi's public IP address. Similarly, I configured the firewall on the home router that directs http requests to the VRE, and another installed on the Pi itself, and can maintain them along with the rest of the system.

The limited processing power of the Pi will continue to constrain the project in important ways, but its integration into AWS speaks to its larger meaning as a full stack project. It offers a model cyber-infrastructure that unites theory and practice in addition to hands-on control of the means of production by the scholar-author without sacrificing power and reach. It represents a macrocosm of big data, big enterprise, and big Internet, miniaturized to a level where individual scholarly agency is regained, if only to a degree. This agency is perhaps most apparent in the inclusion of a Virtual Machines section to the VRE, which migrated content from another of my projects, Academic AMI (academicami.org). This migration more than merely consolidated my technical work and reduced the fragmentation of my scholarly identity across multiple online services. Academic AMI was produced in 2011, in response to a lack of easy-to-access "sandpit" servers. Any time I wanted to experiment with a new tool, test a new plug-in, or demonstrate how a web application could be used in teaching or research, I needed to configure multiple local environments (for each participant) or use an online service to set up a public-facing server. Amazon Machines Images (AMIs) allow me to package up complete operating systems, replete with their own web server and web application, and run them online in less than five minutes. A workshop with 40 participants can thus learn how to use Omeka or Open Journal Systems in the cloud with very little technical overhead.

This approach allowed me to self-provision a minor but functional analogue to Australia's Nectar Cloud, to which New Zealand had no parallel at the time. (It is of some significance that academicami.org actually predated the Nectar Cloud and several similar services around the world.) jamessmithies.org is now more than a mere blog; it is beginning to assume some characteristics of a full-fledged VRE, including "cloud infrastructure on demand" and a downloadable virtual machine that can be either run on a local computer or distributed to groups in need of a standardized operating system and digital humanities toolset. More work is planned to fulfill some of my other needs as a researcher and teacher: integration of my zotero .org library so my intellectual interests are more transparent to visitors; aggregated search across datasets I use on a regular basis; and experiments with visualization and machine learning. Unlike many digital humanists who will either choose or be forced to spread that kind of activity across multiple platforms, at the end of my career I hope to have a single project that consolidates and presents a lifetime of digital scholarship. This aim is perhaps the larger challenge posed by jamessmithies .org. For people with the requisite skills, does a minimal computer + open source web framework + cloud service integration amount to the ultimate VRE?

The need for ongoing maintenance suggests not. Conceived as a decades-long personal project, jamessmithies.org is likely to stay live for some time as a by-product of intellectual and technical engagement, but it is far from a model for general use. This chapter is intended as a project report, not a "how to" guide. The Pi needs to remain plugged in for the site to remain live, the tools used to build it are relatively advanced technologies and need to be updated on a regular basis, improvements in functionality are constrained by my limited programming skills, and depending on Amazon is problematic. The project's intellectual grounding in postphenomenology provides an intriguing perspective on this situation. When all is said and done, it offers an object lesson in human-thing entanglement. The Pi and the VRE that sits atop it are entwined with its author in intellectual, cultural, technical, and epistemological terms. Its affordances can only be enjoyed with ongoing care and attention, perhaps not unlike a farmer's tools; the natural rhythms of human interaction with (and dependence on) technology is returned as a consequence of experimentation. Conceived in this way, the knowledge created from the system and presented using it become almost indistinguishable from the system itself. It presents a stark reminder about the relationship between the modern self and digital technology (Verbeek 9).

The value of the project as a digital humanities experiment is further illustrated in the unexpected insight the Pi/VRE offers about bots and the algorithmic nature of an online, digital world. Bots (short for "robots") take many forms, but are essentially automated software programs that perform tasks on the Internet for their designers. Those tasks range from performing indexing for search services such as Google and Bing to writing cyber-fiction and publishing it on Twitter (Meyer 2013). Digital humanists have started exploring the potential of bots to create new forms of knowledge by surfacing random snippets from the Trove newspaper archive (Sherratt

2013) and building politically oriented "protest bots" (Sample 2014). Other bots are more malicious and scan the Internet for vulnerable web servers to integrate into massive "botnets," which can then be used to send spam or flood other websites with requests in denial-of-service attacks. In a worst-case scenario even the lowliest Raspberry Pi could be enlisted in an attack on the cyber-infrastructure of a nation-state.

Every website on the Internet is subjected to ongoing probing by these bots to find weaknesses, but owners remain unaware because attempted attacks are only recorded in server logs accessible by system administrators. Online services such as Wordpress, Blogger, and Medium keep those logs far from end users, making it impossible to see which bots are casing your website. This distance is inconsequential in many ways and merely illustrates the good sense of using supported services to ensure your online security, but it hides an important feature of the digital world: the vast, algorithmic swarms of bots that go about their business behind the scenes. jamessmithies.org is regularly visited by Googlebot (indexing for Google), Baidu Spider (indexing for the Chinese Baidu search engine), and other friendly enough bots. But it is also subject to attack by Morfeus Fucking Scanner, The Beast, and others that scan for vulnerabilities they can exploit to gain access. The Pi thus unexpectedly acts as a honeypot for research into the algorithmic world beneath the surface of the web, problematizing my understanding of the Internet as a human-centered domain and driving home the potential unsustainability of the project as a whole. While projecting intentionality onto bots would be foolish, jamessmithies.org illustrates an empirical research finding that arose due to the full stack design of its VRE: an unforeseen affordance unlikely to be a feature request in a formal requirements definition workshop. Such machine-inspired serendipity justifies ongoing engagement with a lowly Pi.

## NOTES

I would like to thank the reviewers of this chapter for their wide-ranging and insightful remarks.

1. See "Getting Started," *Smithsonian X 3D*, http://3d.si.edu/article/getting-started.
2. See "Usage Statistics and Market Share of Operating Systems for Websites, July 2015," *w3techs*.

## BIBLIOGRAPHY

Academic AMI. https://academicami.org/.

Benkler, Yochai. "Coase's Penguin, Or, Linux and 'The Nature of the Firm.'" *The Yale Law Journal* 112, no. 3 (2002): 369–446.

Brown, Bill. *A Sense of Things: The Object Matter of American Literature*. Chicago, Ill.: University of Chicago Press, 2003.

———. "Thing Theory." *Critical Inquiry* 28, no. 1 (October 2001): 1–22.

Churchman, C. West. "Guest Editorial: Wicked Problems." *Management Science* 14, no. 4 (1967): B141–2.

Dieter, Michael, and Geert Lovink. "Theses on Making in the Digital Age." In *Critical Making*, ed. Garnet Hertz. Hollywood, Calif.: Garnet Hertz, 2014.

Digital Public Library of America (DPLA). https://dp.la/.

DigitalNZ. https://digitalnz.org/.

Dourish, Paul, and Genevieve Bell. *Divining a Digital Future: Mess and Mythology in Ubiquitous Computing*. Cambridge, Mass.: MIT Press, 2014.

Farquhar, Adam, and James Baker. "Interoperable Infrastructures for Digital Research: A Proposed Pathway for Enabling Transformation." Conference poster at *Digital Humanities*, July 3, 2014. https://figshare.com/articles/Interoperable_Infrastructures_for_Digital_Research_A_proposed_pathway_for_enabling_transformation/1092550.

Fuller, Steve. *Kuhn vs. Popper: The Struggle for the Soul of Science*. New York: Columbia University Press, 2004.

"Getting Started." *Smithsonian X 3D*. http://3d.si.edu/article/getting-started.

Greenfield, Adam. *Everyware: The Dawning Age of Ubiquitous Computing*. Berkeley, Calif.: New Riders, 2010.

Hodder, Ian. "The Entanglements of Humans and Things: A Long-Term View." *New Literary History* 45, no. 1 (2014): 19–36.

Humanities Networked Infrastructure (HuNI). https://huni.net.au/.

Ihde, Don. *Postphenomenology and Technoscience: The Peking University Lectures*. Albany, N.Y.: SUNY Press, 2009.

Kirschenbaum, Matthew. *Mechanisms: New Media and the Forensic Imagination*. Cambridge, Mass.: MIT Press, 2007.

Mackenzie, E. S., J. McLaughlin, A. Moore, and K. Rogers. "Digitising the Middle Ages: The Experience of the 'Lands of the Normans' Project." *International Journal of Humanities & Arts Computing* 3, no. 1/2 (March 2009): 127–42.

McCullough, Malcolm. *Ambient Commons: Attention in the Age of Embodied Information*. Cambridge, Mass.: MIT Press, 2013.

———. *Digital Ground: Architecture, Pervasive Computing, and Environmental Knowing*. Cambridge, Mass.: MIT Press, 2005.

McPherson, Tara. "Designing for Difference." *differences* 25, no. 1 (January 2014): 177–88.

Meyer, Robinson. "@Horse_Ebooks Is the Most Successful Piece of Cyber Fiction, Ever." *The Atlantic*, September 24, 2013.

Montfort, Nick, and Ian Bogost. *Racing the Beam: The Atari Video Computer System*. Cambridge, Mass.: MIT Press, 2009.

Plattner, Hasso, Christoph Meinel, and Larry Leifer, eds., *Design Thinking: Understand—Improve—Apply*. Berlin: Springer, 2011.

Preda, Alex. "The Turn to Things: Arguments for a Sociological Theory of Things." *The Sociological Quarterly* 40, no. 2 (April 1999): 347–66.

Przybylla, Mareen, and Ralf Romeike. "Physical Computing and Its Scope—Towards a Constructionist Computer Science Curriculum with Physical Computing." *Fizikiniai*

*Skaičiavimai Ir Jų Apimtis—Link Konstrukcionistinės Informatikos Kartu Su Fizikiniais Skaičiavimais Ugdymo Programos Kūrimo* 13, no. 2 (July 2014): 241–54.

QueryPic. http://dhistory.org/querypic/.

Raisinghani, Mahesh S., Ally Benoit, Jianchun Ding, Maria Gomez, Kanak Gupta, Victor Gusila, Daniel Power, and Oliver Schmedding. "Ambient Intelligence: Changing Forms of Human-Computer Interaction and Their Social Implications." *Journal of Digital Information* 5, no. 4 (2006). https://journals.tdl.org/jodi/index.php/jodi/article/view/149/147.

Raley, Rita. "Digital Humanities for the Next Five Minutes." *differences* 25, no. 1 (2014): 26–45.

———. *Tactical Media*. Minneapolis: University of Minnesota Press, 2009.

"Raspberry Pi." *Wikipedia,* June 26, 2015.

Ratto, Matt. "Critical Making: Conceptual and Material Studies in Technology and Social Life." *The Information Society* 27, no. 4 (July 2011): 252–60.

Raymond, Eric S. *The Cathedral & the Bazaar: Musings on Linux and Open Source by an Accidental Revolutionary.* Sebastopol, Calif.: O'Reilly Media, Inc., 2001.

Rittel, Horst W. J., and Melvin M. Webber. "Dilemmas in a General Theory of Planning." *Policy Sciences* 4, no. 2 (1973): 155–69.

Sample, Mark. "A Protest Bot Is a Bot so Specific You Can't Mistake It for Bullshit: A Call for Bots of Conviction." Author's blog. May 30, 2014. https://medium.com/@samplereality/a-protest-bot-is-a-bot-so-specific-you-cant-mistake-it-for-bullshit-90fe10b7fbaa#.3gdza9ctg.

Sherratt, Tim. "QueryPic." *Wraggelabs Emporium: Digital Tools for Discerning Historians,* April 15, 2012. http://wraggelabs.com/emporium/trove-tools/newspaper-search-summariser.

———. "Trove Build-a-Bot." *GitHub,* August 29, 2013. https://github.com/wragge/trovebuildabot.

Smithes, James. http://jamessmithies.org/.

Statista. "Pinterest: Unique U.S. Visitors 2015." *Statista* (2015). www.statista.com/statistics/277694/number-of-unique-us-visitors-to-pinterestcom.

Terras, Melissa. "Present, Not Voting: Digital Humanities in the Panopticon: Closing Plenary Speech, Digital Humanities 2010." *Literary and Linguistic Computing* 26, no. 3 (2011): 257–69.

Toomey, W. "First Edition Unix: Its Creation and Restoration." *IEEE Annals of the History of Computing* 32, no. 3 (2010): 74–82.

"Usage Statistics and Market Share of Operating Systems for Websites, July 2015." *w3techs.* Accessed June 29, 2015.

Verbeek, Peter-Paul. *Moralizing Technology: Understanding and Designing the Morality of Things*. Chicago, Ill.: University of Chicago Press, 2011.

Weiser, M. "The Computer for the 21st Century." *Scientific American* 265, no. 3 (1991): 94–104.

Zotero. https://www.zotero.org/.

# Mic Jammer

ALLISON BURTCH AND ERIC ROSENTHAL

Mic Jammer is an ultrasonic security system that gives people the confidence to know that their smart phones are non-invasively muted. When pointed at a smart phone, it de-senses the phone's microphone by applying a high-level, ultrasonic signal inaudible to humans but not to technologies.

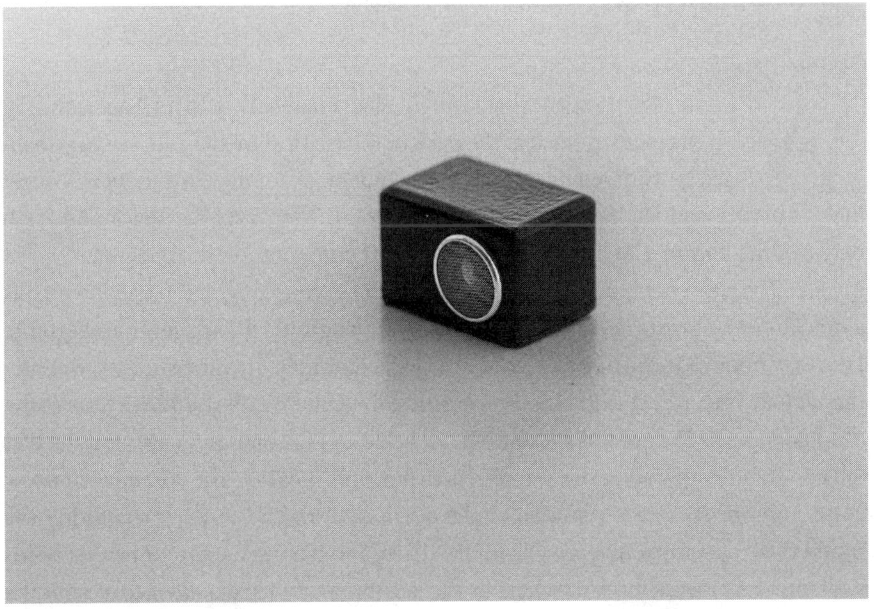

**Figure 11.1.** Mic Jammer. Format: Ultrasonic security system. Materials: Smart phones, printed circuit boards, ultrasonic signals, and various electronic components, including an ultrasonic speaker. Allison Burtch and Eric Rosenthal. Courtesy of Allison Burtch.

# The Making of a Digital Humanities Neo-Luddite

MARCEL O'GORMAN

*There is no hard dividing line between hammer and poem when it comes to making (and studying) culture.*

—Steven E. Jones, *Against Technology*

*Ned Ludd's anger was not directed at the machines, not exactly. I like to think of it more as the controlled, martial-arts type anger of the dedicated Badass.*

—Thomas Pynchon, "Is It O.K. to Be a Luddite?"

"Who wants to take the first swing?" Sledgehammer in hand, I am standing on the loading dock at the back of the Critical Media Lab, staring down at a bewildered dozen graduate students from the University of Waterloo's Experimental Digital Media (XDM) program. Their eyes dart back and forth between the hammer and the dusty Pentium III computer on the concrete floor at my feet. For a moment, there is silence, and then nervous laughter. Someone sneaks a quick photo of me as I smile provocatively at the group. Then a few hands go up. I daresay none of those hands ever held a sledgehammer. The first student, wearing mandatory eye protection, takes a powerful swing, and we all shudder a little at the thud and crash. The second student opens a cleft in the computer case, and the box falls on its side, revealing the soundboard, fan, and speaker. The reluctance is now gone, and one by one the students take a whack at the machinery, shattering the motherboard, compacting the CD-ROM drive, and flaying the tin frame that holds it all together. Pieces fly everywhere as the last few students take their turn with the sledgehammer. When the ritual is over, bits of plastic, silicon, and tin are strewn across the floor. The Pentium III looks like it was put through a trash compactor—or something worse, something much more violent and insidious. I prop up what is left of the box in the same place where we started the ritual. The fan hangs by a sad, single wire. "How did that make you feel?" I ask.

In 1995, when Kirkpatrick Sale picked up a sledgehammer and smashed the monitor and keyboard of an IBM PC in front of a bemused crowd at New York City Hall, he was transported by the experience. As he recalls in an uncomfortable *Wired* interview with Kevin Kelly (2005), "It was astonishing how good it made me feel! I cannot explain it to you" (Kelly and Sale). The somewhat less zealous students in my "Digital Abstinence" seminar[1] did not report feeling "good"—let alone "badass," to cite Pynchon (1984)—about their Luddistic actions. Whereas Sale revels in "the spewing of the undoubtedly poisonous insides [of the CRT monitor] into the spotlight," my students expressed concern about the potentially toxic bits of lead and mercury from the brittle, exploding circuit boards. Other students saw the whole exercise as a waste; the computer could have been used as the guts of a retro arcade cabinet. Or better, it could have been donated to a community organization. The parts could have been upcycled to invent experimental devices.

Clearly, I was not dealing with a group of Luddites, or at least not the machine-smashing brand of Luddite. However, these students signed up for the class because they shared a suspicion about the excessive role of digital media in their lives. Over the course of the term, they would create pinhole cameras and learn to patiently develop photo paper in a darkroom. They would also explore "digital abstinence" by making Arduino-based devices, such as Adam Cilevitz's (2015) prototype for a digital chastity belt, an ironic and humorous device that speaks to the eroticism of handheld device usage.[2] While the students would certainly not call themselves Luddites, the work they completed is by all means neo-Luddistic. Is it possible to imagine a version of digital humanities (DH) based on the same sort of make-oriented, neo-Luddistic practices? How would it work, and what would it accomplish?

At the opening of his interview with Kevin Kelly, Sale notes, "We modern-day Luddites are not, or at least not yet, taking up the sledgehammer and the torch and gun to resist the new machinery, but rather taking up the book and the lecture and organizing people to raise these issues" (Kelly and Sale). He unabashedly claims that contemporary Luddites "confine their resistance . . . to a kind of intellectual or political resistance." Sale clearly distances himself from the arson and murder with which some bands of Luddites were guilty, but perhaps he goes too far in his intellectual position. As his technophilic interviewer was well aware, intellectual resisters armed with books do not hold the same cultural capital as computer resistors developed at the rate of Moore's Law. Smashing a desktop computer with a sledgehammer was ridiculous in 1995 when the real "enemy" of the Luddites was the Mosaic browser. In the same vein, technologies are already deep into obsolescence cycles by the time humanities scholars publish articles about them. With these issues in mind, the DH neo-Luddism I propose intervenes directly in the production of technoculture rather than responding to it post hoc and primarily in a medium (books) to which technoculture is resistant. DH neo-Luddites do not abandon scholarly writing; they supplement it by creating critical objects-to-think-with that provide alternative models for digital media production—models that do not respond dutifully to the demands for efficiency and commercialization that characterize prevailing conceptions of "innovation."

Rather than picking up the sledgehammer, DH neo-Luddites might emulate the habits of Friedrich Kittler (1996): "At night, after I had finished writing, I would pick up the soldering iron and build circuits" (in Griffin 731). This quote has been used by various DH scholars (including myself) to encourage a make-oriented approach to scholarship. It was not used by Stephen Ramsay, however, when he suggested at the 2011 Modern Language Association convention that "Digital Humanities is about building things" ("Who's In and Who's Out"). In fact, soldering and building circuits—let alone writing—did not make it to Ramsay's list of DH *technai*, which included "data mining, xml encoding, text analysis, gis, Web design, visualization, programming, tool design, database design" ("On Building"). Wrapped up in my call for a DH neo-Luddism is an expanded definition of DH beyond the traditional humanities computing tasks on Ramsay's list.[3]

I am not entirely prepared to follow Gary Hall's (2012) polemical provocation that "There Are No Digital Humanities," but I agree with his point that all humanities research has persisted and evolved in a digital context. The subset of the humanities cited by Ramsay is a recent and specific response to institutional and cultural pressures. However, this response, which we have come to call digital humanities, does not account for all things digital in humanities research. As Hall notes, "The (supposedly predigital) humanities can be seen to have *already had* an understanding of and engagement with computing and the digital."

With this context in mind, I describe the work of Kittler and other media theorists—whether they solder or not—as digital humanities research. Kittler is a special case, due to his tactile[4] approach to media. To understand the depth and range of his research, consider that he not only wrote media theory but was also a maker who "bought parts from all over the world, had building instructions sent to him, screwed, soldered, glued parts together" (Gringmuth). Although Kittler does not make the connection explicit, his tinkering cannot be separated from his archaeological media theories. I am calling for a version of DH that makes the connection explicit, and does so to provide modes of digital production that are not complicit with technocapitalism and also resist appeals to progress for the sake of progress.

By challenging prescribed notions of DH, I fall into the trap of self-definition. As Rita Raley (2014) suggests in "Digital Humanities for the Next Five Minutes," this trap is at once "semantic and substantive, practical and ideological, individual and tribal, and wholly academic" (28). It is also, in her words, a waste of "bandwidth" (28). Still, my attempt to carve out a place for neo-Luddism as a humanities research practice requires looking carefully at those practices, already listed by Ramsay, that usually come to mind when we hear "digital humanities." Raley's qualification of self-definition as "wholly academic" also corresponds with a problem noted by Hall, Alan Liu (2012), and others, namely that the growth of DH results from broader institutional needs to, in Raley's terms, "make knowledge useful" (32). This utilitarian process bypasses the humanities' core commitment to be careful, critical, and even contemplative about culture. Such a commitment is often inefficient or defies institutional demands for commercializable innovation. Raley suggests that, rather than acceding to the technocratic pressures of university administration, DH might provide a space to "tinker with the symbolic order of computing, such that it is not ultimately constrained by an agenda of efficiency, rationality, and optimization" (40). This anti-bureaucratic view of DH obviously falls in line with a neo-Luddistic ideology, but neo-Luddism requires a concerted effort to think outside of bureaucratic academia altogether and consider culture at large, including the problems posed by a technocratic apparatus that values efficiency above all else and is driven by narratives of progress and innovation. As Thomas Pynchon suggests in his 1984 essay, "Is It O.K. to Be a Luddite?" the Luddistic work of William Blake, Lord Byron, and various gothic novelists was an admittedly "irrational" response to an "emerging technopolitical order that might or might not know what it was doing." While neo-Luddism may seem romantic, or even futile, the vocal and visible attempt at resistance is what matters.

In *Against Technology: From the Luddites to Neo-Luddism,* Steven E. Jones (2006) identifies three specific "hats" of contemporary neo-Luddism, based on color categories used to identify hacker ideologies: green (eco-critics), red (leftists), and black (anarchists). These categories are not discrete. Two or more may go hand in hand. Green neo-Luddites such as Langdon Winner and Bill McKibben are concerned about technology's environmental impacts. Red neo-Luddites, a category that might also include Winner and McKibben, resist the local and global economic disparities engendered by the neoliberal logic of technological innovation. Scholars such as Jacques Ellul might fall into this category, but so would any activist who attempts to find life outside of technocapitalist consumption. As for the black hat neo-Luddites, consider Chellis Glendenning's (1990) ridiculously simple proposal that "all technologies are political," enmeshed as they are in bureaucratic and economic networks of production and consumption. Keeping in mind the political thrust of technological innovation, as I write this chapter Canadian prime minister Justin Trudeau is touring my innovation-frenzied campus, meeting with start-ups, promising funds for tech research and development, and celebrating the city's new Google headquarters as the shape of things to come (Outhit). I would really like to see teams of DH scholars working in the same physical space as tech start-ups, sharing tools to build digital products and services that challenge the market-driven understanding of "innovation." This work might not require black hat anarchy, but it would certainly require DH scholars to consider their work within the broader scope of technocapitalist production.

Neo-Luddism provides examples of how DH might move beyond its "wholly academic" practices to intervene in broader culture. Neo-Luddistic practices are motivated by political concerns found in humanities fields, such as feminism,

Marxism, and eco-criticism, that work outside or alongside DH. They offer scholars opportunities to reconnect with humanities and social science methodologies that pay close attention to the "critical frameworks and politicized histories" that DH has ignored (Lothian and Phillips). DH neo-Luddism thus responds to Geoffrey Rockwell's (2013) statement that we should focus less on "what we have been" than on "what we could be," a suggestion that Raley also supports. However, one possibility for reimagining DH is to resurrect some historical humanistic concerns that DH has neglected. And, as I have noted, many of those concerns fall in line with neo-Luddism. Before pointing to a way forward, I would like to consider how traditional DH scholarship *has not* been neo-Luddistic. This exercise demonstrates the need for DH to adopt some political frameworks it otherwise ignores in the name of tool building, and to engage more critically with the technocapitalist practices it so willingly adopted.

What would a neo-Luddistic assessment of traditional DH scholarship look like? First, consider the green hat perspective. DH is criticized for generating numerous research tools that are rarely, if ever, used by the scholars for whom they were created. Claire Warwick (2011) points specifically to this problem in "Studying Users in Digital Humanities." Her findings show that roughly one-third of DH projects from several prominent online archives remain unused by their intended audiences. A green hat neo-Luddite might ask about the resources that went into these projects. How much equipment was purchased, and how much e-waste was produced? What is the environmental cost of storing these resources, maintaining them, and making them available online? How much of that equipment went unused, cobwebbed perhaps in a lonely DH laboratory tucked away in the basement of a humanities building? Of course, asking such questions risks ignoring the possible pedagogical or even cognitive benefits of producing unused DH projects or vaporware. We might just as easily question the waste produced in the publication of a scholarly monograph. The point is that DH neo-Luddism takes into account its environmental footprint. Following Warwick's advice, this practice at least means accounting for audience needs and habits.

The image of expensive computer equipment going unused in the name of DH research also brings to mind economic dimensions of the field. Since their inception, DH and humanities computing were viewed as two of the most viable methods for earning grant funding from government organizations and private companies. As Matthew K. Gold (2011) observes,

> At a time when many academic institutions are facing austerity budgets, department closings, and staffing shortages, the digital humanities experienced a banner year that saw cluster hires at multiple universities, the establishment of new digital humanities centers and initiatives across the globe, and multimillion-dollar grants distributed by federal agencies and charitable foundations. (ix)

Alan Liu's assertion that DH is driven by a questionable economic rationale ("The State of the Digital Humanities")—one that might draw scholars away from critical and speculative research for the sake of landing a lucrative budget to fund an "instrumental"[5] DH project rooted in institutional logics of progress and efficiency—is difficult to deny. One need only mention "big data" to summon the specter of seductive grant money for humanities researchers who might otherwise pursue non-digital projects that would go unfunded. There is no question that most DH work is complicit with the prevailing economic and corporate ideologies that drive technological innovation, and many DH scholars acknowledge this alliance. The problem is that such research risks flying in the face of critical practice and might proceed without questioning its own ideology, ethics, or sustainability. In this case, a neo-Luddistic approach is useful, since it provides a critical framework for understanding the various ideologies that inform digital work in the humanities.

A neo-Luddite assessment might at once critique DH's lack of concern for the environment, its uncritical adoption of corporate ideologies, and—keeping in mind the black hat—its willingness to serve an institutional and political climate that views the humanities as an inefficiency to be fixed. While I am by no means calling for anarchy, I side with Raley's contention, once again, that we should make space in the humanities—call it DH or not—for opportunities to "tinker" with technology without being constrained by goals of efficiency and commercialization (40). This reprioritization is precisely what the original Luddites promoted. Several scholars have attempted to rescue Luddism from its negative connotations. Following the work of Kirkpatrick Sale, Nichols Fox (2002), David Noble (1993), and others, Jones suggests that the original Luddites were not a motley crew of random anarchists who were raging against the machine. Instead, they were a fairly well-organized movement of craftspeople and laborers who were being squeezed by a specific set of economic and political circumstances. They were not resisting a general technological zeitgeist; rather, "they were protecting their trade—which, more than a job, was a culture, an economy, and a group of coworkers, a labor 'gang,' their social identity in the community as well as a technique or set of practices" (Jones 48). The original Luddites, Jones reminds us, were not anti-technological at all; in fact they

> were themselves technologists—that is, they were skilled machinists and masters of certain specialized technes (including the use of huge, heavy hand shears, complicated looms, or large, table-sized cropping or weaving machines), by which they made their living. That living and their right to their technology was what they fought to protect, not some Romantic idyll in an imagined pretechnological nature. (9)

One might make a similar claim about humanities scholars who resist the lure of humanities computing and DH. For them, the problem with DH is not its technophilia, but its focus on making tools for the sake of making tools. Such a focus threatens the culture, economy, and social identity of humanities researchers. Many non-DH scholars are fighting to protect a culture and way of life that depend on specific technologies and labor practices, including writing technologies, critical writing skills, close reading, and space for contemplative thought within a world otherwise littered with digital distraction. DH neo-Luddites take these concerns seriously; but rather than picking up sledgehammers or avoiding digital tools altogether, they use soldering irons and other analog and digital technologies to build objects-to-think-with.

DH neo-Luddism, then, emerges alongside the burgeoning maker movement; however, it does so with a critical eye toward what, why, and how things are made. Jones's description of contemporary neo-Luddites may help us to better understand the recent explosion of the maker movement. As he suggests, today's "Neo-Luddites look to the Luddites for the moral authority of working-class experience, a grounding in material realities that seem increasingly elusive in today's alienated, technologically mediated, virtual economy" (8). Regardless of whether they consider themselves to be neo-Luddites, this group of handiworkers searches for an authentic, hands-on experience that cannot be achieved in the cubicle at a tech company. Consider, for example, the title of Mark Frauenfelder's recent book, *Made by Hand: Searching for Meaning in a Throwaway World* (2010). As editor-in-chief of *Make* magazine, Frauenfelder champions the idea that making things off-screen helps to counter a certain, perhaps undertheorized, *malaise* associated with digital culture, a diagnosis proposed more rigorously by philosopher Bernard Stiegler (2010). Several champions of the maker movement, including Kevin Kelly, Mark Hatch (2014), and Chris Anderson (2012), assert the same claim. In *Makers: The New Industrial Revolution*, Anderson suggests that "digital natives are starting to hunger for life beyond the screen" (18). However, the maker movement uncritically heroizes the individualism of white-collared tinkerers[6] and fails to acknowledge its crass complicity with technocapitalism. As Evgeny Morozov (2014) suggests in a sharply angled assessment of maker culture,

> A reluctance to talk about institutions and political change doomed the Arts and Crafts movement, channelling the spirit of labor reform into consumerism and D.I.Y. tinkering. The same thing is happening to the movement's successors.

For this reason, grassroots makerspaces lauded by Frauenfelder, Anderson, and others are recognized as entrepreneurial opportunities. Consider the TechShop franchise run by Hatch, for instance. By the same token, the open hardware 3-D printer manufacturer Makerbot, which embodied a new cottage industry for revolutionary tool making and independent manufacturing, was bought by the Stratasys corporation. Even Arduino, which started as a loosely organized, non-commercial, open-source microcontroller platform shared by communities of makers, was scarred by secretive copyrighting, corporate greed, and an international brand war.[7]

In an essay that has come to define the Arts and Crafts Movement, William Morris (1884) suggests that "a man at work, making something which he feels will exist because he is working at it and wills it, is exercising the energies of his mind and soul as well as of his body." Much like contemporary neo-Luddites, Morris contrasts this exercise to the hopeless toil of working with new machines, which "cause a certain amount of misery among the workers whose special industry it may disturb." As Morozov notes, the make-oriented impulse of the Arts and Crafts Movement serves as an iconic example of resistance to technological innovation; however, the movement's inability to directly impact politics and institutions led to its ultimate demise. For this reason, the make-oriented work of scholars such as Anne Balsamo (2011), David Gauntlett (2011), Daniela Rosner and Sarah Fox (2016), and Matt Ratto, Sara Ann Wylie, and Kirk Jalbert (2014) should be a specific focus of DH neo-Luddites. Gauntlett suggests that his pedagogical practices might lead to "a whole new way of looking at things, and potentially to a real political shift in how we deal with the world" (19). Balsamo states that her own design work seeks to "inspire imaginations that are as ingenious in creating new democratic cultural possibilities as they are in creating new kinds of technologies and digital media" (7). These scholars work conscientiously within institutions to alter the landscape of digital media production. Ratto, Wylie, and Jalbert's emphasis on "critical making"[8] as a research platform is especially useful in this context, as it champions not just making, but making as a form of "technoscientific critique" (86). Indeed, DH neo-Luddism may be conceived as a speculative design practice[9] that resists institutional demands for efficiency and marketability in digital media production. The trick is to wield these design practices toward the greatest possible impact, both institutionally and culturally. Returning once again to Pynchon, "What is important here is the amplifying of scale, the multiplication of effect."

Unlike the Arts and Crafts Movement, DH neo-Luddism adopts the tools of the prevailing technoculture as a means to engage politically with that culture and its institutions. The equivalent for Morris and his companions would have been tinkering with steam-powered machines and electricity rather than turning to medieval handicraft. Of course, DH neo-Luddites, specifically those with media archaeological interests, might also adopt older technologies in their practices, but only to investigate contemporary technoculture. In my class on "Digital Abstinence," for example,[10] I asked students to make a functional pinhole camera using a shoebox, coffee can, or some other recycled container. They followed instructions on online discussion boards, shared design strategies, learned how to drill a pushpin into tin, and took a crash course in traditional darkroom film processing, which required interaction with people and spaces outside of their department. The slow and anticipatory process of exposing photo paper to light without being able to observe immediate results was complemented by the equally painstaking exercise of immersing the prints in chemical baths that—in rare moments of success, and often after several failed attempts—exposed, stopped, and fixed ghostly images onto the paper. The point of this non-digital project was to provide students with a conspicuously tangible counterpoint to digital photography as well as a time for reflection. Many students noted that this reflection was a rare opportunity in their otherwise busy schedules.[11] The project led to some fruitful discussions, both online and in seminar, about digital media and instant gratification, participatory culture and cognitive capital, the pleasure and plight of being an anticipatory animal, and technological care or *sorge,* all informed by readings from Stiegler, Susan Sontag, and Martin Heidegger, among others.

By all means, the course was a neo-Luddite project. But does it qualify as a DH project? My first reaction to this question might be "Who cares?" As long as the handicraft led to critical reflection and productive discussions that challenged the logic of efficiency and innovation that dominate academic institutions and surrounding technocultures, the label of DH is not necessary. On the other hand, by taking on the mantle of DH research, this project challenges some of the unquestioned motivations and contexts of many DH practices, including those on Ramsay's list.

The goal of discussing the pinhole camera assignment and practices like it is to underscore that—not to put too fine a point on it—DH neo-Luddism, like DH more generally, need not be defined as building digital tools. DH might thrive just as well on the creation of analog objects such as homemade radios, conductive play dough, and even media theory essays—as long as these objects-to-think-with are created in the context of digital culture, with the purpose of questioning technocratic ideologies that are uncritical in their modes of digital production and that constrain innovation to the standards of efficiency and marketability.

## NOTES

1. The "Digital Abstinence" course, conducted in the Critical Media Lab at the University of Waterloo, involved a combination of readings, lectures, and seminar presentations, leading to a final design project and critical essay.

2. A sampling of the student projects from this class can be viewed at http://criticalmedia.uwaterloo.ca/crimelab/?p=1482.

3. Ramsay's understanding of DH as a screen-oriented practice persists in an important article written with Geoffrey Rockwell, entitled "Developing Things: Notes toward an Epistemology of Building in the Digital Humanities." The article makes an excellent, thing-oriented argument for the role of prototypes in DH work. However, the "things" envisioned by Ramsay and Rockwell are limited to visualizations, concordances, and tools for text analysis. My hope is to expand the meaning of "building" and "things" in DH so that they are not entirely screen-oriented, but might include hardware prototypes, analog-digital hybrids, and so on.

4. On the notion of "tactile media," see Rosner and Fox as well as Sayers and the Maker Lab.

5. Liu's unique take on instrumentality is that "the digital humanities can most profoundly advocate for the humanities by helping to broaden the very idea of instrumentalism, technological, and otherwise" ("Where Is Cultural Criticism in the Digital Humanities?").

6. On this topic, see Chachra. The issue of race and gender in makerspaces is also tackled with a hands-on approach in the work of Rosner and Fox.

7. See Banzi's view of this controversy at makezine.com.

8. "Critical making" is also used to describe critically acute speculative design techniques taught at the Rhode Island School of Design. See Somerson and Hermano.

9. On speculative design, see Dunne and Raby.

10. I am not attempting to treat this classwork as an ultimate example; it serves merely as a relay to inspire other projects. Examples abound, including "residual media" in Charles Acland's anthology and the High-Low Tech group at MIT Media Lab.

11. Many scholars have written about speed and the absence of reflection in contemporary culture. See, for example, Connolly. More recently, Berg and Seeber tackled the issue of speed and scholarship in *The Slow Professor*.

## BIBLIOGRAPHY

Acland, Charles, ed. *Residual Media*. Minneapolis: University of Minnesota Press, 2005.

Anderson, Chris. *Makers: The New Industrial Revolution*. New York: Crown, 2012.

Balsamo, Anne. *Designing Culture: The Technological Imagination at Work*. Durham, N.C.: Duke University Press, 2011.

Banzi, Massimo. "Massimo Banzi: Fighting for Arduino." *makezine.com*, March 18, 2015. http://makezine.com/2015/03/19/massimo-banzi-fighting-for-arduino.

Berg, Maggie, and Barbara Seeber. *The Slow Professor: Challenging the Culture of Speed in the Academy*. Toronto: University of Toronto Press, 2016.

Chachra, Debbie. "Why I Am Not a Maker." *The Atlantic*, January 23, 2015. www.theatlantic.com/technology/archive/2015/01/why-i-am-not-a-maker/384767.

Cilevitz, Adam. "The Digital Chastity Belt." 2015. http://criticalmedia.uwaterloo.ca/crimelab/?p=1482.

Connolly, William. *Neuropolitics: Thinking, Culture, Speed*. Minneapolis: University of Minnesota Press, 2002.

Dunne, Anthony, and Fiona Raby. *Speculative Everything: Design, Fiction, and Social Dreaming*. Cambridge, Mass.: MIT Press, 2013.

Fox, Nichols. *Against the Machine: The Hidden Luddite Tradition in Literature, Art, and Individual Lives*. Washington, D.C.: Island Press, 2002.

Frauenfelder, Mark. *Made by Hand: Searching for Meaning in a Throwaway World*. New York: Penguin, 2010.

Gauntlett, David. *Making Is Connecting: The Social Meaning of Creativity, from DIY and Knitting to YouTube and Web 2.0*. Cambridge: Polity, 2011.

Glendenning, Chellis. "Notes Toward a Neo-Luddite Manifesto." *The Anarchist Library*. 1990. http://theanarchistlibrary.org/library/chellis-glendinning-notes-toward-a-neo-luddite-manifesto.

Gold, Matthew K. "The Digital Humanities Moment." In *Debates in the Digital Humanities,* ed. Matthew K. Gold, ix–xvi. Minneapolis: University of Minnesota Press, 2012. http://dhdebates.gc.cuny.edu/debates/text/2.

Griffin, Matthew, Susanne Herrmann, and Friedrich A. Kittler. "Technologies of Writing: Interview with Friedrich A. Kittler." *New Literary History* 27, no. 4 (1996): 731–42.

Gringmuth, Sven. "Notes on 'Of Gods and Scripts Around the Mediterranean—Symposium in Memoriam Friedrich Kittler.'" *ZKM Blog*. 2012. https://web.archive.org/web/20150906115146/http://blog.zkm.de/en/insights/but-life-long-enough.

Hall, Gary. "There Are No Digital Humanities." In *Debates in the Digital Humanities,* ed. Matthew K. Gold. Minneapolis: University of Minnesota Press, 2012. http://dhdebates.gc.cuny.edu/debates/text/21.

Hatch, Mark. *The Maker Movement Manifesto: Rules for Innovation in the New World of Crafters, Tinkerers and Hackers*. New York: McGraw-Hill, 2014.

High-Low Tech. MIT Media Lab. http://highlowtech.org/.

Jones, Steven E. *Against Technology: From the Luddites to Neo-Luddism*. New York: Routledge, 2006.

Kelly, Kevin, and Kirkpatrick Sale. "Interview with the Luddite." *Wired,* June 1, 2005. http://www.wired.com/1995/06/saleskelly.

Liu, Alan. "The State of the Digital Humanities: A Report and a Critique." *Arts and Humanities in Higher Education* 11, no. 1–2 (2011): 8–41.

———. "Where Is Cultural Criticism in the Digital Humanities?" In *Debates in the Digital Humanities,* ed. Matthew K. Gold, 490–510. Minneapolis: University of Minnesota Press, 2012. http://dhdebates.gc.cuny.edu/debates/text/20.

Lothian, Alexis, and Amanda Phillips. "Can Digital Humanities Mean Transformative Critique?" *E-Media Studies* 3, no. 1 (2013). http://journals.dartmouth.edu/cgi-bin/WebObjects/Journals.woa/1/xmlpage/4/article/425.

Morozov, Evgeny. "Making It." *The New Yorker,* January 13, 2014. www.newyorker.com/magazine/2014/01/13/making-it-2.

Morris, William. "Useful Work Vs. Useless Toil." *William Morris Internet Archive,* originally published 1884. www.marxists.org/archive/morris/works/1884/useful.htm.

Noble, David. *Progress without People: In Defense of Luddism*. Chicago, Ill.: Charles H. Kerr, 1993.

O'Gorman, Marcel. *Necromedia*. Minneapolis: University of Minnesota Press, 2015.

Outhit, Jeff. "Trudeau Brings Tech Funds on Waterloo Visit." *TheRecord.com,* January 15, 2016. www.therecord.com/news-story/6232600-trudeau-brings-tech-funds-on-waterloo-visit.

Pynchon, Thomas. "Is It O.K. to Be a Luddite?" *New York Times,* October 28, 1984. www.nytimes.com/books/97/05/18/reviews/pynchon-luddite.html.

Raley, Rita. "Digital Humanities for the Next Five Minutes." *differences* 25 no. 1 (2014): 26-45.

Ramsay, Stephen, and Geoffrey Rockwell. "Developing Things: Notes toward an Epistemology of Building in the Digital Humanities." In *Debates in the Digital Humanities,* ed. Matthew K. Gold. Minneapolis: University of Minnesota Press, 2012. http://dhdebates.gc.cuny.edu/debates/text/11.

———. "On Building." Author's website. January 11, 2011. http://stephenramsay.us/text/2011/01/11/on-building.

———. "Who's In and Who's Out." Author's website. January 8, 2011. http://stephenramsay.us/text/2011/01/08/whos-in-and-whos-out/.

Ratto, Matt, Sara Ann Wylie, and Kirk Jalbert. "Introduction to the Special Forum on Critical Making as Research Program." *The Information Society* 30 (2014): 85–95.

Rockwell, Geoffrey. "Inclusion in the Digital Humanities." Author's website. July 22, 2013. www.philosophi.ca/pmwiki.php/Main/InclusionInTheDigitalHumanities.

Rosner, Daniela K., and Sarah E. Fox. "Legacies of Craft and the Centrality of Failure in a Mother-Operated Hackerspace." *New Media & Society* 18, no. 4 (2016): 558–80.

Sayers, Jentery, and the Maker Lab in the Humanities. "Kits for Cultural History." *Hyperrhiz* 13 (2015). http://hyperrhiz.io/hyperrhiz13/workshops-kits/early-wearables-essay.html.

Somerson, Rosanne, and Mara L. Hermano, eds. *The Art of Critical Making.* Hoboken, N.J.: Wiley, 2013.

Stiegler, Bernard. *Technics and Time 3: Cinematic Time and the Question of Malaise.* Translated by Stephen Barker. Stanford, Calif.: Stanford University Press, 2010.

Ulmer, Greg. *Teletheory: Grammatology in the Age of Video.* New York: Routledge, 1989.

Warwick, Claire. "Studying Users in the Digital Humanities." In *Digital Humanities in Practice,* ed. Claire Warwick, Melissa Terras, and Julianne Nyhan, 1–22. London: Facet Publishing, 2011.

PART II ][ *Chapter 13*

## Made: Technology on Affluent Leisure Time

GARNET HERTZ

Made: Technology on Affluent Leisure Time is a sticker produced as a parody and critique of *Make Magazine* by O'Reilly Media. It was distributed for free and included as an insert in the first edition of *Critical Making* (Hollywood, Calif.: Telharmonium Press, 2012).

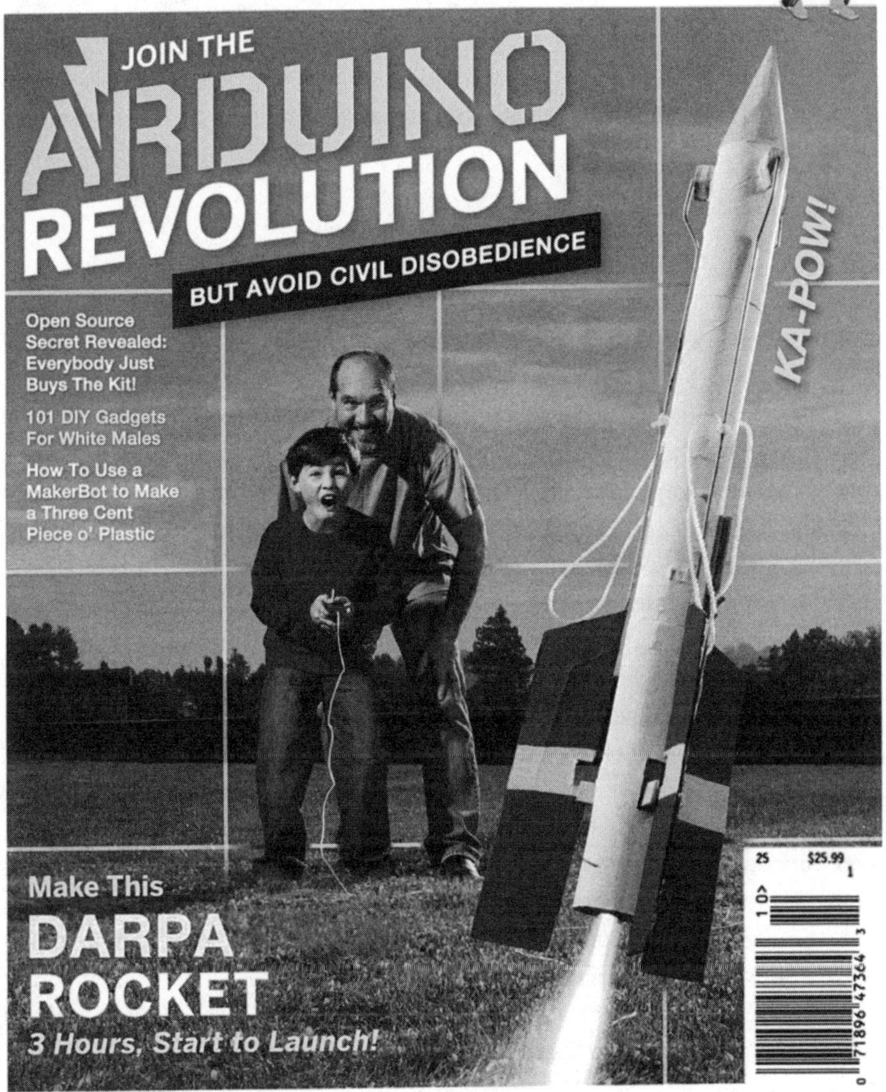


**Figure 13.1.** Format: Full Color Rectangle Vinyl Stickers, UV coated (single-sided). Dimensions: 3.5" × 5". Garnet Hertz. Sticker by the artist.

PART II ][ *Chapter 14*

# Reifying the Maker as Humanist

JOHN HUNTER, KATHERINE FAULL, AND DIANE JAKACKI

This chapter argues that the success of "making" depends on not only physical space but also the intersections between disciplines that encourage critical humanistic discourse. Rather than reifying the digital humanities (DH) maker as a (usually male, usually white, usually economically and socially advantaged) creator, we argue that the DH maker is uniquely positioned to subvert paradigms of class, race, gender, and ableist privilege.[1] Furthermore, we assert that as (digital) humanists, we (with our students) have an opportunity and a responsibility to reclaim the centrality of making to the humanities and its histories. Since the humanities is defined by the production of historically situated critique, critical making deserves prominence in the rhetoric of today's makerspaces. Such prominence could rescue not only DH from residual claims that it is insufficiently "intellectual" but also the humanities from charges that it does not produce anything "useful."[2] After first undoing the presumed discontinuity between traditional humanist practice and contemporary DH makers, we move to some specific examples from our own experience and end by articulating the transformative potential of the DH maker as an enactment of humanistic thought.

The intellectual relationship between making and analyzing has been contested for centuries, and debates around the status of DH making within the contemporary academy are just its latest incarnation. Aristotle's assertion in the *Politics* that "it is impossible to engage in virtuous pursuits while living the life of a vulgar craftsman or hired laborer" crystallizes the old and strongly held prejudice against making things with our hands and in favor of contemplative activities (Aristotle 1.5). It has conditioned the Western academy (and society in general) ever since. Against this assertion, however, is Aristotle's advocacy of "practical wisdom" *(phronesis)* and the benefits of practicing (as opposed to only thinking) virtuous habits (MacIntyre 175–8). A positive concept of a "maker" as a writer and for God as a creator has a pedigree in the English-speaking world dating back to the fourteenth century. A century or so later, "maker" also described a poet (Bawcutt 1–39). At that time, the emphasis was on rhetoric, understood as the scholar's capacity to *make* as the result of reading, analysis, and self-fashioning. For Erasmus in the sixteenth century, the scholar's task was to study ancient wisdom and "store it in our memory once observed, imitate it once remembered, and by constant employment develop an expertise by which we may call upon it instantly" ("Copia" 302). The purpose was not to confine one's thought to the past, but to use thought to create new knowledge for the future. Erasmus's rhetoric also emphasizes the materiality of both language and writing; language is shaped according to the contexts in which it is needed, and it is in every sense something artificial and crafted, not ethereal and abstract. Aristotle denigrated such workmanlike repetitions (even musicians are "vulgar craftsmen" in his estimation [Aristotle 8.5]), but Erasmus has no qualms about stressing the material labor of academic work. The act of writing was much more laborious prior to the invention of fountain pens, modern paper products, and keyboards (Goldberg 61–169).

This debate about the relative value of disembodied thought and embodied practice persists in today's academy, albeit inflected by a twenty-first century Western context. Why is creating an algorithm perceived as "making something new" when compared with writing an essay? The difference in creativity between the two activities is not empirically obvious. Stephen Ramsay and Geoffrey Rockwell (2012) note that making a digital tool is not seen as a "scholarly" activity (77–83) in the same way as writing. On the other hand, algorithms may claim what Johanna Drucker (2012) calls "the cultural authority of digital technology" that emanates from scientific and engineering disciplines (85). They also enjoy a great deal more prestige than traditional humanistic scholarship in the contemporary media environment. The ancient and largely unconscious forces that value intellectual labor over manual work coexist with a social environment where digital skills are deemed essential in secondary schools and fundamental to nearly all academic research outside the humanities. As Max Horkheimer commented in 1937 (in language that could have been lifted from an op-ed article today), "In recent periods of contemporary society the so-called human studies (*Geisteswissenschaften*) have had but a fluctuating market value and must try to imitate the more prosperous natural sciences whose practical value is beyond question" (191). In 2004, Edward Said observed that "no matter who is writing or speaking, where, when, or to whom, the humanities always seem to be in deep and usually terminal trouble" (31). One could trace this rhetoric of crisis all the way back to Erasmus, but especially since 2008 the humanities has witnessed a decline in the number of majors, caused by a toxic combination of economic anxiety, spiraling costs, and media and parental suspicion of the humanities' value in the world.[3] The idea that humanities students should be making real (rather than evanescent) products is a reasonable response to these pressures; it asserts the tangibility of what we do and addresses (in some cases, embraces) the demand to demonstrate "relevance" in our historical moment. However, as history shows, this idea has nothing to do with "making" as something unprecedented or new in humanities education; ever since humanism existed as a self-conscious entity, its scholarly products have been fabricated (Erasmus, *The Correspondence* 261–68).

So where does this ongoing debate leave DH makers in the contemporary academy? Demonstrating that making is "cool" is certainly easy, precisely because it is associated with science and material creation (just as Horkheimer says).[4] Yet, as Debbie Chachra (2015) trenchantly demonstrates in "Why I Am Not a Maker," making also risks replicating some unpleasant assumptions of our socioeconomic reality. Some might claim (echoing Aristotle's denigration of "vulgar craftsmen") that we are "making a virtue of necessity" and turning to digital tools because university students no longer have the reading and writing skills to "do" traditional scholarship as well as their peers a generation ago. But, as Chachra observes, the alternative to making "is usually not doing *nothing*," and making cannot exist without an enormous superstructure of other, less well-paid activities. A similar relationship between critic and practitioner existed in traditional humanist scholarship, as Northrop Frye affirmed in the 1950s, observing that (far from being a paradise for artists) a culture without critics (and the institutional superstructure they imply) "brutalizes the arts and loses its cultural memory" (5). Thus, making in DH is not ontologically different from traditional humanistic scholarship, nor are the issues around it unprecedented in the academy.

With this history in mind, the way forward for *making knowledge informed by technology* is to see a makerspace not only in physical terms but also as an intersection of disciplines: an interdisciplinary matrix that provides a (non-)place for critical creativity and combines elements of the arts, humanities, social sciences, and STEM fields. This matrix is particularly important in a pedagogical environment or makerspace for undergraduates. In one experiment with a pass/fail course embedded within Bucknell University's Humanities and Languages and Cultures Residential Colleges (living/learning communities), second-year students meet weekly to experiment with humanistic thinking and DH. These students (of whom 75 percent are women, and one of whom is visually impaired) experiment with cultural-historical spatial thinking, digital media analysis, artifact curation, and music- and performance-computing. For these students, the process of making begins in thought and imagination, in conversation and debate. It is fed by observation and critique. When they are reassured that DH making is a process, one that may face many failures along the way to a "made" product, students are excited to enter our makerspace. Newly minted on our campus, placed alongside the traditional Craft Center, and equipped with 3-D printers and hardware, this space is a techy parallel to the potter's wheels and paints of its neighbor.

Rather than being intimidated by the hardware and its operators, these students happily repurpose and remediate skills learned by Engineering and Computer Science majors to create DH projects. For them, applying computer languages and software programs from STEM disciplines to the humanities does not somehow validate the latter through the former. Instead, they see the process as dialectical;

code is open to humanistic critique, and critique itself is the product of material forces. This access energizes the students to become the Erasmuses of the twenty-first century. They study and adapt the work of their peers to create new knowledge.

In another example at our institution, two undergraduate student researchers from Computer Science collaborated with a faculty member in Comparative Humanities to produce a searchable database of feature films that is rooted in word forms found within dialogue and paratext. Coding the database and deciding which metadata features were necessary were activities driven by their potential usefulness to scholars. As the collaborators realized very quickly, however, these activities also required making fundamental assumptions about what film research is and what it could be. The acts of programming and knowledge creation converged in processes that encouraged everyone involved to mash-up making and media and to emphasize process as much as product (Hunter, Eyster, and Hartman).

But, in these and other contexts, who are the makers in the humanities? Increasingly, the discourse in global DH revolves around issues of bias in terms of not only gender and race but also language and culture. This dialogue is uncomfortable to a community that has long perceived itself as welcoming and inclusive but in truth has followed the uncritical behaviors of more traditional academic disciplines. And yet, the difficult conversations about inclusivity are leading to responsible policies, many of which are being co-authored by prominent scholar-practitioners in the maker movement.[5] This is a moment when students (and practitioners) in the humanities, as they are reified as makers, are helping scholars and teachers to challenge traditional disciplinary and professional stereotypes within the academy. For example, the international 4Humanities movement (spearheaded by Alan Liu, Geoffrey Rockwell, Melissa Terras, Stéfan Sinclair, and Christine Henseler) presents modes of acting, making, and critiquing in DH that reinforces thinking about the humanities in terms of advocacy. 4Humanities sponsors an advocacy group for students that is founded on empowered peer communication across university campuses.[6] Furthermore, questions about student labor, in particular the slippage between coursework and research apprenticeship, are being foregrounded in ways that explode power dynamics hidden in more traditional humanities disciplines.[7] In all areas of DH making, we need to ensure that students who participate in public-facing work (in whatever medium) have their participation properly mentored and acknowledged.

Two aspects of DH that are of particular concern to all humanists, and that present the biggest challenge to making in the humanities, are access to technology and agency in its application. They are especially important to those of us who think about DH in curricular terms, and so we circle back to the making/thinking opposition with which we began this chapter. Increasingly, DH scholars are interrogating methods and approaches that include rather than exclude: among the first to reconstruct our connections to and with DH are those, such as Moya Bailey (2011), in the position of "square pegs that expose the unacknowledged round holes" within the discipline (Bailey). Leaders in feminist, queer, and critical race studies, such as Kim Gallon (2016), have demonstrated how DH offers "real meaning and significance in the academic universe" and troubles the "very core of what we have come to know as the humanities by recovering alternate constructions of humanity that have been historically excluded from that concept" (Gallon 43, 44). Scholars of race and media such as Amy Earhart and Toniesha Taylor (2016) are using "DIY" DH to reframe our understanding of personhood in historical print and present-day social media discourse (Earhart and Taylor 255). Feminist collectives such as FemTechNet are exploring the embodiment of data production through research projects like Vibrant Lives, led by Jessica Rajko, Eileen Standley, and Jacqueline Wernimont.[8] Meanwhile, members of the Minimal Computing working group of Global Outlook::Digital Humanities (GO::DH) are implementing new ways for communities without access to large institutional infrastructures to engage in DH knowledge making that, as Alex Gil (2015) describes it, is alert to the "hybrid and global future we see being shaped for the scholarly record: parts digital, parts analog" (Gil). All of this scholarship occurs concurrently with the work that George Williams (2012, 2014), Jennifer Guiliano (2014), Erin Templeton, Amanda Visconti (2014), and others are doing across DH and disability studies, challenging DH makers to act more responsibly by considering principles of assistive technology and universal design.[9]

Perhaps this is another watershed moment for the humanities to demonstrate to the world that ours is the proper place to frame discourse about identity, social justice, and even the ineluctable interconnectedness of abstract debates about human rights vis-à-vis technology and the environment. In a recent lecture, Naomi Klein (2016) reminded her audience that confronting issues such as climate change can best be situated in contexts that are familiar to humanists, encouraging us to avoid thinking in terms of isolation and instead complicate the larger "context of austerity and privatisation, of colonialism and militarism, and of the various systems of othering needed to sustain them all" (Klein). Klein's point about the interconnectedness of modes of thought and modes of action that seem (or are positioned) far apart from each other is vital for all humanists, but especially for DH makers. We should be changing the question from who does or does not have access to digital tools to, echoing Gil, "What do we need? . . . What is enough?" (Gil).

In her investigation into the educational and racial politics of makerspaces, Lauren Britton (2015) argues for the activism of organizations such as Techbridge, DIY Girls, and Project H that work in economically disadvantaged communities to increase the participation of underrepresented groups in the maker movement ("Power, Access, Status"). Without student access to computer hardware, software, and collaborative experimental spaces, our expectations for a digitally enriched humanities curriculum replicate expectations of privilege. For instance, the Coachella Valley, California, school district gave disadvantaged students Internet access at night by parking WiFi-equipped school buses in poor neighborhoods. Although the mainstream media celebrated the action as a creative solution to a genuine social problem (Dobo), Britton wants us to see such situations as an indictment of structural inequalities in America and the ways in which the liberatory potential of the World Wide Web is being subverted; and it is through reflecting about making that her call to action is possible.

The academy is pouring resources into the maker movement. Making is high on university agendas.[10] As we grow maker cultures, we must inflect them with the critical insights of gender, race, disability, and design studies that view agency and access as generative foci for technological and pedagogical innovation, environmental and social justice, and storytelling by those who are muted by hegemonic normativity and institutional power. Within DH, we ignite this spark of activism when we interrogate our past as humanists and use that history of critical making to subvert the dominant paradigm of agency. By refashioning the maker as a critical humanist, we can undo existing hierarchies of knowledge and fabricate alternatives to them.

## NOTES

1. For an analysis of these issues and the maker movement in general, see Lauren Britton's excellent series of blog posts (2014, 2015). Britton draws a powerful analogy between the growth of makerspaces and fitness gyms. She points to the physical location of both entities in upper middle class and white neighborhoods as a leading cause for the resulting restriction in access to primarily affluent and white populations.

2. For remarks on the relationships between DH, use, instrumentality, and neoliberalism, see Allington, Brouillette, and Golumbia.

3. See, among many others, Jay, Chapter 1.

4. See Horkheimer 194–97.

5. See, for example, the Digital Humanities Summer Institute Statement of Ethics and Inclusion, led by Jacqueline Wernimont and Angel David Nieves, and the Alliance of Digital Humanities Organizations Conference Code of Conduct.

6. See http://4humanities.org/category/for-the-public/student-voices.

7. See, for instance, A Student Collaborators' Bill of Rights.

8. At Digital Humanities Summer Institute 2016, Jessica Rajko, Stjepan Rajko, and Jacqueline Wernimont of the Vibrant Lives project presented an installation featuring a "web" of woven sensors that vibrated in response to the social media connectedness of the audience's WiFi network.

9. See, in particular, Williams's work using the WordPress plug-in Anthologize as a conversion tool from web text to Braille (2014). See also Hendren.

10. See, in particular, the White House celebration of the National Week of Making in 2014.

**BIBLIOGRAPHY**

*4Humanities: Advocating for the Humanities*. http://4humanities.org.

"A Nation of Makers." *The White House*. 2014. www.whitehouse.gov/nation-of-makers.

Alliance of Digital Humanities Organizations Conference Code of Conduct. http://adho.org/administration/conference-coordinating-program-committee/adho-conference-code-conduct.

Allington, Daniel, Sarah Brouillette, and David Golumbia. "Neoliberal Tools (and Archives): A Political History of Digital Humanities." *Los Angeles Review of Books*. May 1, 2016. https://lareviewofbooks.org/article/neoliberal-tools-archives-political-history-digital-humanities/.

Aristotle. *Politics*. Translated and introduced by C. D. C. Reeve. Indianapolis, Ind.: Hackett Publishing, 1998.

Bailey, Moya. "All the Digital Humanists Are White, All the Nerds Are Men, but Some of Us Are Brave." *Journal of the Digital Humanities*. 2011 Winter: 1, no. 1. http://journalofdigitalhumanities.org/1-1/all-the-digital-humanists-are-white-all-the-nerds-are-men-but-some-of-us-are-brave-by-moya-z-bailey/.

Bawcutt, Priscilla. *Dunbar the Makar*. Oxford: Clarendon Press, 1992.

Bohon, Cory, Jennifer Guiliano, James Smith, George Williams, and Amanda Visconti. "'Making the Digital Humanities More Open': Modeling Digital Humanities for a Wider Audience." *Journal of the Digital Humanities*. 2014 Spring: 3, no. 1. http://journalofdigitalhumanities.org/3-1/making-the-digital-humanities-more-open-modeling-digital-humanities-for-a-wider-audience/.

Boswell, James. *Life of Johnson*, ed. R. W. Chapman, introduced by Pat Rogers. Oxford: Oxford University Press, 2008.

Britton, Lauren. "Democratized Tools of Production: New Technologies Spurring the Maker Movement." *Technology & Social Change Group*. University of Washington Information School, 2014. http://tascha.uw.edu/2014/08/democratized-tools-of-production-new-technologies-spurring-the-maker-movement.

———. "Examining the Maker Movement through Discourse Analysis: An Introduction." *Technology & Social Change Group*. University of Washington Information School, 2014. http://tascha.uw.edu/2014/07/examining-the-maker-movement-through-discourse-analysis-an-introduction.

———. "Power, Access, Status: The Discourse of Race, Gender, and Class in the Maker Movement." *Technology & Social Change Group*. University of Washington Information School, 2015. http://tascha.uw.edu/2015/03/power-access-status-the-discourse-of-race-gender-and-class-in-the-maker-movement.

———. "STEM, DASTEM, and STEAM in Making: Debating America's Economic Future in the 21st Century." *Technology & Social Change Group*. University of Washington Information School, 2014. http://tascha.uw.edu/2014/09/stem-dastem-and-steam-in-making-debating-americas-economic-future-in-the-21st-century.

Chachra, Debbie. "Why I Am Not a Maker." *The Atlantic*, January 23, 2015. www.theatlantic.com/technology/archive/2015/01/why-i-am-not-a-maker/384767.

Digital Humanities Summer Institute Statement of Ethics and Inclusion. Led by Jacqueline Wernimont and Angel David Nieves. http://www.dhsi.org/events.php#ethics+inclusion.

Dobo, Nichole. "WiFi Enabled Bus Connects Students in Poor Calif. Community." *Education Week* (January 2, 2015). http://www.edweek.org/ew/articles/2015/01/02/wi-fi-enabled-bus-connects-students-in-poor-calif.html.

Drucker, Johanna. "Humanistic Theory and Digital Scholarship." In *Debates in the Digital Humanities,* ed. Matthew K. Gold. Minneapolis: University of Minnesota Press, 2012. http://dhdebates.gc.cuny.edu/debates/text/34.

Earhart, Amy E., and Toniesha L. Taylor. "Pedagogies of Race: Digital Humanities in the Age of Ferguson." In *Debates in the Digital Humanities 2016,* ed. Matthew K. Gold and Lauren F. Klein, 251–64. Minneapolis: University of Minnesota Press, 2016.

Erasmus, Desiderius. "Copia: Foundations of the Abundant Style." Translated and introduced by Betty I. Knot. *Collected Works of Erasmus*, vol. 24, ed. Craig R. Thompson, Toronto: University of Toronto Press, 1978.

———. *The Correspondence of Erasmus, Letters 446 to 593 (1516–17).* Edited by R. A. B. Mynors and D. F. S. Thomson. Toronto: University of Toronto Press, 1977.

Frye, Northrop. *The Anatomy of Criticism: Four Essays*, ed. Robert D. Denham. Toronto: University of Toronto Press, 2007.

Gallon, Kim. "Making a Case for the Black Digital Humanities." In *Debates in the Digital Humanities 2016,* ed. Matthew K. Gold and Lauren F. Klein, 42–49. Minneapolis: University of Minnesota Press, 2016.

Gil, Alex. "The User, The Learner and the Machines We Make." *Minimal Computing: A Working Group of GO:DH*. May 21, 2015. http://go-dh.github.io/mincomp/thoughts/2015/05/21/user-vs-learner/.

Goldberg, Jonathan. *Writing Matter: From the Hands of the English Renaissance.* Stanford, Calif: Stanford University Press, 1990.

Hendren, Sara. *Abler.* Author's website. https://ablersite.org/.

Horkheimer, Max. *Critical Theory: Selected Essays*. Translated by Matthew O'Connell. New York: Continuum, 1975.

Hunter, John, Justin Eyster, and Dale Hartman. "The Film Search Engine." 2015. www.filmtvsearch.net/cgi-bin/main.py/moviesearch.

Jay, Paul. *The Humanities "Crisis" and the Future of Literary Studies*. New York: Palgrave Macmillan, 2014.

Klein, Naomi. "Let Them Drown: the Violence of Othering in a Warming World." *London Review of Books* vol. 38 no. 11 (2 June 2016). http://www.lrb.co.uk/v38/n11/naomi-klein/let-them-drown.

MacIntyre, Alasdair. *After Virtue: A Study in Moral Theory.* London: Bloomsbury, 2007.

Miller, J. Hillis. "The Critic as Host." *Critical Inquiry* 3, no. 3 (1977): 439–47.

Minimal Computing Working Group. Global Outlook::Digital Humanities. http://go-dh.github.io/mincomp/.

Ramsay, Stephen, and Geoffrey Rockwell. "Developing Things: Notes toward an Epistemology of Building in the Digital Humanities." In *Debates in the Digital Humanities,* ed. Matthew K. Gold. Minneapolis: University of Minnesota Press, 2012. http://dhdebates.gc.cuny.edu/debates/text/11.

Said, Edward. "The Changing Bases of Humanistic Study and Practice." *Humanism and Democratic Criticism*. New York: Columbia University Press, 2004.

A Student Collaborators' Bill of Rights. http://www.cdh.ucla.edu/news-events/a-student-collaborators-bill-of-rights./.

Vibrant Lives. Led by Jessica Rajko, Eileen Standley, and Jacqueline Wernimont. https://vibrantlives.live/.

Williams, George. "Disability, Universal Design, and the Digital Humanities." *Debates in the Digital Humanities*, ed. Matthew K. Gold, 203–212. Minneapolis: University of Minnesota Press, 2012.

# All Technology Is Assistive: Six Design Rules on Disability

SARA HENDREN

In 1941, the United States Navy commissioned the husband-and-wife team of Charles and Ray Eames to design a lightweight splint to get wounded soldiers safely out of the battlefield. Metal splints of the period were not secure enough to hold the leg still, causing unnecessary death from gangrene, shock, blood loss, and so on. The Eameses had been working on techniques to mold and bend plywood, and they came up with a splint design conforming to the body without a lot of extra joints and parts. The wood design became a secure, lightweight, nestable solution, and the Eameses produced more than 150,000 such splints for the Navy. Over the next decade, they would refine their wood-molding process to create both sculpture and functional design pieces, most notably the celebrated Eames chair.

Graham Pullin (2009), in *Design Meets Disability,* cites this story as an example of a seemingly specialized design problem—improving a battlefield medical aid for wounded soldiers—that inspired a whole aesthetic in modernist furnishings. The chairs launched a thousand imitators and a new ethos of simple, organic lines in household objects. Most people assume that such innovation usually happens in reverse: that a generalized design solution "trickles down" to the narrow confines of adaptive and assistive aids. But, as Pullin points out, the Eames story suggests that disability concerns are in fact an overlooked source of rich aesthetic ideas, with relevance and impact for design far beyond their immediate starting point. More than that, the story demonstrates why everyone should pay more attention to matters of disability.

You might imagine that "disability studies" is just one more category of identity research that has been created primarily for political advocacy, interesting only to those directly affected by issues of accessibility, accommodation, or special rights. But "disabled-ness" is another matter altogether. There are at least two big reasons why disability concerns are everyone's concerns.

First, any us/them distinction between able-minded/able-bodied and disabled is a false divide. After all, how cultures define, think about, and treat those who currently have marked disabilities is how all their future citizens may be perceived if *and when* those who are able-bodied become less abled than they are now, whether by age, degeneration, or some sudden or gradual change in physical or mental capacities. All people, over the course of their lives, traffic between times of relative independence and dependence. So the questions cultures ask, the technologies they invent, and how those technologies broadcast a message about their users—weakness and strength, agency and passivity—are critical ones. And they are not just questions for scientists and policy-makers; they are aesthetic questions, too.

Second, in many cultures—and certainly in the United States—a pervasive, near-obsession with averages and statistical norms about bodies and capacities has become a naturalized form of describing both individuals and populations. But this way of measuring people and populations is only a recent development and worth reconsidering. Disability studies scholar Lennard Davis (2002) writes:

> Before the nineteenth century in Western culture, the concept of the "ideal" was the regnant paradigm in relation to all bodies, so *all bodies were less than ideal.* The introduction of the concept of normality, however, created an imperative to be normal, as the eugenics movement proved by enshrining the bell curve (also known as the "normal curve") as the umbrella under whose demanding peak we should all stand. With the introduction of the bell curve came the notion of "abnormal" bodies. And the rest is history. (*Bending over Backwards* 39)

The bell curve is the source of all talk about how individuals measure up relative to others. In case you doubt this obsession, I invite you to witness conversations among parents of young children—it is all percentiles, and milestones, and being "ahead of the curve" with respect to each month of a child's development. *Exceptional normal-ness* is prized above all else. Measurements reassure anxious caregivers, despite little correlation between them and a lifetime of wellness, healthy relationships, or sustaining work.

Again, Davis reminds us that such standards comprise a *recent* set of cultural ideas, so unquestioned now that they have a way of "enforcing normalcy." Of course, as Davis writes, "It is too easy to say, 'We're all disabled'" (*Bending over Backwards* 31). But a challenge remains: to interrupt cultural assumptions in powerful, creative ways—and to alter wider collective thinking about one's own dependence and independence, and that of others. So how might designers and artists engage these myths about what is normal and make more visible, critical, and expansive technologies?

All technology is assistive technology. What technology are you using that is *not assistive?* Your smartphone? Your eyeglasses? Headphones? Those three examples alone are assisting you in multiple registers: they are enabling or augmenting a sensory experience, or providing navigational information. They are also allowing you to decide whether to be approachable in public; to check out or in on a conversation or meeting in a number of subtle ways; to identify, by your choice of brand or look, with one cultural group and not another.

Making a persistent, overt distinction about "assistive tech" embodies the second-tier do-gooderism and banality that still dominate design work targeted toward "special needs." "Assistive technology" implies a separate species of tools designed exclusively for people with a rather narrow set of diagnostic "impairments"—impairments, in other words, that have been culturally designated as needing special attention, as being particularly, grossly abnormal. But are you *sure* your phone is not a crutch, as it were, for a whole lot of unexamined needs?

Undoing the distinctions between design for disability and design in general yields a couple of benefits: it brings new attention to technologies that are profound in their use and impact on physical and political accessibility. (Advanced replacement limbs,[1] all-terrain wheelchairs,[2] and exoskeletons[3] are evidence of this new attention.) It also brings a productive uncertainty and powerful friction to the task of designing technologies of all kinds. Whether you are designing for an established need or seeking an application for a technical novelty, you might take more time before confidently assigning it to a particular user, or deciding, up front and with confidence, *how* it will be used. A design might be for practical ends, play, or something you have not yet imagined.

Instead of labeling some technologies and not others as assistive, let us start like this: *we are all getting help from the things we make*—all kinds of help, all the time, for our many material, social, educational, and political needs. Private needs and public ones. No one is exempt. *Then* the questions get really interesting: What can a body do (Deleuze 1992)? What needs are you interested in? Who might use which thing for what? Where might the surprises be? How might a familiar thing morph into something else altogether? In the name of good friction, then, I want to suggest some possible dispositions for designers and artists taking a look at ability and disability.

### *1. Invisibility Is Overrated*

The Victoria and Albert Museum's 2005 exhibition, "Hearwear: The Future of Hearing," commissioned designers to reconsider the traditional hearing aid, a long neglected prosthesis known for dubious "flesh toned" plastics and metal circuitry. The designers rejected the idea of these devices as objects of shame.

"The Beauty of Inner Space," a design by Ross Lovegrove, has more in common with jewelry than medical gear. His proposal would have a hearing aid amplify and mute sounds at the user's discretion—highlighting sounds you *want* to hear and canceling out others. And the Svara hearing aid, by BreweryLondon, is a proposal to make amplification gestures blend seamlessly with other movements: moving the necklace's "pendant" up or down, for example, or tucking one's hair behind the ears.

In other words, one strand of design might be devoted to making the hearing aid as discreet as possible—to hide its function from view. But another round of questions becomes more interesting altogether: What might a hearing aid also do—or do instead—that has not been considered?[4]

## 2. *Rethink the Default Bodily Experience*

Researchers at Georgia Tech used a tongue driver—a wireless device that allows those who have high-level spinal cord injuries, and therefore little or no limb movement, to operate computers and their own electric wheelchairs—to reimagine wheelchair navigation for quadriplegic users. Placing wheelchair controls in headsets, say the researchers (Robinson 2012), makes them susceptible to jostling and frequent recalibration. Moving the entire system inside the mouth makes it stable and reliable, and the tongue's receptors are sensitive enough that the user can move a cursor on a screen and direct a wheelchair. Instead of *approximating* a hand movement with joystick directionality, the system exploits a built-in sensitivity goldmine, protected from outside elements. And it can be programmed for many complex commands at once. Sometimes heightened functionality is about reconsidering typical adaptations entirely, inverting the expected sensory mechanism. One could easily picture this system in general use for tasks, like gaming, that typically require hand control.

## 3. *Consider Fine Gradations of Qualitative Change*

I am as much a fan of exoskeletons and bionic limbs as the next person. But designers must also address far subtler changes for bodies over a lifespan. Some of the most interesting ideas pose ways to "edit" environments that already exist, to accommodate more bodies more of the time. Nichola Trudgen's "Wanderest" (2009)[5] is just that kind of edit: a perch for pausing on the otherwise relentlessly forward-looking streetscape. As cities consider their usability for aging populations, this kind of accommodation might be as important as newer, "smarter" nursing home environments. Could small structures like "Wanderest" make streets more navigable and independent living more attainable for a longer period?

So many medical technologies for treatment are just that: medicalized. They operate with the assumption that a change in ability is primarily a biological condition, without thought for the broader ways the built environment can expand and shift to welcome multiple kinds of bodies and experiences.

## 4. *Uncouple Medical Technologies from Their Diagnostic Contexts*

Temple Grandin (2012) is a research scientist in animal husbandry and a well-known self-advocate for people with autism spectrum conditions. She revolutionized the cattle slaughter process, creating far more humane tools and practices for a huge percentage of slaughterhouses across the United States. She grew up a close observer of cattle on ranches and noticed the common use of a "squeeze chute"—a tight chamber that holds a cow still for inoculation. The deep pressure had a calming effect on the animals.

Watching this technology, Grandin intuited her *own* need for an adaptive "hugging machine" that would provide her with a proxy for human touch. For someone whose interpersonal interactions were often confusing, this machine delivered a kind of affection and calming influence that Grandin needed but would not get from a typical human relationship. Artist and MIT professor Wendy Jacob (1998) collaborated with Grandin to modify and replicate the hugging machine in the form of "squeeze chairs"—furniture that gives you a hug.

What happens when a tool used for therapeutic reasons *also* points outward from a diagnostic mode toward something more ambiguous, entering the realm of the poetic? Why should a critical object like the squeeze chair *not* possess more affect or be more responsive? When an object's uses and users become less clearly marked, new stories about that object and its users can suddenly emerge.

### 5. *Design for One*

Michail Vanis (2017), an interaction designer working with a team of fellow students on "the future of work," started to think about his grandmother Despina's retirement from her job as a seamstress—a job she valued for its camaraderie of fellow workers at their sewing machines in a shared physical space. After her retirement, Despina did not need a chair or adaptive machine to sew in her elder years, but she did miss the togetherness of colleagues. So Vanis created "Social Sewing" (2011), a complex of sewing machine avatars that activate when Despina's now far-flung colleagues are also laboring in their post-work contexts. This project is about productive, radical constraints: it narrows the design question to a single user, but it suggests a much wider frame for thinking about the future of work in all its crucial qualitative senses.

### 6. *Let the Tools You Make Ask Questions, Not Just Solve Problems*

The tricky part with popular prosthetic design—bespoke artificial limbs, for example—is an overwhelmingly dominant trend toward making people with atypical bodies "pass" as "normal." Plenty of well-meaning designers set out to redesign an object so that its wearer will not "appear disabled," with the presumption that a preconception of "normal" is always desirable.

Yes, of course, some users want discreet tools. But others roundly reject the notion that all bodies should conform to some standardized or performative ideal. This kind of variability and disagreement should also be a productive friction for designers. Once freed from thinking in terms of creating tools for disability, designers can create personal objects that disrupt our notions of dependence and autonomy.

Jennifer Crupi (2017), an artist and metalsmith, makes a kind of gestural jewelry. Her "Power Gesture" (2013) is an assistive device to rehearse one's self-presentation. It forces its wearer to assume the authoritative position of steepled fingers, held confidently and calmly in front of one's chest, with fingertips on each hand aligned, pressed together, and spread wide apart. Crupi's "Guarded Gesture" (2012), a "necklace" of thick silver wire that ends in two curved resting bowls for the wearer's forearms, externalizes the betrayal of emotions that is so revealing in the crossed-arms stance. These designs express a kind of comedy-with-teeth: Crupi makes a shrewd comment on the sciences of body language and the ways humans say both what they want to express and what they wish to hide.

Questions of utility matter: Does it work efficiently? Is its power maximized? Is it user-friendly? Can it be mass-produced, affordably? But questions outside utilitarian concerns also matter. Whether interrogative design,[6] or critical design (Dunne and Raby 2013), or "design for debate" (Dunne 2008), objects and their stories suggest a para-functionality (Dunne 2005) that renders visible subtler needs and proxies.

Let us hope for objects that raise and suspend questions, and employ them alongside objects designed to solve problems. Then we can have a complex public conversation about needs and desires for interdependence—and about tools that provide assistance to every human body.

## NOTES

Published by Backchannel on October 16, 2014, the first version of this essay appeared at https://backchannel.com/all-technology-is-assistive-ac9f7183c8cd. Thanks to Graham Pullin, Katherine Ott, Mara Mills, and Tim Maly. I am especially grateful for Ott, Serlin, and Mihm's *Artificial Parts, Practical Lives: Modern Histories of Prosthetics*.

1. See DEKA's "Luke Arm," for example.
2. See Action's "Trackchair," for example.
3. See Ekso Bionic's exoskeletons, for example.
4. See more hearing aids in the exhibition covered by Designboom.
5. See Ridden for details about "Wanderest."
6. See the Interrogative Design Group.

## BIBLIOGRAPHY

Action Manufacturing, Inc. "Trackchair." http://www.actiontrackchair.com/.

BreweryLondon. "Svara Hearing Aid." London: Victoria and Albert Museum, 2005.

Crupi, Jennifer. 2017. http://jennifercrupi.com/.

———. "Guarded Gestures." 2012. http://jennifercrupi.com/work-guard2b.html.

———. "Power Gesture." 2013. http://jennifercrupi.com/work-powergesture1a.html.

Davis, Lennard J. *Bending over Backwards: Disability, Dismodernism and Other Difficult Positions,* 1st ed. New York: New York University Press, 2002.

———. *Enforcing Normalcy: Disability, Deafness, and the Body,* 1st ed. New York: Verso, 1995.

DEKA Research and Development Corp. "Luke Arm." http://www.dekaresearch.com/.

Deleuze, Gilles. *Expressionism in Philosophy: Spinoza.* Translated by Martin Joughin. Brooklyn, N.Y.: Zone Books, 1992.

*Designboom.* "Hearwear: The Future of Hearing." http://web.archive.org/web/20061230103540/http://www.designboom.com/contemporary/hearwear.html.

Dunne, Anthony. "Design for Debate." *Architectural Design* 78, no. 6 (November/December 2008): 90–93.

———. *Hertzian Tales: Electronic Products, Aesthetic Experience, and Critical Design.* Cambridge, Mass.: MIT Press, 2005.

Dunne, Anthony, and Fiona Raby. *Speculative Everything: Design, Fiction, and Social Dreaming.* Cambridge, Mass.: MIT Press, 2013.

Ekso Bionics. http://eksobionics.com/.

Grandin, Temple. *Temple Grandin, Ph.D.* 2012. http://www.templegrandin.com/.

"Hearwear: The Future of Hearing." London: Victoria and Albert Museum, 26 July 2005–5 March 2006. http://www.vam.ac.uk/content/articles/p/past-exhibitions-and-displays-2005/.

The Interrogative Design Group. http://www.interrogative.org/about/.

Jacob, Wendy, and Temple Grandin. "The Squeeze Chair." Cambridge, Mass.: Massachusetts Institute of Technology, 1998.

Lovegrove, Ross. "The Beauty of Inner Space." London: Victoria and Albert Museum, 2005.

Ott, Katherine, David Serlin, and Stephen Mihm, eds. *Artificial Parts, Practical Lives: Modern Histories of Prosthetics.* New York: New York University Press, 2002.

Pullin, Graham. *Design Meets Disability.* Cambridge, Mass.: MIT Press, 2009.

Ridden, Paul. "James Dyson Award Finalists Announced." New Atlas, September 15, 2010. http://newatlas.com/dyson-award-finalists-announced/16377/.

Robinson, Abby. "Tongue Drive System Goes inside the Mouth to Improve Performance and User Comfort." *Georgia Tech News Center,* February 20, 2012. www.news.gatech.edu/2012/02/19/tongue-drive-system-goes-inside-mouth-improve-performance-and-user-comfort.

Trudgen, Nichola. "Wanderest." New Zealand, 2009.

Vanis, Michail. 2017. http://mikevanis.com/.

———. 2011. "Social Sewing." http://mikevanis.com/social-sewing.

# PART III

# MAKING AS INQUIRY

# Thinking as Handwork: Critical Making with Humanistic Concerns

GABBY RESCH, DAN SOUTHWICK, ISAAC RECORD, AND MATT RATTO

## *Thinking Is Handwork*

Late one night in the spring of 2015, two members of our lab at the University of Toronto found themselves hunched over a lab bench strewn with skeins of wire insulation and plastic shavings, brainstorming over a seemingly unsophisticated but remarkably complex challenge: How does one go about making a semi-hollow piece of plastic *feel like* a hand-worn chunk of solid ivory?[1] We experimented with a number of shop-room hacks, from buffing the object's striated surface with a mixture of animal fat and carnauba wax until it had the "worn" look and texture of aged ivory, to drilling a hole in its base and filling it with fine sand to simulate how solid ivory *weighes* in one's hand (see Figure 16.1). This exercise was part of an experiment in creating 3-D–printed replicas of ivory busts from a collection at the Art Gallery of Ontario. The busts the replicas reproduce are themselves replicas, originally made with a Victorian-era pantograph (a nineteenth-century precursor to computer numerical control [CNC] and 3-D-printing technologies) invented by Benjamin Cheverton, a notable artist, craftsperson, and engineer, for the Great Exhibition of 1851. Each replica was copied mechanically from much larger marble busts, many hand-carved by Sir Francis Chantrey, the leading portrait sculptor in Regency-era Britain.

Even if, echoing Walter Benjamin (1936), works of art have *always been reproducible,* this particular reproduction process stirred provocations to which critical digital humanists might attend. We might consider how the overwhelmingly upper-class male social network that inspired Chantrey (and, consequently, Cheverton) does not attract significant attention in an art museum filled with works of similar inspiration. Or we could interrogate the vectors along which the Victorian ivory trade, a key facet of British imperialism, produced a medium that continues to haunt museums. With a primary motivation to weigh various techniques that might make

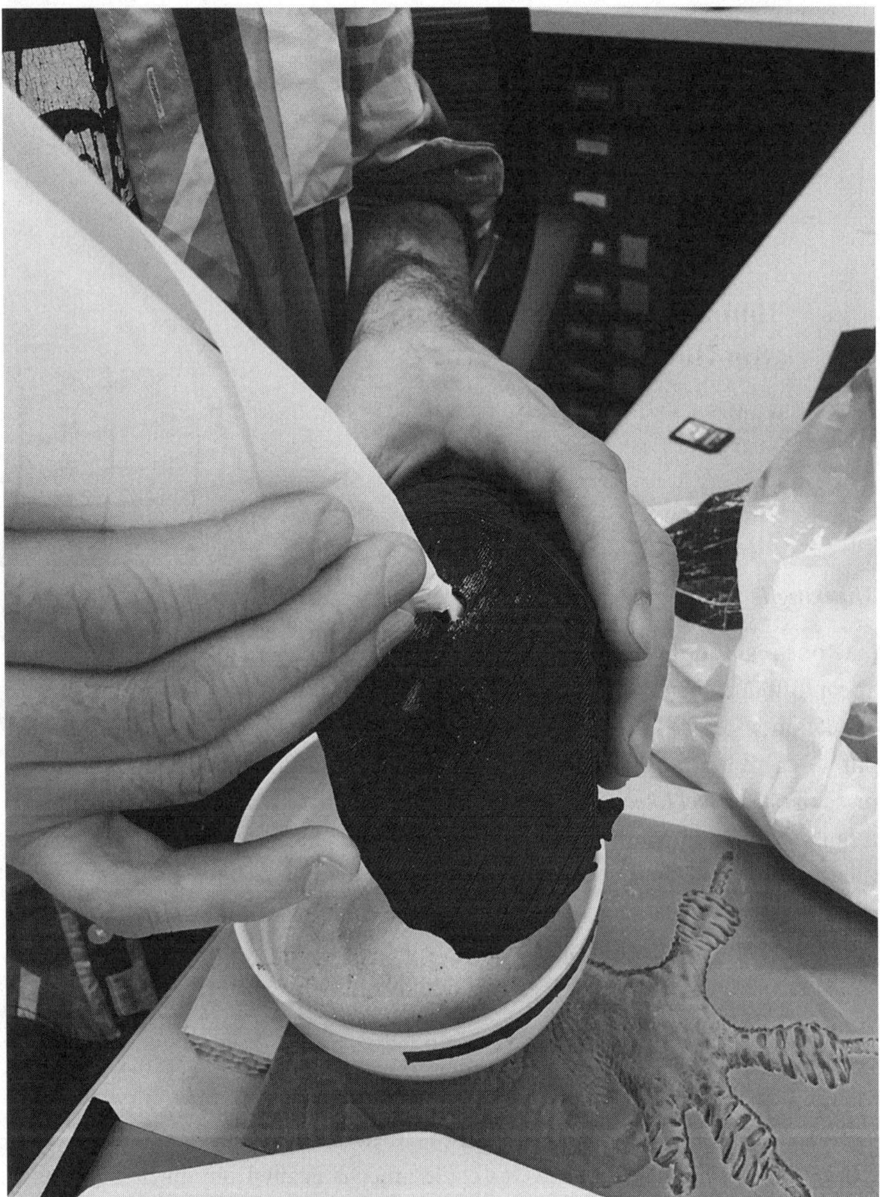

**Figure 16.1.** Gabby Resch experimenting with sand. Photograph by Dan Southwick.

our object feel more or less "real," we had to sift through and across a mangle of practice (Pickering 1993) that requires a diverse array of digital pre-production techniques, exercising our own knowledge of processes—both material and digital—that constitute 3-D printing as a medium and negotiating critical issues of authenticity, curatorial and institutional authority, and the relationship between the materiality of museum artifacts and their digital-material surrogates. These concerns undergird our ongoing experiments in replication.

In this chapter, we describe some ways to think productively about materiality by demonstrating how material interventions trouble theoretical work (and vice versa). We elaborate on opportunities for digital humanists as well as science and technology studies (STS) scholars who are involved (or implicated) in discussions about methods for critical making (Ratto 2011), especially in work that engages with cultural institutions such as galleries, libraries, archives, and museums. We describe recent experiences our lab—composed of members with backgrounds from philosophy of science and Chinese history to electrical engineering and systems administration—had building and deploying objects as well as experiences, most of which used 3-D printing as a medium, in a handful of world-class museums. These projects cut across humanities and STS themes and generally necessitate interdisciplinary tactics. Taken together, they broaden an ecology of iterative software and hardware work, interaction techniques, and scholarly practices that we regularly invoke, adapt, and reimagine. A host of fundamental issues inform this work, including how scientific and cultural knowledge are regularly co-produced in cultural institutions; how infrastructures that cross disciplinary boundaries can share objects, methods, and features along digital and material axes; and how new technologies that afford greater interaction across digital and material spaces change the ways cultural institutions engage their publics. These issues remain open and messy, but we hope our examples will contribute to a necessary dialogue in which many of us are already embedded.

### *Atoms, Bits, Media, Matter*

When we articulate our work somewhere along a material-digital continuum, or through approaches and techniques that blur the material-digital distinction, we fall into a seductive trap. Troubling the dichotomy between material and digital comes naturally in the academy, where we can ruminate endlessly about whether inscribed bits on a hard drive are continuous or discrete, or whether digitality is implemented over a continuous analog substrate (Smith 2003). A significant proportion of our lab's research considers the materiality of digital infrastructures, and we generally operate from a position with which many digital humanists likely agree: that the digital is always material. Computation may be considered "a modeling activity" where correspondences between distinct domains (e.g., digital and material) must be established (Isbell et al. 198). But computation is a phenomenon where real-world effects are not just mirrored in digital space; they are entangled with digital representations. As a computational activity guided by a correspondence theory of representation—where the "closer it is to the real thing, the better" (Lynch 217)[2]—3-D modeling is a site where this entanglement is especially pronounced.

These dialogues are productive and enriching for scholars, but our attempts to unsettle the marked distinction between digital and material culture meet resistance from cultural heritage professionals who have to reconcile this distinction in their work. For many of these professionals, "the digital" is necessary but also threatening. Digital culture can challenge their institutional mandates (e.g., "Why should the public go to a museum when they can see the same content on an iPad at home?" is a familiar refrain, however shortsighted it might be). Rather than thinking of material and digital as distinct entities that meet, overlap, and occasionally blur into each other, we encounter them as entangled phenomena, situated in a gradient along which agential possibilities are distributed among human and non-human entities and cut by a wide and ever-changing array of social, technical, and institutional concerns (Barad 2003). Compounding this digital-material entanglement, we also think of 3-D reproduction as a unique medium that actively figures and influences the processes through which digital objects are reshaped into analog or material ones.

These factors influence how we make critically, especially in humanities contexts. We engage, often unequally, with ideas from STS, critical theory, digital humanities (DH), design, feminist technoscience, human-computer interaction (HCI), maker cultures, and a number of cognate disciplines and movements. As our projects indicate, critical making invokes a reflexive methodological position that interrogates the politics of sociotechnical objects and systems as well as the institutions that we engage and care about—particularly as those institutions are forced to navigate a rupture in how the public perceives their relevance at a time of increasing austerity. In the sense that we draw selectively upon specific methods, requiring hands-on engagement as an additional resource, theory both guides and emerges from the critical making projects our lab undertakes.

This making does not have to be "digital" or even participatory making (as exemplified by the so-called "maker movement"), but it should attempt to reconcile a schism between those who purportedly create digital (and digital-derived) content in institutional contexts and those purportedly tasked with representing and interpreting it (as if these tasks are discrete). For us, "doing theory" with critical making[3] entails moving beyond shallow critical reflection, or mere acknowledgment of the relational ontologies brought to bear on the institutional contexts of our work. However, theory cannot be taken for granted. Many reports seem to give passing reference to theoretical perspectives, rather than demonstrating deep engagement with them. This tendency is especially problematic in projects that illuminate unequal power distributions and then claim to somehow grant greater agential capacity to actors who were previously rendered invisible, mute, or obsolete (as if agency is something we, as makers or scholars, can grant[4]). To avoid this tendency, our projects use theoretical concepts in occasionally utilitarian, but generally non-deterministic, ways to think through the agential possibilities, temporal conditions, and materiality of institutions.

While we do not intend for our critical making methods to be grounded in instrumental logic, we constantly negotiate between instrumental and aesthetic concerns when working with cultural institutions. Considerations abound, including how we can *use* 3-D printing to make museum objects "more interactive."

Traditional value propositions and epistemic commitments we might encounter in scientific and artistic communities—utility and empirical rigidity, on the one hand; expression and empirical flexibility, on the other—are troubled by considerations toward assessment. We are also not strictly beholden to questions of aesthetics, the pragmatics of developing institutional relationships, or arguments about the relative value of processual acts versus evocative objects (although we lean toward the former). Among the most interesting discoveries we have encountered in our engagements with cultural institutions is a heightened sensitivity to how preparing an object for display can be a more important locus of epistemic activity than the exhibited object itself.

We are not going to pretend to have a definition of DH that works for everyone, nor are we as intimately familiar with DH concerns as many readers of this book might be. If we understand critical computational inquiry in the humanities as both the interrogation of digital tools used by humanities scholars and the use of digital tools to interrogate theoretical claims about how cultural reproduction occurs, then we might assume that creating and understanding digital archives of cultural "data" should be a core concern of the H/DH archipelago (given that some of the most mature and robust computational tools reside in this space). What are the intersections of "humanistic concerns and digital capabilities" (Drucker, *SpecLab* 64) where critical making might present valuable insight? Should there be an agreed-upon description of "humanistic concerns" that we can take as a starting point? What might some "acceptable" maker activities for humanities scholars be if such activities use immature technologies that have not received official institutional sanction? Is humanities scholarship better served by taking *the act of* prototyping as a form of pedagogy, or by insisting on the release of full-fledged investigative tools into the wild, where so many of them meet a lonely death? Generally speaking, we have not reconciled our work with claims that tools, if they are to be taken as theories, should be accessible, transparent, and available to peer review, although we tend to agree with such claims (Ramsay and Rockwell 2012). For the most part, we are also sensitive to a critique that using computers to manipulate or interpret humanities data does not always constitute theorizing.

With these points in mind, we propose that 3-D rematerialization (including additive manufacturing such as 3-D printing as well as subtractive manufacturing such as routing and laser cutting) is a kind of visualization technique appropriate for certain humanities concerns. We undertook a handful of recent projects guided by this consideration. One project involved a collaboration between members of our lab and an international team of researchers and artists at the Art Gallery of Burlington. We captured embodied gestural data performed during craft practice and artistically reproduced it through a series of 3-D prints. Another project involved members of our lab collaborating with the Royal Ontario Museum to produce 3-D–printed tactile representations of 2-D digital images that have been included in an annual photography exhibit and are now in the museum's teaching collection. This project, which began by algorithmically displacing and manipulating color values in digital images but ultimately required a significant amount of hand "sculpting" that traversed the material-digital gap, introduced a new mode of sensory engagement for non-sighted (as well as sighted) visitors to the museum. Despite the success of these collaborations, we are not particularly "eager to suspend critical judgment in a rush to visualization" (Drucker, "Humanities Approaches to Graphical Display" 1), likely because prototypes and half-finished iterations generally satisfy the requirements of our work. Beyond the issues listed earlier, a host of possibilities, affordances, and opportunities inherent in 3-D work require greater attention: how, for instance, 3-D–driven investigations inform recent dialogue around "making" in humanities scholarship; what 3-D–based curricula across a full chain of activities—from capture (digitization) to cleanup and design (digital artisanship) to printing (rematerialization) to finishing (material artisanship)—might look like for museum and DH professionals; and how scholars should engage the public in participatory and collaborative 3-D making experiences that promote sustained engagement with cultural materials.

## *The 3-D Museum Medium*

The fact that many museums are already well versed in 3-D scanning and printing technologies (for conservation purposes, at least), and that museums are *already* 3-D in the first place, should temper the hype about 3-D printing as an "ideal" technology for museum-based humanistic inquiry. But there is an interesting—albeit troubling—trend under way in which 3-D printing is positioned as a technology that museums might (and, in some cases, should) embrace to develop new modes of interaction between humans and artifacts (Sportun 2014). While 3-D printing has inhabited a role as one of the preeminent maker technologies, its integration in cultural spaces necessitates a host of critical considerations, including questions about the materiality of the medium (e.g., what happens to all this plastic ephemera, particularly when printing happens on-site, as it off-gases or disperses in the presence of priceless artifacts?), the expertise of operators (e.g., is 3-D printing a black box-able technology, as numerous manufacturers hope, or does it require the kind of tacit knowledge, experience, and care that comes from opening its hardware?), and who it ultimately serves (e.g., are STEM-funding agencies herding museums into initiatives that promote training members of the public to meet the world's crises, and, if so, who in the museum benefits from these neoliberal narratives?). While there is a growing body of creative and playful examples of museum-based 3-D, we can offer scant evidence of the medium's use in critical provocations that challenge the institution itself.

Both the museum world and the public are witnessing a paradigm shift in how museums are perceived (Anderson 2004)—from collections-centered, traditional institutions to visitor-centered, reimagined public institutions. The two paradigms are not mutually exclusive, and some recent evidence suggests that museums might cautiously warm to participatory culture without disregarding their past mandates (Söderqvist 2010). This idea is contested, with evidence of backlash toward the participatory museum. Concomitant with this paradigm shift are challenges to not only curatorial and institutional authority but also the power of objects to tell stories and the very definition of an exhibit. As critical STS scholars with humanistic leanings, we are naturally drawn to projects that illuminate the politics of institutional authority. So how do we reconcile our critical work with the politics of our institutions? Consider the following example.

In 2013, members of our lab collaborated with a team of partners to create and implement a 3-D design and printing experience at the Royal Ontario Museum (ROM). Visitors to the museum were invited to use iPads to create unique pieces of an imaginary Mesopotamian city that were 3-D–printed *in situ* and installed in a dynamic, collective, participatory exhibit. A number of unanticipated situations emerged throughout the run of the exhibit, which was staged on Friday nights as part of a public engagement that turns the museum into a kind of nightclub for thousands of (mostly young) adults. A significant number of participants experimented with deliberately anachronistic designs, many resembling modern skyscrapers. Others collapsed columns into ziggurats or turned temples upside down. One visitor referred to a sleek, modernist obelisk they created as a "Mesopotamian Freedom Tower." This particular example would probably horrify curators or museum interpreters, who are not only accountable to visitor experiences but also responsible for representations of history and culture. We, however, were presented with an opportunity to think critically about how museums use new technologies to structure temporality and present authoritative institutional narratives and, furthermore, to consider whether these narratives are commensurable with claims that technologies like 3-D printing afford the ability to re-create, or even reimagine, the past.

In another example, described in the opening paragraph of this chapter, we prepared touchable models for an exhibit at the Art Gallery of Ontario (AGO). This exhibit, which highlights busts of notable figures such as James Watt (a contemporary of Cheverton), might initially be read through a kind of *Leviathan and the Air-Pump* (1985) network analysis, where scholars look for evidence of epistemic cultures in the material record of the collection. Historiographical work that intersects with critiques of contemporary curatorial regimes is also interesting in this instance. What and whose histories are collected and represented, and how are they troubled when scholars and the public reimagine their mode of interaction with exhibits? The experience of preparing pieces for an exhibit that speaks to historical power dynamics and modes of production, as well as contemporary metaquestions about the role of technology in museum interactions, was illuminating for us. It informed ongoing theoretical discussions members of our lab have about histories of ocularcentric interaction and the politics of touch in memory institutions. Additionally, it forced us, as STS scholars with critical humanistic tendencies, to look inward, at our own practices, relationships, and epistemic commitments. In addition to its use in participatory culture, 3-D printing is increasingly proposed as a technology that affords new modes of interaction that then increase inclusivity or accessibility. For instance, the AGO exhibit included a projected video of our 3-D making process, positioned adjacent to a touchable bust. The video performed a mediating role that called attention to the gallery's willingness to use new technologies for the purposes of accessibility and perceived relevance. A similar video was displayed alongside the tactile models we prepared for the ROM. Museums are beginning to foreground these aspects of 3-D printing in their marketing, suggesting that 3-D printing technology somehow connects them with the past and the future at the same time, while also extending their collections to a wider audience. These uncomplicated narratives can seem scripted or determined by the manufacturers of maker technologies, and we are not entirely comfortable being associated with them.

Returning to the problem of conceptualizing a material-digital entanglement that is attentive to institutional politics, we recognize a growing tendency toward characterizing 3-D–printed objects as digital instructions implemented in a material substrate. This tendency overlooks and often erases the considerable amount of handwork that goes into the digital composition and preparation of printed artifacts. Such handwork includes the embodied act of capturing an object and digitizing it, the somewhat skeuomorphic enactment of a digital drafting station that requires a pressure-sensitive stylus and tablet to digitally sculpt and prepare scanned data, and post-processing work that entails cleaning up random bits of digital noise that get materialized (something the AGO also highlighted in their video display, as their videographer focused on one of our hands trimming residual bits of plastic). But this labor is not just handwork. It requires a more sophisticated temporal understanding of what it means to do material work. The *matter* of 3-D printing resists stability—it desires to disperse, settle, and blend, generating latent chemical effects that humans must be wary of, particularly conservationists who have to weigh how 3-D–printed objects might off-gas, or how the process, if done *in situ*, might emit ultrafine particles into a museum space.[5] Offering assurances that the wild west of 3-D printing is supported by a few decades of anecdotal evidence is insufficient. We must account for why 3-D printing would be an institutional issue in the first place.

## *Making Things Matter Together*

We take Alan Liu's (2012) suggestion that DH can learn from how STS approaches culture, technology, and society. Liu proposes that engaging with STS "would help the digital humanities develop an understanding of instrumentalism—including that of its own methods—as a culture embedded in wider culture" (502). Further, we argue that critical making with humanistic concerns could serve as a bulwark against a tendency by scholars, humanists among them, to replace technological determinism with social determinism (Latour 84). Liu writes, "Only by creating a methodological infrastructure in which culturally aware technology complements technologically aware cultural criticism can the digital humanities more effectively serve humanists by augmenting their ability to engage today's global-scale cultural issues" (502). DH and STS can do work together that might enable us to productively intervene in society. We could devise joint tactics to face the "problem" of digitization. We could expose flawed, deterministic tendencies that pervade our disciplines. We could highlight the troubling conflation of digital literacy with critical sociotechnical and information literacy, when these mean quite different things but are often used interchangeably.

A plethora of worthwhile scholarship exists under the aegis of DH, STS, and even HCI that uses "making" as a productive and reflexive process. Together, we might extend the reflexive modes of engagement that are boundary-agnostic. Surely, some of the "little hacks" we deploy in STS-grounded work can be ported to humanistic contexts. A far more interdisciplinary framing than DH-meets-STS is required, however, if we are going to construct the methodological apparatus that Liu proposes. (This framing would include recognizing projects in adjacent fields like HCI that have pursued similar goals.)[6] For our lab, such framing draws from contemporary museology, interaction design, media theory, and STS's increasingly distant parent, philosophy of science, which, as Willard McCarty notes, hovers in the background of DH (17).

Following Karen Barad, we recognize an "entanglement of matter and meaning" that questions erroneous separations of nature from culture as well as matters of fact from matters of concern (Latour 2005) and care (Puig de la Bellacasa 2011).[7] This entanglement is especially important if matters of fact—nature, raw data, positivist empirical study, and scientific realism, for instance—can no longer be restricted to the natural sciences, and matters of concern culture, social constructivism, and values, for example—have moved beyond the humanities and social sciences. Like Barad, we seek to recognize how the humanities and sciences are already entangled, and to trace diffraction patterns that record the histories of interaction, interference, reinforcement, and difference between them. This approach requires taking into account how each "culture" recognizes another significant entanglement—between *matter* and *relevance*. Do the concerns that matter to us, as humanists and humanities allies, conflict with agendas that define how our work is deemed relevant? We must ask to whom we want to be accountable, as well as how the epistemic products of our work produce a kind of relevance that can be tough to measure. In the interest of staging a "productive intervention in society," we must also ask: What kind of advocacy work do we want to do? Maybe we need to develop pervasive technologies and experiences that, as Liu suggests, "fundamentally reimagine humanities advocacy" (497) and enhance the ability of humanistic scholarship to both communicate and resonate with the general public. In that case, sites such as museums, where the public effectively meets the humanities face-to-face, would be productive sites of intervention.

We must also unbox the epistemic objects (Knorr Cetina 2008) that humanistic and STS-informed making might share, or the boundary objects (Star and Griesemer 1989) that might enable translation across epistemic disjunctures. Critical making, as we propose it, is more a mode of critically reflexive (even transformative) inquiry than a record of scholarly activity. While tracing scholarly knowledge production might be a core concern of both STS and DH, our work is not directly related to it. Writing object biographies of digital making experiences may be a "way of knowing," and situating researchers in these unwieldy biographies may be a political act (Morgan 2012), but we also need to look for theories in prototypes and, following Galey and Ruecker (2010), recognize that our projects may be interpreted as rhetorical devices to "be used in persuasive performances" (Ramsay and Rockwell 78).

Critical making examines objects that are never fixed. Direct material engagement is a "condition for knowing," and this knowing is not only "knowing from a distance" (Dolphijn and van der Tuin 52). It is a combination of distant and close reading, attending to the particulars of institutional artifacts and the networks through which they travel. It provokes thoughtful studies of murky suspensions, where bits of material and digital worlds collide. Moreover, it encourages an examination of the different value propositions associated with reflexive material and semiotic engagement. The projects we have highlighted force us to revisit many of the Benjaminian notions we might entertain about digital reproduction and simulation, while also offering new insights into concerns, such as the increasingly algorithmic nature of DH work, that should interest humanities scholars. Is, for instance, the handwork of 3-D always an alternative to the algorithmic when much of it is done procedurally through computer-aided design?

If STS and DH scholars are going to successfully collaborate using modes of engagement similar to the ones we have described, then we must first examine our own goals. Are we looking to address critical questions or demonstrate them? Are we illustrating how things come to matter, or are we exploring how they come to matter through process? Understanding a critical issue does not automatically count as an intervention, just as a critical intervention does not automatically ensure understanding. We hope that, by mandating direct material engagement as a condition for knowing, a critical making approach to humanistic concerns can do away with some of these unnecessary conflations. The projects mentioned here offer new avenues into the politics of representation, exhibition, memory, and institutional knowledge. At the same time, they serve as platforms for critically interrogating the sociotechnical systems that are increasingly foisted on institutions struggling to demonstrate their relevance.

We need to be mindful of the multiple meanings of *audience* in these endeavors, though. If the benefits to be derived are often for the makers and, potentially, their scholarly audience, then does critical making count as scholarship, pedagogy, advocacy, or all of the above? It is often hard to tell. We can be sure, however, that this is a perfect moment to find oneself hunched over a messy lab bench at two in the morning, mesmerized by the cacophony of Cartesian robots dancing back and forth, and trying to meet some institution's deadline while pondering the entanglements of meaning and matter, subject and object, material and digital, and—of course—handwork and headwork.

## NOTES

1. This heading and the title of this chapter are inspired by two things: a passage on the "thingly character" inherent in Heidegger's assertion that "denken ist/als handwerk" (Simon 188–89) and an Instagram post by Natalie Jeremijenko: https://instagram.com/p/4xDWUcTG7h.

2. And, if so, then how do we reconcile representational theories and 3-D modeling with Johanna Drucker's assertion that "rendering observation (the act of creating a statistical, empirical, or subjective account or image) as if it were the same as the phenomena observed collapses the critical distance between the phenomenal world and its interpretation, undoing the basis of interpretation on which humanistic knowledge production is based. We know this. But we seem ready and eager to suspend critical judgment in a rush to visualization"? ("Humanities Approaches to Graphical Display" 1).

3. See Matthew Kirschenbaum's tweet from January 4, 2013 on making as doing theory: https://twitter.com/mkirschenbaum/status/287280574815666177.

4. See Barad on reworking the notion of agency in ways that are appropriate to relational ontologies, recognizing agency as a matter of possibilities for reconfiguring entanglements: "The notion that there are agents who have agency, or who grant agency, say, to non-humans (the granting of agency is an ironic notion, no?), pulls us back into the same old humanist orbits over and over again. And it is not easy to resist the gravitational force of humanism, especially when it comes to the question of 'agency.' But agency for me is not something that someone or something has to varying degrees" (in Dolphijn and van der Tuin 54).

5. We might consider this phenomenon with regard to Jane Bennett's articulation of a vibrant materiality: "as much force as entity, as much energy as matter, as much intensity as extension" (20).

6. See, for example, Sengers, et al.

7. See Barad in Dolphijn and van der Tuin (50).

## BIBLIOGRAPHY

Anderson, Gail, ed. *Reinventing the Museum: Historical and Contemporary Perspectives on the Paradigm Shift.* Lanham, Md.: Rowman AltaMira, 2004.

Barad, Karen. "Posthumanist Performativity: Toward an Understanding of How Matter Comes to Matter." *Signs* 28, no. 3 (2003): 801–31.

Benjamin Walter. "The Work of Art in the Age of Mechanical Reproduction" (1936). In *Illuminations*, ed. Hannah Arendt, 217-52. New York: Schocken Books, 1969.

Bennett, Jane. *Vibrant Matter: A Political Ecology of Things*. Durham, N.C.: Duke University Press, 2009.

Dolphijn, Rick, and Iris van der Tuin. "'Matter Feels, Converses, Suffers, Desires, Yearns and Remembers': An Interview with Karen Barad." In *New Materialism: Interviews and Cartographies,* ed. Rick Dolphijn and Iris van der Tuin, 48–70. Open Humanities Press, 2012.

Drucker, Johanna. "'Eye-Mind-Design-Production': An Interview with Johanna Drucker." *MATLIT* 1, no. 1 (2013): 169–77.

———. "Humanities Approaches to Graphical Display." *Digital Humanities Quarterly* 5, no. 1 (2011): 1–21.

———. *SpecLab: Digital Aesthetics and Projects in Speculative Computing*. Chicago, Ill.: University of Chicago Press, 2009.

Galey, Alan, and Stan Ruecker. "How a Prototype Argues." *Literary and Linguistic Computing* 25, no. 4 (2010): 405–24.

Isbell, Charles L., Lynn Andrea Stein, Robb Cutler, Jeffrey Forbes, Linda Fraser, John Impagliazzo, Viera Proulx, Steve Russ, Richard Thomas, and Yan Xu. "(Re)defining Computing Curricula by (Re)defining Computing." *ACM SIGCSE Bulletin* 41, no. 4 (2010): 195–207.

Jeremijenko, Natalie. Instagram. July 5, 2015. https://www.instagram.com/p/4xDWUcTG7h/.

Kirschenbaum, Matthew. Twitter. January 4, 2013. https://twitter.com/mkirschenbaum/status/287280574815666177.

Knorr Cetina, Karin. "Objectual Practice." In *Knowledge as Social Order: Rethinking the Sociology of Barry Barnes,* ed. Massimo Mazzotti, 83–97. Farnham, U. K.: Ashgate Publishing, 2008.

Latour, Bruno. *Reassembling the Social: An Introduction to Actor-Network-Theory* (Clarendon Lectures in Management Studies). Oxford: Oxford University Press, 2005.

Liu, Alan. "Where Is Cultural Criticism in the Digital Humanities?" In *Debates in the Digital Humanities,* ed. Matthew K. Gold, 490–509. Minneapolis: University of Minnesota Press, 2012.

Lynch, Michael. "Science in the Age of Mechanical Reproduction: Moral and Epistemic Relations between Diagrams and Photographs." *Biology and Philosophy* 6, no. 2 (1991): 205–26.

McCarty, Willard. *Humanities Computing*. London: Palgrave Macmillan, 2005.

Morgan, Colleen Leah. "Emancipatory Digital Archaeology." PhD dissertation, University of California, 2012.

Pickering, Andrew. "The Mangle of Practice: Agency and Emergence in the Sociology of Science." *American Journal of Sociology* 99, no. 3 (1993): 559–89.

Puig de la Bellacasa, Maria. "Matters of Care in Technoscience: Assembling Neglected Things." *Social Studies of Science* 41, no. 1 (2011): 85–106.

Ramsay, Stephen, and Geoffrey Rockwell. "Developing Things: Notes toward an Epistemology of Building in the Digital Humanities." In *Debates in the Digital Humanities,* ed. Matthew K. Gold, 75–84. Minneapolis: University of Minnesota Press, 2012.

Ratto, Matt. "Critical Making: Conceptual and Material Studies in Technology and Social Life." *The Information Society* 27, no. 4 (2011): 252–60.

Sengers, Phoebe, Joseph Kaye, Kirsten Boehner, Jeremiah Fairbank, Geri Gay, Yevgeniy Medynskiy, and Susan Wyche. "Culturally Embedded Computing." *Pervasive Computing*, IEEE 3, no. 1 (2004): 14–21.

Shapin, Steven, and Simon Schaffer. *Leviathan and the Air-Pump: Hobbes, Boyle, and the Experimental Life*. Princeton: Princeton University Press, 1985.

Simon, Jules. *Art and Responsibility: A Phenomenology of the Diverging Paths of Rosenzweig and Heidegger*. London: Bloomsbury, 2011.

Smith, Brian Cantwell. "The Devil in the Digital Details: Digital Abstraction and Concrete Reality." Unpublished draft, last modified 2003.

Söderqvist, Thomas. "The Participatory Museum and Distributed Curatorial Expertise." *NTM Zeitschrift für Geschichte der Wissenschaften, Technik und Medizin* 18, no. 1 (2010): 69–78.

Sportun, Samantha. "The Future Landscape of 3D in Museums." In *The Multisensory Museum: Cross-Disciplinary Perspectives on Touch, Sound, Smell, Memory, and Space*, ed. Nina Levent and Alvaro Pascual-Leone, 331–41. Lanham, Md.: Rowman and Littlefield, 2014.

Star, Susan Leigh, and James R. Griesemer. "Institutional Ecology, 'Translations' and Boundary Objects: Amateurs and Professionals in Berkeley's Museum of Vertebrate Zoology, 1907–39." *Social Studies of Science* 19, no. 3 (1989): 387–420.

# Bibliocircuitry and the Design of the Alien Everyday, 2012–13

KARI KRAUS

Bibliocircuitry and the Design of the Alien Everyday is a series of student projects that grew out of several book design labs conducted as part of a Fall 2012 course (ENGL 758B Book 2.0: The History of the Book and the Future of Reading) taught by Kari Kraus at the University of Maryland. Using physical books as springboards for computation and mixed media experiments, the student projects realize one of the larger aims of the course: to position bibliotextual scholarship and pedagogy as design-oriented practices that can be used to prototype and imagine the future of the book. The project resulted in a publication by the same name.

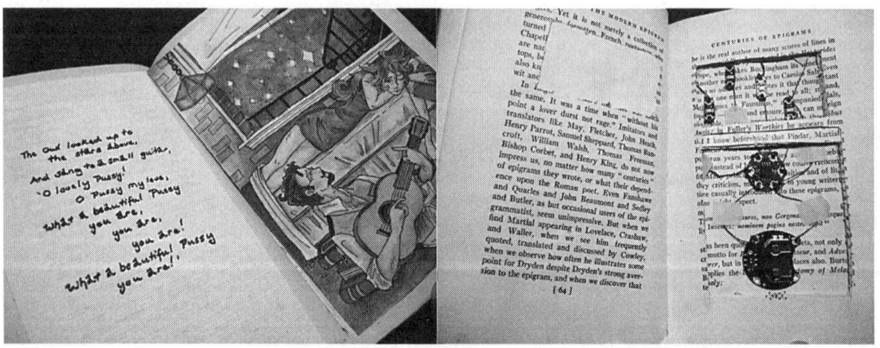


**Figure 17.1.** Illustration of Edward Lear's Owl singing to the Pussycat. An Arduino board embedded in subsequent pages controls light-emitting diodes (LEDs) that make the stars visible outside the Pussycat's window twinkle. Format: Physical computing and mixed media. Materials: Microcontrollers, electronics, mixed media, and physical books. Charity Hancock Balch, Clifford Hichar Moberg, Carlea Holl-Jensen, Kari Kraus, Cameron Mozafari, and Kathryn Skutlin Shutt. Illustration and photograph by Clifford Hichar Moberg.

# Doing History by Reverse Engineering Electronic Devices

YANA BOEVA, DEVON ELLIOTT, EDWARD JONES-IMHOTEP,
SHEZAN MUHAMMEDI, AND WILLIAM J. TURKEL

In this chapter we describe three experiences of collaboratively reverse engineering historical electronic artifacts at the University of Western Ontario's Lab for Humanistic Fabrication, a setting that supports hands-on fabrication and experimentation, programming and computer-aided design, and traditional historical research. Our first case study comes from Elliott's work on the re-creation of wireless effects designed by early-twentieth-century magicians to simulate mind reading. These effects depended on electromagnetic induction, a technique that has recently come to prominence for its applications in radio-frequency ID tagging, wireless charging, and near-field and secure wireless communications, largely driven by interest in the Internet of Things. The second case explores Muhammedi's software re-creation of an analog electronic musical instrument built by the Canadian engineering pioneer Hugh Le Caine. We used a visual programming language to create a low-cost, widely accessible, and suggestive model of Le Caine's device, one that simultaneously helps us to interrogate the digital-analog divide. A final case study focuses on the analog electronic computer—part of a long-dismissed tradition of analog computing that was overshadowed by digital developments. Here, Jones-Imhotep and Turkel make small analog computers to further explore the relation between the digital and the analog and to gain insights about the crucial role of analogs in the history of scientific instrumentation. In all of these cases, we are interested in exploring how collaborative acts of making and experimentation can deepen scholarly and public understanding of history.

We refer to our approach as "humanistic fabrication" and believe that it provides a performative and ontological complement to the epistemological or representational work that comprises most day-to-day practice in historical disciplines. Rather than attempting to reproduce (knowledge of) any particular technological past, our goal is to stage situations that allow us to experience a specific process, moment, or flow.[1] Humanistic fabrication is thus a kind of "ontological theatre," to use the terminology of Andrew Pickering (2010).[2] Our concern is to engage with the world rather than to create representations of it. Sometimes we do learn things that we can put into words, but this "entail[s] a *detour,* away from performance and through the space of representation, which has the effect of *veiling* the world of performance from us" (Pickering 20, emphasis in original). So rather than writing about humanistic fabrication, we typically share this research practice with colleagues, students, and the general public by offering dozens of collaborative, hands-on workshops each year: in classrooms and hackerspaces; at libraries, museums, and conferences; and during intensive venues such as the Digital Humanities Summer Institute (DHSI). We also document our performances in online forums, on our own websites, and in GitHub, so that others may be encouraged to stage comparable performances of their own. Take this chapter as an offering in a similar spirit (Turkel and Elliott 2014).[3]

In addition to terms like "re-making" or "re-creating," we use the expression "reverse engineering" to focus on the exploratory, experiential, and performative aspect of our work. What is important to us is immersing ourselves in a setting where we are collaboratively and actively engaged with design, intention, material constraint, and the "adjacent possible"[4]—with process rather than product. Within the history of technology, scholars have long privileged large-scale industrial technologies as sites to understand social transformation (Hughes 1983). But electrical or transportation infrastructures lend themselves poorly to experimental, hands-on exploration. By shifting the scale to smaller, often more intimate objects such as household technologies and personal computing devices, re-making or reverse engineering can provide unusual insights about the micro-level contours that shape our broader historical understandings. And in the absence of historical evidence about the design, use, and impact of material devices, those practices can help us to reenact and reimagine portions of the historical worlds they occupied and the meanings they held (Turkel 2011).

### *Case 1: Mind Reading with Magnetic Induction*

In a 1909 book debunking spiritualistic phenomena, an amateur magician named David Abbott (1977) wrote of experiments using induction to transmit voices. Abbott's brother-in-law, an engineer at Western Electric, had recently seen a wireless telephony device demonstrated at White City.[5] Abbott adapted this device to the purpose of illusion, concealing a coil and telephone receiver in the body of a papier-mâché kettle. During the performance of one of Abbott's magical acts, voices were transmitted via a hidden Dictaphone to an accomplice in another room. The accomplice, in turn, could speak into a telephone transmitter that was attached to a large coil hidden under the performance room. Through induction, the coil transmitted the accomplice's voice into the body of the kettle. Held anywhere in the performance space, the kettle appeared to speak to Abbott and his audience. He soon modified the method to suit stage magic. Instead of direct contact, a coil on one's person was all that was needed to get voices out of a receiver. Moving about freely, the performer could surreptitiously receive information at any time, while the audience remained entirely unaware. The induction method soon spread beyond Abbott's own performances. By the 1930s, he had produced talking tea kettles for magicians around the world. They were joined by talking vases, lamps, Buddha statues, and mind reading sets available by mail order from suppliers such as Thayer Magic in California.

Magicians put induction to work for a variety of purposes, yet they abandoned the technique fairly quickly, despite much practice and refinement in the early twentieth century. With the current renewal of interest in near-field effects and communications, we were motivated to revisit these experiences and techniques, particularly to explore questions regarding their aural history. The attempt to recapture the historical experience of sound has received considerable scholarly attention in the last two decades (Corbin 1998; Johnson 1996; Thompson 2004). But these valuable studies have privileged scholarly imagination over the historically minded re-creation of objects and effects. What might these induction devices and effects have sounded like? If a kettle or vase was supposedly a spirit voice, then how could a spirit plausibly sound? For the performers who were literally wrapping themselves in the technology, what was it like to receive information? And, with contested claims over the effectiveness of magnetic induction, can we determine which methods might have worked best and under what circumstances?

In the case of stage magic, the original device or exact replicas are often not available. They have been lost or destroyed, are held in private collections, or are otherwise beyond our resources to acquire or study. Nevertheless, it is possible to experiment with these technologies in a way that is sensitive to existing sources. Elliott's prior work on the technology and culture of stage magic has shown that there is a great deal to be learned by attempting to re-create these devices in some form (Elliott, MacDougall, and Turkel 2012). One major insight involves intentional lacunae in historical records. Some explanations for magical illusions are incomplete or incorrect—descriptions and drawings might be missing crucial elements, components might not function as depicted, and generalizations were used to omit details while still revealing most elements of a secret. Stage magicians balanced the need to keep their own methods secret with a desire to gain reputation or notoriety amongst their peers, and they delighted in revealing the secrets of competitors and publicly debunking mediums. When a magical apparatus is built according to the directions given in historical sources, it often does not work exactly as claimed, but one does not learn that until actually trying to rebuild the apparatus.[6]

Even when the historical sources were not intentionally designed to mislead, they assume a fair degree of tacit knowledge, and experimentation with small models has been useful for bringing some of this experience into sharp relief. For example, the original descriptions of how to accomplish levitation effects often do not include information about sets, accompanying props, backdrops, lighting, and other details that were essential for proper performance. Attempting to restage small-scale forms of the performance quickly brings those issues to the forefront, as elements that are supposed to be hidden are blatantly obvious, lighting casts unforgiving shadows that reveal how an effect is accomplished, or backdrops signal actions that were supposed to be concealed. Model-scale experiments can also be recorded and examined after the event and compared with recordings where conditions were controlled or altered.

Elliott's models of induction illusions use wire coils, circuits, audio pickups, and telephone transmitters that allow him to record and measure the results of transmitting at various powers and volumes, with stationary and moving receivers, and with varying orientations between the receiver and the transmitter coil. These models are by no means replicas of the originals, but they give him a sense of how the originals may have worked, what they may have sounded like, and how to provide a more nuanced interpretation of extant representational sources of past magical performances. And they allow him to share these more embodied and tacit understandings with other people in a workshop setting. At the end of the day, Elliott has not provided definitive answers to any of the questions that motivated his exploration, but we would not expect him to, any more than we would expect the players or audience of *Hamlet* to come to a satisfactory conclusion about the meaning of life. What we do learn from performative engagements like these is that they are, for us at least, very much worth doing. They give us a nuanced feeling for past technologies and an imaginative sense of historical milieu that we have not found any other way to access. As Michael Polanyi wrote in *The Tacit Dimension* (2009), "*We can know more than we can tell*" (4, emphasis in original). Humanistic fabrication allows us to share some of what we cannot put into words.

### *Case 2: Translating the Sonde into Code*

Reverse engineering and simulating an analog hardware device in the form of digital software provides a distinct set of opportunities for hands-on learning. In this section we describe Muhammedi's re-creation of the Sonde, one of Hugh Le Caine's lesser-known devices for composing and producing electronic music. Born in 1914, Hugh Le Caine was a Canadian pioneer in the field of electronic music (Young 1989). He studied applied science at Queen's University and spent many years working for the National Research Council as a physicist. Throughout that time he was an avid creator of musical instruments. He is most famous for inventing the Sackbut, one of the world's first synthesizers, in 1945. When he switched to being a full-time musician in 1954, Le Caine was able to create a host of new electronic instruments, including the Touch Sensitive Organ (1955), the Multi-track Tape Recorder (1955), the Oscillator Bank (1957), and the Serial Sound Structure Generator (1965).

The Sonde was one of Le Caine's final projects before he retired, adapted from a previous instrument of his, the Tone Mixture Generator. The Sonde's key feature was its ability to produce 200 sine waves simultaneously, ranging from five to 1,000

Hz in five-Hz increments (Le Caine and Ciamaga 1970). Using matrix generation, 10 convertor oscillators spaced by 100 Hz were connected with 20 fixed oscillators ranging from zero to 95 Hz. By subtracting the frequencies of the combined sine waves, multiple sine waves could be heard at once. The amplitudes of each of the 200 generated tones could be controlled independently using a vertical slider in addition to an overall volume control. This interface afforded the creation of complex sine-tone mixtures, eliminating the need to continuously record and combine individual sine waves by dubbing. Ultimately, the Sonde reduced the cumbersome tape hiss generated when recording multiple sounds over the same reel.

For this project, Muhammedi used a visual programming language called Max 6, in which code consists of symbolic messages and audio data communicated in real-time between a collection of objects using virtual "patch cords." Max is a particularly appropriate choice for this project, since the language was originally developed by electronic musicians using the metaphor of a network of analog devices connected by physical patch cords. Many software objects in Max directly correspond to the electronic equipment of analog studios: sine wave oscillators, switches, filters, oscilloscopes, and so on. The Sonde itself was one such analog electronic device.

Working in software has many well-known advantages. The first is drastically reduced costs. Adding another sine wave oscillator to a software synthesizer is basically free, whereas building another electronic module is definitely not. Although there is a licensing fee for programmers who want to code in the Max language, a runtime module can be used to freely distribute a Max program to as many people as possible.[7] The second advantage is accessibility: the software re-creation allows anyone to utilize and experiment with the digital version. Individuals are free to generate their own sounds, increasing the opportunities for public interaction and engagement. The final benefit is that software has very different affordances than hardware. As we explored different ways to represent the components of the Sonde, we continually confronted these differences. In his interface, for example, Le Caine used a multi-pole, multi-position crossbar switch once commonly used for telephony. How closely should we attempt to model this piece of now unfamiliar technology? Real analog equipment has a warm and somewhat unpredictable sound that is now highly valued among electronic musicians. Should we add additional code to simulate that?

Le Caine's original instrument used 30 physical oscillators wired to telephone switches, run through a final filter, and then amplified to create the desired sound. In the early 1970s, the University of Toronto Electronic Music Studio improved upon the Sonde, replacing the sliders of the original prototype with a grid of printed circuit keys (Le Caine and Ciamaga 1970). Since we were prototyping in software, implementing versions of both interfaces was relatively easy, and it gave us a glimpse of some changes occurring in electronic music composition during the late 1960s and early 1970s. At the same time, we recognize that our simulated instruments have none of the tactility of the originals.

Complex sine tone mixtures are readily generated in software, and their sound is familiar to anyone who listens to contemporary ambient electronic music. Although Le Caine anticipated the use of computers for music creation, he never embraced the world of computer-generated music. Gayle Young argues that Le Caine's understanding of music was rooted in analog terms: "His dislike of stepped systems and disinterest in computers was linked with his inclination toward analogue systems, an inclination that went deeper than a simple use of available (analogue) techniques to what could be called analogue imagination" (166). Le Caine was certainly aware of how computer scientists might improve upon the Sonde but felt that such improvement would alter his own appreciation for analogue musical instruments. In our case, working with digital simulations of Le Caine's creation continually drew our attention to material aspects—especially the cadence of adjusting controls to produce desired effects—that we had not yet considered and also led us to experiment with analog synthesis and live electronics (Collins 2010). We cannot be sure what tacit features Le Caine most appreciated when composing with the Sonde, but we do have a new appreciation for some of the possibilities the device may have afforded, and we hope that others who play with it have a similar experience.

### *Case 3: Thinking with Analogs*

There was a time when electronics meant something other than digital. For decades spanning the middle of the twentieth century, making electronics meant building analog machines. Like their namesakes in literature and biology, electronic analogs sought to establish correspondences and harmonies. In place of tropes and organisms, however, they took phenomena like time and motion and rendered them as physical quantities—voltages, positions, and currents. Analogs in the humanities and the natural sciences served the interests of explanation, classification, and clarification. Electronic analogs, by contrast, served the interests of calculation, modeling, and intervention. They found their way into everything from music synthesizers to automata, and ultimately computers. Through that remarkably simple premise—that one object might stand for another—analog computers sought to represent the flux of the world, as well as the possibilities for controlling it, through the continuous variation of electrical values.

What happened to analog computers? One account, often repeated in the history of computing, suggests that they died out because they were not fast enough and did not lend themselves to the kinds of pressing applications that digital machines handled easily. That view turns out to be inaccurate in important ways. As historian David Mindell (2002) explains: "Analog and digital arose together, as distinct but related approaches to representing the world in machines. In general, historians of computing have neglected analog computing, viewing it primarily as an obsolete predecessor to digital. . . . On the contrary, we have not yet begun to understand the history and significance of analog computing, especially the relationship between analog and digital machines" (10). Up to the 1960s, analog computing was faster, more advanced, and more obviously applicable to problems of machine control than were digital computers (Edwards 1997). Analog computers were also easier to integrate with the analog world of things. While digital computing handled discrete entities well, analog computing was the better match for continuous and fluid systems. Analog devices were well suited for measurement and instrumentation, simulation of movement, visualization via pen plotters and oscilloscopes, and control of actuators such as servo-mechanisms (Paynter 1955). One author of a text on analog circuits suggested that a problem with their widespread adoption was the lack of a compelling and inexpensive visual output display (Smith 1971). By contrast, the analog computers at the heart of electronic music synthesizers produced compelling audification (rather than visualization) and thus became quite popular in devices such as the Moog synthesizer (Pinch and Trocco 2004).

In many ways, then, digital computing was a solution in search of a problem (Pinch and Bijker 2004). And even as they eventually supplanted many analog devices, digital devices continued to be shaped by techniques originally developed around analog machines (Williams 1991). This tendency is especially common in places where digital devices have to interface with users in a material world. Analog signals like sound, light intensity, and mouse movements are digitized by cell phones, cameras, and personal computers; that digital information, in turn, has to be converted back into the sounds we hear, the images we see, and so on. Today, solid state analog devices are ubiquitous (Turkel 2011).

In re-creating analog electronic computers, we attempt to understand what has been lost in the overriding emphasis on contemporary technologies and to experience some of the richness and complexity of a time when electronics were not exclusively or necessarily reduced to the digital. Additionally, the practice materializes one of the central arguments of technology studies from the last three decades—that the development of technology involves historical contingencies. The decline of analog was never as necessary, or absolute, as the standard story would have us believe. Rebuilding analog computers is an attempt to trace out what Andrew Pickering (2010) has called "sketches of another future." Beyond the physical devices produced, our acts of construction generate insight into current scholarly issues and practice. We aim, then, to arrive at that long-standing argument about contingency in a novel way—through the performative engagement with electronic artifacts. In addition to contributing to the history of electronics and to broader methodological questions within the field of technology studies, both our subject matter and approach provide innovative opportunities for teaching within and beyond the classroom setting.

Analog computing is an exemplary subject for staging hands-on historical investigation, because there are often a number of different ways to accomplish a particular goal with analog circuitry. For example, one of the central components of analog computing (both before and after the invention of the transistor) was a device known as an operational amplifier (Frederiksen 1988; Jung 2004). Op amps, as they are commonly known, were created by combining a number of vacuum tubes or transistors into a module with certain properties. In the ideal case, the op amp was a kind of universal building block. By adding a few additional parts, it could be turned into any number of other useful devices to perform mathematical operations such as summing, averaging, integrating, differentiating, or computing logarithms (Paynter 1955). Op amps were also designed so that they could be substituted for one another without affecting the function of the larger circuits of which they were a part. Real op amps, of course, fell short of the ideal. Analog circuit designers faced opportunities and constraints that cannot be fully understood without exploring the electronic behavior of the circuits that they built.

To understand those opportunities and constraints, we designed and built a small analog computer loosely based on the Heathkit EC-1, which was sold by the Heath Company in kit form beginning in 1959. The original kit used lethal voltages and now-scarce components, so our re-creation is really an "analog" of the original. Working from the design, construction, and programming processes laid out in the schematic and instruction manual for the Heathkit EC-1, we substituted readily available, lower-voltage electronic components and integrated circuits to arrive at a system that works in the same fashion (Heath Company, *Operational Manual*; *Heathkit Assembly Manual*). Along the way we studied a number of contemporary physical artifacts and texts from mid-twentieth-century analog computing, solving typical electronics problems using the methods most familiar to analog computer designers and programmers of the 1950s and 60s (Johnson 1956; Korn and Korn 1956; Paynter 1955). Commercially available kits such as the Heathkit EC-1 generally attempted to teach electronics via moralized, highly scripted assembly projects. And somehow these kits conveyed the implicit knowledge essential to electronics construction. Our building of analogs, by differently skilled collaborators, helps us to understand the process by which kits taught the kind of "fingertip" specialized knowledge that cannot be learned from books.

Our performative engagement with analog devices is paired with representational work geared to both academic and broader audiences. Within the scholarly realm, we are interested in critically reinterpreting the role of analog devices in the history of computing and scientific instrumentation and expanding upon the value of hands-on methods within the humanities (Jones-Imhotep and Turkel; Turkel and Jones-Imhotep; Turkel, Muhammedi, and Start 2014). In addition, we are producing schematics for a series of open-source electronic construction modules that invite others to explore analog computing. These modules could be adopted within history and social science classes about technology, and perhaps even within electronics curricula. They could further serve as independent projects that would engage enthusiasts of making in both a hands-on electronics activity and thinking about social-historical issues surrounding computing.

## *Conclusion*

In this chapter we have briefly described our experiences collaboratively reconstructing stage magic illusions, electronic musical instruments, and analog electronic computers in settings where the emphasis is on performative engagement with the world. In doing this work, we are not invested in making exact reproductions. Even if we could somehow create them, they would have very different meanings and affordances for us than for their original creators and users (Turkel 2011).[8] When we share these experiences with members of the general public, they seem to find them as fun and absorbing as we do. Academic participants lose themselves in these playful explorations, too, although some feel an obligation afterwards to try to make their new understandings more explicit. Here we outline four trajectories to connect our work to more traditional kinds of knowledge representation.

First, the affective. The fact that doing this kind of work is fun and compelling (to the point where some people have a hard time believing it *is* work) suggests that the scholarly study of play and games may have something to teach us about what is happening in these settings. Our view of our work as "ontological theatre" establishes some common ground with theories of performance. Our various audiences have found our model-scale stagings (of magic illusions, for example) to be particularly captivating, something we relate to a widespread fascination with miniatures, dollhouses, and puppet theatres, as well as an interest in microworlds more generally. On a more intimate level, we have often found that we experience a sense of loss or absence as we engage more deeply with forms of life we think are now gone. Jentery Sayers[9] suggests that this sense may be produced by the acts we are engaged in, rather than the things themselves, an idea we plan to pursue in future work.

Second, the artifactual. The philosopher Davis Baird (2004) points out that "'Craft knowledge,' 'fingertip knowledge,' 'tacit knowledge,' and 'know-how' are useful concepts in that they remind us that there is more to knowing than saying. But they tend to render this kind of knowledge ineffable. Instruments have a kind of public existence that allows for more explicit study" (18). Baird argues that an artifact may act as a model, as a device that creates phenomena, as an instrument for measuring or computing, or as some combination of the three. Like texts, models can provide representations. Physical devices, however, can also "constitute knowledge in a different, nonrepresentational way. Such instruments work epistemologically in a manner that draws on pragmatist conceptions of knowledge as effective action. A fundamental difference, however, is that with instruments, the action has been separated from human agency and built into the reliable behavior of an artifact" (12). Hands-on exploration provides technology studies scholars with a way to acquire technical and scientific knowledge that is tacit and embodied, and that can be learned best through experimentation, trial, and error (Collins 2009).

Third, the material. We have a preference for certain kinds of components and workflows. Whenever possible we work with modular and reusable systems,[10] we favor reclaimed and recycled materials, and we mercilessly compost, reuse, or continue to hack the things we have already made. This approach not only allows us to embrace the accidents and failures that are crucial elements of design thinking; it also enables us to maintain our focus on process rather than product and to offer frequent workshops. We document as much as possible, and we version and share our software on GitHub and elsewhere. Our work can thus be situated both as a kind of commons-based peer production (Benkler 2006) and as part of the so-called maker movement (Charny 2011).

Fourth, academic fellow travelers. Our engagements can be seen as a kind of "research-creation," because they "typically integrate a creative process, experimental aesthetic component, or an artistic work as an integral part of a study" (Chapman and Sawchuk 2012). When we do make the detour through the space of representation, we engage in what Philip Agre (1997) calls "a critical technical practice—a technical practice for which critical reflection upon the practice is part of the practice itself" (xii). The artifacts we make might be seen as "provotypes" (Mogensen 1992). Although they are never exact re-creations of historical objects, provotypes have the ability to provoke "discussion about current practice through practice" (Donovan and Gunn 2012). In re-creating historical technologies, we raise both historical and historiographical questions about the role and salience of material cultures. Our practice of historical reverse engineering is related to the present-oriented scholarship of critical making. Like reverse engineering, critical making combines the methods of "two typically disconnected modes of engagement in the world—'critical thinking,' often considered as abstract, explicit, linguistically-based, internal and cognitively individualistic; and 'making,' typically understood as material, tacit, embodied, external, and community-oriented" (Ratto and Hockema 52). In this way, reverse engineering electronic devices teaches us about their inner workings and, when complemented by careful historical analysis and traditional sources, gives us a glimpse into the decisions, constraints, and contingent choices of their designers and makers. But it also combines creation and critical analysis to expand our understanding of how scholarly knowledge is generated and communicated (Galey and Ruecker 2010). Each performative engagement opens new fields for play, experience, and discovery; teaches us things we can put into words and things we cannot; and creates shareable artifacts that can be mobilized and studied in their own right.

## NOTES

1. See Turkel; and Elliott, MacDougall, and Turkel.

2. Pickering's work and ours also build on Latour's concept of the "nonmodern."

3. If the idea of "ontological theatre" is too abstruse, then compare this kind of work to so-called food porn. The point of such pictures is *not* knowledge production; it is that one might be inspired to create and consume something similar. As to how it tastes, *à chacun son goût*.

4. This phrase comes from Stuart Kauffman by way of Steven Johnson.

5. White City was a large fair on the south side of Chicago, in operation from 1905 to the 1950s.

6. There is a bit more detail about the process of building model-scale illusions in Elliott, MacDougall, and Turkel, and a lot more in Elliott's forthcoming doctoral dissertation.

7. It would also be straightforward to translate the Max code to Pure Data (aka Pd), a closely related, open-source dataflow language. We have not yet done this.

8. For a more philosophical treatment, see Nagel.

9. Personal communication, January 2016. In addition to the work described here, we also collaborated with Sayers and members of the Maker Lab at the University of Victoria on the development of kits for cultural history. See Belojevic; Sayers.

10. Favorites include LEGO, Ardunio microcontrollers, VEX robotics kits, littleBits electronics, Phidgets modules, MaKey MaKey boards, MakeDo cardboard tools, and MakerBeam extruded aluminum.

## BIBLIOGRAPHY

Abbott, David P. *David P. Abbott's Book of Mysteries*. Omaha, Neb.: Modern Litho, 1977.

Agre, Philip E. *Computation and Human Experience*. Cambridge: Cambridge University Press, 1997.

Alexander, C. *The Life and Mysteries of the Celebrated Dr. "Q."* Los Angeles, Calif.: Alexander Publishing, 1921.

Atkinson, William Walker. *Mind-Power: The Secret of Mental Magic*. Chicago, Ill.: Advanced Thought Publishing, 1912.

Baird, Davis. *Thing Knowledge: A Philosophy of Scientific Instruments*. Berkeley, Calif.: University of California Press, 2004.

Belojevic, Nina. "Kits for Cultural History." Maker Lab for the Humanities, University of Victoria, September 20, 2013. http://maker.uvic.ca/kch.

Benkler, Yochai. *The Wealth of Networks*. New Haven, Conn.: Yale University Press, 2006.

Blondel, Christine, and Matthias Dörries, eds. *Restaging Coulomb: Usages, Controverses et Réplications Autour de la Balance de Torsion*. Florence, Italy: Leo S. Olschki, 1994.

Ceruzzi, Paul. *A History of Modern Computing*. Cambridge, Mass.: MIT Press, 1998.

Chapman, Owen, and Kim Sawchuk. "Research-Creation: Intervention, Analysis and 'Family Resemblances.'" *Canadian Journal of Communication* 37, no. 1 (2012): 5–26.

Charny, Daniel. "Thinking of Making." *Power of Making*. London: Victoria and Albert Museum, 2011.

Cohen, Daniel, and Roy Rosenzweig. *Digital History: A Guide to Gathering, Preserving, and Presenting the Past on the Web*. Philadelphia, Pa.: University of Pennsylvania Press, 2006.

Collins, Harry. *Tacit and Explicit Knowledge*. Chicago, Ill.: University of Chicago Press, 2010.

Collins, Nicholas. *Handmade Electronic Music: The Art of Hardware Hacking,* 2nd ed. New York: Routledge, 2009.

Corbin, Alain. *Village Bells: Sound and Meaning in the 19th-century French Countryside.* New York: Columbia University Press, 1998.

Donovan, Jared, and Wendy Gunn. "Moving from Objects to Possibilities." In *Design and Anthropology,* ed. Wendy Gunn and Jared Donovan, 121–34. Burlington, Vt.: Ashgate, 2012.

Edwards, Paul N. *The Closed World: Computers and the Politics of Discourse in Cold War America.* Cambridge, Mass.: MIT Press, 1997.

Elliott, Devon, Robert MacDougall, and William J. Turkel. "New Old Things: Fabrication, Physical Computing, and Experiment in Historical Practice." *Canadian Journal of Communication* 37, no. 1 (2012): 121–28.

Frederiksen, Thomas M. *Intuitive Operational Amplifiers.* New York: McGraw-Hill, 1988.

Galey, Alan, and Stan Ruecker. "How a Prototype Argues." *Literary and Linguistic Computing* 25, no. 4 (2010): 405–24.

Haring, Kristen. *Ham Radio's Technical Culture.* Cambridge, Mass.: MIT Press, 2006.

Heath Company. *Heathkit Assembly Manual: Educational Electronic Analog Computer Model EC-1.* Benton Harbor, Mich.: Heath Company, 1960.

———. *Operational Manual for the Heath Educational Analog Computer Model EC-1.* Benton Harbor, Mich.: Heath Company, 1959.

Heering, Peter. "Regular Twists: Replicating Coulomb's Wire-Torsion Experiments." *Physics in Perspective* 8, no. 1 (2006): 52–63.

Hopwood, Nick, and Soraya de Chadarevian. "Dimensions of Modelling." In *Models: The Third Dimension of Science,* ed. Soraya de Chadarevian and Nick Hopwood, 1–15. Stanford, Calif.: Stanford University Press, 2004.

Hughes, Thomas Parke. *Networks of Power: Electrification in Western Society, 1880–1930.* Baltimore, Md.: Johns Hopkins University Press, 1983.

Johnson, Clarence L. *Analog Computer Techniques.* New York: McGraw-Hill, 1956.

Johnson, James H. *Listening in Paris: A Cultural History.* Berkeley, Calif.: University of California Press, 1996.

Johnson, Steven. *Where Good Ideas Come From.* New York: Riverhead, 2010.

Jones-Imhotep, Edward. "Icons and Electronics." *Historical Studies in the Natural Sciences* 38 (2008): 405–50.

Jones-Imhotep, Edward, and William J. Turkel. "Image Mining for the History of Electronics and Computing." In *Seeing the Past: Augmented Reality and Computer Vision,* ed. Kevin Kee. Under consideration.

Jung, Walter G. *Op Amp Applications Handbook.* Burlington, Mass.: Newnes, 2004.

Korn, Granino, and Theresa M. Korn. *Electronic Analog Computers,* 2nd ed. New York: McGraw-Hill, 1956.

Latour, Bruno. *We Have Never Been Modern.* Cambridge, Mass.: Harvard University Press, 1993.

Le Caine, Hugh, and Gustav Ciamaga. "The Sonde: A New Approach to Multiple Sinewave Generation." *Journal of the Audio Engineering Society* 18 (1970): 536–39.

Mindell, David A. *Between Human and Machine: Feedback, Control and Computing before Cybernetics*. Baltimore, Md.: Johns Hopkins University Press, 2002.

Mody, Cyrus, and David Kaiser. "Scientific Training and the Creation of Scientific Knowledge." In *Handbook of Science and Technology Studies,* 3rd ed., ed. Edward J. Hackett, Olga Amsterdamska, Michael E. Lynch, and Judy Wajcman, 377–402. Cambridge, Mass.: MIT Press, 2007.

Mogensen, Preben. "Towards a Provotyping Approach in Systems Development." *Scandinavian Journal of Information Systems* 4 (1992): 31–53.

Nagel, Thomas. "What Is It Like to Be a Bat?" *Philosophical Review* 83, no. 4 (1974): 435–50.

Paynter, H. M., ed. *A Palimpsest on the Electronic Analog Art*. Boston, Mass.: George A. Philbrick Researches, 1955.

Pickering, Andrew. *The Cybernetic Brain: Sketches of Another Future*. Chicago, Ill.: University of Chicago Press, 2010.

Pinch, Trevor, and Frank Trocco. *Analog Days: The Invention and Impact of the Moog Synthesizer.* Cambridge, Mass.: Harvard University Press, 2004.

Pinch, Trevor J., and Wiebe E. Bijker. "The Social Construction of Facts and Artifacts: Or How the Sociology of Science and the Sociology of Technology Might Benefit Each Other." In *The Social Construction of Technological Systems: New Directions in the Sociology and History of Technology,* ed. Wiebe E. Bijker, Thomas P. Hughes, and Trevor Pinch, 17–50. Cambridge, Mass.: MIT Press, 1989.

Polanyi, Michael. *The Tacit Dimension*. Chicago, Ill.: University of Chicago Press, 2009.

Ratto, Matt, and Stephen Hockema. "Flwr Pwr: Tending the Walled Garden." In *Walled Garden,* ed. A. Dekker and A. Wolfsberger, 51–60. The Netherlands: Virtueel Platform, 2009.

Sayers, Jentery. "Kits for Cultural History." *Hyperrhiz* 13 (Fall 2015). http://hyperrhiz.io/hyperrhiz13/workshops-kits/early-wearables-essay.html.

Sayers, Jentery, Devon Elliott, Kari Kraus, Bethany Nowviskie, and William J. Turkel. "Between Bits and Atoms: Physical Computing and Fabrication in the Humanities." In *The New Companion to the Digital Humanities,* ed. Susan Schreibman, Ray Siemens, and John Unsworth, 3–21. Hoboken, N.J.: Wiley, 2016.

Sibum, Heinz Otto. "Experimental History of Science." In *Museums of Modern Science: Nobel Symposium* 112, ed. Svante Lindqvist, 77–86. Canton, Mass.: Science History Publications, 1999.

———. "Reworking the Mechanical Value of Heat: Instruments of Precision and Gestures of Accuracy in Early Victorian England." *Studies in History and Philosophy of Science* Part A, 26, no. 1 (1995): 73–106.

———. "Working Experiments: Bodies, Machines and Heat Values." In *The Physics of Empire,* ed. Richard Stanley, 29–56. Cambridge, U.K.: Whipple Museum of the History of Science, 1994.

Smith, John I. *Modern Operational Circuit Design*. New York: Wiley-Interscience, 1971.

Thompson, Emily. *The Soundscape of Modernity: Architectural Acoustics and the Culture of Listening in America, 1900–1933*. Cambridge, Mass.: MIT Press, 2004.

Turkel, William J. "Hacking History, from Analog to Digital and Back Again." *Rethinking History* 15, no. 2: 287–96, 2011.

Turkel, William J. and Devon Elliott. "Making and Playing with Models: Using Rapid Prototyping to Explore the History and Technology of Stage Magic." In *Pastplay: Teaching and Learning History with Technology*, ed. Kevin Kee, 175–98. Ann Arbor, Mich.: University of Michigan Press, 2014.

Turkel, William J. and Edward Jones-Imhotep. "Sensors and Sources: How a Universal Model of Instrumentation Affects Our Experiences of the Past." In *Varieties of Historical Experience,* ed. Charles Stewart and Stephan Palmie. Under consideration.

Turkel, William J., Shezan Muhammedi, and Mary Beth Start. "Grounding Digital History in the History of Computing." *IEEE Annals for the History of Computing* 36, no. 2 (2014): 72–75.

Wiley, Barry H. *The Indescribable Phenomenon: The Life and Mysteries of Anna Eva Fay*. Seattle, Wash: Hermetic Press, 2005.

Williams, Jim, ed. *Analog Circuit Design: Art, Science, and Personalities*. Burlington, Mass.: Butterworth-Heinemann, 1991.

Young, Gayle. *The Sackbut Blues: Hugh Le Caine Pioneer in Electronic Music*. Ottawa: National Museum of Science and Technology, 1989.

# Electronic Music Hardware and Open Design Methodologies for Post-Optimal Objects

EZRA TEBOUL

This chapter develops a brief historical and theoretical overview of hardware hacking within the context of electronic music instruments, suggesting how component-level analysis of some specific artifacts can help scholars to appreciate accelerating shifts in musical production as well as larger cultural trends. The chapter does not promote hardware hacking as an optimal solution for every musician. Rather, it recognizes hacking as a long-lasting and self-sustaining technocultural practice. This recognition is achieved in part by developing an adapted understanding of Anthony Dunne's "post-optimal electronics" (2005). Such understanding investigates what makes electronic instrument design unique, how each artist bends the traditions of engineering and fabrication for their purposes, and offers possibilities for relating audio technologies to our modern culture of invention. In short, taking a closer look at audio technology's technocommunal aspects informs modern trends in composition, invention, and scholarship.

The development of contemporary electronic music is closely related to the tinkering practices enabled by kits in early-twentieth-century industrialized countries.[1] Containing all the parts and instructions necessary to put together some electronic device, these kits allowed for reverse engineering to be a personal and possibly untrained experience.[2] Originally aimed at amateur radio enthusiasts, they evolved to provide people with accessible, simple, yet effective audio systems and, occasionally, instruments such as theremins.[3] In turn, hobbyist publications empowered young enthusiasts. For instance, Robert Moog and Donald Buchla started as teenagers building electronics kits, suggesting that electronic music is deeply rooted in the do-it-yourself (DIY) practices that made it possible.[4] It is only natural, then, for contemporary composers to engage directly with the physicality of electronic music by designing and building their own equipment or modifying existing devices. Developing a creative, experiential understanding of signal processing is one way, for example, to acquire an additional connection to the artifacts involved in music making.

With kits evolving from somewhat hazardous vacuum-tube circuits to inexpensive solid-state devices in the late sixties, the limiting factor for engaging directly and safely with electronics for music became dedication, not prior knowledge. Quoting Nicolas Collins (2006), "Rule #17: If it sounds good and doesn't smoke, don't worry if you don't understand it" (225). Educational publications also shifted from paper (electronotes and popular electronics)[5] to the network of online resources available to the electronics tinkerer today. Since schematics are often sufficient to produce a close equivalent of a device, even the early web message boards were good enough to enable amateur or small-scale circuit building.[6] Online information and advice on fabricating your own musical electronics have existed since the late nineties (one of the first posts on the diyaudio.com forum is dated from 2000). "It's never been easier to hack. . . . Tim Berners-Lee birthed the World Wide Web and a hundred fuzztones flowered" (228). The consequence of cheap tools, cheap parts, accessible information, and a lack of centralized authority is a variety of alternative visions for an exploded field of personal electronic music devices. Approaches range from respecting best practices outlined by engineering scholars to working purely by intuition,[7] with musically successful innovations coming from both sides of this spectrum. If Moog's machines helped to kickstart modern electronic music, then Buchla's instruments became essential to avant-garde composers such as Morton Subotnick, and entire genres are now based on specific hardware hacking techniques.[8]

A compelling instance is the work of Jessica Rylan, a former Buchla employee who founded the now-defunct Flower Electronics[9] brand in 2006 and ran it until 2013. Rylan's products included mostly standalone analog synthesizers, reminiscent of Buchla's colorful banana jack-wielding modulars[10] and David Tudor's unmarked electronics. Rylan's approach is explicitly an expansion of traditional circuit design. Describing her design methodology, she writes:

> During the period of time when I was designing circuits, I tried to incorporate a scientific approach into my design work. However, I used this strategy alongside other strategies including intuition, limitation challenges (for a year I didn't use an oscilloscope or a digital meter), and making design decisions visually (either based on what the components looked like, or how the schematic looked aesthetically). (Teboul Appendix 199)

Rylan's "personal synth" is full of small originalities at the circuit level that make it a unique, performable, and personal device. These originalities include voltage control of the wave-shaping circuit within the 8038-based oscillator, or a voltage controlled amplifier implemented with zener diodes, which exhibit nonlinear behaviors and allow for an unusual, nonlinear filtering characteristic. Such developments are materializations of an exploratory engineering—a multifaceted tinkering.[11]

Similarly, Ben and Louise Hinz of Dwarfcraft Devices[12] have developed a personal and commercially viable approach to audio-effects boxes and eurorack-format synthesizer modules. Starting from Collins's *Handmade* recommendations, a few years of experimentation led Dwarfcraft to become an appreciated brand. An early device, the "Robot Devil," contained a version of a Nic Collins circuit (Collins 155), itself obtained from Craig Anderton's (2003) formative publication (Anderton 173). In this case, however, most of Collins's advice was ignored and seemingly unusual modifications were made, with protection diodes removed and gain values set well beyond the recommended range. The result is nevertheless an original and usable device,[13] which is emblematic of many popular signal processing devices currently on the market.[14]

In effect, with each new device comes a new iteration of experimental design practice, a multifaceted and heterogeneous ecosystem for invention[15] based on what is accessible to the designer of the next step. Each step does not necessarily represent technological progress. Instead, it is the materialization of another personal vision of electronic music. Had the field of electronic instrument design had a clear direction or a more rigid structure (like amateur radio), this explosion of visions and methodologies arguably could have been stifled. However, the musical context surrounding these developments is important: loosening the assumption of what was "desirable" in electronic instruments came with a wider acceptance of musicians from various skill levels in both academic (Cardew's Scratch Orchestra, for example) and popular (or punk) forms of music.

This history and methodology draw clear connections with the open-source hardware community.[16] Actors and networks of actors are often comparable: tools are usually of the electronics, fabrication, design, and graphic variety; spaces include communal, personal, or professional shops; and the imagined communities usually solidify in online presences (forums and data sharing platforms, for instance) and occasional physical events, such as knobcon and the National Association of Music Merchants (NAMM). These connections do not necessarily suggest that open-source will develop splintered, local versions of technology, but they do offer precedents as to how creative minds approach technical freedom.

If the genealogy, reality, and legitimacy of these silicon luthiers,[17] or heterogeneous designers,[18] has been established, then consider the individuality of the auditory experience: the quality of a sound is determined by the listener based on internal factors (tastes) and external influences (context). As sound sources, instruments will be judged on similarly subjective, variable, and personal levels. That is, *the quality of creative devices is not reducible to a set of objective metrics* (such as the size, power consumption, and storage capacity for a hard drive). Those metrics may be of interest but must be considered alongside the experiential connection a person and their audience have to the artifact. Of course, extremely high-quality components may be used in personal instruments and may increase reliability or comfort; however, the persistence of vacuum-tube amplifiers[19] and analog synthesizers[20] attests to a tendency to become attached to "inefficient" technologies.[21] Theoretical discussions of electronic music instruments explicitly acknowledge the shortcomings or incongruities of hardware as ultimately inspiring for their designers and audiences.[22]

This concept of purposefully challenging people through design relates directly to Anthony Dunne's theory of post-optimal electronics: "if user-friendliness characterizes the relationship between people and the optimal electronic object, then user-unfriendliness, a form of gentle provocation, could characterize the post-optimal object" (Dunne x). Characterizing electronic music hardware as a class of post-optimal objects offers a tool to discuss the development of so many individualized visions of electronic music, as the term encapsulates much of what makes those devices catalysts of poetic experiences. Building your own electronic instrument, even if it is not necessarily the most technologically advanced tool available, provides an inherent personal connection, as well as an intuitive understanding of the device that might serve the interests of composition. Rylan notes that this connection is no guarantee of musical or technical quality, yet it can be inspiring and effectively open new compositional or performative paths (Teboul 200).

A post-optimal vision of electronic music also has ideological implications. Opening up, modifying, and copying devices should be justifiable if it can benefit the final artistic product, and yet the majority of available devices do not carry that ideal through their design: enclosures are often designed to prevent consumer servicing, and warranties are voided unless either the device is inspected by an approved technician or authorized firmware is uploaded. These restrictions force electronic instruments back into an "optimal" vision of technology, where better metrics justify replacements and minimize personal connections to devices. Such optimization mimics greater cultural trends of material consumption in industrialized economies.

Concerns in discussions of music technology, including discussions about authors, origins, interface designs, and their subsequent use/reuse/misuse, have been and continue to be addressed by scholars and scholarly organizations.[23] However, the technological components themselves are often ignored in these discussions. This inattention to components is important because electric instruments and the artifacts they contain are embedded with personal connections to their original designers. Electronics are possible only because of an industrialized and standardized manufacturing market premised on individual labor. In this market, the building blocks of instruments are largely shared from one device to the next, through components (such as resistors, capacitors, inductors, and transistors[24]) as well as circuits (consider "standard circuit" topologies discussed in electronics textbooks[25]). These dependencies explain the sensation among audio electronics designers that entirely novel designs are extremely rare, and they further justify the connection with open-source design: if most audio devices are a new take on an old concept, then acknowledging lineage is ethically preferable to claiming originality. It is also instructive.

The underlying paradox of techno-artistic practices is that engaging with the physicality of electronic music is an important source of inspiration and motivation for practitioners. The works of David Tudor, his students, and a variety of contemporary practitioners from Peter Vogel to MSHR (Birch Cooper and Brenna Murphy) attest explicitly to this inspiration.[26] Breaking down the black boxes of electronic music has motivated the creation of many pieces across the professional-accessible spectrum. Yet few practitioners acknowledge how the subsystems they make explicit all contain personal connections to components made by other designers. The original intentions for those small elements, circuit topologies, and associated materials all subtly influence the system in which they are used, even if they are co-opted. Dealing with these components directly, instead of relying on graphical user interfaces or computer screens, also helps practitioners to better understand subsystem functionalities and their histories. For instance, consider how the liner notes by engineer Forrest Warthman for Tudor's *Neural Synthesis* (1995) offer extensive insight on the genesis of the piece itself and its technological significance precisely because they discuss the components involved. The notes cover the development of the chips used to simulate neuron functions and how Tudor's creative intuition guided the project. Warthman includes the following comment on the links between music and technology:

> Audio oscillators have a subtle but long history in Silicon Valley. Many local engineers date the beginning of the semiconductor industry to the 1938 development by Bill Hewlett and David Packard of their first product, an audio oscillator, in a downtown Palo Alto garage.[27]

With such a fortuitous connection, the details of individual components appear all the more important. Who designed the components? In which system were they were originally used? How were they packaged? Why did resistors evolve from carbon compositions to other materials? Can these subsystems be approximated with alternatives that are interesting to practitioners?

These concerns may seem superfluous; however, this care for low-level detail is primordial in some of the professional audio world. It is also central to post-optimal electronics. Recording and mastering engineers often spend a considerable amount of time experimenting with capacitors for a particular section of a filter or amplifier. To them, those choices matter, and the quality of their system is a significant element of their professional reputation.[28] By becoming more aware of the origins and implications of the component choices, musicians can expand the connection between a particular device and its sonic products. The framework of post-optimality therefore shifts the conversation from a technical level to an experiential one, opening a discussion that is often mired with elitism ("a professional degree validates your opinion") and classism (for instance, the sound systems associated with component-level care are expensive).

Ultimately, then, this chapter extends the current exchanges on electronic instrument design by widening the focus to personal relationships and acknowledging the deep intuitive understanding many gain through experimentation, without abandoning a parallel genealogy of the musical systems and individual components that make them. This sociotechnological understanding of electronic music hardware is in many ways related to previous, more generalized accounts of invention,[29] but those sociological or historical studies rarely deal directly with circuits. Post-optimality and poetics serve this vision by demonstrating how technologies facilitate tasks in a variety of ways, some of which need not involve scientific progress or innovation. Musicians and audiences are unique, and the objects that bind them together benefit from crystallizing that uniqueness through attention to context.

## NOTES

1. In effect, homemade electronic music inherited kit culture's traditionally white cis male population. See Haring on radio and Rodgers on music technology as traditionally gendered spaces.

2. For more on the culture of kits, see Haring, Chapter 7.

3. Theremins are particularly emblematic of the history of electronic music. Also, Moog began his synthesizer business by selling assembled versions of kits. For more on Moog and Buchla, see Pinch.

4. For a history of making in musical electronics, see Teboul, Chapter 2.

5. Archives available at http://electronotes.netfirms.com and www.americanradiohistory.com/Popular-Electronics-Guide.htm.

6. See diyaudio.com, diystompboxes.com, and synthtopia.com alongside schematic websites such as www.hylander.com/moogschematics.html. A proper discussion of the particularities of intellectual property laws relative to copying the functional elements of musical devices is beyond the scope of this chapter. For an informal discussion, see www.muzique.com/clones.htm.

7. For a discussion of various philosophies of circuit bending, see Ghazala.

8. See Collins; Kelly; and Novak.

9. See Rylan et al. at www.flowerelectronics.com.

10. See www.buchla.com.

11. For a more complete analysis of Rylan's "personal synth," see Teboul, Chapter 3, Section 2.

12. See Ben and Louise Hinz at www.dwarfcraft.com.

13. For additional details and references, see Teboul, Section 3.3.1. For an in-depth analysis of musical electronics as post-optimal objects, refer to Teboul, Chapter 3.

14. See, for instance, the Earthquaker Devices Bit Commander, the Death By Audio Robot, and the Electro Harmonix Octave Multiplexer.

15. The biological connotations of this term appear particularly appropriate considering the real-time, personalized and fragile nature of the communal platforms that empower homemade electronic music, echoing Eriksen's use of the word mushrooming (24). The online instrument maker communities are born, evolve, invent tools, influence each other, develop points of view, die, and leave artifacts behind that slowly decay.

16. See Gibb, Introduction.

17. See Collins; and Teboul.

18. Heterogeneous designers are a creative version of Law's Heterogeneous Engineers (see Law in Bijker).

19. See Barbour; and Hamm.

20. See, for example, the panel discussion at the San Francisco MusicTech Summit on May 17, 2010, archived at https://archive.org/details/ResurgenceOfAnalogSynthesizers.

21. For an in-depth discussion of cultural change as an alternative to technological progress in addressing functional imperfections (reverse salients), see McSwain in Braun.

22. See Rovan discussing Evens (2005).

23. See Pinch; Kelly; Rodgers; and Novak.

24. This is most obviously exemplified by the integrated circuit, a packaged and unmodifiable black box.

25. For example, consider topologies for comparators, integrators, negative feedback-based operational amplifiers, and Darlington pairs. See Horowitz, Hill, and Hayes; and Langford-Smith.

26. See Collins; and Issue 14 of the *Leonardo Music Journal* for a practical history of examples.

27. See www.davidtudor.org/Articles/warthman.html.

28. See Teboul, Sections 3.8, 4.9, and A.1 for an in-depth discussion of the topic based on an interview with Sang-Wook Nam, mastering engineer.

29. See specifically the literature emerging from Bijker's work.

## BIBLIOGRAPHY

Anderton, Craig. *Electronic Projects for Musicians.* New York: Amsco Publications, 2003.

Barbour, Eric. "The Cool Sound of Tubes." *Spectrum, IEEE* 35, no. 8 (1998): 24–35.

Bijker, Wiebe E., Thomas P. Hughes, Trevor Pinch, and Deborah G. Douglas. *The Social Construction of Technological Systems: New Directions in the Sociology and History of Technology.* Cambridge, Mass: MIT Press, 2012.

Collins, Nicolas. *Handmade Electronic Music: The Art of Hardware Hacking.* New York: Routledge, 2006.

———. "A Solder's Tale: Putting the 'Lead' Back in 'Lead Users.'" *IEEE Pervasive Computing* 7, no. 3 (2008): 32–38.

Dunne, Anthony. *Hertzian Tales: Electronic Products, Aesthetic Experience, and Critical Design*. Cambridge, Mass.: MIT Press, 2005.

Eriksen, Timothy. "Old Folks' Concerts: The Meaning and Mushrooming of an Antiquarian Music Craze, 1853–1856." PhD dissertation, Wesleyan University, 2015.

Evens, Aden. *Sound Ideas: Music, Machines, and Experience*. Minneapolis: University of Minnesota Press, 2005.

Ghazala, Reed. *Circuit-Bending: Build Your Own Alien Instruments*. Hoboken, N.J.: Wiley, 2005.

Gibb, Alicia. *Building Open Source Hardware: DIY Manufacturing for Hackers and Makers*. Boston, Mass.: Addison-Wesley, 2015.

Hamm, Russell O. "Tubes Versus Transistors—Is There an Audible Difference?" *Journal of the Audio Engineering Society* 21, no. 4 (1973): 267–73.

Haring, Kristen. *Ham Radio's Technical Culture*. Cambridge, Mass.: MIT Press, 2007.

Hinz, Ben, and Louise Hinz. Dwarfcraft Devices. http://www.dwarfcraft.com/.

Horowitz, Paul, Winfield Hill, and Thomas C. Hayes. *The Art of Electronics*. Vol. 2. Cambridge: Cambridge University Press, 1989.

Kelly, Caleb. *Cracked Media: The Sound of Malfunction*. Cambridge, Mass.: MIT Press, 2009.

Langford-Smith, Fritz. *Radiotron Designer's Handbook*. 4th ed. Sydney, Australia: The Wireless Press, 1953.

McSwain, Rebecca. "The Social Reconstruction of a Reverse Salient in Electrical Guitar Technologies: Noise, the Solid Body, and Jimi Hendrix." In *Music and Technology in the Twentieth Century*, ed. Hans-Joachim Braun, 186-198. Baltimore: Johns Hopkins University Press, 2002.

Novak, Daniel. *Japanoise: Music at the Edge of Circulation*. Durham, N.C.: Duke University Press, 2013.

Pinch, Trevor J., and Trocco, Frank. *Analog Days: The Invention and Impact of the Moog Synthesizer*. Cambridge, Mass.: Harvard University Press, 2009.

Rodgers, Tara. *Pink Noises: Women on Electronic Music and Sound*. Durham, N.C.: Duke University Press, 2010.

Rovan, Joseph Butch. "Living on the Edge: Alternate Controllers and the Obstinate Interface." In *Mapping Landscapes for Performance as Research: Scholarly Acts and Creative Cartographies,* ed. Shannon Rose Riley and Lynette Hunter, 252–59. New York: Palgrave Macmillan, 2009.

Rylan, Jessica, et al. Flower Electronics. http://www.flowerelectronics.com/.

Teboul, Ezra. "Silicon Luthiers: Contemporary Practices in Electronic Music Hardware." Master's thesis, Dartmouth College, 2015.

Tudor, David. *Neural Synthesis Nos. 6-9*. New York: Lovely Music, 1995.

PART III ][ *Chapter 20*

# Glitch Console

NINA BELOJEVIC

Glitch Console is a hacked or "circuit-bent" Nintendo Entertainment System that links the consumer culture of video game platforms to issues of labor, exploitation, and the environment. Player experience is interrupted by various types of glitches, which dramatically affect and "haunt" game play without crashing the system itself. Circuit bending, or the practice of serendipitously modifying the behavior of electronics by soldering new connection points on a circuit board, also encourages a creative, hands-on approach to media theory and platform studies. For both the player and the artist/hacker, the Glitch Console directs attention to materials and operations.

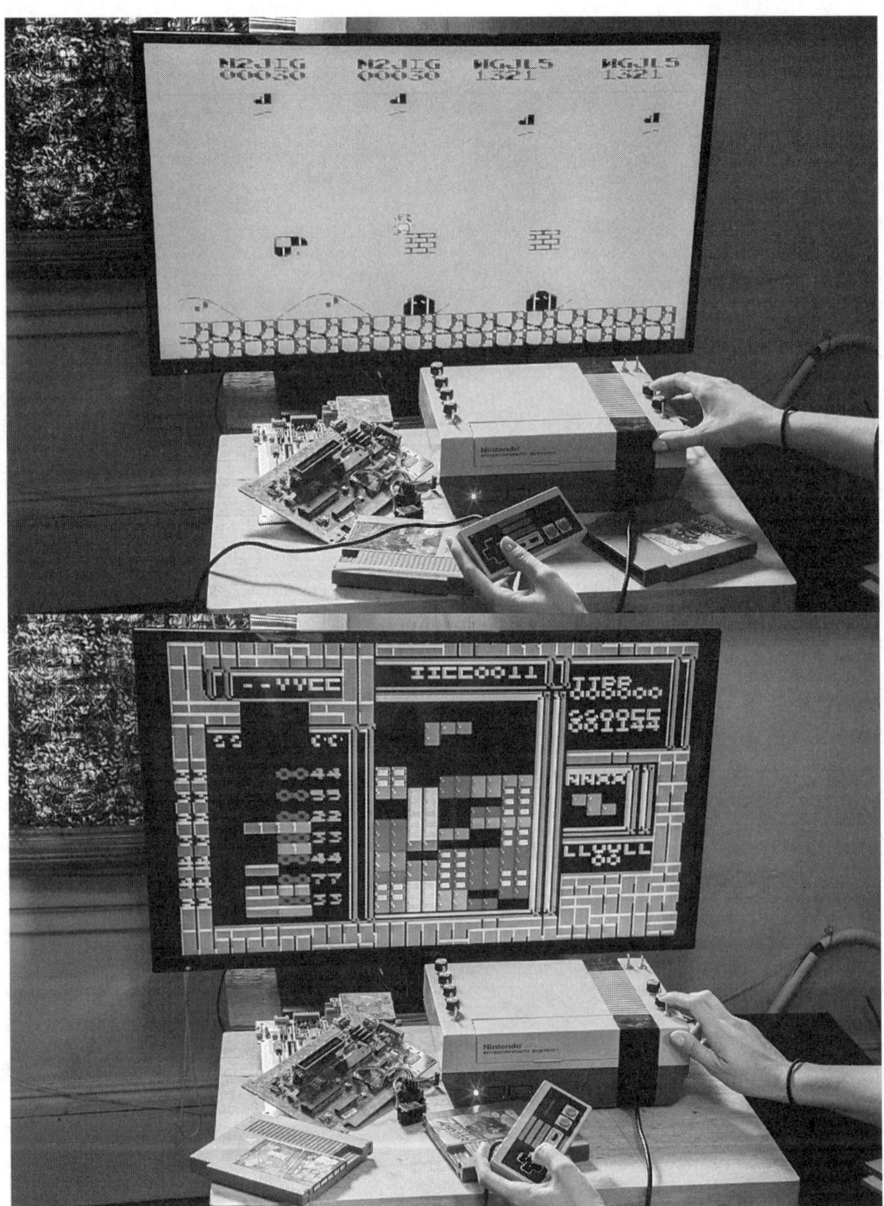


**Figure 20.1.** Glitch Console. Format: Hacked video game console. Materials: Nintendo Entertainment System, game cartridges, soldering iron, and various electronic components. Nina Belojevic. Photograph by Rhoderick Lising.

# Creative Curating: The Digital Archive as Argument

JOANNE BERNARDI AND NORA DIMMOCK

*Re-Envisioning Japan: Japan as Destination in 20th Century Visual and Material Culture* (*REJ*) conjoins a collaboratively built digital environment with the physical, personal collection of travel, tourism, and educational ephemera from which it evolved (Bernardi). Documenting changing images of Japan and its place in the world in the early to mid-twentieth century, the digital archive is comprised of artifacts but is in itself an artifact, a creatively curated representation of representations. Digital environments enable us to see things differently, and, as *REJ*'s title suggests, the project capitalizes on this virtue. Its direction has been shaped by the convergence between innovative scholarship in material culture studies and digital humanities (DH), giving it purpose as a recuperative project grounded in a uniquely syncretic relationship between material and digital worlds. History is not exclusively embedded in words; objects also resonate with historical voice, and digital space allows the objects in the *REJ* collection to resonate in ways that are not easily contained by the written word alone. The project's focus on the material remains of the past offers opportunities to rethink large historical processes through the careful consideration of seemingly trivial objects, uncover and explore past lives and individual interactions, and test assumptions about the present by interrogating the past.

*REJ* depends on collaboration between the authors. As a professor of Japanese and Film and Media Studies at the University of Rochester (Joanne Bernardi) and director of the university's Digital Humanities Center (Nora Dimmock), we each bring different perspectives, experience, and areas of expertise to the project, shaping it in ways that challenge conventional modes of scholarly communication and knowledge production. *REJ* is about making—making a physical collection of objects, a critical digital archive, and a new perspective on the past through digital scholarship. Collaboration challenges us to question the conventional definitions of our disciplinary domains, humanities scholarship, and librarianship, forcing us to negotiate not only the unique narratives that historical objects carry but also the traditional structures created to categorize and contain them.

The core *REJ* team includes two staff members of the Digital Humanities Center who specialize in digital imaging and programming. They have been involved in *REJ* since it became a collaborative project in 2011. In addition, undergraduate and graduate students, a postdoctoral fellow specializing in metadata curation for visual and material culture, and other library staff members have contributed to the project in important ways.[1] Together we have worked toward building a digital site that embodies scholarship and functions as a versatile pedagogical and research tool, facilitating access to and analysis of a unique collection of primary sources. Expanding into digital space has allowed us to experiment with different ways to present the collection's wide variety of media in order to best accommodate a diversity of formats. These media range from postcards, photographs, stereographs, and glass lantern slides to travel brochures, guidebooks, sheet music, and small-gauge films.

*REJ* seems to confirm Peter N. Miller's (2014) observation in "How Objects Speak" that "the digital, far from killing the material world, seems only to have intensified our attachment to it." The complementary process of creating the best possible digital copies for each medium and object and designing the most effective digital environment for their presentation is contingent upon interaction between the digital and physical worlds. The ongoing process of building the *REJ* digital archive has made us more sensitive to how objects inform us of the past, and how digital tools can intercede to make that awareness immediate and deep. Online collections like *REJ* invite us to interrogate enduring and dominant historical narratives. As Miller notes, these narratives have become abstracted over time, detached from earlier practices that interpreted the past through the world of things. *REJ* gives us access to the world of tangible things marked by traces of human touch, opening up possibilities to comprehend life in twentieth-century Japan on a granular level through narratives of personal use and encounters embodied by everyday objects. Due to the flexibility and scale of the digital environment, we can also look for patterns and relationships that add nuance to our understanding of the encounters between diverse cultures and societies over time (Manovich).

In this chapter we focus on our effort to move beyond creating a digital presence for ephemeral objects toward redefining the digital archive as critical scholarship. The first section, "The Physical Archive," describes *REJ*'s genesis as object-based research through the creation of a personal research and teaching collection of ephemeral objects. *REJ*'s early development helped establish the Digital Humanities Center's digitization program. The second section, "The Digital Archive," details the correlation between the project's expansion into a digital space and the development of new practices for incorporating a wide range of material culture objects into digital scholarship. In the third and final section, "The Archive as Matter," we outline plans for *REJ*'s future.

### *The Physical Archive*

*REJ* was motivated by Joanne Bernardi's previous research on silent Japanese cinema in the context of the country's rapid-fire cultural transformations during the first decades of the twentieth century. Her engagement with visual images lost to time led to a preoccupation with the relationship between objects and history: how material loss affects the history-making process, the role of objects and images in forging global connections, and the relationship between material culture (as discrete physical artifacts and historical evidence) and the written word as historical narrative. The *REJ* collection began in 2000 with her search for photographic images of early twentieth-century Japan that could bring the landscape and life of that period into sharper focus.[2] She sought out images of Japan that could complement her familiarity with early and silent films from Europe, the United States, and (to a much lesser extent) other parts of the world, providing a better understanding of Japan's place in that world. She was not looking for photographic images in books—"disembodied" photographic images as illustrations—but rather photographs as objects, "time-bound physical artifacts" (Sandweiss), like moving images themselves.

The Internet's unprecedented capacity to facilitate access to a wide range of material culture on a massive scale was key to the development of this project. Postcards from the 1900s–30s that were readily available through online auctions seeded the physical collection. Bernardi was initially drawn to postcards as visual records of place, especially the urban landscapes more likely to have been captured on film. She soon came to appreciate the many other ways that postcards connect us to the past: as traces of relationships, such as picture postcard exchanges between pen pals or missives that were often deeply personal; as visual records of Japan's presence at world's fairs and expositions in Europe and America; and as glimpses of Japan's rising profile in the international world order ("Our Allies" and "Flags of All Nations"). She even discovered images of a surprising number of imaginary Japans, such as the Japanese Village in Massachusetts (Wonderland Amusement Park at Revere Beach), described in a caption as a "15 minute tour of the Flowery Kingdom," complete with its own "Mt. Geisha."

Writing about the complicated origins of the early travel film genre, Tom Gunning (2006) describes turn-of-the-century and early twentieth-century travel and its relationship to travel imagery as "a means of appropriating the world through images," noting the role postcards played in this phenomenon (27). The nature of postcards as embodiments of image and movement (travel by people and the circulation of things) as well as evidence of place helped determine *REJ*'s focus on objects belonging to broadly defined categories. The contours of the collection's conceptual, chronological, and generic parameters were refined with less interest in superlative collecting than in exploring the range and variety of ephemeral objects encountered, salvaged, and offered for sale from the "infinite archive of the past."[3]

Travel- and education-related objects form the bulk of the collection and fall into working categories that complement each other in useful ways.[4] "Tourist Japan" was an early title for the project, linking the virtual armchair traveler reading about Japan with tourists moving through physical space. The words "tourist" and "tourism" can denote passive consumers and mindless consumption, but they can also be flexible and inclusive. The rise of twentieth-century tourism is central to understanding twentieth-century cultural flow and identity; the tourist perspective is personal, allowing for a multiplicity of narrative perspectives.[5]

Each encounter with a used object brought the past into sharper focus through the material evidence of personal experience. Victoria Kelley (2015) describes objects looked at from this perspective as "bearers of trace, scarred with the markers of time and use" (Kelley). When postcards issued by Japanese and U.S. shipping companies led to the discovery of travel brochures and other tourism ephemera, these things evoked a connection with the past that was stunningly direct. Such artifacts are not just evidence of a particular mode of transportation, travel, and leisure at a specific historical moment. In addition to their evidentiary value, informing us of the cultural, political, and economic systems that produced them, they are immediate links to the people who used them. In fact, the criteria for selecting objects for the *REJ* collection were increasingly determined by an impulse to better understand the people and acts behind the objects, as well as the layered contexts for their production and circulation. A distinction—and a balance—between the particular (the object, the detail, the personal) and the general (the object's historical context, the larger picture, the object in public space) was necessary to maintain a focus on the objects themselves. This distinction and balance were also conducive to teaching and learning.

A productive, reciprocal relationship exists between digital scholarship and pedagogy. "Tourist Japan," a course first designed in 2002 to complement Bernardi's research, fulfills the function of mediating between *REJ*'s personal and public dimensions. This Japanese studies course uses travel and tourism culture to illuminate the relationship between Japan's modernization processes and identity formation. Students work with objects in the *REJ* collection as an alternative approach to understanding twentieth-century Japan and patterns of human interaction and cross-cultural exchange. Haptic appreciation of the *REJ* collection plays a key role in class, as students explore how the meaning of things changes over time and according to context. They learn how material culture both embodies and acts on public and personal biases by curating their own digital exhibits using objects in the collection. Curation becomes an exercise in material culture studies and digitally mediated humanistic inquiry.[6]

Library collaboration, which began in 2011, was motivated by the need to make the *REJ* collection more accessible to students in "Tourist Japan." Nora Dimmock, then head of the Multimedia Center, took on the project of digitizing objects in the *REJ* collection so they could be more easily studied, reused, and re-contextualized by students in the course. She joined the project at a critical turning point. *REJ* almost came to a standstill when it became clear that the draft outline for a book manuscript failed to reflect the project's premise and scope as object-based scholarship. A conventional book format could only accommodate a limited number of illustrations, and the wide range of media and the complex relationships between individual objects would need to be crowbarred into a limited number of chapters. A book format also impeded timely collaboration with researchers working in other disciplines who could enrich the collection's interpretation by studying it from different perspectives. It thus became increasingly evident that digitization and online access facilitating a curated presentation of the collection in a meaningful context would be the best way to share this work.

## *The Digital Archive*

*REJ* and the Digital Humanities Center both began at roughly the same time, each evolving from a need to expand the boundaries of not only physical and virtual space but also traditional modes of scholarly communication. Since their inception, each has been in a constant state of transformation, scaling up slowly based on the availability of human, capital, and intellectual resources. *REJ* and the Digital Humanities Center have yet to reach their full potential, but together they comprise a faculty-library collaboration developing over the course of three distinct phases, with the third and final phase just beginning.

The first phase was all about creating: the collaboration between the library and *REJ*, the website, and the digital project. The collaboration began as an extension of the library's reserves processing program. *REJ* needed a circulation point where students in "Tourist Japan" could access a selection of materials from the collection to complete digital exhibit curation assignments. Like many academic libraries in 2010, only one librarian provided DH support on an ad-hoc basis (Posner 44). As the head of the library's Multimedia Center, Dimmock straddled the fence between providing traditional library services and entering into new collaborations with faculty that might require long-term commitment of staff time and library resources.

In the beginning, digitization was cobbled together because the library had no commitment beyond copying services. The staff produced JPEG copies on inexpensive flatbed scanners at a resolution of 150 dots per inch (DPI) and uploaded them to a website created by central university IT staff. As collection items were dropped off to be scanned, staff stockpiled them to work on later, during lulls in digitizing material for course reserves and special projects. The library lacked formal structures to support digital scholarship during this phase of development. Staff essentially created a program to support the project surreptitiously because it made sense and helped forge new library practices at the same time.

The second phase of the project focused on building a new platform for the digital project as well as a new digital humanities focus in the library. At this time,

Rochester was using digital humanities methods and projects to augment traditional scholarship by adding a lab section to a traditional humanities course. This structure allowed faculty and library collaborations to flourish. *REJ* expanded that model to include support for individual faculty research. Such an expansion required deft negotiation with the library's network and systems administration units for server space for high-quality images and a fresh WordPress install. More important, it emphasized the need for a digitization center for faculty research. At every evolution, *REJ* challenged the status quo in a way that was instrumental to establishing a legitimate digital humanities program, converting the Multimedia Center into the Digital Humanities Center and transforming library practice from knowledge organization to knowledge creation.[7]

In 2013, the development of the current *REJ* WordPress site was constrained by a major factor. The designer/developer assigned to the project was a temporary staff member who could not devote the time needed to fully understand *REJ* as a large-scale, ongoing work of digital scholarship. Grateful for any assistance, we failed to exert sufficient editorial control over the design process, resulting in a trade-off between interface aesthetics and functionality.[8] *REJ*'s overall design is beautiful, but the overly customized WordPress theme is nearly impossible to change. This design makes the archive seem inert, masking its continuous transformation as new resources, objects, and data are added. Another problem with the current platform is its purely visual navigation. Adding metadata to the images would require a manual edit of each image in the interface, a process too cumbersome to manage. The decision to focus solely on the images and not display the metadata was a lost opportunity to place the images in context.

The process of creating the basic architecture for the *REJ* digital archive established a pattern of careful negotiation between the objects in the physical collection, their digital surrogates, and the digital environment developed for them. In addition to the complex connections between individual objects in the *REJ* collection, this negotiation between physical and digital worlds makes the project unique. The online archive's structure was designed from the start to mirror the decisions made while collating, classifying, and cataloging objects in the physical collection. The *REJ* digital archive's five core heterarchical categories (three based on function and two on format) reflect the original taxonomy expressly devised for the *REJ* physical collection. In the WordPress platform, these categories are translated into five galleries ("Edification & Information," "Leisure & Entertainment," "Moving Images," "Postcards," and "Tourism & Travel") that are then divided into subcategories. The result is a *visualization* of the curatorial deliberations that shaped the physical collection. In digital space, taxonomy functions as a powerful rhetorical tool, unmasking the curatorial process of creating the collection as well as its capacity to make meaning. This initial step in building the online archive was a critical point in the project's development as scholarship. We realized a coherent and comprehensive visualization of an abstract conceptual framework that was difficult, if not impossible, to express through words on paper.

*REJ*'s success and the popularity of Rochester's digital humanities lab courses persuaded the library to make a significant investment in DH, funding both new and upgraded staff positions (a GIS Research Specialist, Digital Humanities Programmer, and Digitization Specialist) in spring 2013 and establishing a digitization program in the center. This support was also the result of a shift in institutional priorities from viewing digitization as a supplemental activity offered by staff to recognizing it as a core function of the center's team. The team now had access to a high-resolution camera and copy stand as well as high-quality scanners with the ability to color-correct and produce preservation quality, 600-DPI TIFFs. The digitization workflow for *REJ* transitioned from a low- to high-priority project at the center. The library's commitment also led to more institutional support: a grant funding the inspection, repair, and digitization of 180 small-gauge films in the *REJ* collection. This grant also covered the cost of digitizing 46 specially commissioned live recordings of songs in the sheet music collection.

When we began populating the site in 2014, we made decisions about representation through considerations of interface, display, and materiality. Displaying the collection's wide range of formats to best represent physical objects in a two-dimensional environment was challenging. Many team meetings led to discussions about representing material objects and how to incorporate them into *REJ*. We decided to use a page-turning app, for example, to display sheet music and other multi-page publications. Postcard fronts and backs are scanned separately and then stitched together so both sides can be displayed simultaneously. We also incorporated light box features that allow people to zoom in on individual images. The films are a unique feature, and we have recuperated, repaired, and digitized 180 titles so far. They represent critical intersections between small-gauge film, tourism, and education through the 1970s. We categorized them by gauge in the main navigation scheme, but they are accessible within each of these subcategories on a custom-built timeline, allowing people to search for them according to their date of creation.

At some point during this work we realized the digitization workflow was driving the design, just as the original WordPress platform drove the site architecture. Our focus was on creating a critical mass so that we could determine the digital archive's capabilities. We were moving from one format to another in an attempt to fill out the archive's framework, which we could then use to demonstrate and discover how researchers and scholars might use the digital environment and its materials.[9] We were looking to the archive itself to give us a better understanding of its potential as digital scholarship. The archive evolved through a process of repeatedly asking ourselves what we wanted it to achieve. In this respect, its design was analogous to that of any artifact created through problem definition (a perceived gap in knowledge) and the iterative exploration of possibilities to solve that problem in the best possible way (Ulrich). In the early stages of our collaboration, we considered the online space to be a "digital component" of a "twin project" also involving a scholarly monograph. In hindsight, this approach was problematic. The implication that a digital entity cannot stand alone as scholarship hobbled *REJ*'s development at the intersection of material culture studies and digital humanities practice. Digital mediation initially facilitated access, investigation, instruction, and interpretation by others, but it was also a catalyst for meaning-making. Curation in digital space made the relationships between individual objects more obvious, revealing new possibilities for research and opportunities to rethink familiar questions. All collections excite us with their promise of discovery; online digital collections like *REJ* do so with unprecedented immediacy.

### *The Archive as Matter*

*REJ* is now entering its third phase of development as a digital archive. This phase could be characterized as re-envisioning *REJ*. One challenge before us is how to position the project to contribute to the larger global research ecosystem defined by projects such as the Digital Public Library of America (DPLA) and the Advanced Research Consortium's catalogue. These projects represent the second generation of federated digital collections. First-generation projects start with databases, which ingest digital assets for discovery through a common web interface. Second-generation projects like DPLA start with metadata, which is aggregated across multiple databases and then accessed through a search interface that points to assets stewarded by individual memory institutions. The metadata for *REJ* exists, but it is not attached to each digital asset. With second-generation discovery in mind, we plan to migrate *REJ* to the Omeka content management platform. Omeka is built on a robust and extensible metadata-driven framework and offers several advantages over the current WordPress architecture. During this third phase, our focus will be on exposing the scholarship inherent in the curatorial process and developing the technology with a critical lens.

The *REJ* physical collection contains about 3,500 artifacts of material culture, and roughly 75 percent of it has been digitized and made available online. As we transition the digital archive to Omeka, stewardship of the physical collection will transition to the library's Department of Rare Books and Special Collections. This transition will facilitate enhanced metadata, make the physical collection more accessible, and guarantee its preservation. In contrast to the *REJ* physical collection, the *REJ* digital archive is still young. Its life as scholarship has only begun. At this transitional moment, we need to regroup and reconsider the digital archive's ostensible future and its shelf life—where it might be in 20 or 30 years.

Carole L. Palmer's (2004) concept of the thematic research collection, which she describes as "specialized scholarly resources built for research support," is a useful way to think of the *REJ* digital archive as we further develop it. *REJ*'s digital environment has many of the key attributes that Palmer identifies: it is electronic, "extensive but thematically coherent," "structured but open-ended" (growing the archive's architecture and its functionality is a prime objective), and "anchored" by a "core set of primary sources." Palmer attends to the correspondence between thematic research collections and laboratory (or even collaboratory) settings familiar to the sciences: both contain research material and the tools to work with it. Thus, in both instances "scholarship is embedded in the product and its use." However, much work remains to be done on *REJ* to create what Palmer calls a "contextual mass," which "prioritizes the values and work practices of scholarly communities." Collaboration has been an important objective for us throughout the project, and we are thinking of how to make the digital archive fully interactive, encouraging scholarship through contributions by registered users. We are also thinking of new tools to enhance research capability as well as ways to dynamically present fragile objects and less common media (e.g., film strips and Viewmaster slides). A spatial tool for researchers to create historic travel itineraries and new content based on the enhanced presentation of fragile objects (such as travel guides and maps) are in the works.

In addition to maximizing *REJ*'s scholarly impact by extending it with enriched metadata and contextual mass, we are planning an open-access, web-based publishing platform that will promote multimodal digital scholarship across disciplines. This publishing platform and journal will focus on object-based scholarship and pedagogy. Its working title, *Routes,* is inspired by James Clifford's 1997 eponymous book about the complexities of cultural mobility and cultural encounters in the modern world. In this context, "routes" suggest the circulation of objects, trade, and pathways through collections and websites.[10] The journal's first issue will focus on projects using the *REJ* collection. The fluid, recombinatory capacity of a digital environment complements the exploratory and interpretive methods of inquiry intrinsic to the study of material culture. With digital technology's capacity to enhance engagement with the material world, we hope to encourage reuse of the *REJ* archive and collection as well as a deeper appreciation of the intrinsic link between past lives and our present day.

## NOTES

1. See Bernardi, *Re-Envisioning Japan* (Credits) for a list of the individuals who have contributed to the project since its inception.

2. When she began collecting objects for what was to become the *Re-Envisioning Japan* collection, Bernardi had just completed a book about nonextant films from Japan's silent era. She worked with metatextual and ancillary primary sources (e.g., scenarios, historiographical sources, trade publications, and fan magazines), and in this context surviving photographic images such as frame reproductions and publicity photographs acquired singular resonance.

3. This term is borrowed from Hitchcock's post to the "Voices of the People" online symposium on *The Many-Headed Monster* history blog.

4. The process of devising categories and determining their relationship is described in more detail at *Re-Envisioning Japan*.

5. See, for example, Urry and Larsen's work on the tourist gaze.

6. The syllabus for the current iteration of this course is available at *Re-Envisioning Japan*. An important venue for developing *REJ*, this course has evolved dramatically in correspondence with the project's digital expansion. It is currently taught as a heuristic digital humanities lab in which students digitally and physically interact with the *REJ* digital archive as well as the objects in the collection. It is open (no prerequisites) to both graduate and undergraduate students. Parented by the Department of Modern Languages and Cultures (Japanese and Comparative Literature), it is cross-listed with the Film and Media Studies Program and the Department of English. Students interact with *REJ* objects to author their own Omeka exhibits as windows on Japan's past.

7. See Nowviskie, who has written extensively about how academic libraries and librarians have responded to the need for the academy to accommodate new modes of digital scholarship and knowledge production, referring to covert operations like the University of Rochester's Digital Humanities Center in its early stages as "path[es] to production for scholarly R&D" (53).

8. See Clement, Hagenmaier, and Knies, who assert that working in the digital medium influences editorial practice in a way that forges strong connections between the work of scholars, librarians, and archivists. Effective communication across the boundaries of disciplinary practice is a key factor in determining the success of large-scale digital collaborations like *REJ*.

9. Rhyne supports making a complete collection available online to offer researchers access to a more comprehensive understanding of the subject. This type of thinking also drove the production of images for *REJ*'s digital archive.

10. The authors are grateful to Kyle Parry, 2015–2017 CLIR Postdoctoral Fellow in Data Curation for Visual and Cultural Studies, University of Rochester, for helping us with *REJ*'s redesign and to refine our vision for this journal.

## BIBLIOGRAPHY

Bernardi, Joanne. *Re-Envisioning Japan: Japan as Destination in 20th Century Visual and Material Culture*. Rochester, N.Y.: University of Rochester Digital Scholarship Lab, River Campus Libraries. First Word Press iteration (2013–16): http://humanities.lib.rochester.edu/rej. New Omeka site (2017): https://rej.lib.rochester.edu/.

Clement, Tanya, Wendy Hagenmaier, and Jennie Levine Knies. "Toward a Notion of the Archive of the Future: Impressions of Practice by Librarians, Archivists, and Digital Humanities Scholars." *The Library* 83, no. 2 (2013): 112–30.

Gunning, Tom. "The Whole World within Reach: Travel Images without Borders." In *Virtual Voyages: Cinema and Travel*, ed. Jeffrey Ruoff, 25–41. Durham, N.C.: Duke University Press, 2006.

Hitchcock, Tim. "Sources, Empathy and Politics in History from Below." *Voices of the People,* July 15, 2015. http://manyheadedmonster.wordpress.com.

Kelley, Victoria. "Time, Wear and Maintenance: The Afterlife of Things," chapter 16 in *Writing Material Culture*, ed. Anne Gerritsen and Giorgio Riello. London: Bloomsbury, 2015.

Manovich, Lev. "How to Compare One Million Images?" Author's blog. http://manovich.net/index.php/projects/how-to-compare.

Miller, Peter N. "How Objects Speak." *The Chronicle of Higher Education,* August 11, 2014. http://chronicle.com/article/How-Objects-Speak/148177.

Nowviskie, Bethany. "Skunks in the Library: A Path to Production for Scholarly R&D." *Journal of Library Administration* 53, no. 1 (2013): 53–66.

Palmer, Carole L. "Thematic Research Collections." In *A Companion to Digital Humanities,* ed. Susan Schreibman, Ray Siemens, and John Unsworth. Oxford: Blackwell, 2004. http://www.digitalhumanities.org/companion.

Posner, Miriam. "No Half Measures: Overcoming Common Challenges to Doing Digital Humanities in the Library." *Journal of Library Administration* 53, no. 1 (2013): 43–52.

Rhyne, Charles S. "Images as Evidence in Art History and Related Disciplines." In *MW97: Museums and the Web 1997*. May 2, 2007. www.museumsandtheweb.com/mw97/speak/rhyneint.html.

Sandweiss, Martha A. "Artifacts as Pixels, Pixels as Artifacts: Working with Photographs in the Digital Age." *Perspectives on History* (November 2013). https://www.historians.org/publications-and-directories/perspectives-on-history/.

Ulrich, Karl. *Design: Creation of Artifacts in Society.* Philadelphia, Pa.: University of Pennsylvania Press, 2005–2011.

Urry, John, and Jonas Larsen. *The Tourist Gaze 3.0*. London: Sage, 2011.

# Reading Series Matter: Performing the SpokenWeb Project

LEE HANNIGAN, AURELIO MEZA, AND ALEXANDER FLAMENCO

When poets participate in the formal mechanism known as the poetry reading, sometimes embedded within the larger context of a reading series, they also participate in and sometimes break social and literary conventions. A similar break occurs when digital tools are used to record what was intended to be ephemeral. Consider a poetry reading series that took place at Sir George Williams University (now Concordia University) in Montreal between 1966 and 1974. This series, simply referred to as "the Poetry Series," was recorded on 65 reel-to-reel tapes, containing over one hundred hours of audio and featuring some of North America's most influential schools of postmodern poetry, including work by members of the Beats, Black Mountain, New York School, San Francisco Renaissance, and TISH, a Canadian poetry collective. In 1999, 25 years after the series ended, these tapes were discovered in an English Department Chair's office at Concordia University; they were then deposited in the university archive, and by 2013 they were digitized, transcribed, and re-presented, or *un*-archived, online at spokenweb.ca, a Social Sciences and Humanities Research Council-funded research project that explores methods of scholarly engagement with literary sound recordings.

SpokenWeb uses the robustness of new media to uncover and investigate the lost genealogy of a poetry reading series and its place within the larger history of institutional literary events. This investigation considers the effects of recording technology on cultural production since the 1950s, when magnetic tape devices were popularized in Canadian universities. The Poetry Series tapes are a case study for scholarly speculation on the influence of new media in literary studies, on the importance of embodied voice and materiality, and for discussing concepts such as "paraphonotext" (Filreis 2015), "performance" (Taylor 2003), and "archival effect" (Manoff 386)[1] as they relate to poetry and literature. Digital archive projects such as PennSound, the Walt Whitman Archive, UbuWeb, Slought Foundation, the Emily Dickinson Archive, and SpokenWeb are examples of how digital content management systems allow mixed media to be consolidated and presented to facilitate the exploration of cultural material that exists at the periphery of the digital world. SpokenWeb uses its corpus to raise questions about the nature of poetry performance, or what Charles Bernstein (2009) calls the "ghostly presence" of disembodied voices (962), and the effects generated when documentary residues of a reading series reenter public space.

In this chapter, we detach from a (phono)textual-centric perspective and approach SpokenWeb as a digital venue for exploring the implications of, in Jason Camlot and Darren Wershler's (2015) terms, "making the reading series discernible." Through digitization, SpokenWeb transformed the Poetry Series from a collection of archival documents lacking both metadata and historical transparency to a properly contextualized moment in Canadian literary history. As the Poetry Series tapes demonstrate, the contexts and concepts that surround archival documents require a space outside the archive itself—a space where they can be re-presented not just as archival documents but as a comprehensive collection of literary recordings that depend on digital technologies for narration and circulation as much now as they depended on analog technologies for their original production in the 1960s and 70s. While analog media such as print or magnetic tape are transparent and accessible in their own way (as material objects with unique relationships to the technologies that produced them), digitization creates connections within the complex network of institutions and desires that make media meaningful. Just as analog technology made the Poetry Series tapes possible between 1966 and 1974, digital technology and educational institutions allow us to return to the past anew in the twenty-first century.

Since 2013, SpokenWeb has organized two conferences and three reading events that used the Poetry Series tapes to explore methods for engaging with recorded sound. Two key terms for approaching these critical performances are "un-archiving" and "re-presentation" (Camlot and McLeod).[2] "Re-presentation" refers to the retrieval, remediation, contextualization, and dissemination of archival materials. Closely related, "un-archiving" makes analog material discernible as both an object of study and an accessible audio file. These terms contribute to what Camlot and Wershler call "the development of new critical methods and vocabularies, new tools, and new modes of presenting and disseminating knowledge." The Poetry Series tapes are objects of scholarly study because they are preserved in different media formats (e.g., magnetic tape, WAV, and MP3), heard, transcribed, uploaded to SoundCloud, tethered to WordPress, and displayed at SpokenWeb. Each of these format migrations and content transformations ushers in another meta-level of transmission and analysis. SpokenWeb responded to these transformations with three critical gestures to examine how the material traces of a poetry reading series are presented and disseminated.

The first gesture is preservation. As Christine Mitchell (2015) notes in her media archaeology of SpokenWeb, the Sir George Williams University (now Concordia) Instructional Media Office (IMO) recorded and stored the Poetry Series readings even though it was not entirely sure how or why the tapes might be used. Because the IMO staff was often concerned more with preservation than usability, the survival and usefulness of the tapes depended on collaborative efforts between records management personnel and humanities scholars. And yet, preservation processes do not necessarily guarantee historical value. Before the SpokenWeb tapes were digitized and transcribed, their content was contextually opaque, preserved in human memory and inert documentary materials—press releases, reviews, photographs, and the analog tapes themselves—housed in the school's archive. This inertia is partly why Camlot, SpokenWeb's principal investigator, referred to the Poetry Series (even after its tapes had been digitized) as "a perfectly useless collection—hundreds of hours of audio that someone would actually have to listen to in order to find out what [was] there" (Filreis, Camlot, and Evans). The matter of utility is of primary importance when approaching this reading series and its recordings, first as materializations of ephemeral performances and then as digital renditions of them. The endeavor to update an analog audio archive into a digital form does not necessarily resolve concerns about usefulness. As Wendy Chun (2008) notes, "Digital media, through the memory at its core, was supposed to solve, if not dissolve, archival problems such as degrading celluloid or scratched vinyl, not create archival problems of its own" (153). So how does SpokenWeb operate as a useful repository, and what are the implications of preserving a so-called ephemeral literary event?

SpokenWeb's second gesture responds to these two questions by resuscitating phonographic or disembodied voices and then studying the consequences (Bernstein 962). While the reel-to-reel tapes extend the series' ephemerality, turning the readings and thus the authors' voices into what Chun calls an "enduring ephemeral," their digitization renders this extension even more accessible. As Marlene Manoff (2010) notes, "Our notions of the past are shaped by our exposure to various selections or packagings of historical artifacts, by hybridized versions of older cultural objects, and by new media that incorporate and frame pieces of the past" (388). SpokenWeb mediates its audience's engagement with the Poetry Series by arranging its content into a media assemblage for discovery online. More important, the project exemplifies how projects like the Poetry Series are useful because they help to qualify and even develop the digital vocabulary of literary scholars who are studying historical materials such as poetry readings in new contexts. As a repository, SpokenWeb is shaped by the instinct to create but likewise exists as a unique cultural artifact that "[describes] and [understands] the new ways in which we experience reality" (386). In fact, SpokenWeb is digital research-creation[3] in its own right, as it produces critically reflexive discourse from what were supposed to be ephemeral events, demonstrating its role—and embodying its third gesture—as a performed archive.

In 2013, SpokenWeb and the Concordia Department of English invited a group of archivists, oral historians, librarians, developers, and literary scholars to participate in a two-day mini-conference called Approaching the Poetry Series. Each participant was asked to present work that explored methodological and/or technical approaches to documentary sound recordings of literary performances. There was, however, a creative/critical constraint: each participant was asked to engage directly with SpokenWeb, integrating specific examples from the Poetry Series to explore ongoing work about, say, avant-garde poetics or the digital re-presentation of literary artifacts. Most of the presentations were developed, peer reviewed, and published in a special issue of *Amodern,* called "The Poetry Series." While the *Amodern* papers focus on the first and second gestures in the genealogy of SpokenWeb, the re-presentations and "new live events" organized in the later stages of the project focus on mediality and the relations between new and old media, forcing audiences of live performances and digital archives to rethink media experience, performance, and the objects through which an archival impulse and narrative continuity are reconciled. Consider an example.

In 2012, George Bowering and David McFadden participated in the inaugural Performing the Spoken Word Archive event, which invited those who read in the Poetry Series to return to Montreal and re-read alongside their former selves. Two years later, in 2014, Daphne Marlatt and Diane Wakoski were featured in the second installment. And in 2015, as part of the Can Lit Across Media conference, a "recording party" was hosted in Concordia University's de Sève Cinema. Billed as All the Poets in Town, the party featured over 30 readings, mostly by Montreal poets, of single poems, each no longer than three minutes. After informing the audience of these constraints, Camlot gave a disclaimer during his opening remarks: the de Sève Cinema had been wired. Microphones were onstage, directed toward the audience as well as the readers, placed throughout the theatre, and installed on the building's exterior to pick up some sounds of Montreal's Grand Prix Weekend. This self-reflexive gesture encouraged audience members to think of the event as both a display of poetic virtuosity and a poetry reading *about poetry readings*. By inviting "all the poets in town" to give brief readings, the event directed attention away from a unidirectional exchange between speaker and listener (common to many poetry readings) and toward the event's convivial nature (the idea of forming a community around poetry's oral and aural dimensions). By installing microphones in unusual places, such as in the audience and outside the building, the event worked to "make audible" or give discernible presence to aspects of the poetry reading, such as sounds of the audience and venue, that tend to be neglected. These sounds are so often captured accidentally, at the edge of a microphone's range. Audio-acoustic technicians monitored and recorded the event from a sound booth at the back of the cinema so that the tracks could be made available on SpokenWeb for listening, interpretation, mixing, and alteration at a later date. By including the sounds of the audience and venue alongside the poets' and speakers' voices, the All the Poets in Town recording party *performed* the poetry reading as not simply a demonstration of authorship and orality but also a community-forming event within a larger aural context, inherently connected to the space- and time-capture technologies that surround it.

In a similarly critical fashion, the theaters in which the Performing the Spoken Word Archive events took place resembled art exhibitions: documents from the university archive—photographs, newspaper clippings, and posters—were put on display, allowing audience members to move through the space and interact with some of the Poetry Series documentary material. Guests partially assumed the role of archivists, piecing together a moment in literary history. The event also featured listening stations, which gave audience members access to the full versions of the original Bowering and McFadden and Marlatt and Wakoski readings as well as other Poetry Series recordings, affording even deeper immersion in history. Audience members who wished to share their experiences were given an opportunity to do so: "Inspired by the community memory clinics organized by the Centre d'histoire de Montréal, SpokenWeb designed a 'memory booth' and set it up at the back of the project's public events to record the thoughts, stories and remembered experiences of audience members" (Clarkson and High). By allowing audience members to record their experiences—by giving them their own "venue" for hearing—the Performing the Spoken Word Archive events retrieve audience members, if only in part, from the passive interlocutory role often assumed in exchanges between speaker and audience. As they incorporate digital re-presentations of archival documentary material into new live events, audience members are forced to reconsider their understanding of what it means to collectively gather and listen to poetry performance.

Not only did the Performing the Spoken Word Archive events invite and at times force their participants to rethink and reengage with poetry performance, the act of preserving spoken performances, environmental sounds, individual reactions, and prerecorded materials through various media also underscored the relationship between text and spoken word. The recording parties and performances showcased and further contributed to building comprehensive collections of audio that prompted their participants to conceptualize text as something less tangible than a written document. True, this audio could not exist without the technology that preserves, replays, and consequently solidifies it by virtue of its medium. Still, the content is foremost the substance of vocal expression, which is inherently fleeting. The recording parties and performances thus enabled their participants to reflect on aural documents and consider the position in which they existed as participants who were actively contributing to the production and reproduction of text, and ultimately making traces for future examination, provided anyone is willing to listen.

Marlatt, Wakoski, Bowering, and McFadden all commented on how uncanny it was to recite poetry alongside their former voices.[4] They laughed and showed signs of embarrassment and nostalgia, sometimes cringing at the ghostly recitations of their past selves, as though their sense of individuality were being folded in time. Both poet and audience witnessed the illusory closing of a temporal gap, as if the recorded voices were emitting from physical bodies. And yet, the grainy textures of the recorded voices reminded everyone of discontinuity. Poet and audience experienced time-axis manipulation—the same experience ushered in at the start of the twentieth century by the very electromechanical media that made playback and editing possible. Similarly, the All the Poets in Town recording party encouraged both poets and audience members to question the place of media in literary studies.

Poetry readings will continue to be performed and preserved in different ways, and the media formats through which these events are preserved and disseminated will continue to call attention to how robust new media actually is. In light of digital media's inherent instability, how enduring databases will prove to be is at best unclear. Nevertheless, each time the SpokenWeb recordings are re-presented as part of an event such as an academic conference or a poetry happening, both the poetry reading and its interpretation become self-conscious, self-referential, and self-reflexive activities. To think about the implications of re-presenting a literary reading series, the SpokenWeb project—using a defined collection of literary sound recordings—experiments with the possibilities of poetry performance in the wake of digital sound studies, and in doing so establishes a critical discourse about a very particular literary phenomenon: poetry readings and the larger series of which they are often a part. As Camlot and Wershler observe, "The data of the poetry series can be approached up close and at a distance . . . [T]he aggregation of data from multiple, historically parallel reading series . . . may prove to provide a complimentary macro-analysis of the data, a potentially informative mode of 'Distant Listening.'" The genealogies of poetry readings and reading series are areas of research that have been underheard, underaddressed, underrepresented, and underperformed in literary scholarship. This, however, is beginning to change, as processes of uncovering, un-archiving, and digitally re-presenting archival material are helping to stitch together important pieces of cultural fabric.

## NOTES

1. We prefer the term "performance" over "reading" in light of the many ways in which poetry can be performed and understood, and in reference to what Diana Taylor refers to as "vital acts of transfer, transmitting social knowledge, memory, and a sense of identity through reiterated, or what Richard Schechner has called 'twice-behaved behavior'" (2–3). This "twice-behaved behavior" can be the reading of a poem or the starting point for other forms of embodied art, such as dancing, theater, happenings, and so on.

2. We understand these two terms as they were used in this two-day conference, which sought to examine "the complex ways in which media records and re-presents literary events."

3. For a discussion on the history and polity behind the term "research-creation," see Manning and Massumi 84–89.

4. A comprehensive collection of these and other oral-history interviews can be heard at http://spokenweb.concordia.ca/oral-literary-history.

## BIBLIOGRAPHY


Bernstein, Charles. "Making Audio Visible: The Lessons of Visual Language for the Textualization of Sound." *Textual Practice* 23, no. 6 (2009): 959–73.

Camlot, Jason, and Darren Wershler. "Theses on Discerning the Reading Series." *Amodern 4: The Poetry Series* (2015). http://amodern.net/article/theses-reading-series.

Camlot, Jason, and Katherine McLeod. "Can Lit Across Media: Un-Archiving the Canadian Literary Event." Conference promotional poster, January 19, 2015. http://spokenweb.ca/blog/cfp-can-lit-across-media-un-archiving-temporal-literary-event.

Chun, Wendy Hui Kyong. "The Enduring Ephemeral, or the Future Is a Memory." *Critical Inquiry* 35 (2008): 148–71.

Clarkson, Ashley, and Steven High. "Playing with Time: Oral History and Literary Studies in the SpokenWeb Project." *Amodern 4: The Poetry Series* (2015). http://amodern.net/article/playing-time.

Emily Dickinson Archive. http://www.edickinson.org/.

Filreis, Al. "Notes on Paraphonotextuality." *Amodern 4: The Poetry Series* (2015). http://amodern.net/article/paraphonotexuality.

Filreis, Al, Jason Camlot, and Steve Evans. "Beyond the Text: Literary Archives in the 21st Century." *Amodern 4: The Poetry Series* (2015). http://amodern.net/article/beyond-text.

Manning, Erin, and Brian Massumi. *Thought in the Act: Passages in the Ecology of Experience.* Minneapolis: University of Minnesota Press, 2014.

Manoff, Marlene. "Archive and Database as Metaphor: Theorizing the Historical Record." *portal: Libraries and the Academy* 10, no. 4 (2010): 385–98.

Mitchell, Christine. "Again the Air Conditioners: Finding Poetry in the Institutional Archive." *Amodern 4: The Poetry Series* (2015). http://amodern.net/article/again-air-conditioners.

PennSound. Charles Bernstein and Al Filreis, eds. University of Pennsylvania. http://writing.upenn.edu/pennsound/.

Slought Foundation. https://slought.org/.

SpokenWeb. Jason Camlot et al., eds. Concordia University. http://spokenweb.ca/.

Taylor, Diana. *The Archive and the Repertoire: Performing Cultural Memory in the Americas.* Durham, N.C.: Duke University Press, 2003.

UbuWeb. http://ubu.com/.

The Walt Whitman Archive. Ed Folsom and Kenneth M. Price, eds. University of Nebraska-Lincoln. http://whitmanarchive.org/.

# Loss Sets

AARON TUCKER, JORDAN SCOTT, TIFFANY CHEUNG, AND NAMIR AHMED

Working with Ryerson University's Digital Media Experience Lab, the Ryerson Geospatial Maps and Data Centre, and the Ryerson Centre for Digital Humanities, the Loss Sets 3-D Poetry Project translates poems co-written by Jordan Scott and Aaron Tucker into sculptures. The poems are first turned into coordinates along the X, Y, and Z axes, after which (under Tucker, Namir Ahmed, and Tiffany Cheung's direction) those points are imported into the 3-D modeling software, Rhino, where the models are rendered with the Grasshopper plug-in. The pieces are further manipulated using information such as latitude, longitude, and spot height from the Columbia Icefields. The poems are originally generated under the theme of "loss," and the icefield data is incorporated with that theme to examine and resist the utopian impulses around 3-D printing "replacing" any object, especially as technologization relates to the natural world. Using these multiple data sets, a sculpture is "carved away" from a six-inch cube, and those results are then printed in 3-D.

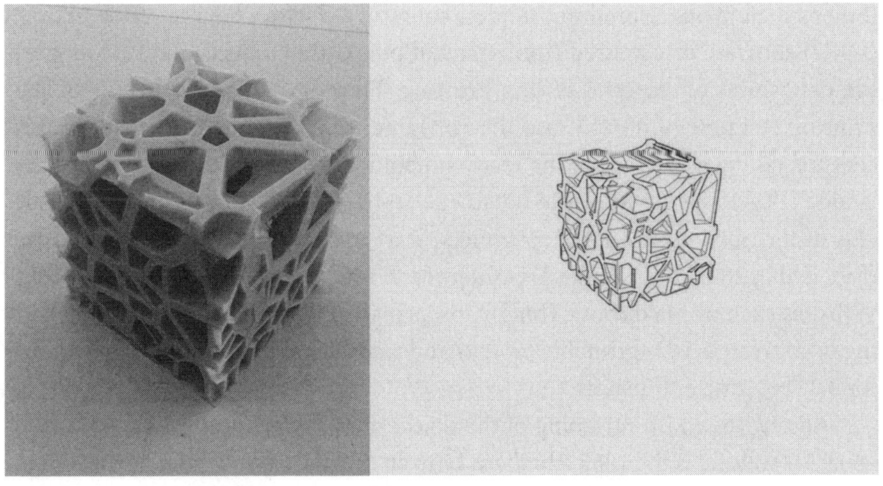

**Figure 23.1.** Loss Sets. Format: 3-D–printed sculptures. Materials: PLA and ABS plastic filament, poetry, and Columbia Icefield data. Aaron Tucker, Jordan Scott, Tiffany Cheung, and Namir Ahmed. Photograph by the artists.

# Dialogic Objects in the Age of 3-D Printing: The Case of the Lincoln Life Mask

SUSAN GARFINKEL

"Smithsonian Now Allows Anyone To 3D Print (Some) Historic Artifacts," declared a headline on the *Forbes Tech* blog page (Mack). "These New 3D Models Put the Smithsonian's Most Renowned Items in Your Hands," explained another, at the website of *Smithsonian Magazine* (Stromberg). Both appeared in November 2013, when a simultaneous press release and conference announced the launch of "Smithsonian X 3D," an initiative to scan significant museum artifacts and turn them into three-dimensional digital models to either view online or download and 3-D–print via a new portal website.[1] "The future has arrived," tweeted Mythbusters host Adam Savage (2013). "Is 3-D a Game Changer?" asked the newsletter of the American Historical Association (Varin).

3-D printing is an additive process whereby deposits of a suitably mutable material—powdered metal, heated plastic, biomatter, or chocolate, for instance—are built up on a platform and solidified layer by layer to create three-dimensional forms. Computer models constructed with computer-aided design (CAD) software or captured from scans of preexisting objects are used to guide the deposition of material during printing. First developed in the 1980s, 3-D printing technology moved into the consumer market early in the twenty-first century, taking advantage of the ready suitability of such thermoplastics as polylactide (PLA) and acrylonitrile butadiene styrene (ABS). Following on the success of the open-source RepRap project, start-ups such as MakerBot Industries (founded in 2009) today sell 3-D printers for home use at prices well under $1000. Websites such as Makerbot's Thingiverse provide convenient platforms for sharing user-created 3-D–printable models and also act as sites of online community for 3-D printing enthusiasts.

Among the most intriguing of the object models to appear on the Smithsonian X 3D website is the 1865 Abraham Lincoln life mask (see Figure 24.1): intriguing because the mask itself is a copy of a copy of a copy, even before it became a 3-D model to be copied via printing yet again; intriguing because it nevertheless so

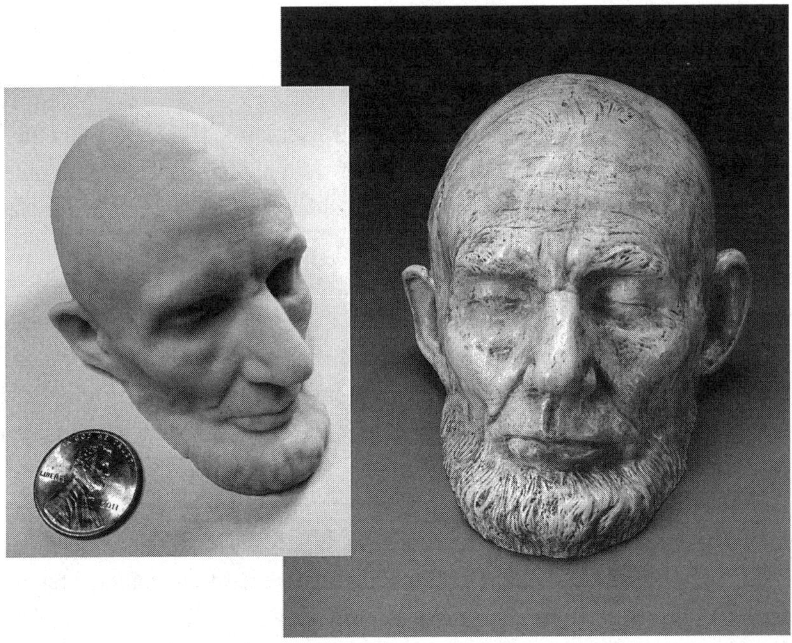

**Figure 24.1.** Left: Reduced-size 3-D print of Smithsonian X 3D "Lincoln Life Mask (Mills)" print-ready model (photo: Author); Right: Clark Mills, Abraham Lincoln life mask, c. 1917 cast after 1865 original. National Portrait Gallery, Smithsonian Institution (photo: Smithsonian).

powerfully retains a sense of presence, of aura—of Lincoln—through its multiple transformations. Unlike the earlier 1860 Lincoln life mask, taken before his election as president (and also provided at Smithsonian X 3D), this second mask embodies the visage of a poignantly burdened national leader at the end of a long and divisive Civil War. "It is impossible to look at this cast of Lincoln's face—gaunt and careworn—and not think that it is a death mask," write its caretakers (Smithsonian X 3D, "Introduction"). Indeed, taken less than two months before his nation-wrenching assassination, this later likeness timelessly foreshadows yet fully inhabits the universalizing tragedy of Lincoln's lost life.

The Smithsonian's curators seem to struggle with terminology as they seek to explain the life mask's derivative physical nature yet palpable psychic presence. The manner of its creation by sculptor Clark Mills is detailed clearly enough under the heading "Process" in a website section devoted to a "Tour" of the object:

> It is thought that Mills cast the original [1865] mask at the White House using a process that involved greasing the president's whiskers and applying oil over his face . . . Mills then spread a thin coat of plaster paste over Lincoln's face, leaving open only a small space under the nostrils so the president could breathe. The plaster dried in only fifteen minutes. Mills asked Lincoln to twitch his facial muscles until the mask broke into pieces and fell into a towel that Mills

> held. The pieces were then reassembled to form the finished mask. (Smithsonian X 3D, "Process")

Yet the object that has been scanned for Smithsonian X 3D is not in fact the "finished mask" just described—which, if made of the original pieces reassembled would create a negative space, a mold, of the president's face, its operative surface facing inward.

Confusingly for the curators' prose, the terms "life mask" and "death mask" typically refer to a solid casting made after the fact from an original hollow mold of the face—and the curators have left out the step where that casting of the mold was completed. Plus, the object that was scanned for the Smithsonian's 3-D model is also several generations and several decades removed from any actual plaster that touched Lincoln's face: the Smithsonian's "1865" life mask is a later plaster copy of a plaster impression taken from Mills's original mold. As detailed on the "Provenance" page of the "Tour," at the death of Clark Mills in 1883, the original 1865 life mask was given by Mills's son to Lincoln's former private secretary, after which time multiple copies were made from it in both plaster and bronze. Soon after, Mills's son also presented a plaster copy created from the original to the Smithsonian. *This* cast—meaning the scanned one—the curators explain, "was created in 1917 from the original mask that was given to the Smithsonian Institution in 1889" (Smithsonian X 3D, "Provenance"). In order to create the 1917 copy, of course, another here-unmentioned intermediate mold would also have been made. Face becomes mold becomes imprint becomes mold becomes imprint—and then becomes a scanned 3-D model, download, and print, circa 2015. All but Lincoln's face itself are copies.[2]

Even more than they struggle with the terminology of process, the Smithsonian's curators struggle to contain the mask's aura with their language. They title one section of the tour "A Window into Lincoln's Thoughts" with no explanation for how such direct revelation might operate. Under a subsequent heading, "Devotion to the Cause," they observe that "as Lincoln looks out, frozen in time with hollowed cheeks and with every line and wrinkle on his face recorded, we cannot help but think about the enormity of the challenge he had faced" (Smithsonian X 3D, "Devotion to a Cause"). In fact—and not surprisingly given the process of creation they have depicted—it is clear when viewing the mask that Lincoln's eyes are fully *closed*. The curators' wording is a literal mistake but less so an affective one: despite its closed eyes, the life mask seems to open wide to us some fundamental Lincoln-ness, viscerally other, but also eminently humane, exposing him to us while simultaneously hiding him behind the visage of our own interpretations. It both defies context and cannot exist without it.

I offer these details to explain the curators' conundrum, for even at this remove we still read the life mask as Lincoln, not a mask. Though derivative, it does not hide its subject: the mask reveals what it represents. The 3-D–enabled viewer on the Smithsonian's website enhances this conflation of mask and Lincoln, allowing us to virtually *touch* and turn and move the pixel projection that simulates its form. Likewise, this transformed object-formation still always emerges as Lincoln when we produce it on 3-D printers, either reduced in size or at scale (Figure 24.1), and hold a newly made copy derived of these many other copies in our hands. What confounds us, perhaps, is the strangeness of the thing that is a life mask in our age when such morbidly sentimental objects are odd or novel. It is the intimacy of touch: as we use our hands to rotate the virtual model so, too, do we heft this chunk of printed plastic, incongruously perceiving through our fingertips *this* thing to have touched Lincoln's face. Like the contents of Lincoln's pockets surviving at the Library of Congress, this vestige of his once-embodied humanness evokes utter fascination.[3] So like and yet different from the ubiquitous copper pennies and five-dollar bills that render Lincoln's face a tokenized and omnipresent memorial, the life mask and its copies are tangible in a startlingly intimate way.

Search Flickr, Twitter, or even Facebook, and you will find user photographs of 3-D prints of the Smithsonian's 1865 Lincoln life mask model. Often they are white like plaster, though brightly colored hues are almost as common. Sometimes they are full-sized, though more frequently they are reduced to just a few inches wide. Sometimes you can see the parallel contours of an imperfect 3-D–printing process overwhelming Lincoln's likeness. Often, the image posted deliberately foregrounds some feature of the model's nascent physicality: the 3-D print is still in process, the newly finished object is held in a hand or posed with a coin beside it for scale. Sometimes there are modifications: over at Thingiverse, a user has turned the original Smithsonian model into a Christmas ornament by adding a loop to the top of its head (UndeadManatee). This is not to suggest that the life mask was not evocative, even transformative, before it was published as a printable 3-D model in November 2013, nor that 3-D–printed copies are either more, or less, authentic than other copies made by more traditional means. Instead, the life mask's widely shared digitization, coupled with the ready option to create a new instance of a known-to-be-singular original, opens up a heterogeneous process to more makers, more viewers, more iterations, and more contexts: the possibilities transcend what is probable.

The Lincoln life mask example is exceptional, of course—except when it isn't. The 3-D capture, modeling, sharing, downloading, and printing of even the most mundane physical object constitutes a process at once specific yet far-reaching in its capacity: a discursive, performative, and dialogic one. In his formative analysis of literary genres, theorist Mikhail Bakhtin (1981) explores the multiply elastic environment of language, arguing that language in use is always dialogic, residing as it does in a complex swirl of contexts. Any meaning-in-the-moment is embedded in and overlaid with a rich array of its prior and emergent meanings, both consonant and contradictory. "No living word," writes Bakhtin, "relates to its object in a *singular* way" (276). Rather, he argues, the object in context "is entangled, shot through with shared thoughts, points of view, alien value judgments and accents," which are built on both "the inexhaustible wealth and contradictory multiplicity of the object itself" and "the socially heteroglot multiplicity of its names, definitions and value judgments" as invoked in prior usage (276, 278). Language, as lived interaction, merely complicates the dialogic object's already abundantly situated meanings.

Material culture scholars such as Bernard L. Herman (1992) have long made a case for a discursive approach to the study of material life: "Because objects occupy multiple contexts through time and perception, their meanings are always multifoliate and fluid. . . . Artifacts, like the totality of expressive culture, are multifunctional in their expressive content with a single object often imbued with an array of potential meanings" (5). As Herman contends, "In the discourse of objects we confront the fact that material culture does not passively reflect cultural process" (5). Given that objects, like language, so routinely exceed their meanings, the term dialogic object as I explore it here is surprisingly underused given its powerful implications. All objects are dialogic, their meanings emergent in the physical and cultural contexts that frame them—just as contexts reciprocally, and recursively, arise through the presence of objects.[4]

The ease with which 3-D–printed copies of cultural artifacts invite us to engage the object's dialogic nature is striking: by virtue of heightened circulation they are ready sites of discourse; moving broadly among and across contexts, they allow for the flexible dissemination, amplification, and re-creation of meanings. They are souvenirs, miniatures, remixes, recreations, memories, and inventions. They are technologically immediate yet affectively timeless, melding the past with the present with the future according to the needs and knowledges of their makers, users, and viewers. Like all objects, they actively constitute culture and its processes. In her intriguing discussion of the vibrancy of matter beyond human agency, political theorist Jane Bennett (2010) coins a phrase: *the thing formerly known as an object*. "Thing-power," she writes, "gestures toward the strange ability of ordinary, man-made items to exceed their status as objects and to manifest traces of independence or aliveness, constituting the outside of our own experience" (xvii). Things defy comprehension because they offer us too little, or too much. From one perspective they confound us because they lack words to define themselves and could seemingly mean anything. From another perspective, they lack words and are therefore not subject to the complications and uncertainties that language invites.[5] Here is Bakhtin's contradictory multiplicity realized in a material frame.

If objects are things in context—physical, cultural, historical, aesthetic—then the 3-D print's trajectory from original artifact to 3-D model to printed copy at once complicates and clarifies the shifting terrains, both physical and meaningful, that all material entities inhabit. Its transformations—of state, form, material, location, environment—especially bring to light the ways all material objects function across time, space, and context. The much-copied Lincoln life mask model compounds this visibility by virtue of its dense web of cultural-historical associations and its manifold replications, but this instance is a difference of scale, not of kind. Thus, while the finished 3-D print resides at a moment of cultural and technological convergence, it is no revelation in its own right. Instead, by foregrounding the dialogic nature of all cultural objects, it becomes a compelling vehicle for the larger exploration of discursive material forms while also imprinting the ethos of our own cultural-historical moment. When we grasp that final 3-D print in our hands, it is a palpable affirmation that all objects are dialogic reinstantiations, ever available to reshape our world.

As Walter Benjamin (1969) so famously indicated, in the age of mechanical reproduction a work of art's authentic aura is at once destroyed and liberated. Thus we know Lincoln through the contours of his life mask even as each 3-D–printed copy fails its test of authenticity. If meaning is emergent in context, made in this moment, and the next one, on and on, there are yet still processes—of mind, of culture, of environment, of physics—that preserve continuities of meaning across each semiotic gap. Objects, in their material thingness, continue to exist over time, which has the effect on us of embodying history: our history, the object's history, the planet's history. Because it is simultaneously discerned anew while also embodying our perceived continuity with the past, the object continuously reinvents itself in its own likeness. The process is not unlike the workings of "invented tradition" identified by Eric Hobsbawm (1983), except our emphasis here is on the invention of continuity rather than the veracity of a particular past. "The souvenir both mourns and celebrates the gap between object and context of origin," writes literary critic Susan Stewart (1984) in her masterful book *On Longing* (164). "The souvenir must be removed from its context in order to serve as a trace of it" (150). In its materiality the 3-D print appeals to and satisfies our nostalgic desire for connection, for authentic experience, yet we do not doubt it is a replica. "We do not need or desire souvenirs of events that are repeatable," Stewart elaborates (135). "Rather, we need and desire souvenirs of events that are reportable . . . through narrative the souvenir substitutes a context of perpetual consumption for its context of origin" (135). Our fascination with the powerful uniqueness of Lincoln is, in this way, earnestly indulged through the easy reproduction of each compelling copy of his likeness. "It is within an exuberant world of copies," suggests Hillel Schwartz (2014), "that we arrive at our experience of originality" (175).

Based in the array of its meaningful contexts, the dialogic object is at once multiple and distinct. In *The Dialogic Imagination* Bakhtin argues that, with the rise of the novel, author and hero newly share a temporal plane "and may enter into dialogic relations and hybrid combinations" with each other as contemporaries (27–28). With "the original formally present author in a zone of contact with the world he is depicting," Bakhtin writes,

> For the first time in artistic-ideological consciousness . . . every event, every phenomenon, every thing, every object of artistic representation loses its completedness, its hopelessly finished quality and its immutability that had been so essential to it in the world of the epic "absolute past" . . . Through contact with

> the present, an object is attracted to the incomplete process of a world-in-the-making, and is stamped with the seal of inconclusiveness (28–30).

For us, the 3-D–printed copy is inherently incomplete simply because its authorizing original and intermediary model are, of necessity, exterior to its own physicality. Each is intrinsically a version of the others, reinforcing Bakhtin's world-in-the-making with its dynamic multiplicity, with the way that it keeps creating meanings.

Here, we are not simply claiming that the dialogic object is in dialogue with people, though of course in part it is. Rather, the object is in dialogue with its multiple contexts, so that the actions and perceptions of those who shape, foreground, or inhabit those contexts interrelate with the object by sharing formational meanings. No single mediator can perceive, contain, or synthesize all contexts: interpretation is contingent, based in the time, place, and position of the subject, and in the affordances the object employs. Our interpretive role necessarily brings us into negotiation with all of those contexts, even those that may be out of view. Yet our object encounters, if wholly contingent, do not lack specificity. Like anthropologist Clifford Geertz's (1973) seminal "thick description" or dramatist Richard Schechner's (2002) foundational version of "performance," our encounter with an object's significance is not just between us and its visible contexts; it is a triangulation between us and our understanding of how its visible context relates to many others. It is "our own construction of other people's construction" (Geertz 9), and it is "twice-behaved" (Schechner 52).[6]

Copies—3-D prints or otherwise—bring meaning back to the original just as the original grounds and situates its abundant copies. "To say that a work of art grows in originality in proportion to the quality and abundance of its copies is nothing odd," write Bruno Latour and Adam Lowe (2011) in "The Migration of the Aura, or How to Explore the Original Through Its Facsimiles" (279). Much as for a poem or play, each concrete performance reflects both process and product, how the two work together. To quote Charles Péguy via Derrida, as they do, "If we stop interpreting, if we stop rehearsing, if we stop reproducing, the very existence of the original is at stake" (279). Latour and Lowe further suggest that "the real phenomenon to be accounted for is not the delineation of one version from all others but the whole assemblage of one—or several—original(s) *together with* its continually rewritten biography" (278). Surely the Lincoln life mask—so clearly an entity that holds aura across its composite state of original, 3-D model, and 3-D copy—qualifies here. "Students of material culture argue for the primacy of the artifact as a historical document or text, but that primacy is limited by the realities of [recoverable] context," argues Herman (10). If the original lives in both its copies and contexts, as well as in the stories that adhere to them, then the dialogic process across the whole assemblage of versions, environments, and interpreters is inevitably made visible. Taken together, the original-model-copy composite functions as a discontinuous yet meaningfully coherent entity whose digital interlude—material dissolving into virtual in order to be created once again—invites us to foreground the continuities and gaps in its significance, to explore both as foundational qualities of *things*. As objects retreat from a material authentic they gather ever more layers of experience and meaning—arraying their multiplicity for ready use in further dialogic encounters across time and space.

If performance is the creation of meaning through use, then objects, as material expressions, are surely performances in their own right (Garfinkel). When folklorist Richard Bauman and anthropologist Charles Briggs (1990) identify the "situational" context of performance, they are focused on the rising conditions of the moment. Building in part on Bakhtin's sociolinguistics, they explore the concept of *entextualization*, a transformational process whereby discrete units of discourse are rendered extractable from their interactional setting (73). This shift of attention, they argue, "represents a major step towards achieving an agent-centered view of performance" (69). "Consider for a moment," they write,

> why researchers have had to make such an issue of contextualization, to devote so much effort to establishing that the form, function, and meaning of verbal art cannot be understood apart from context. The reason is precisely that verbal art forms are so susceptible to treatment as self-contained, bounded objects separable from their social and cultural contexts of production and reception. (72)

If scholars of verbal performance have most often sought to show how expressive meaning is firmly anchored, Bauman and Briggs argue an opposite tack, asking "what it is that makes verbal art decenterable despite all these anchoring counterforces" (73). If we extend this observation of the de- and re-contextualization of verbal genres to all separable and bounded forms, we soon see entextualization at work for the Lincoln 3-D model and its prints: they are surely neither "self-contained" nor "separable from their social and cultural contexts"—except when the decentering processes of discourse substantively transform and realign their meanings, creating junctures of new stability. Indeed, through time and circumstance, the transmutations of circulating objects are essential to keeping culture moving and alive.[7]

Yet, "thingification—" writes science studies scholar Karen Barad (2003), "the turning of relations into 'things,' 'entities,' 'relata,'—infects much of the way we understand the world and our relationship to it. Why do we think that the existence of relations requires relata?" ("Posthuman Performativity" 812). Like Bennett, among other scholars sometimes labeled new materialists, Barad argues that matter itself plays an active role in creating the world. It is neither dependent nor secondary. In her far-reaching theorization of what she terms *agential realism*—a "performative metaphysics" based in the rejection of dualities between observer and observed, words and things, objects and their boundaries—Barad proposes "a posthumanist refiguration of the nature of materiality and discursivity and the relationship between them" (818). Drawing on the work of quantum physicist Neils Bohr, she posits *phenomena* as the basic epistemological components of the world. "The primary ontological units are not 'things' but phenomena—dynamic topological reconfigurings / entanglements / relationalities / (re)articulations. And the primary semantic units are not 'words' but material-discursive practices through which boundaries are constituted" (818). Phenomena, Barad writes, "are constitutive of reality," while the world "is an ongoing open process of mattering through which 'mattering' itself acquires meaning and form in the realization of different agential possibilities" (817–18). For Barad, "Matter is not immutable or passive. . . . Matter is always already an ongoing historicity" (821).[8]

Bauman and Briggs on one side, Barad on the other: they both converge on the same coin but at incompatible faces. At the very moment words take on the tangible qualities of objects, objects are disbound from the tyranny of linguistic formulations, and meaning coalesces in the middle. Yet as Bill Brown (2004) writes in his formative discussion of "thing theory,"

> The very semantic *reducibility* of *things* to *objects*, coupled with the semantic *irreducibility* of *things* to *objects*, would seem to mark one way of recognizing how, although objects typically arrest a poet's attention, and although the object was what was asked to join the dance in philosophy, things may still lurk in the shadows of the ballroom and continue to lurk there after the subject and object have done their thing, long after the party is over. (3)

Material objects, for all our contemplation, are still a conundrum—which is also "the resistance of the object[,] . . . the impossibility of its being exhausted by a word," that Bakhtin so long ago identified (276).

If part of an object's meaning lives in its contexts, the converse must also hold: part of the meaning of context is borne by objects. They implicate each other. Material objects, like the building blocks of all cultural discourse, emerge in meaning as they are encountered. Because of this, and despite their seemingly static materiality, they are precisely as emergent as any other container of human meaning, be that a sentence, a song, or a sensation. 3-D–printed copies are no different in this regard. What they do for us, though, is expose more readily to view a field of possibilities that was already there, awaiting our detection: virtuality's state change allows us to see that the contexts of objects change along with their materiality. Speed, scale, material, use, locale: all these can change more rapidly or unexpectedly than what previous generations experienced as part of their customary life-world. Our digital moment also works to bring multiple strands of scholarship closer together: literary scholars study things while material culturalists work to engage semiotics while digital humanists interrogate the anthropocene while we all set up maker labs to, well, make things. Recognized or not, the intended or unintended potential uses of objects, or environments, are all latent affordances, quietly waiting to drive meaning forward.

In the dialogically expansive world of meaning revealed by the culture of 3-D copies, an expansive range of cultural affordances enable multiplicity. In our ever more computerized age, writes Schwartz, "creation and imitation, invention and repetition may become as indistinct as knowing is from copying" (204).

As the Smithsonian's Lincoln life mask model shows us, 3-D printing opens to view a Bakhtinian moment in cultural materiality. Through its immediacy, the attention it gathers, and the plasticity it brings to processes of memory, 3-D printing has the potential to put makers of material objects in dialogue with their no-longer-immutable, no-longer-impossibly-distant sources. For the dialogic object—that is, any object—a formerly absolute and immutable past dissolves into a configurable present available for further renegotiation. The 3-D-printed copy of the 3-D model of the significant original artifact, in its layers and tangles of dialogic multiplicity, invites a uniquely sustained attention to the object's raw world-making potential.

## NOTES

1. Other high-profile museums to release 3-D models in this time frame include the Metropolitan Museum of Art and the British Museum.

2. An image of the Smithsonian's 1889 life mask, whose plaster surface is darkened with paint to resemble bronze, can be found by searching at http://americanhistory.si.edu/collections. On the creation and subsequent history of the plaster Lincoln life masks and their copies see Volk, "The Lincoln Life-Mask and How It Was Made," Ostendorf, "A Relic from His Last Birthday," and Stewart, "An Anthropologist Looks at Lincoln."

3. "The contents of Abraham Lincoln's pockets on the evening of his assassination" are part of The Alfred Whital Stern Collection of Lincolniana, Rare Books and Special Collections Division, Library of Congress. For an image, see www.loc.gov/item/scsm001049. The Stern collection also includes a bronze cast of the 1865 Mills life mask: www.loc.gov/item/scsm001047.

4. The specific term "dialogic object" appears in the "Introduction" (1–6) and also as a section heading in Riggins, *The Socialness of Things*. For a noteworthy use of the term "dialogic object" within the field of semiotics, see Kent, "Dialogic Semiotics."

5. For examples from each perspective see, for example, Glassie, *Folk Housing in Middle Virginia,* and Prown, "Mind in Matter," and compare these to Brown, "Thing Theory," as well as Ingold, "Materials against Materiality" and "Writing Texts, Reading Materials."

6. For Geertz, "what we call our data are really our own constructions of other people's constructions of what they and their compatriots are up to" (9). For Schechner, "twice-behaved behavior is generated by interactions between ritual and play." (56)

7. There is a rich multidisciplinary scholarship on the commodification and circulation of objects, especially in history and anthropology, which goes beyond the scope of the present conversation. For one influential example, see Appadurai, *The Social Life of Things*.

8. For a far-reaching exploration of her theories, see Barad, *Meeting the Universe Halfway*.

**BIBLIOGRAPHY**

Appadurai, Arjun. "Introduction: Commodities and the Politics of Value." In *The Social Life of Things: Commodities in Cultural Perspective,* ed. Arjun Appadurai, 3–63. Cambridge: Cambridge University Press, 1986.

Appadurai, Arjun, ed. *The Social Life of Things: Commodities in Cultural Perspective.* Cambridge: Cambridge University Press, 1986.

Bakhtin, M. M. *The Dialogic Imagination: Four Essays,* ed. Michael Holquist, translated by Caryl Emerson and Michael Holquist. Austin, Tex.: University of Texas Press, 1981.

Barad, Karen. *Meeting the Universe Halfway: Quantum Physics and the Entanglement of Matter and Meaning.* Durham, N.C.: Duke University Press, 2007.

———. "Posthumanist Performativity: Toward an Understanding of How Matter Comes to Matter." *Signs* 28, no. 3 (2003): 801–31.

Bauman, Richard, and Charles L. Briggs. "Poetics and Performance as Critical Perspectives on Language and Social Life." *Annual Review of Anthropology* 19 (January 1990): 59–88.

Benjamin, Walter. "The Work of Art in the Age of Mechanical Reproduction." In *Illuminations: Essays and Reflections,* ed. Hannah Arendt, translated by Harry Zohn, 217–51. New York: Schocken, 1969.

Bennett, Jane. *Vibrant Matter: A Political Ecology of Things.* Durham, N.C.: Duke University Press, 2010.

Brown, Bill. "Thing Theory." In *Things,* ed. Bill Brown, 1–22. Chicago, Ill.: University of Chicago Press, 2004.

Chemero, Anthony. "An Outline of a Theory of Affordances." *Ecological Psychology* 15, no. 2 (2003): 181–95.

Fleming, E. McClung. "Artifact Study: A Proposed Model." *Winterthur Portfolio* 9 (January 1974): 153–73.

Garfinkel, Susan. "Recovering Performance for Vernacular Architecture Studies." *Perspectives in Vernacular Architecture* 13, no. 2 (2006/7): 106–14.

Geertz, Clifford. "Thick Description: Toward an Interpretive Theory of Culture." In *The Interpretation of Cultures: Selected Essays,* 3–30. New York: Basic, 1973.

Gibson, James J. "The Theory of Affordances." In *The Ecological Approach to Visual Perception,* 127–43. Boston, Mass.: Houghton Mifflin, 1979.

Glassie, Henry H. *Folk Housing in Middle Virginia: A Structural Analysis of Historic Artifacts.* Knoxville, Tenn.: University of Tennessee Press, 1975.

Herman, Bernard L. "Introduction: The Discourse of Objects." In *The Stolen House,* 3–14. Charlottesville: University of Virginia Press, 1997.

Hobsbawm, Eric. "Introduction: Inventing Tradition." In *The Invention of Tradition,* ed. Eric Hobsbawm and Terence Ranger, 1–14. Cambridge: Cambridge University Press, 1983.

Ingold, Tim. "Materials against Materiality." *Archaeological Dialogues* 14, no. 1 (2007): 1–16.

———. "Writing Texts, Reading Materials. A Response to My Critics." *Archaeological Dialogues* 14, no. 1 (2007): 31–38.

Kent, Thomas. "Dialogic Semiotics." *The American Journal of Semiotics* 6, no. 2/3 (1989): 221–37.

Latour, Bruno, and Adam Lowe. "The Migration of the Aura, or How to Explore the Original Through Its Facsimiles." In *Switching Codes: Thinking through Digital Technology in the Humanities and the Arts,* ed. Thomas Bartscherer and Roderick Coover, 275–97. Chicago, Ill.: University of Chicago Press, 2011.

Mack, Eric. "Smithsonian Now Allows Anyone To 3D Print (Some) Historic Artifacts." *Forbes / Tech.* November 13, 2013. www.forbes.com/sites/ericmack/2013/11/13/smithsonian-now-allows-anyone-to-3d-print-some-historic-artifacts.

MakerBot Industries. https://www.makerbot.com/.

Nye, Benjamin D., and Barry G. Silverman. "Affordance." In *Encyclopedia of the Sciences of Learning,* ed. N. M. Seel, 179–83. New York: Springer, 2012.

Ostendorf, Lloyd. "A Relic from His Last Birthday: The Mills Life Mask of Lincoln." *Lincoln Herald* 75 (1973): 79–85.

Prown, Jules David. "Mind in Matter: An Introduction to Material Culture Theory and Method." *Winterthur Portfolio* 17, no. 1 (1982): 1–19.

RepRap. http://reprap.org/.

Riggins, Stephen Harold, ed. *The Socialness of Things: Essays on the Socio-Semiotics of Objects.* New York: Mouton de Gruyter, 1994.

Savage, Adam. Tweet of November 13, 2013. https://twitter.com/donttrythis/status/400652819532746752.

Schechner, Richard. *Performance Studies: An Introduction.* New York: Routledge, 2002.

Schwartz, Hillel. *The Culture of the Copy: Striking Likenesses, Unreasonable Facsimiles.* New York: Zone Books, 2014.

"Smithsonian Releases 3-D Collection and Launches New 3-D Explorer." *Newsdesk: Newsroom of the Smithsonian.* November 13, 2013. http://newsdesk.si.edu/releases/smithsonian-releases-3-d-collection-and-launches-new-3-d-explorer.

Smithsonian X 3D. "Tour: Looking at Clark Mills' Life Mask of Abraham Lincoln." 2013. http://3d.si.edu/tour/looking-clark-mills-life-mask-abraham-lincoln.

Stewart, Susan. *On Longing: Narratives of the Miniature, the Gigantic, the Souvenir, the Collection.* Baltimore, Md.: Johns Hopkins University Press, 1984.

Stewart, T. D. "An Anthropologist Looks at Lincoln." In *Annual Report of the Board of Regents of the Smithsonian Institution,* 419–38. Washington, D.C.: Government Printing Office, 1952.

Stromberg, Joseph. "These New 3D Models Put the Smithsonian's Most Renowned Items in Your Hands." *Smithsonian Magazine,* November 13, 2013. www.smithsonianmag.com/smithsonian-institution/these-new-3d-models-put-the-smithsonians-most-renowned-items-in-your-hands-180947679.

Thingiverse. https://www.thingiverse.com/.

UndeadManatee. "Abraham Lincoln Christmas Ornament." November 9, 2014. http://www.thingiverse.com/thing:536545.

Volk, Leonard W. "The Lincoln Life-Mask and How It Was Made Reprinted from the Century Magazine for December, 1881: By Permission of the Century Company." *Journal of the Illinois State Historical Society* 8, no. 2 (1915): 238–59.

# PART IV

# MAKING SPACES AND INTERFACES

# Feminist Hackerspaces: Hacking Culture, Not Devices (the zine!)

AMY BUREK, EMILY ALDEN FOSTER, SARAH FOX, AND DANIELA K. ROSNER

*This chapter includes edited contents of a zine that was inspired by and sourced from research originally published in "Hacking Culture, Not Devices: Access and Recognition in Feminist Hackerspaces," by Sarah Fox, Rachel Rose Ulgado, and Daniela K. Rosner of the Human Centered Design and Engineering Department at the University of Washington. Illustrations in the original publication are by Emily Alden Foster. Editing and layout of the original publication are by Amy Burek.*

*A chance encounter between Burek (a hackerspace member) and Fox at a local short-run publication festival led to collaboration on a zine—a self-published magazine typically made with a photocopier—that knit together content from the published paper with local histories of feminist print production. Reprinted here (with adaptations to accommodate a book's format), the zine is an effort to circulate scholarship and continue conversations from the field.*

In putting this zine together (see Figure 25.1), we wish to open a dialogue about the culture being made in and around feminist hackerspaces. Our research has started to reveal important connections between the work being done within these spaces and larger developments in corporate technology cultures. Members have reframed a concern for women's access to technical industries as one of recognizing technical work already there, destabilizing the unmarked categories of technical labor. Our hope is that this zine can help spur a wider discussion of the practices and criticisms that are happening in these spaces. In doing so, we recognize that there is no solid view of what it means to be a hacker or a feminist. We instead wish to highlight the multiple views and practices, including technical work and feminist activism, that can take place under the auspices of the hackerspace.

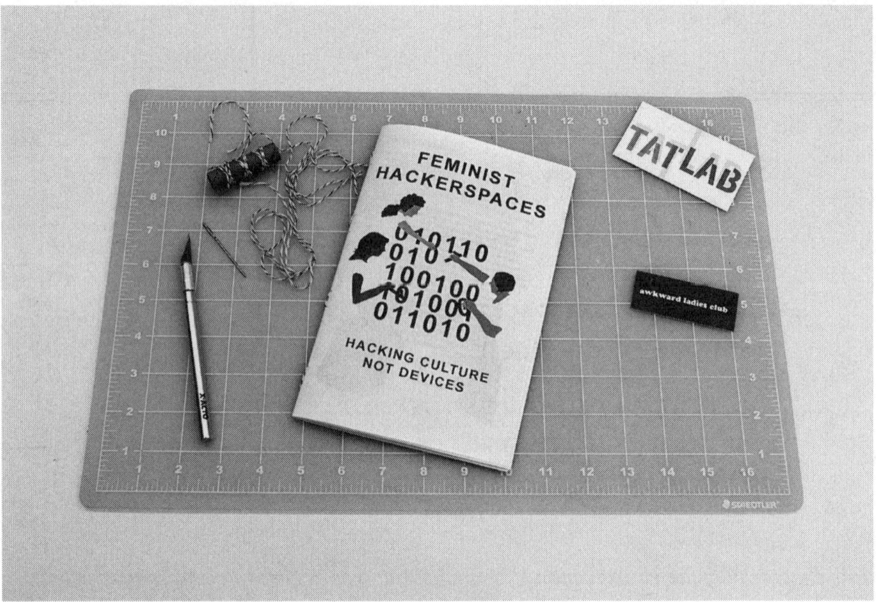


**Figure 25.1.** One of the zines just after assembly. Courtesy of Amy Burek, Emily Alden Foster, Sarah Fox, and Daniela K. Rosner.

## *What Is a Hackerspace?*

Hackerspaces are collectively run workspaces that act as places for people to socialize and collaborate on projects. These spaces are often run by a community of people who share common interests or hobbies, such as hardware hacking, programming, DIY science, and making. Hackerspaces have resources, like communal computers, electronics prototyping tools and components, 3-D printers, and laser cutters, allowing members to experiment and create. Knowledge is also shared between members in the form of workshops, skillshares, lectures, and casual social events. According to scholars of technology and human-computer interaction, while these spaces can enable grassroots entrepreneurism and technical innovation, they often remain tied to particular people (often white, male, and college-educated) and ideas of what counts as technical work.

## *What Are Feminist Hackerspaces?*

The women developing feminist hackerspaces have described their aims to support women's creative and professional pursuits. They hope to provide a place for those who identify as women and those who support feminism to gather, share ideas, be creative, and network professionally. Although they all differ in their implementations, these spaces share a core tenet that women and other marginalized people should be welcomed to perform technical practice without being subjected to discrimination or abuse.

Inspired by the opening of the mother-oriented Mothership Hackermoms (Berkeley, California), organizers of Seattle Attic formed the first feminist hackerspace in Washington in 2012. Following suit after fruitful conversations at Adacamp 2013 (a conference for women in open technology), organizers in San Francisco established Double Union, and Flux was opened later that year in Portland, Oregon.[1]

As in many hacker communities, members of feminist hackerspaces tend to engage in activities associated with traditional ideas of "hacking"—technical practices such as electronics prototyping and programming. In women-oriented and feminist spaces, a significant amount of time tends to be dedicated to learning other creative and practical techniques, such as writing, fiber arts, visual arts, and fermenting and canning foods.

Professional networking can also be a part of feminist hackerspace communities; however, not all members self-identify as "hackers" or work in technical industries. Some of the spaces observed actively recruit members outside of the tech industry in an effort to diversify their membership and the skills valued.

### *Why Do Members Find Feminist Spaces Necessary?*

Early feminist hackerspaces have focused on the need for places of safety and shared values. In the words of one organizer, "As a woman in technology, it's like, I'm already part of a like a 10, 20 percent group so it doesn't really take a lot to turn me off. So I think like I'm just more sensitive to like things like the space sucking and being dark and gloomy."

Women who have spent time in typical hackerspaces have reported discomfort and vulnerability. (See Figure 25.2.) Stories of harassment that have occurred in these spaces have circulated widely within female and feminist tech circles:

> [A woman] was working on something and this kid next to her was like bragging to her about how he had gotten a woman online to show him her breasts by threatening to hurt a kid. And she was like "What is going on here? Why are you telling me this?" And she looked at the guy who runs the space and pays the rent here and was like "Are you going to do anything about this?" And then, like, he didn't.

### *Membership*

Most feminist hackerspaces vet potential new members through nomination and/or voting processes. At some spaces, in-person meetings during an open house are required before membership decisions are made. In addition to sharing feminist ideals in line with a hackerspace's mission, members are expected to act respectfully toward each other regardless of their background or level of technical skill. Applications are also a chance to emphasize the expectation that new members will agree to the same fundamental rules and possess similar values.

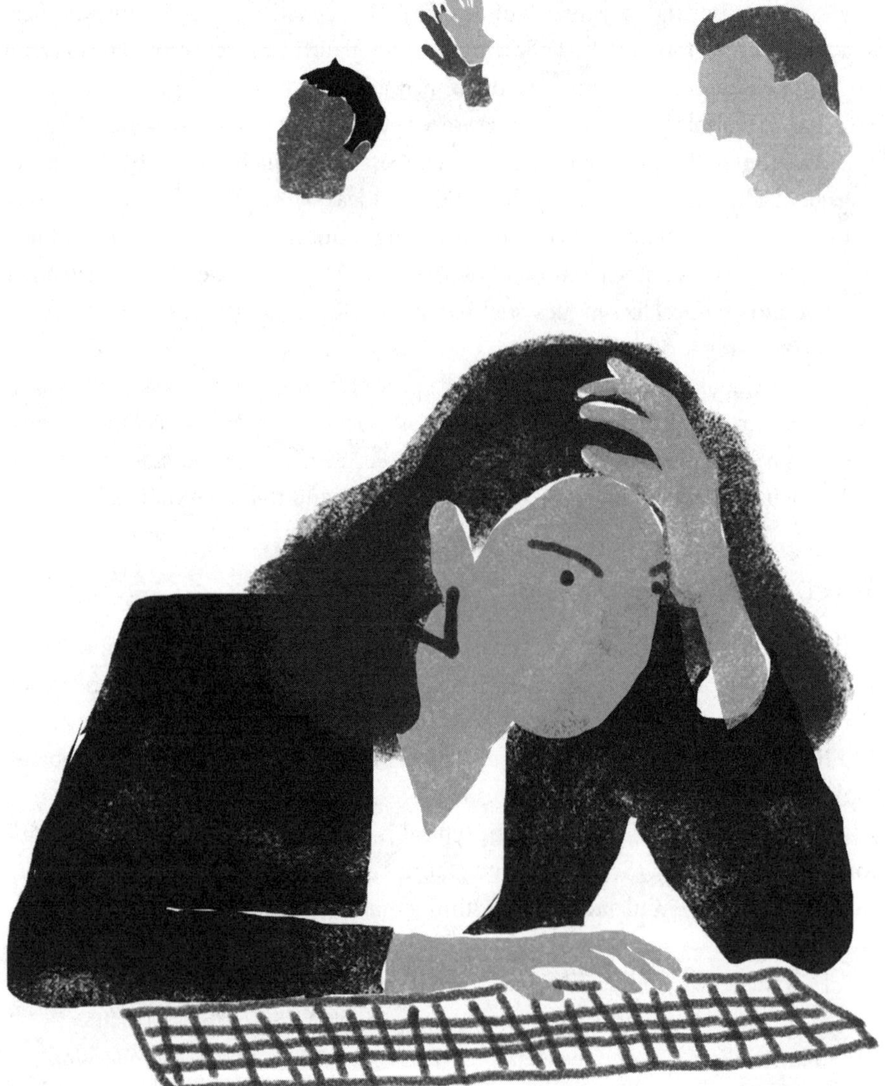

**Figure 25.2.** A programmer leaning over a keyboard with her head in her hand as two men high-five in the background. Featured in *Feminist Hackerspaces: Hacking Culture, Not Devices (the zine!)*. Courtesy of Amy Burek, Emily Alden Foster, Sarah Fox, and Daniela K. Rosner.

### *Access*

Members set the boundaries of who can access their space. At least one feminist hackerspace chooses not to disclose their address online. New visitors to such a space would require the guidance of a current member to find it. A space in Oakland chose a location somewhat removed from transit to and from San Francisco in order to better serve its immediate, local community. Many spaces set rules for who can attend certain events (e.g., members-only, members and guests, or open to the general public).

### *Codes of Conduct*

One organizational aspect that all feminist hackerspaces share is a clear code of conduct. Why are such guidelines necessary for a communal space? Codes of conduct provide safeguards against harassment and allow those in marginalized communities to feel supported. The goal is to allow open conversation about shared values concerning topics such as gender, identity, inequality, and inclusion without having to justify or "explain" viewpoints when faced with situations of abuse. As Sophie Toupin, a feminist scholar and member of a feminist hackerspace in Montreal, explains, "When feminist and anti-oppression politics are not explicitly part of the ethos of a space whether virtual or physical, the burden of education will often be placed upon the people who are living these oppressions."[2] Reading through a code of conduct before joining or entering a space allows new or prospective members to ensure that a space aligns with their personal values. It also allows new members to join spaces feeling confident that they will be treated ethically.

### *What Are the Spaces Like?*

Walking into a feminist hackerspace, you might find large, sturdy worktables and couches or other comfortable furniture. Members may be using laptops, working together on shared pieces of equipment, or reading books and zines from a space's library. As described by one space member, the goal is to have "a space where you can come into your own but also watch other people learn and grow." A space of comfort that supports cooperation is key!

### *Hackerspace Inventories*

Hackerspaces pool resources to purchase tools and equipment for members to share and use for personal projects. Here are some of the tools you might find at a feminist hackerspace (see Figure 25.3):

- 3-D printers
- Laser cutters, vinyl cutters, and wood cutters
- Raspberry Pi and other electronics
- Soldering irons
- Sewing machines
- Bookmaking tools
- Screenprinting supplies
- Dremels and other power tools

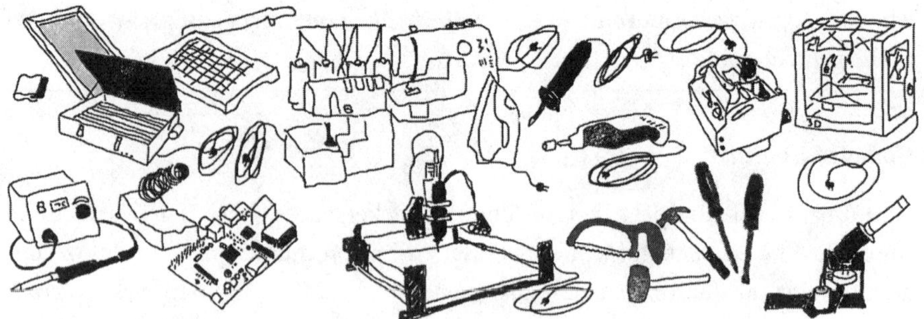

**Figure 25.3.** A line of hacker tools including a soldering iron, paper cutter, screen printing screen, sewing machine, CNC router, and various hand tools. Featured in *Feminist Hackerspaces: Hacking Culture, Not Devices (the zine!)*. Courtesy of Amy Burek, Emily Alden Foster, Sarah Fox, and Daniela K. Rosner.

- Hammers, screwdrivers, and other hand tools
- Button makers
- Knitting needles and crochet hooks

### *Hacking Is Fun*

Many of the activities happening at feminist hackerspaces can be quite similar to those happening at other hackerspaces around the world. In addition to working together to learn how to use shared equipment such as 3-D printers and computer-operated cutting tools, workshops on topics such as these can be found on the calendars of feminist hackerspaces:

- Circuit building
- Wikipedia editing
- App development
- Programming skill share

Most spaces hold both private events and workshops open to the public or guests of members. Whether an event is closed or open usually depends on the activity (such as working on the space's own app or wiki) and the comfort level of the host and/or the participants. Some events may specify whether or not men are allowed to attend.

### *Hacking Is Crafting*

Perhaps like non-feminist spaces, hacking includes technical work like circuit-building workshops, video game jams, Wikipedia editing, app development, and programming skillshares. Hacking also expands to include crafting, making, and political and identity work. This merging of hackerspace activities with traditionally feminized forms of craft-based practices destabilizes dominant categories of technical work to recognize the technical practices that are already taking place. Below are some examples of craftwork that happen in feminist hackerspaces (see Figure 25.4):

- Writing workshops
- Fermenting and canning foods
- Sewing instruction
- Candle making
- Figure drawing
- Stamp carving

## *Hacking as an Identity*

The word "hacking" can suggest many things: rebellion, technical prowess, problem solving, or engaging in engineering activities as an amateur rather than as a professional. If you have seen the 1995 techno-classic film *Hackers,* you know that hacking can also refer to the practice of breaking into computers or stealing data for noble or nefarious purposes. The term can also be used to suggest a certain amount of technical skill, as one member noted: "I think the term can kind of really be pretentious, you're just working on your iOS app all day . . ."

Since feminist spaces expand hacking to include crafting, making, and political and identity work, hacking becomes more than just tinkering with electronics—it is also an opportunity to look inward for means to build and maintain a sense of purpose. Feminist hackerspaces have become sites for members to gather and discuss workplace issues, personal identities, and goals through workshops on topics such as impostor syndrome or "failure clubs." The forms of sharing and innovation that occur here might go underappreciated in contexts outside of the feminist hackerspace.

## *The Problems with "Hacking" and "Making"*

Like the word "feminist," the terms "hacker" and "maker" may not properly represent people of color and economically disadvantaged groups who have been excluded or are unable to take advantage of popular DIY movements.

Founder of LOLspace, a people-of-color–led hackerspace in Oakland, Jen Mai Wu, explains:

> [Hacking is] like a rebranding of stuff that has been going on for a long time [ . . . ] You make your jams, whatever. You grow your own food. Now people are doing that, and they're kind of like boutique, expensive stuff [ . . . ] I noticed that a lot of the people who were benefitting from the maker movement who kind of were able to liberate themselves from the job that they didn't like and were able to do something like take a hobby and turn it into something they really loved.

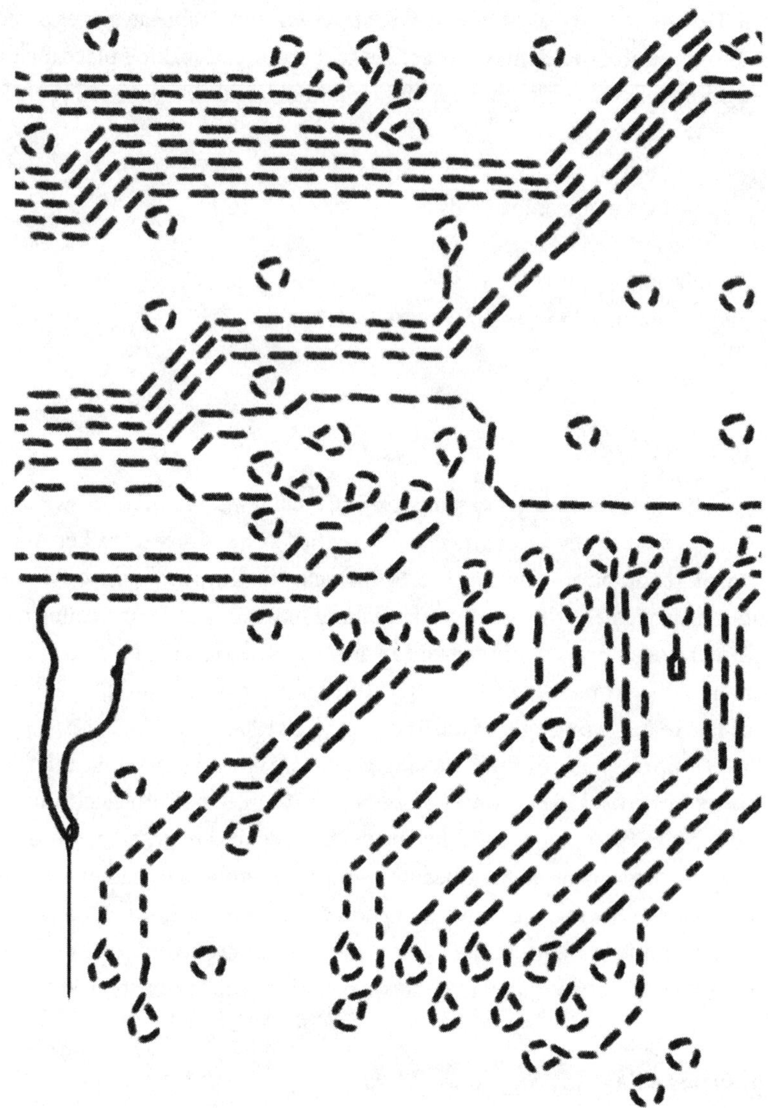

**Figure 25.4.** An illustration of sewn circuitry. Featured in *Feminist Hackerspaces: Hacking Culture, Not Devices (the zine!)*. Courtesy of Amy Burek, Emily Alden Foster, Sarah Fox, and Daniela K. Rosner.

Some spaces have moved away from the term "hacker" (particularly in space names) due to its associations with (white and Asian) masculinist tech culture in an effort to promote inclusion.

### *What Makes These Spaces Feminist?*

Labeling a space as feminist allows members to share a language and a set of ideals. It is also a mechanism to keep out people with fundamentally different worldviews. One interviewee and space organizer notes:

> You'll keep away a lot of people you don't want. It creates a very explicit filter, which will push people away, which will be very nice.

### *What Is Intersectional Feminism?*

With its own political and historical context, the term "feminist" has the potential to deter some people whom spaces wish to include. A president of one feminist hackerspace described her concern about the use of the word:

> Where I hesitate around calling it a feminist hackerspace is a feminist has a lot of nice white lady baggage around it . . . So we try to make it clear with the rest of the way that we put ourselves forward that that's not [what] we're going for.

Many spaces emphasize the importance of intersectional feminism. In fact, all of the spaces observed called themselves intersectional either on their websites or in interviews. Coming out of critical race theory, intersectional feminism acknowledges that many factors influence social prejudice and injustice, and these factors interact with each other. Oppression varies in degree and intensity depending on factors such as race, class, gender, ability, and sexual orientation.[3]

The term "intersectional feminist" is used by groups to distance themselves from past feminist movements that were less concerned with issues facing women who were non-white, or who possessed varying degrees of ability or economic access (just to name a few). The use of the term is indicative of an interest in having memberships that are diverse and inclusive by considering difference, privilege, and injustice.

### *The Future of Feminist Hackerspaces*

The membership base of many feminist hackerspaces remains mostly white, mostly college-educated, and mostly middle class. As members work toward becoming more racially, ethnically, and socioeconomically diverse, they must acknowledge the legacies of marginalization within feminist activism that result in such a lack of diversity.

The number of feminist hackerspaces continues to grow in the United States (e.g., Hacker Gals in Kalamazoo, Michigan, and Spanning Tree in Washington, D.C., both formed in 2014). Feminist and women's groups have also expanded within traditional hackerspaces (e.g., Miss Baltazar's Laboratory in Vienna, Austria, and Anarchafeminist Hackerhive in San Francisco are some of the earliest examples).

If you can't find a group that fits your needs, you can always start your own! For more about how, you can read about feminist hackerspace design patterns[4] on the Geek feminism wiki or Liz Henry's article about the process of founding Double Union.[5]

### *Where Are Feminist and Women's Hackerspaces (in the United States)?*

- Mothership Hackermoms, Berkeley, California[6]
  Membership open to mothers of every gender.
  *"We give mothers of every gender the time and space to explore DIY craft and design, hacker/maker culture, community workshops, entrepreneurship, and all manner of creative expression—with on-site childcare. Our HackerSprouts program teaches children the creative process through educational childcare and STEAM-based workshops. HackerMoms creates families that build together."*

- Double Union, San Francisco, California[7]
  Membership open to women (trans, cis, queer, straight, and not-fitting-into-those-labels/other).
  *"Our mission is to create a community workshop where women can work on projects in a comfortable, welcoming environment."*

- Seattle Attic, Seattle, Washington[8]
  Membership open to all women, cis and trans.
  *"We are a feminist, woman-centered, trans- and queer-inclusive space for tinkerers, makers, crafters, and hackers of all genders. Our goal is to offer a safe, non-intimidating environment, tools, and a supportive, friendly community to help feminist makers and hackers learn and build."*

Through material and discursive engagement, members of these spaces contest widely understood forms of hacking and technology development. By reframing activities rarely associated with technical work (e.g., weaving and identity workshops), they open up hacking to a wider set of individuals and make room for practices that do not sit neatly within wider corporate or popular hobbyist technology cultures.

## NOTES

This work was supported under NSF CAREER #1453329.

1. Flux closed in July 2014.

2. See more at http://dpi.studioxx.org/en/feminist-hackerspaces-safer-spaces.

3. To learn more about intersectionality, we recommend reading the work of people such as Kimberlé Crenshaw, Patricia Hill Collins, and bell hooks.

4. See http://geekfeminism.wikia.com/wiki/Feminist_hackerspace_design_patterns.

5. See https://modelviewculture.com/pieces/the-rise-of-feministhackerspaces-and-how-to-make-your-own.

6. See http://mothership.hackermoms.org.

7. See http://www.doubleunion.org.

8. See http://seattleattic.com.

PART IV ][ *Chapter 26*

# Fashioning Circuits, 2011–Present

KIM A. BRILLANTE KNIGHT

Fashioning Circuits uses wearable media as a lens to consider the social and cultural valences of bodies and identities in relation to fashion, technology, labor practices, and craft and maker cultures. A public humanities project, it combines scholarship, university coursework, and community partnerships.

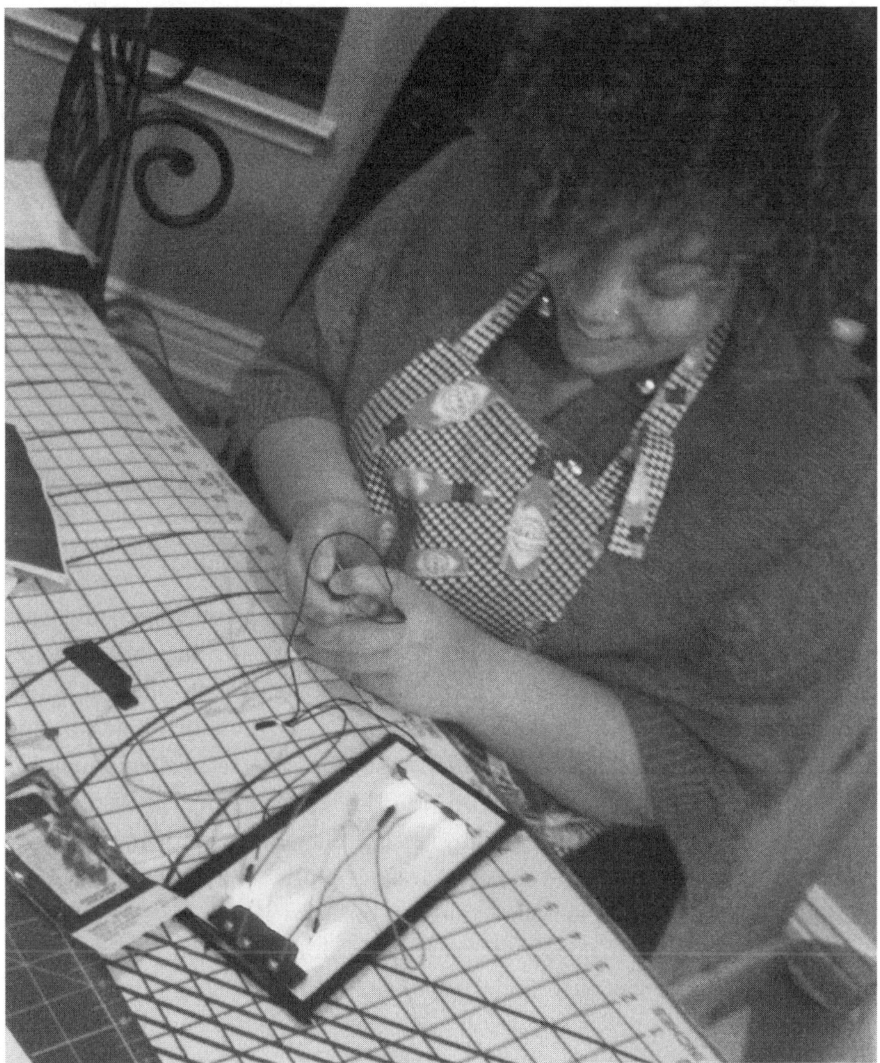

**Figure 26.1.** This photo was taken in fall 2011 as Brianni Nelson, one of Fashioning Circuits' co-founding students, finished soldering her first circuit. Her smile and gasp of surprise when the LEDs lit up suggest that this kind of humanities "making" assignment has important pedagogical implications. Format: Public humanities project. Materials: Electronics, coding, sewing, social contexts, and cultural theory. Founder and Director: Kim A. Brillante Knight. Co-founding Students: Brianni Nelson, Elisa Pequini, Amy Pickup, Tameka Reeves, and Mattie Tanner. Research Team: Lisa Bell, Jessica Knott, Jodi Madera-Prado, Andrew J. Miller, Laura Pasquini, and Lari Tanner. Community Team: B Cavello, Sunnye Childers, Lance King, Harrison "Hal" Massey, Patti McLetchie, Sydnie Montgomery, Karla Y. Muñoz, and Lauren Shafer. Photograph by Kim A. Brillante Knight and Brianni Nelson.

# Making Queer Feminisms Matter: A Transdisciplinary Makerspace for the Rest of Us

MELISSA ROGERS

## *A Makerspace of Our Own*

With maker methodologies gaining popularity in the humanities, how might we imagine queer feminist investments in and engagements with making? What do queer feminist approaches to making look like in academic environments where entrepreneurial maker movements extend the optimistic promise of transforming education through pedagogies of "invent to learn?" Science, Technology, Engineering, and Math are slowly becoming STEAM (STEM + Art), and "innovation" will supposedly rescue the increasingly obsolescent humanities for a future of corporate universities.[1] In a landscape of knowledge production where institutional resources are up for grabs for some kinds of work and as constricted as ever for others, what counts as "making" is highly contested. The hierarchies of value that manage divisions of scholarly and artistic labor also adjudicate which forms of making *matter*.

To elaborate on these issues, this chapter showcases a series of Interactive Textiles workshops that I ran in the spring of 2014 in the Women's Studies Multimedia Studio at the University of Maryland, College Park (UMD). The Multimedia Studio is a multipurpose room where members of the campus community can explore how the politics of making are entangled with gender, race, sexuality, class, and ability. Connecting these small, intimate workshops to my research and pedagogy, I demonstrate how attention to practices of queer feminist cultural production not only deepens our understandings of why making matters to the humanities but also expands narrow definitions of "the digital." Such expansion makes digital humanities work legible by determining what is *digital enough* for a capital-letter "DH" project.[2] I argue that, rather than producing "things," the activities in the Women's Studies Multimedia Studio produce *space* for modes of thought that put pressure on what matters in digital humanities scholarship and teaching. Theorizing how making practices shape, and are shaped by, complex identities and forms of power enables us to use digital humanities methods toward transformative ends, reverse engineering and hacking the hierarchies that structure our thinking about technology and culture.[3] The necessity of feminist, queer, and antiracist spaces for making in the midst of the buzz around entrepreneurship and innovation cannot be underestimated. Such spaces can help us to critically assess how these discourses differently privilege or disadvantage us depending on our social locations and also notice and value how people who are marginalized or oppressed have historically needed to be innovators, entrepreneurs, and hackers of daily life in order to survive, inventing and appropriating specific making practices to cohere their communities and nourish their creativity with few resources.

Since its establishment in 2011 by composer, sound artist, and electronic music historian Tara Rodgers, the Multimedia Studio has hosted numerous classes, events, and workshops, bringing together transdisciplinary audiences from across the University of Maryland campus and beyond. It acts as both the digital hub of the Women's Studies department and a bridge between Women's Studies and Design Cultures and Creativity (DCC, formerly Digital Cultures and Creativity), a living-learning honors college in which students collaboratively explore issues in emerging media through access to labs in their dormitory that facilitate a workshop-style curriculum. The unique and evolving relationship between the honors college and the department brings together DCC's emphasis on cutting-edge digital technologies with Women's Studies' focus on social justice, intersectionality, and feminist arts activisms. The Studio provides undergraduate and graduate students in Women's Studies and the College of Arts and Humanities the opportunity to engage with the analytical and hands-on tools of cultural production, while also piquing DCC students' interest in Women's Studies courses, feminist science and technology studies, and queer and antiracist artists and theorists. While most of the Studio's equipment is oriented toward the production of sound and high-quality audio, the space also serves as both an informal gathering spot for those who are investigating the relationships between technology, media, and culture and a home for a grassroots collection of resources such as zines, books, and films about feminist art- and media-making, digital or otherwise.

As the graduate student coordinator for the Studio between 2013 and 2015, I regularly held sessions of my Introduction to Women's Studies: Women, Art, and Culture class in the space. I also organized zine workshops, a pop-up makerspace for the Humanities Intensive Learning and Teaching institute held by the Maryland Institute for Technology in the Humanities (MITH), and regular meetings of the Multimodal Working Group with graduate student colleagues in Women's Studies, American Studies, and English. While facilitating the use of the Studio by students and faculty, I was immensely privileged to be able to use it as a laboratory for my own dissertation research as, over the course of my graduate career, my interests shifted from the cultures surrounding do-it-yourself (DIY) zine production to the connections between self-proclaimed maker movements and contemporary fiber craft as practiced by queer artists. I thought about myself in relationship to the Studio's activities as a participant-observer involved in the development of a queer feminist praxis, taking notes and reflecting on what was happening there, photographing events, periodically sketching maps and plans, and talking to various stakeholders formally and informally about what they desired from the Studio and what could be improved. Such forms of witnessing are invaluable for not only the university administration and management of makerspaces and other community-oriented initiatives but also the use of making as a method in the humanities, combining experimental fabrication processes with writing and research practices that are already familiar to humanists. I draw on my experience teaching classes and leading workshops in the Multimedia Studio to show how, with relatively few resources in comparison to high-tech makerspaces on campus, making as a methodology came to matter. What, then, can a queer feminist framework of making that originates in Women's Studies tell us about what is valued, explicitly and implicitly, in digital humanities?

The Women's Studies Multimedia Studio is not explicitly a makerspace or hackerspace; it is both something more and something less. A 28'–by-16' wheelchair-accessible room located in a separate building from the departmental office proper, its high ceiling, two tall windows, and bright red soundproofing panels offset the institutional atmosphere created by the fluorescent lighting and beige cinderblock walls. The presence of an old orangey couch, a coffee table, and a long shelving unit lend a lounge-like feel to the room, and the two desktop Mac computers, drum kit, and electronic keyboard suggest that the space is something different from a classroom. Although DCC students use it as a "studio" in a more traditional sense—as a space for the practice and production of music—I am interested in how the uses of the Multimedia Studio can value these older modes of media production associated with the fine arts and creative industries while also making space, quite literally, for newer trajectories of practice that are currently emerging from maker movements and digital humanities. Here, I think through how practices of knitting and crochet draw attention to feminized forms of creativity, and how these and other fiber crafts might open avenues into queer feminist making in the humanities.

A small but growing literature about makerspaces and hackerspaces run by feminists, queers, and people of color reveals that gender, sexuality, race, and class are fraught issues in contemporary maker cultures.[4] While little of this work focuses on university spaces, it nevertheless provides useful insights into everyday forms of political praxis, demonstrating a range of approaches to making that are committed to or animated by social justice. Most relevant for my purposes is Sarah Fox, Rachel Rose Ulgado, and Daniela K. Rosner's "Feminist Hackerspaces: Hacking Culture, Not Devices" (2015), whose authors interviewed the organizers of feminist hackerspaces on the West Coast of the United States. They argue that hacking is "a technological imaginary, a set of deeply held ideas and norms subject to failures and partial readings" (1). By not defining "hacking" purely in terms of dismantling and modifying technological devices, the authors and their participants show how the practice is embedded in the labor of craft as well as the shaping of feminist identities (6–7). This is a welcome approach in which "hacking practice becomes less about the resulting products . . . than the cultural shifts they engender" (12). Such a model of hacking, and making more broadly, is particularly useful for humanities research that examines the values and assumptions built into the technologies we use as well as the cultures that produced them.

In describing the Interactive Textiles workshop series below, I retain Fox, Ulgado, and Rosner's attention to the cultural, spatial, and craft practices that shape feminist spaces for making. Spaces such as the Women's Studies Multimedia Studio can foster critical interventions into digital humanities by redefining the digital through transdisciplinary praxis. Having a makerspace of our own—a space dedicated to the production of feminist, queer, and antiracist knowledge through the making of art and media—matters in the imagining of multiple futures for digital humanities.

### *Interactive Textiles and Transdisciplinary Making in the Humanities*

Craft processes such as knitting and crochet traverse disciplinary boundaries. They are the subjects of art history, folk, computational, and feminist discourses as well as practical *methods* for making in the arts and humanities. They can help us access forms of creative knowledge that have been feminized and devalued as well as industrialized, outsourced, and made invisible. These marginalized, hybrid knowledges are the basis of the queer feminist pedagogy that I attempt to practice in and outside the Women's Studies classroom, and which I brought to the Interactive Textiles workshop series with DCC students. A queer feminist approach to making centered in craft—in this case fiber crafts—opens fissures of meaning in "the digital" and confronts our assumptions around what the term encompasses.

The Interactive Textiles workshops had two goals: to allow computer science and engineering students to explore, in a low-stakes environment, methods of making to which they may not have been exposed, and to provoke questions about how the meanings attached to the kinds of making that we practice today are collectively negotiated in relationship to gender, race, sexuality, and class. The series focused on the labor of fiber crafts, the people we associate with such labor, and the materiality of the media involved in the making of wearable technologies. Although Interactive Textiles was advertised as a "design camp" (one of several working groups from which DCC students choose each semester), I assumed that participants would know more about the language and technical aspects of design than I did. I also knew that this particular set of honors students had little exposure to the vocabulary of feminist, queer, or critical race theories outside of their required electives and that, because many of them had taken a full complement of Advanced Placement exams before enrolling at UMD, they might be less likely to take more humanities courses beyond requirements they had already met. I therefore needed to use widely accessible examples of art activism to get participants interested, while also challenging them to think beyond disciplinary frameworks that value high-tech approaches, sleek and streamlined design, and neatly packaged solutions.

The paragraph-length workshop descriptions included in the Google calendar that students used to register for the design camps emphasized open-ended exploration of a range of tools and materials, prototyping as an iterative routine, and the basic techniques and terminology of knitting and crochet. Each of the workshops was meant to stand on its own, covering a different aspect of designing with textiles and culminating in the third and final session on prototyping wearable technology using the LilyPad Arduino, an open-source hardware platform designed by Leah Buechley and the High-Low Tech group at the Massachusetts Institute of Technology (MIT) Media Lab. Importantly, I centered the workshops in craft practices rather than physical computing, with which DCC students already have some experience. By making the series less about creating a finished product with the LilyPad and more about the processes of textile work, I sought to resist the fetishization of digital technologies evident in both the mainstream maker movement and digital humanities. I also wanted to reorient the participants' attention toward ancient crafts whose relatively recent association with femininity and amateurism has caused them to be undervalued and overlooked.[5] Avoiding the uncritical celebration of the digital that dominates discussions of wearables and the Internet of Things, I focused on how wearable technology is not new, and how advances in textiles and fashion industries have always driven technological innovation.[6] This approach was reflected in the decision to use the language of "interactive textiles" rather than "electronic textiles,"[7] highlighting how textiles are *already* interactive without the addition of circuitry or hardware.[8] We interact with textiles in their construction, manipulating them with our fingers or "digits," but they also interact with us in everyday ways that we often fail to notice: keeping us warm and dry, bringing aesthetic pleasure (and other feelings) to the public and private spaces we inhabit, creating interfaces between our bodies and everyone else, and revealing much about the gendered, racialized, sexual, and classed ways we move through the world.

The workshops thus engaged the category of "the digital" on craft's terms, challenging participants to repeatedly ask, "why 'digital'?" and " 'digital' how?" In the queer feminist pedagogy I am prototyping, craft is praxis—an epistemological framework from which to approach the meanings of design and fabrication *and* a method for making textiles and other real objects. Craft, as one approach to making in the humanities, invites us to consider what we want digital technologies to *do* in combination with much older and still ubiquitous modes of cultural production. Such a combination can foster in our students an attitude toward technology that is both curious and critical, better equipping them to live and work in a world that is increasingly mediated by networked quantification, surveillance, and "smart" objects incessantly gathering data.

The Interactive Textiles workshops drew between four and six participants from DCC. I provided them with a Dropbox folder with two recommended readings: Betsy Greer's short essay, "Craftivist History" (2011), on her use of the term craftivism, and Maria Elena Buszek's interview with Margaret Wertheim, "Crochet and the Cosmos" (2011), on the creation of the *Crochet Coral Reef* (2005–), one of the largest distributed crafting projects in the world. In my brief presentations I drew on the creative place-making practices of yarn bombing, guerilla knitting, and other forms of craftivism to give a sense of how fiber crafts are being used to expose and subvert the hierarchies of value that determine what counts as art.[9] I also gave an overview of how artists are utilizing computing, visualization and modeling, and digital fabrication to transform their craft-based processes, and vice versa.[10]

Building on lesson plans about feminist art movements developed for Introduction to Women's Studies: Women, Art, and Culture, I asked participants to describe the associations they have with craft. They conjured familiar images: dried pasta and string necklaces attached to the contentious term "arts and crafts," ageist and bourgeois stereotypes of "spinsters" and "little old ladies" with houses full of decorative lace doilies and tea cozies, and crocheted thrift store afghans in garish colors. These comments confirm that some fiber crafts are intimately entangled in the domestic as the overdetermined site where white, middle-class femininity is responsible for propping up the nuclear family and the nation's racial order. At the same time, fiber and other indigenous and ethnic craft practices have been plundered by colonial regimes, anthropologists, and museums, constructing some cultural traditions as the primitive others to Western art history or precursors to modern modes of making.[11] To counter the stereotypical notions of craft that students bring with them to workshop or classroom spaces, I drew examples from the growing body of work by queer studio crafters such as Sheila Pepe, Allyson Mitchell, L. J. Roberts, Josh Faught, Aubrey Longley-Cook, and John Paradiso, some of whom do not just make art but also theorize and write about the relationship between art, craft, sexuality, and gender.[12] Using craft's excessive baggage for their own purposes, these artists mobilize the multiple meanings of the term to bring gendered labor, trans embodiment, and queer subjectivities into public spaces while challenging hegemonic definitions of art. Thus, in Interactive Textiles as in the Women's Studies classroom, gender, race, sexuality, and class formed the core of our conversations about "good" and "bad" taste, gentrification and domesticity, and creative labor in and beyond art worlds. In the context of my classes, I used these issues to anchor analysis of museums, collecting practices, and controversies over public arts funding.

After a discussion of the tools and terminologies of knitting and crochet, grounded in the assortment of materials I brought with me, we used finger knitting and crocheted chains to understand the structure of the most basic stitches. Finger and arm knitting are accessible methods for quickly creating knitted rope and fabric without using needles. They require no specialized tools or skills; the loops that make up individual knit stitches are wrapped around the fingers or arms with any kind of yarn and pulled through one another by hand. Online tutorials are numerous; and, once the basic steps of finger knitting are mastered, making large lengths of knitted rope in under an hour is easy. Because finger knitting is frequently taught to children, many students realize that they have done it before or that they are able to teach it to their peers. Its simplicity, however, does not make it any less "real" or "authentic" than traditional forms of knitting; it is a variation on the process. Similarly, its ability to elicit childlike pleasure does not make it any less valuable as a teaching tool. On the contrary, such pleasure frequently surprises students, especially those who adamantly insist that they are not "creative" or "artistic" or have anxiety around "being bad at crafts." The fun and instant gratification of these activities can build confidence and generate curiosity about more complex or difficult processes, while evoking questions about how we were steered toward or away from specific kinds of making over the course of our lives. How is it that certain forms of creativity become more or less available to us, as gendered, racialized, sexual, and classed subjects of various ages and abilities? How is it that we come to see some types of making as valuable while others seem childish, silly, or useless? In workshops as well as humanities classrooms, embracing what is fun and playful about making spurs deeper inquiries about cultural and aesthetic values.

The Interactive Textiles workshops built on these activities, using knitting looms to think about what sort of objects could be made from knitted fabric. We also talked about different gauges or weights of yarn, the difference between synthetic and natural fibers and their consequences for projects, and the use of other materials, especially "plarn," plastic yarn made by cutting plastic shopping bags into strips, loops, or long spirals, which can be used as is or lightly knotted together and rolled into a ball. Plarn is an abundant, versatile, yet finicky material, somewhat prone to breaking.

Neither a classroom nor a lab, the Multimedia Studio provided a meeting ground for the transdisciplinary perspectives of Women's Studies and DCC and allowed for freeform discussions during materials and tool exploration. The small size of the workshops made the series feel like an experimental knitting circle; the participants were openly curious about the possible end results of techniques they had never tried. The looms removed some of the intimidation around learning to use knitting needles, and the plarn lowered the stakes of failure because it is such an ordinary and forgiving material, helpful for reusing large quantities of plastic bags that easily become trash. This reuse sparked a conversation around "sustainability" as a buzzword, the effectiveness of ecological activism, and what constitutes an environmental approach to making. We also had a lively discussion about the Institute for Figuring's *Crochet Coral Reef* project, to which over eight thousand women have contributed crocheted "corals" to be exhibited at museums and galleries around the world in order to raise awareness of coral reef destruction due to pollution and global warming.[13] The project has not only "allowed the entry of housewives and prisoners, as well as scientists, mathematicians and skilled crafters, into some of the most prestigious venues on Earth" (Wertheim and Wertheim 23) but also engaged, via craft, enormous numbers of people in collectively reimagining the conditions for sustaining life on our planet. Donna Haraway (2015) describes the project as an "SF worlding," writing, "The *Crochet Coral Reef* is palpable, polymorphous, terrifying and inspiring stitchery done with every sort of fiber and strand, looped by thousands of people in dozens of nations, who come together to stitch care, beauty and response-ability in play tanks" (11).[14]

The *Crochet Coral Reef* exemplifies the kinds of questions I hoped the Interactive Textiles series would provoke. Christine Wertheim (2015), one of the creators of the Institute for Figuring, writes, "Crochet reefs are the products of a digital technology" (90). Tracing the history of the digital from the fingers or digits to classical numerals and contemporary binary computation, Wertheim argues that there has been a "mental erasure about [the digital's] roots in the human body. Enfolded within this transformation is both an amnesia and a wider story of conceptual blindness that continues to limit our understanding and appreciation of traditions generally seen as 'feminine'" (90). She goes on to show how "digital crafts," such as knitting, crochet, weaving, lacemaking, and others, rely on iteration, algorithms, and written or visual code, elements usually associated with high-tech devices but which compose the patterns that comprise crafted objects: "By playing through the code, the crafter brings an object into being" (90). Fiber crafts materially encode information in their media and structure—*they matter*.

Wertheim's essay counters the popular assumption that feminine handicrafts are mindless simply because they are repetitive or may be derived from instructions, and that they are frivolous because their aesthetics might be categorized as "decorative," a classification used to dismiss women's creativity as not being serious, substantial, or conceptually rigorous. Furthermore, her use of "digital technology" to describe crochet and other feminized fiber crafts leaves room for a rather queer reading of the digital, defamiliarizing it by reminding us of its forgotten origins in the body while also asserting that technologies are multiple, dynamic, and cultural rather than only computational.[15] Her insistence on these terms is not mere associative punning or wordplay; it is a feminist project of reclamation and revaluing. By drawing connections between crochet, biology, mathematics, physics, and computer science, Wertheim and her collaborators subvert the hierarchies of value that keep these domains separate.

In doing so, Wertheim offers a compelling argument for the practice of craft as a method for making in the humanities. In craft, she writes, "activities often theorized as mutually exclusive are performed simultaneously: reading and doing, thinking and making, learning about a structure while materially embodying it" (90). She and her sister Margaret (2015), cofounder of the Institute, claim that "most Crochet Reefers eschew formal patterns" and prefer instead "a kind of material play, constructing organically with their hands while drawing on a library of algorithms they come to know in their fingers as well as in their brains. Such *digital intelligence* mediates a process of figuring in which knowledge resides in both body and mind" (Wertheim and Wertheim 21, emphasis in original). Craft's ability to break down the Cartesian mind-body dualism is frequently noted in theories of multidisciplinary craft, and its capacity to playfully undermine binaries makes it an intriguing companion for queer theorists. Ann Cvetkovich (2012), writing about craft in the context of the politics of depression, femininity, and queer artistic production, extends this premise in a slightly different direction: "Crafting is about a way of being in the world that requires not just knowledge but practice" (168). For Cvetkovich, craft's embodied performativity provides a powerful antidote to reductive oppositions between consumerism and feminism, aesthetics and activism, complicity and resistance. As she argues, "Engaged in a deep dialogue with women's culture through forms of practice that perform thinking by doing, crafting self-consciously questions what constitutes feminism and what constitutes the political" (168). Fiber crafts thus enable a "thinking by doing" that links STEM fields, arts and humanities, and movements for social justice.

How might humanities practitioners cultivate the kind of digital intelligence that the Wertheims and Cvetkovich describe? What kinds of labor would this cultivation require of educators? Humanities makerspaces and activities like those explored during Interactive Textiles offer space to develop craft knowledge alongside and through the frameworks of transdisciplinary fields and, importantly, the time to understand that learning is an ongoing, embodied *practice* that cannot be confined to the quarter, semester, or academic year. While the workshops offered opportunities beyond shallow dabbling in a process, even a months-long project did not provide enough time to inculcate craft as a habitual practice among students who already possessed high levels of technical expertise. For making to be integrated into the humanities, especially when it involves time- and labor-intensive practices such as fiber crafts, we must not only rethink the environments where learning happens but also the timeframes across which it unfolds. We also need to consider how, though immensely valuable, DIY approaches to pedagogy often put the burden of materials and tools provision on the instructor, even when an institutionally supported space such as the Women's Studies Multimedia Studio is available for use. Integrating making into the humanities behooves us to find new ways to support precarious academic labor by, for example, graduate students and adjunct faculty who, given time, resources, and fair compensation, could be educational innovators. Being entrepreneurial within corporatizing universities is incumbent on precarious laborers, who also have the most to lose in deviating from the curricular status quo. As both a graduate student and adjunct who has had to be resourceful in teaching craft as a method, I am all too aware that our understandings of and attitudes toward academic labor need to change if digital humanities are to be truly transformative of our teaching and learning.

## *Crafting Futures for Digital Humanities*

The future of digital humanities is not a given. As we have seen in the long-standing debates over naming, origin stories, field formation, boundary work, and inclusion that are taking place in the panels of national conferences, on the pages (and screens) of major publications, and in the hallways between offices and classrooms, the "big tent" of digital humanities and what it encompasses have never been clear. We might take comfort in this fact, as it means we do not have to settle for a metaphor evoking containment, bigness, circus performance, or lofty prowess.[16] Instead, what other habitats might we craft for the future of our digital work? What kinds of homes or dwelling places, to reference the domesticities that haunt the craft practices I describe here, do we want to construct for digital humanities? I have argued that spaces such as the Women's Studies Multimedia Studio at the University of Maryland make room for transdisciplinary praxis and reimagine the digital technologies we value. They also reorient digital humanities to different subjects and subjectivities, different bodies, different tools and media, and different practices of knowledge production. In Interactive Textiles, participants and I were able to attend to craft and thus to texture, messiness, softness, touch, embodiment, entanglement, slowness—a queerer version of the "digital" than one designed to be sleek and smooth, clean, cold, quick, and impersonal. This is not to say that one should, or ever could, supplant the other; indeed, my point is precisely that we need to make room for multiple versions of the digital, multiple ways of being digital humanists, and multiple modes of making because of the multiple worlds we inhabit.

The power to create capacious, undomesticated, queer futures for digital humanities, futures characterized by their plasticity and their possibilities instead of their predictability, is at our fingertips. Digital humanities offer more yarn to spin and more stories for the making. How we choose to do so matters.

### NOTES

1. Smith argues compellingly that, contrary to the discourse circulating in higher education, the humanities are not in crisis. Smith also demonstrates the inadequacy of the language of profit, cost, and "value" in describing humanities projects. During also offers a useful summary of common arguments "defending" the humanities from their perceived obsolescence and calls for less moralizing about the state of the humanities.

2. Here, I follow Bianco's example, referring not to "the digital humanities" (or capital-letter DH) but digital humanities plural, sans the article. I use Bianco's essay as a point of departure for my own inquiry into the politics and ethics of the institutionalization of making in the university, and the boundary work behind its naming. She asks, "What quick, concatenating, and centrifugal forces have so quickly rendered the many under the name of one, *the* digital humanities? What's in this name, its histories, legacies, and privileged modalities that assert centrality over and against differentials?" (97).

3. I borrow the language of transformation from the #TransformDH collective, who use the radical and activist traditions associated with feminist theory, queer theory, critical race theory and ethnic studies, and disability studies to think through and intervene in digital politics. Some of the founders of the collective write, "We wonder how digital practices and projects might participate in more radical processes of transformation—might rattle the poles of the big tent rather than slip seamlessly into it. To that end, we are interested in digital scholarship that takes aim at the more deeply rooted traditions of the academy: its commitment to the works of white men, living and dead; its overvaluation of Western and colonial perspectives on (and in) culture; its reproduction of heteropatriarchal generational structures" (Lothian and Phillips).

4. Many mainstream publications about gender, race, and sexuality in makerspaces take an "add and stir" approach to diversifying spaces that assumes that, simply by increasing the number of women, people of color, or queers in makerspaces, a culture of sexism, racism, and homophobia will be overturned. See, for example, Guthrie. Others, however, take a more nuanced approach to the issue of changing the masculinist and elitist environments of makerspaces. These include Henry, "The Rise of Feminist Hackerspaces and How to Make Your Own," as well as Toupin, "Feminist Hackerspaces as Safer Spaces?"

5. This kind of fetishism is evident in the flagship publication of the maker movement, *Make: Magazine,* and its online platform (makezine.com), as well as its online store, Maker Shed. *Make* focuses on high-tech gadgetry by offering guides to complex and expensive projects that can be completed using CNC routers, 3-D printers, laser cutters, and even heavy-duty equipment more traditionally associated with construction and carpentry. In attempting to pander to a demographic who may not have access to or interest in these specialized technologies, Maker Media recently created *Craft: Magazine*, which prominently features women, fiber crafts, and projects for children and the home on the covers of its ten issues. Rather than recognizing the long-standing practical and conceptual connections between the maker movement and craft communities of practice, the creation of a new publication ostensibly marketed toward women only serves to further divorce craft from the nebulous category of "making," explicitly associating craft with the feminine, the childish, and the domestic while also using craft purely as a marketing device. In the maker movement as in the art world, then, craft becomes supplementary to "the real thing," in this case making.

6. Ryan writes, "It is a commonplace among archaeologists, anthropologists, and even historians that textiles and garments (and the construction of these) exist alongside other technologies that drive cultural change in all periods" (17). She argues, "Textile technologies drove the industrial revolution. In the early eighteenth century, textile industry inventions, such as the programmable mechanical loom developed by Basile Bouchon, Jacques de Vaucanson, and Joseph-Marie Jacquard, are today considered progenitors of the development of computer technologies and have become part of their mythos. As a record of change and material advancement, textiles and dress are intrinsically bound up with technological invention" (20).

7. Ryan parses the nomenclature of wearable technologies and writes that the terms "electronic textiles" and "e-textiles" often refer to " 'embedded technologies,' the actual circuitry or devices worked into a garment or fabric" (96), which has found an industry niche in athletic wear.

8. I am grateful to Jarah Moesch, one of the graduate assistant instructors at DCC at the time of the workshops and a personal friend of mine, for her support of and feedback on the series, especially her suggestion of the phrase "interactive textiles" to name what I was trying to accomplish. Our conversations and ongoing collaboration critically shaped the workshops and my thinking on craft.

9. Greer defines craftivism broadly as a combination of crafting and activism. Juxtaposing the practices of craftivism with direct action and other traditional forms of protest, she writes, "As craftivists, we foment dialogue and thus help the world become a better place, albeit on a smaller scale than activists who organize mass demonstrations. . . . As craftivists, we are also permission-givers, helping to breathe life into artistic practices that some people may think are obsolete by showing their relevancy and poignancy" (*Craftivism* 124).

10. One excellent site for the exploration of the relationship between craft and computing is bitcraftlab.com, as well as its Twitter account, @bitcraftlab. Another fantastic resource is Kim A. Knight's site for Fashioning Circuits, a project whose goals are "to explore the ways in which fashion and emerging media intersect and to work with community partners to introduce beginners to making and coding through wearable media." In addition to thinking about knitting in relationship to coding, crafters, artists, and makers are combining animation, pixilation, and embroidery; using 3-D printing to create textiles out of plastic and other materials; and hacking or designing machines and software for knitting, embroidery, and weaving.

11. While her essay is not about art history, Nakamura's "Indigenous Circuits" provides another critical perspective on the ways indigenous craft circulates and is transformed through cultural imperialism, showing how, in the 1960s, Navajo women were represented as the ideal laborers for manufacturing electronics because of their presumed "docility, manual dexterity, and affective investment in native craft" (921). She argues, "Indian-identified traits and practices such as painstaking attention to craft and an affinity for metalwork and textiles were deployed to position the Navajo on the cutting edge of a technological moment precisely because of their possession of a racialized set of creative cultural skills in traditional, premodern artisanal handwork" (925). Nakamura's essay raises crucial questions about the relationships between craft, racialization, digital technologies, and labor, demonstrating that the creative value of craft practices can be marshaled in service of racial projects as well as technological innovations. Nakamura's article was published several months after Interactive Textiles, or it would have been required reading.

12. There is now an extensive literature on queering craft (and crafting queerness), partially as a result of these artists' work. Most useful for my purposes are Pepe; Roberts; and Auther. For more on how craft came to be seen as supplementary or inferior to art, see Auther, *String Felt Thread;* and Adamson, *Thinking Through Craft.*

13. See http://theiff.org/current.

14. Haraway uses "SF" to shorthand "string figures, science fact, science fiction, stitched fantasies and speculative fabulation" (11). Haraway describes parts of this formulation in a speech to the Science Fiction Research Association (2013), and Katie King adds "speculative feminisms" to the list in her essay, "A Naturalcultural Collection of Affections: Trandisciplinary Stories of Transmedia Ecologies Learning."

15. While I do not have space to do so here, I want to read "the digital" through its queerest and most speculative associations. The digital, especially when understood in relationship to the hands, calls to mind same-sex and especially lesbian sexual practices such as fingering and fisting. Conceptualizing the digital in this manner could reorient us away from heteronormative understandings of sexual practice that focus myopically on binary sex and gender or genitalia, and toward Foucault's famous formulation in the *History of Sexuality* Vol. I, of "bodies and pleasures" whose limitless combinations need not be restricted to simplistic understandings of the "truth" of sexual desire. In "Making Queer Love: A Kit of Odds and Ends," I argue that craft is an erotic practice whose digital or handmade qualities can free us up for new ways of queering love.

16. I am grateful to Martha Nell Smith, whose repeated insistence that we "mind our metaphors" has fundamentally shaped my thinking about the politics of doing digital humanities work, and who pointed out to me that the metaphor of the "big tent" contains and sets limits around this work as much as it enables it.

## BIBLIOGRAPHY

Adamson, Glenn. *Thinking Through Craft*. London: Bloomsbury, 2007.

Auther, Elissa. "'He Is Survived by His Longtime Companion': Feeling in the Work of Josh Faught." *Art Practical* 6, no. 3 (2015). www.artpractical.com/feature/he-is-survived-by-his-longtime-companion-feeling-in-the-work-of-josh-faught.

———. *String Felt Thread: The Hierarchy of Art and Craft in America*. Minneapolis: University of Minnesota Press, 2009.

Bianco, Jamie "Skye." "This Digital Humanities Which Is Not One." In *Debates in the Digital Humanities*, ed. Matthew K. Gold, 96–112. Minneapolis: University of Minnesota Press, 2012.

bit.craft.lab. http://bitcraftlab.com/.

Buszek, Maria Elena. "Crochet and the Cosmos: An Interview with Margaret Wertheim." In *Extra/Ordinary: Craft and Contemporary Art,* ed. Maria Elena Buszek, 276–90. Durham, N.C.: Duke University Press, 2011.

Cvetkovich, Ann. *Depression: A Public Feeling*. Durham, N.C.: Duke University Press, 2012.

During, Simon. "Stop Defending the Humanities." *Public Books.* http://www.publicbooks.org/nonfiction/stop-defending-the-humanities, 1 March 2014, accessed 15 April 2014.

Foucault, Michel. *The History of Sexuality,* Volume 1: An Introduction. Trans. Robert Hurley. New York: Vintage, 1990.

Fox, Sarah, Rachel Rose Ulgado, and Daniela K. Rosner. "Hacking Culture, Not Devices: Access and Recognition in Feminist Hackerspaces." In *Proceedings of the 18th ACM Conference on Computer Supported Cooperative Work and Social Computing*, 56–68. Vancouver, B.C., March 14–18, 2015. http://dl.acm.org/citation.cfm?id=2675133.2675223.

Greer, Betsy. *Craftivism: The Art of Craft and Activism*. Vancouver, B.C.: Arsenal Pulp Press, 2014.

———. "Craftivist History." In *Extra/Ordinary: Craft and Contemporary Art*, ed. Maria Elena Buszek, 175–83. Durham, N.C.: Duke University Press, 2011.

Guthrie, Georgia. "Where Are the Women in Makerspaces?" *Make: Magazine*, April 7, 2013. http://makezine.com/2013/04/07/where-are-the-women/.

Haraway, Donna. "SF: Science Fiction, Speculative Fabulation, String Figures, So Far." *Ada: A Journal of Gender, New Media, and Technology* 3 (2013). http://adanewmedia.org/2013/11/issue3-haraway/.

———. "Sym-chthonic Tentacular Worldings: An SF Story for the Crochet Coral Reef." Foreword in *Crochet Coral Reef*. Los Angeles, Calif.: The Institute for Figuring, 2015.

Henry, Liz. "The Rise of Feminist Hackerspaces and How to Make Your Own." *Model View Culture*, February 3, 2014. https://modelviewculture.com/pieces/the-rise-of-feminist-hackerspaces-and-how-to-make-your-own.

King, Katie. "A Naturalcultural Collection of Affections: Transdisciplinary Stories of Transmedia Ecologies Learning." *The Scholar and Feminist Online* 10, no. 3 (2012). http://sfonline.barnard.edu/feminist-media-theory/a-naturalcultural-collection-of-affections-transdisciplinary-stories-of-transmedia-ecologies-learning/0.

Knight, Kim A. et al. Fashioning Circuits. http://fashioningcircuits.com/.

LilyPad Arduino. *High-Low Tech*, Leah Buechley and the MIT Media Lab. Cambridge, Mass.: Massachusetts Institute of Technology. http://highlowtech.org/?p=34.

Lothian, Alexis, and Amanda Phillips. "Can Digital Humanities Mean Transformative Critique?" *E-Media Studies* 3, no. 1 (2013). http://journals.dartmouth.edu/cgi-bin/WebObjects/Journals.woa/1/xmlpage/4/article/425.

Nakamura, Lisa. "Indigenous Circuits: Navajo Women and the Racialization of Early Electronic Manufacture." *American Quarterly* 66, no. 4 (2014): 919–42.

Pepe, Sheila. "The Margin You Feel May Not Be Real." *The Brooklyn Rail*, April 2, 2014. www.brooklynrail.org/2014/04/criticspage/the-margin-you-feel-may-not-be-real.

Roberts, L. J. "Craft, Queerness, and Guerilla Tactics: An Extended Maker's Statement." In *Loop: Knitting Now*, ed. Jessica Hemmings. London: Black Dog Publishing, 2010.

———. "Put Your Thing Down, Flip It, and Reverse It: Reimagining Craft Identities Using Tactics of Queer Theory." In *Extra/Ordinary: Craft and Contemporary Art*, ed. Maria Elena Buszek, 243–59. Durham, N.C.: Duke University Press, 2011.

Rogers, Melissa. "Making Queer Love: A Kit of Odds and Ends," *Hyperrhiz* 13 (Fall 2015). http://hyperrhiz.io/hyperrhiz13/missives-of-love/queer-love-essay.html.

Ryan, Susan Elizabeth. *Garments of Paradise: Wearable Discourse in the Digital Age*. Cambridge, Mass.: MIT Press, 2014.

Smith, Martha Nell. "The Humanities Are Not a Luxury: A Manifesto for the Twenty-First Century," *Liberal Education* (Winter 2011): 48–55.

Toupin, Sophie. "Feminist Hackerspaces as Safer Spaces?" *.dpi: Feminist Journal of Art and Digital Culture* 27. http://dpi.studioxx.org/en/feminist-hackerspaces-safer-spaces.

Wertheim, Christine. "Matter and Form." In *Crochet Coral Reef*, ed. Margaret Wertheim. Los Angeles, Calif.: The Institute for Figuring, 2015.

Wertheim, Margaret, ed. *Crochet Coral Reef*. Los Angeles, Calif.: The Institute for Figuring, 2015.

Wertheim, Margaret, and Christine Wertheim. "Introduction: Iterate, Deviate, Elaborate." In *Crochet Coral Reef*, ed. Margaret Wertheim. Los Angeles, Calif.: The Institute for Figuring, 2015.

# Movable Party

WENDY HSU, STEVEN KEMPER, JOSEF CAMERON TAYLOR,
LINDA WEI, AND JACOB ALDEN SARGENT

Movable Party is a bicycle-powered system for participatory musical performance designed and built by Los Angeles-based maker collective, Movable Parts. Taking design inspirations from Taiwan's street sound innovations, the collective made the system to instigate ad hoc, emplaced social interactions as a form of creative friction against urban sprawl. The system consists of three stationary bicycles, each equipped with rear-wheel hub motors that generate enough energy to power a medium-sized public address system. The bicycles are also equipped with sensors to track rear-wheel speed as well as rider position. Mapped to musical parameters in software, sensor data from riders' gestures and movements transform the bicycles into interactive musical instruments.

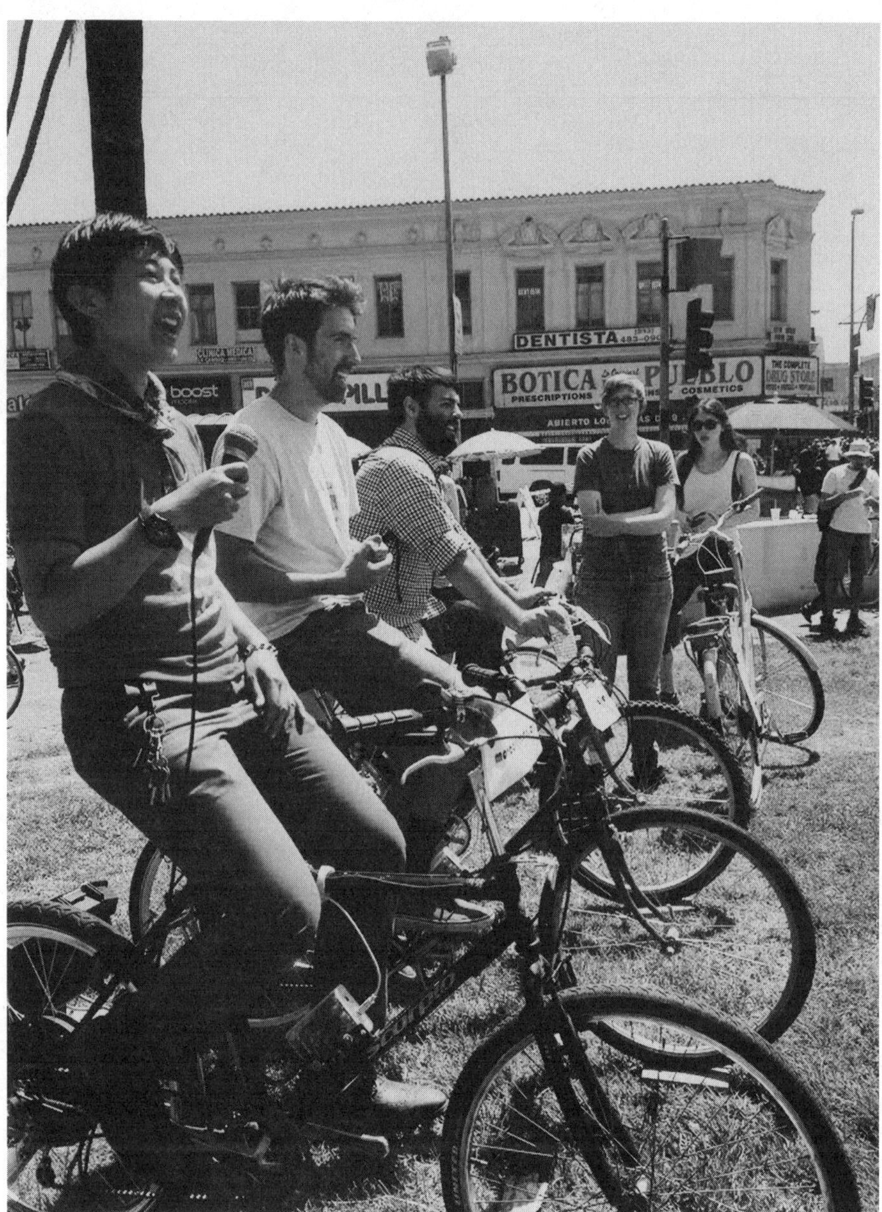


**Figure 28.1.** Movable Party. Format: Participatory musical performance. Materials: Bicycles, sensors, Arduinos, hub motors, power inverter, charge controller, battery, laptop, and PA system. Wendy Hsu, Steven Kemper, Josef Cameron Taylor, Linda Wei, and Jacob Alden Sargent. Photograph courtesy of the artists.

PART IV ][ *Chapter 29*

# Disrupting Dichotomies: Mobilizing Digital Humanities with the MakerBus

KIM MARTIN, BETH COMPTON, AND RYAN HUNT

As demonstrated by the popularity of *Make: Magazine,* Maker Faires, and maker-inspired curricula, makerspaces and maker culture have gathered significant attention in recent years. Although these concepts are increasingly familiar, many makerspaces (also known as fab labs, hackerspaces, and DIY centers) are often found in basements of university campuses or off the beaten path of popular downtown streets. As makerspaces gain traction, their role in supporting their local communities and acting as social spaces for their members has become clearer (Taylor, Connolly, and Hurley). For instance, many of them are becoming mobile, shifting from dark basements and hidden streets into the wider public sphere through the use of vehicles. Maker projects in themselves, these vehicles help instill a love of creative play by carrying materials to help a wider population engage with maker culture. We manage one such vehicle: the MakerBus, a school bus based in Southern Ontario. Since starting this project in April 2013, we have responded to questions we did not think we would encounter in our time as graduate students: how do we continue to remain critically aware of the maker technologies we use and provide? How do we maintain our academic interests surrounding the maker movement, yet also strive to make a difference in our local communities? And how do we negotiate our roles as "experts" in a field where we have so much more to learn?

After briefly introducing the concept of mobile makerspaces and the MakerBus, this chapter explores perceived dichotomies that we have faced and continue to face. We feel that academic scholarship often neglects personal experience, which is central to critical work. Thus, we offer our experiences with the MakerBus as a window into a public-facing communications project in order to inform future like-minded projects and diversify current maker discourse. Through our unique point of view as humanities graduate students overseeing the MakerBus project, we provide a reflexive take on two common dichotomies: the academy or the community, and experts or amateurs.

### *Mobile Makerspaces*

A makerspace is "a general term for a place where people get together to make things" (Roslund and Rodgers). In the spirit of DIY, makers use these spaces to share a variety of skills—from sewing, woodworking, and laser-cutting to artistic practices and computer programming. Mobile makerspaces take this concept on the road, packing all the equipment into a vehicle and going out into communities to foster engagement. While no two makerspaces are the same, one common goal of mobile makerspaces is to provide access to resources and offer educational experiences to their communities (Moorefield-Lang). Instead of requiring individuals to visit a library or university campus, mobile makerspaces go directly to them. The current literature on mobile makerspaces is narrated largely by those involved in their creation: communications personnel for libraries and museums, teachers looking to extend school programming, university groups of STEM advocates, and independent organizations (including nonprofits, charities, and social enterprises) (Craddock; de Boer; Gierdowski and Reis; Moorefield-Lang).

With no direct ties to a particular university, library, museum, or school, the MakerBus is an independent organization. It is also a retrofitted 1989 school bus that carries an eclectic collection of technologies—such as virtual reality and augmented reality viewers, drones (or quadcopters), 3-D scanners, and 3-D printers—that are often affiliated with the maker movement. One aspect of our work involves partnering with charities and nonprofits to offer creative approaches to digital literacy education in our city. We are different from other mobile makerspaces because we aim to include arts, humanities, and social sciences content in our explorations.[1] We visit libraries, schools, and museums and work with children, teens, and adults alike. We have designed adult literacy modules about drones and podcasting ("Maker Curriculum Modules"), held fashion shows of wearables and handmade clothing, and even attempted to set a world record. Not all of these activities occur on board the bus; however, the MakerBus is the symbol that drives our community-focused project.

### *The Academy or the Community*

Academic scholarship predominantly frames community involvement through terms such as "knowledge mobilization,"[2] "community outreach," and "public engagement."[3] While these terms have been used to describe work that is reciprocal in nature, in practice they are mostly unidirectional—academics remain producers of knowledge, and community members (or "the public") remain consumers of curated academic information. This perceived dichotomy shapes what both parties (i.e., scholars and community partners) bring to the table.

Our work with the MakerBus disrupts this dichotomy in two ways. First, our interactions with the larger maker community shaped our personal academic interests. More specifically, 3-D printing and 3-D modeling altered Beth Compton's

Ph.D. path. She knew little about either topic prior to her work with the MakerBus. She now explores issues of representation and replication in cultural heritage management through interviews with research participants in the Circumpolar North. Having to negotiate gender dynamics as a female co-founder of the MakerBus led Kim Martin to a post-doctoral fellowship examining the role of gender in makerspaces. Meanwhile, Ryan Hunt decided to leave the academy and now balances community engagement via the MakerBus with discussions of the MakerBus in academic contexts, including this very chapter.

Second, our paths as scholars inform our community-based, collaborative work, providing a critical lens when advocating for maker technology and digital literacy. For example, the Innov8 project saw the MakerBus partner with a literacy advocacy program, a local church, and an adult education institute. Each group contributed a unique knowledge set to the larger goals of the project (Dumlao and Janke). Literacy Link South Central's focus on literacy information and training, combined with their awareness of London's underprivileged social areas, led them to create digital literacy programming with a focus on 18- to 35-year-olds. The local church and adult education institute provided a connection and attentiveness to the interests of potential participants. The MakerBus provided a creative take on digital literacy around maker technologies such as 3-D printing and augmented reality, demonstrating how they are more than mere gadgets for uncritical consumption or entertainment.

In 99 percent of Ontario elementary and secondary schools, students have access to computers with Internet access (Chen). However, research shows that access alone does not equate directly with increased scholastic confidence or performance (Chen). More technology is not necessarily better; how resources are used matters most. While providing at-risk and underserved groups with access is an important MakerBus mandate, we also encourage people to evaluate their relationship with technology. The Innov8 project was the result of finding "common ground" and could not have happened without a critical assessment of digital literacy techniques and maker technology (Sandy and Holland). As a group we worked through past literacy programming and concluded that many of the learning objectives could be met with maker technologies. For instance, instead of teaching someone how to use a search engine, we presented them with a Makey Makey, provided instructions for set-up, and then asked them to look online to locate either new games to play or other uses for this technology.[4] With the maker technology as the focus, Innov8 participants wanted to understand how things worked. They also learned the requisite digital literacy skills through curiosity instead of a step-by-step tutorial. This unique approach to digital literacy training would have been difficult to achieve without voices and contributions across the academy and community.

Through the MakerBus project we built a network that connects nonprofit, charity, corporate, government, and academic initiatives, each of which is motivated by a diverse array of interests. Our network and the way we draw upon these partnerships are unique to our community and the individuals with whom we work. We believe our project must be viewed within a broader ecosystem of existing local projects and complementary services responsive to local needs. This integrated and unifying approach treats academic and community expertise as equally valuable.

### *Experts or Amateurs*

A core ethos of the maker movement is to challenge traditional views of the expert, recognizing that everyone, from aerospace engineers to kindergartners, has skills to share (Martinez and Stager). This sentiment of collaborative, peer-to-peer learning turns students into teachers and amateurs into experts. As Kuznetsov and Paulos point out, DIY culture is driven by creativity and open information exchange. In these communities, expertise is not derived from formal education or training alone, but also by "hobbyists and enthusiasts who critique and learn from each others' work, giving rise to the *expert amateur*" (8). Such expertise in amateurism results from dialogue with the maker community, gaining knowledge from sharing knowledge, and participating in iterative creative processes. One of the goals of the MakerBus is to help our community members realize their potential as expert amateurs by leading them to engage with maker technology in ways that pique their unique, individual interests. Another goal is to challenge normative assumptions about expertise, including assumptions about who experts are and where expertise is developed.

Despite this goal, our backgrounds in higher education, combined with the leadership roles we have undertaken by virtue of running the MakerBus, often give the impression that we are maker experts. Part of what makes the MakerBus desirable to organizations like libraries and schools is the perceived expertise of its team members in maker and educational technologies. Aware of this paradox (that we use our status as experts to challenge assumptions of expertise), we are transparent about our own knowledge, or lack thereof. For example, in a recent set of workshops with teacher-librarians from the local school board, we discussed our relationship with our 3-D printer. Assembled from a kit over a period of months on a kitchen table, we learned how 3-D printers work by building (and often failing to build) our first printer. By telling this story, we were being honest about our perceived expert status, acknowledging that we gained familiarity with 3-D printers and their use through trial-and-error experimentation.

The use of specific maker technologies (e.g., 3-D printers and 3-D scanners) requires us to gain detailed knowledge about them, and working with the public means sharing this information in a variety of settings. Some people consider this knowledge to be expertise, but we treat it as a platform: information that will inspire others to expand their own experiences with the tools we have at hand. For instance, in our 3-D printing workshops, we demonstrate the printer, the software it requires, and numerous 3-D scanning methods. Then, instead of working to achieve a fixed set of learning outcomes, the group discusses their personal interests and skill sets and how both may relate to 3-D printing. We have yet to leave one of these workshops without learning from the participants and witnessing the participants learn from one another.

From its outset, the MakerBus has challenged dichotomies. Acting simultaneously as academics and community members, we have felt tensions between perceived expertise and amateurism, at times feeling like amateur professionals or professional amateurs. Our professional training in library and information sciences, archaeology, and history, respectively, all influence the direction of the MakerBus project, but the humanistic skills we obtained through our education are rarely employed academically in the day-to-day running of the MakerBus.

The MakerBus and, in our experience, a great many makerspaces reflect Kuznetsov and Paulos's idea that DIY culture has given rise to the "expert amateur." While none of us has formal training in science education, curriculum design, or emerging technologies, we have gained "expert" status in many different community circles through our continued work with the project. Drawing upon elements of our academic training, experience working with diverse groups, and a healthy sense of trial and error, we hope to continue inspiring critical dialogue about maker technologies and pedagogies that encourages people to share their unique skills, ideas, and perspectives, making everyone an expert amateur. By seeking and valuing divergent expertise to the benefit of all parties, and by recognizing that knowledge mobilization is reciprocal, we are well positioned to forge new directions and create, above all else, meaningful change.

## NOTES

1. See Geek Bus (http://geekbus.com), one of the better-funded mobile makerspaces in North America, as an example of a STEM-only organization.

2. For the Social Sciences and Humanities Research Council's definition of "knowledge mobilization," see www.sshrc-crsh.gc.ca/funding-financement/programs-programmes/definitions-eng.aspx#km-mc.

3. The National Endowment for the Humanities' "Digital Projects for the Public" grants support projects that contribute significantly to the public's engagement with the humanities. See www.neh.gov/grants/public/digital-projects-the-public.

4. A Makey Makey is a small circuit board that, when connected to a computer via a USB and to conductive material via alligator clips, creates an interface alternative to a standard keyboard and mouse.

## BIBLIOGRAPHY

Chen, Bodong. "Exploring the Digital Divide: The Use of Digital Technologies in Ontario Public Schools. Explorer Le Fossé Numérique: L'Usage Des Technologies Numériques

Dans Les Écoles Publiques de L'Ontario." *Canadian Journal of Learning and Technology* 41, no. 3 (2015). www.cjlt.ca/index.php/cjlt/article/view/926/450.

Craddock, IdaMae Louise. "Makers on the Move: A Mobile Makerspace at a Comprehensive Public High School." *Library Hi Tech* 33, no. 4 (2015): 497–504.

de Boer, Jeroen. "The Business Case of FryskLab, Europe's First Mobile Library FabLab." *Library Hi Tech* 33, no. 4 (2015): 505–18.

Dumlao, Rebecca J., and Emily M. Janke. "Using Relational Dialectics to Address Differences in Community-Campus Partnerships." *Journal of Higher Education Outreach and Engagement* 16, no. 2 (2012): 151–76. http://openjournals.libs.uga.edu/index.php/jheoe/article/view/793.

Gierdowski, Dana, and Daniel Reis. "The MobileMaker: An Experiment with a Mobile Makerspace." *Library Hi Tech* 33, no. 4 (2015): 480–96.

Kuznetsov, Stacey, and Eric Paulos. "Rise of the Expert Amateur: DIY Projects, Communities, and Cultures." In *Proceedings of the 6th Nordic Conference on Human–Computer Interaction: Extending Boundaries (NordiCHI '10)*, 295–304. Reykjavik, Iceland, 2010. http://dx.doi.org/10.1145/1868914.1868950.

"Maker Curriculum Modules." *Literacy Link South Central*, 2014. www.llsc.on.ca/node/159.

Makey Makey. http://www.makeymakey.com/.

Martinez, Sylvia, and Gary Stager. "The Maker Movement: A Learning Revolution." *ISTE*, July 21, 2014. www.iste.org/explore/articledetail?articleid=106.

Moorefield-Lang, Heather Michele. "When Makerspaces Go Mobile: Case Studies of Transportable Maker Locations." *Library Hi Tech* 33, no. 4 (2015): 462–71.

Roslund, Samantha, and Emily Puckett Rodgers. *Makerspaces*, ed. Kristen Fontichiaro. Ann Arbor, Mich.: Cherry Lake Publishing, 2014.

Sandy, Marie, and Barbara A. Holland. "Different Worlds and Common Ground: Community Partner Perspectives on Campus-Community Partnerships." *Michigan Journal of Community Service Learning* 13, no. 1 (2006): 30–43.

Taylor, Nick, Philip Connolly, and Ursula Hurley. "Making Community: The Wider Role of Makerspaces in Public Life University of Dundee." In *Proceedings of the SIGCHI Conference on Human Factors in Computing Systems (CHI '16)*. San Jose, Calif. 2016. http://dx.doi.org/10.1145/2858036.2858073.

## Designs for Foraging: Fruit Are Heavy, 2015–16

CARL DISALVO, TOM JENKINS, JONG WON (KARL) KIM, CATHERINE MESCHIA, AND CRAIG DURKIN

Design for Foraging explores the appropriation of precision technologies for ad-hoc urban agricultures. Fruit Are Heavy is a custom-designed, low-fidelity sensing platform to infer the ripeness of fruit in trees by monitoring the relative droop of branches as the fruit matures. The project uses research-through-design to speculate on diverse economies and propose alternative configurations of so-called smart cities.

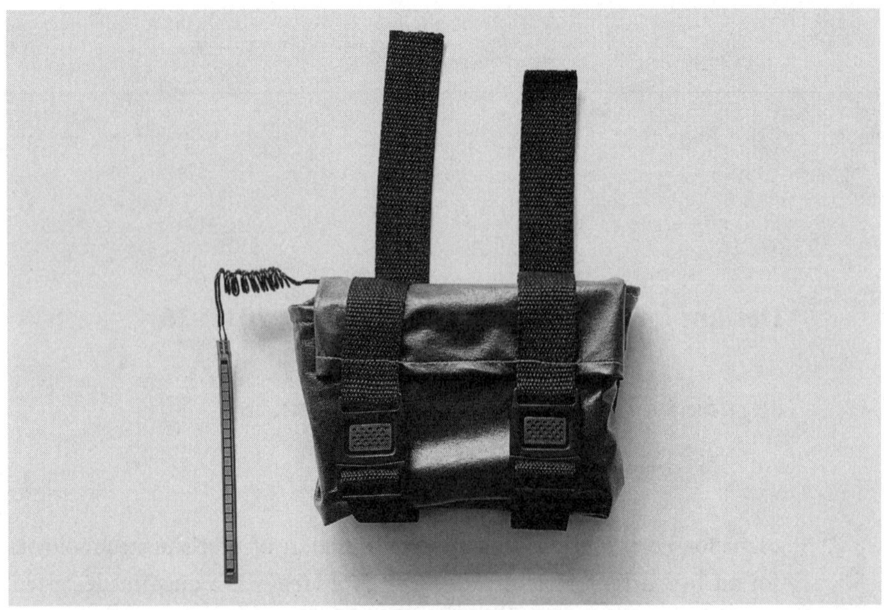

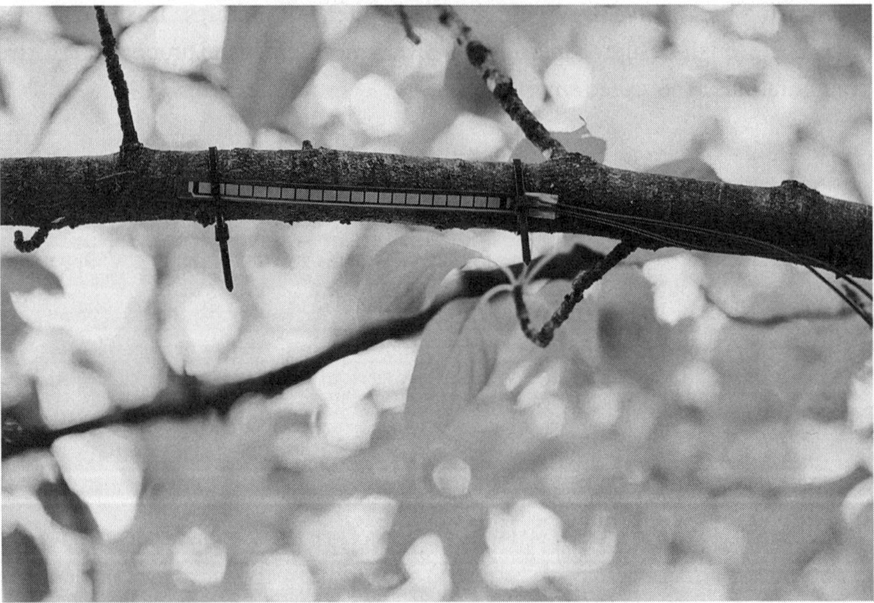

**Figure 30.1.** Designs for Foraging: Fruit Are Heavy. Format: Prototype sensor system and service. Materials: Custom electronics, flex sensor, apple trees, and apples. Carl DiSalvo, Tom Jenkins, Jong Won (Karl) Kim, Catherine Meschia, and Craig Durkin. Photograph courtesy of Sean MacKey.

# Experience Design for the Humanities: Activating Multiple Interpretations

STAN RUECKER AND JENNIFER ROBERTS-SMITH

This chapter deals with two central propositions. The first is that the humanities has an opportunity to create a new kind of experience design that is fundamentally different in its goals from experience design in industry. In order to reliably appeal to customers, commercial experience designers strive for consistency. Whether working with retail outlets or amusement parks, they attempt to produce a customer experience that is similar for everyone who enters. There is, for example, a well-defined "Disney experience" that strives to keep a trip to any Disney location within the discourse of the brand. Cinderella should not take a vaping break where anyone can see her, and Belle cannot decide to go blonde this month. Such occurrences would compromise the brand, and that is fair enough. But one side effect of consistency is that, aside from the inevitable hermeneutic of suspicion, visitors are rarely if ever encouraged to experience Disney from different perspectives. For the humanities, however, encouraging people to experience culture from different perspectives is a core value: we seek to enrich the object of study by layering multiple, simultaneous, valid interpretations onto it. Conceiving a form of experience design that expresses this value should therefore be possible.

Our second proposition is that there are forms of activation resulting from cultural experiences that range from the immediate physiological reaction to the long-term creative response. By using the word "activation," we refer to the various physical and psychological states of response to a stimulus. With these states of response in mind, humanities experience design should accommodate the fact that the time scale of responses to cultural experiences stretches conceivably from the instant to the lifetime. It should thus encourage immediate, medium, and long-term responses from, for instance, someone attending a cultural venue or event. Whether this proposal for a humanities experience design is widely accepted, our own goal for this practice is to explore new ways of designing experiences to engage audiences in complex acts of interpretation as they move into and out from cultural performances and venues.

In some respects, interpretation is a part of living; it cannot be escaped, because people make sense of their environments to greater or lesser degrees as they move through the day. However, we may speak of an "interpretive experience" within the particular context of a cultural event. It involves a reflexive cognitive response that differs from the unexamined response of simple, superficial, or straightforward reading. Interpretation in the humanities is typically described as the application of some theoretical lens; the lenses are not mutually exclusive, but instead increase our understanding of the object of study as each in turn is articulated and applied. For example, someone might experience a production of *Macbeth,* such as the Punchdrunk company's famous immersive, environmental adaptation, *Sleep No More* (2011), and interpret it through feminism, formalism, psychoanalysis, postmodernism, queer theory, and so on. Although *Sleep No More* varies somewhat in how each audience member experiences it, such variation does not necessarily imply an individual's use of multiple interpretive lenses.

### *Hypothesis 1. The goal is an enriched interpretive experience.*

To enhance the experiences of their audiences, cultural and educational institutions have been leaders in adopting emerging technologies to provide context for the cultural content they offer. Museums, for example, have for decades used audio guides and video commentary to communicate interpretations of artifacts while audiences are viewing them. Recently, augmented reality apps such as the Museum of London's *Streetmuseum*—a recognized leader in the field of cultural heritage (Jeater; Zolfagharifard)—have extended delivery systems to include mobile and other emerging technologies. When the camera of a mobile phone is directed at a London monument, *Streetmuseum* overlays a curated historical image of the same site. The results are both beautiful and intellectually provocative (see Figure 31.1).

Like most systems that use emerging media to enhance audience experience,[1] *Streetmuseum* invites audiences to "customize" an augmented reality exhibition by enabling them to select the kinds of content they prefer (choosing nearby historical sites from a Google map), reorganize content in ways predefined by the app's designers (creating "trails" by routing favorite historical sites on a Google map), and endorse or "share" content (sending images the app creates to social media). This kind of engagement facilitates a predictable flow of artifacts and expert opinion from the museum to app users and then to social media, extending the reach of the museum's virtual exhibition space and the size and diversity of its audience.

Typically, then, technological enhancements to audience experience have numerous features. First, they overlay or operate in parallel to embodied, material experiences. The technological enhancements are not replacements, as they are in virtual reality, but augmentations. Second, they communicate expert interpretations of artifacts or events. In order to understand what they are seeing or experiencing, members of the audience can benefit from exposure to previous

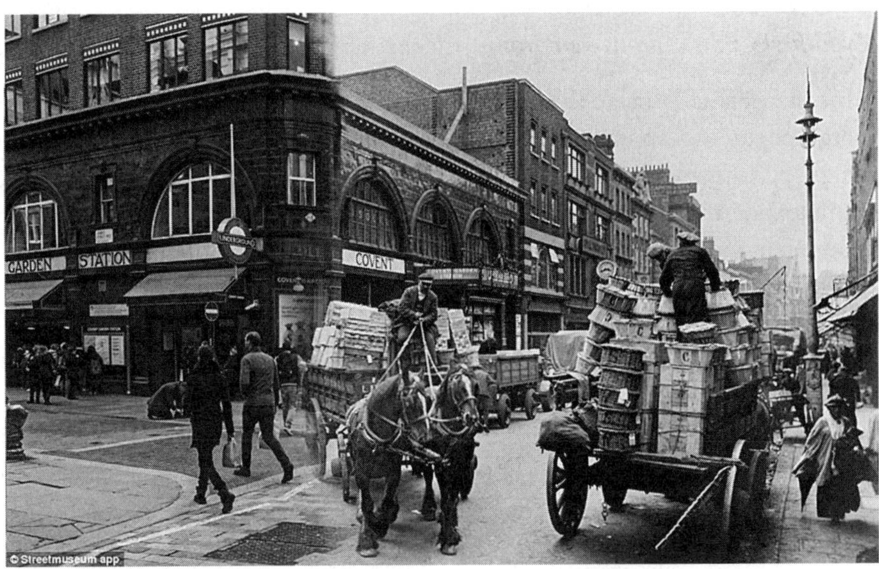


**Figure 31.1.** Covent Garden Station in the Museum of London's Streetmuseum. Screenshot of *Streetmuseum* app.

valid interpretations. Third, at least in some cases, technological enhancements allow audiences to customize and endorse exhibits through their own comments. Fourth, they ask audiences to facilitate the process of engaging a broader public, whether by spreading knowledge of the experience through their own social networks or contributing to the body of public commentary associated with the artifact or event.

We see an opportunity for scholars in the humanities to extend this approach in the service of an important, long-standing goal of humanities research and education, namely to increase audiences' ability and interest in producing their own interpretations of cultural phenomena from a variety of theoretical or experiential perspectives. To that end, we propose the design of what we call "interpretive environments" rather than discrete technological tools or systems. Our interpretive environments integrate embodied, material, and virtual experiences (so that each affects the others). They activate differing—even conflicting—interpretations of artifacts or events, hopefully by the same audience members. They enable audiences to generate and communicate new cultural insights. Finally, they position audiences as agents rather than facilitators of interpretive acts. One strategy for moving forward involves integrating location-based, augmented reality, and motion-capture technologies into the design of material, embodied interpretive experiences for existing cultural events.

***Hypothesis 2. Interpretive environments can activate interpretive experiences.***

Since our goal is to make the habitual practice of interpretation compelling for more people, our approach involves three theoretical dimensions: experience design, performance studies, and hermeneutics. Experience design gives particular attention to the temporal movement of a participant through an event. One common framework taught to students of experience design is the 5Es. Originally developed through the study of rituals, the 5Es emphasize aspects of experience that surround the core experience. A person may begin by seeing or hearing various forms of enticement to come to the event; then enter, experience, and exit the event; and finally extend the experience through various reminders, such as souvenirs, recordings, and social media activities.[2] Further, experience designers ask what makes an experience compelling. Many experiences are mundane and should stay that way: for instance, very few people would want a consistently compelling trip to the post office or grocery store. However, for some kinds of events, including cultural events, the goal is to make the experience important and even memorable. The aspects of a compelling experience, as taught to experience designers, are that it should be some combination of fresh, immersive, accessible, significant, and transformative (Kumar).

The field of performance studies, on the other hand, privileges other aspects of experience. It acknowledges embodied cultural practice as a mode of knowledge production, preservation, and transmission.[3] It focuses on the repertoire of acts that instantiates the values and expertise of a community through repetition, witness, and instruction. People perform for and teach one another acts ranging from domestic tasks, such as cooking, to rituals that reconfigure social relationships, such as marriages, to codes of conduct, such as oral histories, to self-consciously structured reflections, such as sports, dances, songs, or plays. Such acts take a range of forms from the most quotidian to the most stylized (Taylor 20). As a community's understanding of itself shifts, its repertoire of cultural performances shifts in parallel. Diana Taylor (2003) and others have demonstrated the hermeneutic power of cultural practice by tracing its suppression during the Latin American conquest in particular, and the process of "transculturation" by which the practices of the Mexica and conquering Spaniards merged over time (Taylor 17, 79–109). In an interpretive environment, interpretation is expressed and adopted as a value, but also embodied, repeated, witnessed, and taught.

Finally, hermeneutics is the theorization and interpretative practice of symbolic human communication and non-symbolic human experiences (Ramberg and Gjesdal; Ramsay). The practice, if not always the theory, of hermeneutics tends to suggest that multiple valid interpretations can coexist, and that seeing an object of study through various lenses is beneficial. As Paul Ricoeur (1988) and others have noted, hermeneutics emphasizes the problematics of the text, or the points where further explanation is necessary. Also, every text carries with it its own hermeneutic of suspicion, and ambiguity is the nature of language, so that even the most straightforward communication opens itself to alternative readings. An interpretive environment, then, activates problematics.

In combination, experience design, performance studies, and hermeneutics suggest that an interpretative environment can encourage compelling interpretations by:

- ushering participants along a temporal route into and out from the core cultural experience that is their focus;
- providing a fresh, immersive, accessible, significant, and/or transformative experience along the way;
- modeling acts of interpretation (so that interpretation can be taught and learned);
- presenting participants with explicit interpretive problems, or gaps in meaning, that can be explored physically; and
- providing opportunities for participants to repeat (new) acts of interpretation, modeling them in turn for others.

### *Hypothesis 3. The conceptual ontology of cultural experiences is greater than their instantiation.*

When we attend a symphony, we know that the music we hear exists beyond the context of this particular performance. The composer and process of composition are historically situated. Perhaps previous performances existed, and they varied in their particulars from the current performance. The performers may be different; the conductor, even if the same, may have new ideas about the music; the audience will likely differ from previous audiences; and so on. These levels of conceptual ontology may be modeled and layered onto one another. For example, people familiar with library and information studies will likely know of the Functional Requirements for Bibliographic Records (FRBR), a conceptual ontology for library catalogs (1998). As Barbara Tillet suggests, this ontology recognizes the significant differences between four aspects (item, manifestation, expression, and work) of a cultural object:

> Even in everyday language, we tend to say a "book" when we may actually mean several things.
>
> For example, when we say "book" to describe a physical object that has paper pages and a binding and can sometimes be used to prop open a door or hold up a table leg, FRBR calls this an "item."
>
> When we say "book" we also may mean a "publication" as when we go to a bookstore to purchase a book. We may know its ISBN but the particular copy does not matter as long as it's in good condition and not missing pages. FRBR calls this a "manifestation."

> When we say "book" as in 'who translated that book,' we may have a particular text in mind and a specific language. FRBR calls this an "expression."
>
> When we say "book" as in 'who wrote that book,' we could mean a higher level of abstraction, the conceptual content that underlies all of the linguistic versions, the story being told in the book, the ideas in a person's head for the book. FRBR calls this a "work." (Tillet 2–3)

FRBR has not been universally accepted or applied, even in library and information studies, and it is not the only possible layering of ontologies. However, it is a good example of the kind of thinking we have in mind. Returning for a moment to the symphony, we can say that it emerges from the composer's ideas (the work) that are realized through the score (an expression), which is embodied in the edition of the score used for this concert (a manifestation) and exemplified by the particular copy of the score printed on a certain paper stock that perhaps contains some notes, dog-ears, or other signs of use (an item). Similarly, the symphony performance itself is a designed event. The orchestra has an idea (the work) of how to interpret the score, and they reach an understanding of what this interpretation implies for the conductor and musicians (an expression). This understanding is embodied in a performance (a manifestation), which is exemplified by a performance on a given night (an item). These distinctions are important because they play a role in the act of interpretation.

Using this FRBR-based analysis, we now have four ontological categories associated with the music before it is performed, and four more associated with the performance. Any of these eight ontological levels can be subject to evaluation, discussion, and critique. Acknowledging this fact, audience members will often refer to a specific performance (an item) as an important—perhaps the most important—aspect of the experience overall. This specificity does not, however, remove from consideration the other seven levels of conceptual ontology. Shifting awareness across all eight levels encourages audience members to make multiple, valid interpretations.

### *Hypothesis 4. Experience design may produce a range of impacts, including long-term ones.*

User experience studies in the humanities have engaged mixed-mode qualitative and quantitative methods (including surveys, semi-structured interviews, screen capture, and sideshadowing) drawn principally from the social sciences and design (Dobson et al.; Ruecker et al.; Roberts-Smith et al.). These methods have been effective in evaluating experimental prototypes, especially when assessment protocols are designed to encourage what Teresa Dobson et al. call "generative feedback," or responses "that invite one to step away from the ideas instantiated in the prototype and consider the broader context, such as the values inherent in, say, a disciplinary approach to knowledge and knowledge mobilization as evidenced by the responses of readers" (6). Dobson et al.'s approach, particularly its treatment of study participants as co-creators of critical insight and knowledge through both participatory (Schuler and Namoika) and cooperative design (Greenbaum and Kyng), aligns well with the goals of interpretive environments. It also takes seriously Louise Phillips and Agli Zavros's (2013) suggestion that "participants themselves should be counted as members of the research team" (Dobson et al. 12).

However, applying some of the controls expected in the social sciences and design is difficult when we design interpretive environments intended for public audiences in non-academic cultural organizations. In the lobby of the Stratford Festival, for example, where audiences move freely among numerous experiences, including a bar, shop, and mobile trumpet fanfare, some interpretive experiences may not be easily isolated from others. We also need to measure forms of impact that we do not normally consider but may be meaningful to those responsible for the event. These forms might include ticket sales, return visits of identifiable audience members, the emotional responses of audience members, and endorsements in social media.

Since interpretive environments aim to increase audience interest and ability to engage in complex acts of interpretation, those interpretations must be assessed in terms of their aesthetic value, idiosyncrasies, and demonstrated knowledge of cultural events. We therefore propose a new protocol for impact assessment that accommodates the following range of responses, from the immediate to the long-term:

- involuntary physiological (such as fight/flight responses, laughter, tears, and anxiety),
- voluntary embodied (such as dancing, singing, and applause),
- descriptive perception (noticing new things without necessarily explaining them),
- directed perception (discerning which new things are most important),
- comparative perception (noticing differences and similarities with cognate experiences),
- speculative perception (wondering what would happen if the experience were designed differently),
- passive imagination (accepting immersion in a fiction offered by the experience),
- active imagination (co-creation of a fiction supported by the experience),
- generative interpretation (producing a new idea for the interpreter about what an experience means and why it matters), and
- creation (writing, directing, performing, or otherwise making a new, original experience).[4]

Some of these responses (e.g., voluntary embodied) can be directly observed, while others (e.g., speculative perception) rely on reporting of some kind. The responses are all important with respect to enjoying a cultural experience, but the last three require a cognitive action that is less reactive or more generative than the rest. Similarly, any of these responses may be immediate, medium-term, or long-term since, for example, involuntary physiological responses may be experienced while remembering a cultural event as well as during it, and creative cognitive effort might be made simultaneously (consciously or unconsciously) with the original experience of an event as well as afterwards. Consequently, our new assessment protocol will necessarily emphasize qualitative self-reporting, including the kinds of "critical," "evocative," and even performed personal narratives that have been employed in the field of autoethnography (Burdell and Swadener; Ellis; Spry).

### *Hypothesis 5. New interpretive environments should not compete with the environment to be interpreted.*

We assume that experience design for the humanities will not occupy center stage, but should instead encourage an interpretive stance toward other, central cultural experiences. However, in strengthening this perspective, we might argue that all interpretive environments occur physically and/or mentally around the edges of a primary cultural experience.

The physical side is a practical necessity for many cultural experiences, since any discussion of interpretation can interfere with other audience members' experiences. Such discussions therefore tend to take place outside the performance venue, perhaps in the lobby or in a restaurant, bar, or coffee shop, where people gather after the show to discuss what they just experienced. Many such places near cultural venues will display historical playbills, posters, or photos of performers, each of which associates the restaurant with the area and culture. These venues also remind their clientele that the performance they just experienced is not an isolated event. In this respect, they help to activate interpretive discussion, if only through comparative perception.

The mental side involves the necessary step away from total immersion and toward a more critical understanding of the event. This form of reflection can occur during or after the performance and does not require discussion with other people. It does, however, occupy a mental track or conceptual channel where primary perception and naive understanding of what is happening are supplemented with a secondary awareness and more nuanced understanding of what is implied. People with specialized training in the humanities will often conduct complex acts of interpretation while immersed in an experience, but for some the immersion is enough to process at the time.

### *Hypothesis 6. An interpretive environment is a space between the dominant cultural discourse of the moment and a cultural phenomenon that is the focus of the experience.*

Interpretive environments are interfaces between discourse and experience. In some cases, such as an art exhibit dedicated to canonical works, the cultural experience may reinforce the dominant worldview. In other instances, it may directly oppose the dominant worldview, which is then supported by its defining other. A third possibility is that the cultural experience offers alternatives to the dominant cultural discourse. In all cases, the interpretive space can be opened in a generative manner, and the interpretive environment plays a role by sitting between the audience's everyday experience of the world and the experience of the world offered by the cultural event. Deliberately designing these transitional spaces to increase their generative hermeneutic potential is the challenge for experience design in the humanities. As Johanna Drucker (2014) points out, such design is a central concern for speculative computing. Perhaps we can take the lead of critics such as Jerome McGann (2001) and Stephen Ramsay (2011), who suggest the benefits of various forms of defamiliarization, whether through deformation (McGann) or algorithmic criticism (Ramsay).

### *Hypothesis 7. Any interpretive discipline may contribute to the design of interpretive environments.*

The humanities may be best positioned to design interpretative environments, and—as a branch of the humanities that concerns itself with making—digital humanities could have an important role to play. The grounding humanities discipline (e.g., English, history, or cultural studies) will influence the kind of making that is done, and collaboration with adjacent disciplines, such as psychology, sociology, design, and education, is possible. Many of these disciplines are already active in public humanities, where, to quote Miriam Bartha, the concept of serious work is twofold:

> "Serious work" in the humanities thus invokes two discourses simultaneously. It refers to critical and creative intellectual, political, and cultural work that makes a social difference and it refers to what counts and can be made to count, academically, as "serious work"—i.e., rigorous scholarship. (86)

Experience designers in the humanities should aim for both forms of production but not concern themselves with creating new Disneylands; other core cultural experiences, such as symphonies, plays, films, and operas; or venues, including museums or art galleries. We would like to see attempts to make new experiences that activate interpretation from multiple perspectives. As "serious work" that is supplementary, secondary, or liminal, interpretive experience design could emerge as a discipline in its own right, with appropriate assessment measures and best practices. Or it could enrich and extend the outcomes of any scholarly or cultural endeavor, since it creates the conditions for both specialist and non-specialist participants to engage reflexively and critically in what might otherwise be habitual or unexamined activities.

As an example of the experience design we have in mind, consider the "hermeneutobooth," a pilot project we are developing. It will consist of a physical structure that sits in the lobby of a theater and provides a partially sequestered space for reflection integrated into the lobby's overall design. People who are about to attend a play will be invited into the booth, where they will be asked to make a video recording of their answers to questions related to the play's themes. Each question will be unique, and all questions will demand multiple answers. Sometime after the performance, participants will be sent copies of the video recordings they have made and invited to update their answers, either by email or with a new video recording, in response to their experience of the play. This fairly simple activity aims to fulfill the goals and parameters we outline for interpretive experience design, while directing interpretive energies toward the play instead of the hermeneutobooth.

### *Conclusions and Future Directions*

One of our unaddressed questions is where interpretive environments overlap with critical or speculative designs (e.g., by Dunne and Raby) that provoke people to engage their critical faculties. If critical or speculative design proves to be useful, then we will need to consider how it not only provokes but also activates multiple, simultaneous, valid interpretations. Another question concerns the role of propinquity: For interpretive environments to be effective, must they occupy a spot in space and time that is close to the central event, or can they be designed for remote application? We might, for instance, envision an experience intended for the lobby before an opera. On the other hand, we might consider a virtual or augmented reality experience that could take place anywhere. Most important, can experience design that activates interpretation fulfill the role we propose for it in this chapter, or will it best be deployed in combination with other strategies, such as public information campaigns, new kinds of games or toys, or more widespread education related to the core values of the humanities? Each of these combinations leads us into new possibilities for inquiry as we work toward developing a more robust model.

#### NOTES

1. For an example in Canada, see Kevin Kee and vxFusion Ltd.
2. See Kumar.
3. See Roach; and Piccini.
4. Byrne and Alexander cite a parallel taxonomy of degrees of participation commonly used by development agencies (4).

**BIBLIOGRAPHY**

Bartha, Miriam. "Serious Work: Public Engagement and the Humanities." *Western Humanities Review* 64, no. 3 (2010): 85–104.

Burdell, Patricia, and Beth Swadener. "Critical Personal Narrative and Autoethnography in Education: Reflections on a Genre." *Educational Researcher* 28, no. 6 (1999): 21–26.

Byrne, Elaine, and P. M. Alexander. "Questions of Ethics: Participatory Information Systems Research in Community Settings." In *Proceedings of the 2006 Annual Research Conference of the South African Institute of Computer Scientists and Information Technologists on IT Research in Developing Countries* (SAICSIT '06), ed. Judith Bishop and Derrick Kourie, 117–26. South African Institute for Computer Scientists and Information Technologists, Republic of South Africa (2006).

Dobson, Teresa M., Monica Brown, Dustin Grue, Ernesto Peña, Geoff Roeder, and the INKE Research Team. "The Interface Implications of Understanding Readers." In "The Future of Reading," ed. Stan Ruecker, special issue, *Interdisciplinary Science Reviews* 40, no. 1 (2015): 3–16.

Drucker, Johanna. *Graphesis: Visual Forms of Knowledge Production*. Cambridge, Mass.: Harvard University Press, 2014.

Dunne, Anthony, and Fiona Raby. *Speculative Everything: Design, Fiction, and Social Dreaming*. Cambridge, Mass.: MIT Press, 2013.

Ellis, Carolyn. "Evocative Autoethnography: Writing Emotionally about Our Lives." In *Representation and the Text: Re-Framing the Narrative Voice*, ed. W. Tierney and Y. Lincoln, 115–39. Albany, N.Y.: State University of New York Press (1997).

Greenbaum, Joan M., and Morten Kyng. *Design at Work: Cooperative Design of Computer Systems*. Mahwah, N.J.: Erlbaum, 1991.

The International Federation of Library Associations and Institutions. Functional Requirements for Bibliographic Records. Munich: K.G. Saur Verlag, 1998.

Jeater, Meriel. "Smartphones and Site interpretation: The Museum of London's *Streetmuseum* Applications." In *Archaeologists and the Digital: Towards Strategies of Engagement*, ed. Chiara Bonacchi, 66–82. London: Archetype Publications, 2012.

Kee, Kevin, and vxFusion Ltd. *Niagara 1812: An iHistoryTour*. 2010. www.ihistorytours.com.

Kumar, Vijay. *101 Design Methods: A Structured Approach for Driving Innovation in Your Organization*. Hoboken, N.J.: Wiley, 2012.

McGann, Jerome. *Radiant Textuality: Literature after the World Wide Web*. London: Palgrave, 2001.

Phillips, Louise, and Agli Zavros. "Researchers as Participants, Participants as Researchers." In *The Role of Participants in Education Research: Ethics, Epistemologies, and Methods,* ed. Warren Midgley, Patrick Alan Danaher, and Margaret Baguley, 52–63. New York: Routledge, 2013.

Piccini, Angela. "An Historiographic Perspective on Practice as Research." *Studies in Theatre and Performance* 23, no. 3 (2003): 191–207.

Punchdrunk, Emursive, and Rebecca Gold Productions. *Sleep No More.* Dirs. Felix Barrett and Maxine Doyle. McKittrick Hotel: New York, 2011.

Ramberg, Bjørn, and Kristin Gjesdal. "Hermeneutics." *The Stanford Encyclopedia of Philosophy: Winter 2014 Edition*, ed. Edward N. Zalta. http://plato.stanford.edu/archives/win2014/entries/hermeneutics.

Ramsay, Stephen. *Reading Machines: Toward an Algorithmic Criticism*. Champaign, Ill.: University of Illinois Press, 2011.

Ricoeur, Paul. "Philosophical Hermeneutics and Theology." *Theology Digest* 24, no. 2 (1988): 155.

Roach, Joseph. *Cities of the Dead: Circum-Atlantic Performance*. New York: Columbia University Press, 1996.

Roberts-Smith, Jennifer, Teresa Dobson, Sandra Gabriele, Stan Ruecker, and Stéfan Sinclair, with Annemarie Akong, Matt Bouchard, Shawn DeSouza-Coelho, David Lam, Omar Rodriguez, and Karen Taylor. "Literary Theory and Theatre Practice: *Watching the Script* and the *Simulated Environment for Theatre*." Poster presented at Digital Humanities 2010, King's College, London, July 7–11, 2010.

Ruecker, Stan, Ali Grotkowski, Sandra Gabriele, Jennifer Roberts-Smith, Stéfan Sinclair, Teresa Dobson, Annemarie Akong, Sally Fung, and Omar Rodriguez. "Abstraction and Realism in the Design of Avatars for the Simulated Environment for Theatre." *Visual Communication Journal* 12, no. 4 (2013): 459–72.

Schuler, Douglas, and Aki Namioka. *Participatory Design: Principles and Practices*. Mahwah, N.J.: Erlbaum, 1993.

Spry, Tami. "Performing Autoethnography: An Embodied Methodological Praxis." *Qualitative Inquiry* 7, no. 6 (2001): 706–32.

*Streetmuseum*. Museum of London. www.museumoflondon.org.uk/Resources/app/you-are-here-app/home.html.

Taylor, Diana. *The Archive and the Repertoire: Performing Cultural Memory in the Americas*. Durham, N.C.: Duke University Press, 2003.

Tillet, Barbara. "What Is FRBR? A Conceptual Model for the Bibliographic Universe." Washington, D.C.: Library of Congress Cataloging Distribution Service, 2004. www.loc.gov/cds/downloads/FRBR.PDF.

Zolfagharifard, Ellie. "Streets of London Now . . . and Then: Stand Still and Picture Yourself in History with App that Creates Hybrid Images of Present and Past." *Mail Online*. February 27, 2014. www.dailymail.co.uk/sciencetech/article-2567739/Streetmuseum-app-creates-hybrid-images-London.html.

# *AIDS Quilt Touch*: Virtual Quilt Browser

ANNE BALSAMO, DALE MACDONALD, AND JON WINET

The AIDS Quilt Touch (AQT) Virtual Quilt Browser is one of several interactive experiences based on the AIDS Memorial Quilt. In free-browse mode, viewers can explore the Quilt by zooming and panning across the 25-gigapixel image. In Narrative Threads mode, they can follow pathways that present stories about individual panels and the cultural significance of the Quilt. Other AQT applications include a story-making platform, a digital guest book, and interactive timelines.

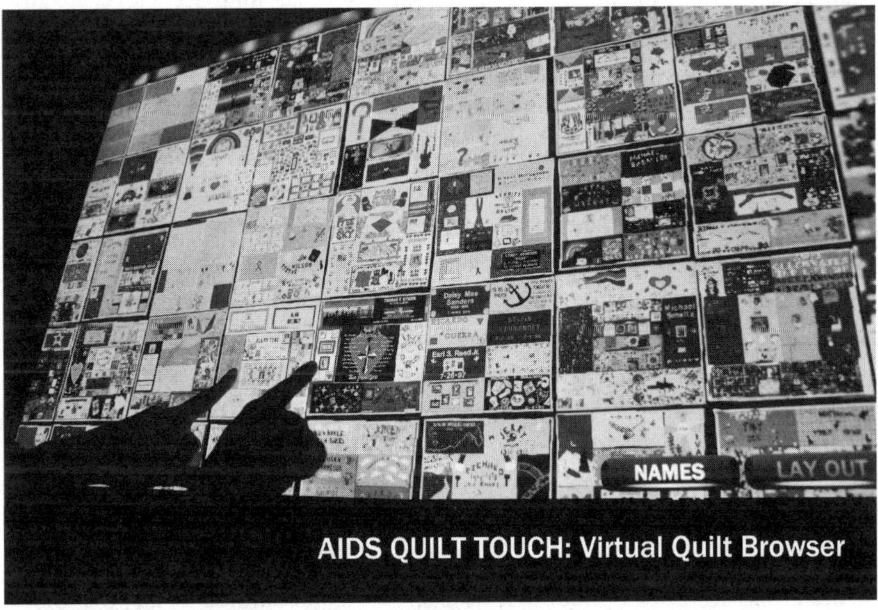


**Figure 32.1.** AIDS Quilt Touch: Virtual Quilt Browser. Format: Public interactive for use on a gesture-based tabletop display. Anne Balsamo, Dale MacDonald, and Jon Winet. Photograph courtesy of the artists.

PART IV ][ *Chapter 33*

# Building Humanities Software That Matters: The Case of the *Ward One* Mobile App

HEIDI RAE COOLEY AND DUNCAN A. BUELL

An estimated ten thousand people gathered at the state house grounds in Columbia, South Carolina, on the morning of July 10, 2015. They gathered with anticipation; they gathered despite record heat. At 10:00 a.m. "the flag" would be—swiftly and with little ceremony—lowered and transported to the Confederate Museum located a mile away. Some dozens might have been there supporting the flag; the vast majority, black and white together, were there to witness a historic event, to symbolically turn from a divisive past toward a future whose hallmarks might be justice, social equity, and mutual respect among citizens. More than a century and a half after the end of the Civil War, more than 50 years after the flag had been raised to the staff on the state capitol dome as a symbol of resistance against the civil rights movement, and 15 years after a legislative compromise took it from the dome to place it at a different prominent position on the state house grounds, "the flag" would come down—and that mattered.

We write in the weeks just after joining that joyful crowd to witness the removal of the Confederate battle flag and the pole from which it flew. Newly laid sod has replaced the concrete slab that anchored that pole and the wrought iron fence that enclosed it. The moment has passed, but we are aware that its record lives on in hours of news footage, numerous newspaper articles, and myriad forms of social media. While the wave of interest in the flag's removal has subsided, racial tensions remain palpable across the country.[1] This historic moment, our present, provides a context for our collaborative efforts to make humanities software that matters at the University of South Carolina (USC). These efforts engage students and community members to develop software that presents routinely unacknowledged histories in order to cultivate a more sophisticated understanding of the various forces that have shaped and continue to shape the local landscape. In our efforts, we aspire to provoke reconsideration of the past in the present in hopes of transforming how a community—in this case, Columbia, South Carolina—imagines a shared future.[2]

For the past four years, we have been developing critical interactives that bring unacknowledged histories of social inequity to visibility. August 2014 saw the completion of the prototype *Ghosts of the Horseshoe,* a mobile application for the iPad that presents the history of slavery that made possible South Carolina College (established in 1801), now the heart of the University's Columbia campus.[3] Known as the historic Horseshoe, the old campus core is a "surprisingly intact and well-preserved 'landscape of slavery,'" according to our local public historians (Thomas Cooper Library). Slaves molded, transported, and laid the bricks that form the structures on the historic campus, and they maintained and served in those buildings in the years preceding the Civil War. Mobilizing the affordances of the geolocative touchscreen device and Augmented Reality (AR) functionality, *Ghosts* confronts its interactors with the fact that they walk unwittingly amidst ghosts, many of whom will forever remain unnamed even as their labor gave shape to the structures that populate the historic grounds.

Our current critical interactive project is a mobile application called *Ward One* (see Figure 33.1) that foregrounds the 1960s displacement of a predominantly African American community. Around the country, urban renewal programs empowered local officials to declare large swaths of land "blighted areas." Families were evicted and businesses closed—often to the benefit of universities and colleges eager to expand. The Ward One district, several of whose neighborhoods and businesses lay adjacent to USC, fell victim to this process.[4] The university took advantage of the opportunity, acquiring, for example, property upon which it constructed the enormous Coliseum in 1968. In 1974 USC took possession of Booker T. Washington High School, established in 1916 as one of the few schools in Columbia for African American students. While the main building of the former high school was recently renovated and currently houses USC's Department of Theater and Dance, the two brick wings of the old school were torn down. The bricks from those structures now pave one of two elliptical driveways that define the historic Horseshoe site.

Not surprisingly, very few visitors, students, staff, or faculty know this history. Nor do they realize that a group of former Ward One community members maintain an organization that refuses to forget the old neighborhood. These individuals grew up in shotgun houses lining streets and alleys where university structures (including the Koger Center of the USC music school) now stand; they attended Celia Dial Saxon School, now the site of USC's Strom Thurmond Wellness Center; they congregated at churches where the Coliseum and the just-completed building for the USC business school now stand; they graduated from Booker T. Washington High School. The "old Ward One" is alive, and the *Ward One* project encourages the University's current students to collaborate with former Ward One residents in presenting their stories, memories, and strength of spirit.

A proof of concept version of *Ward One* was produced during a 14-week, team-taught "Critical Interactives" course in spring 2015 that enrolled 19 undergraduate and graduate students from computer science, public history, media arts, film and media studies, and English. The class presented its work on April 21, 2015, in the

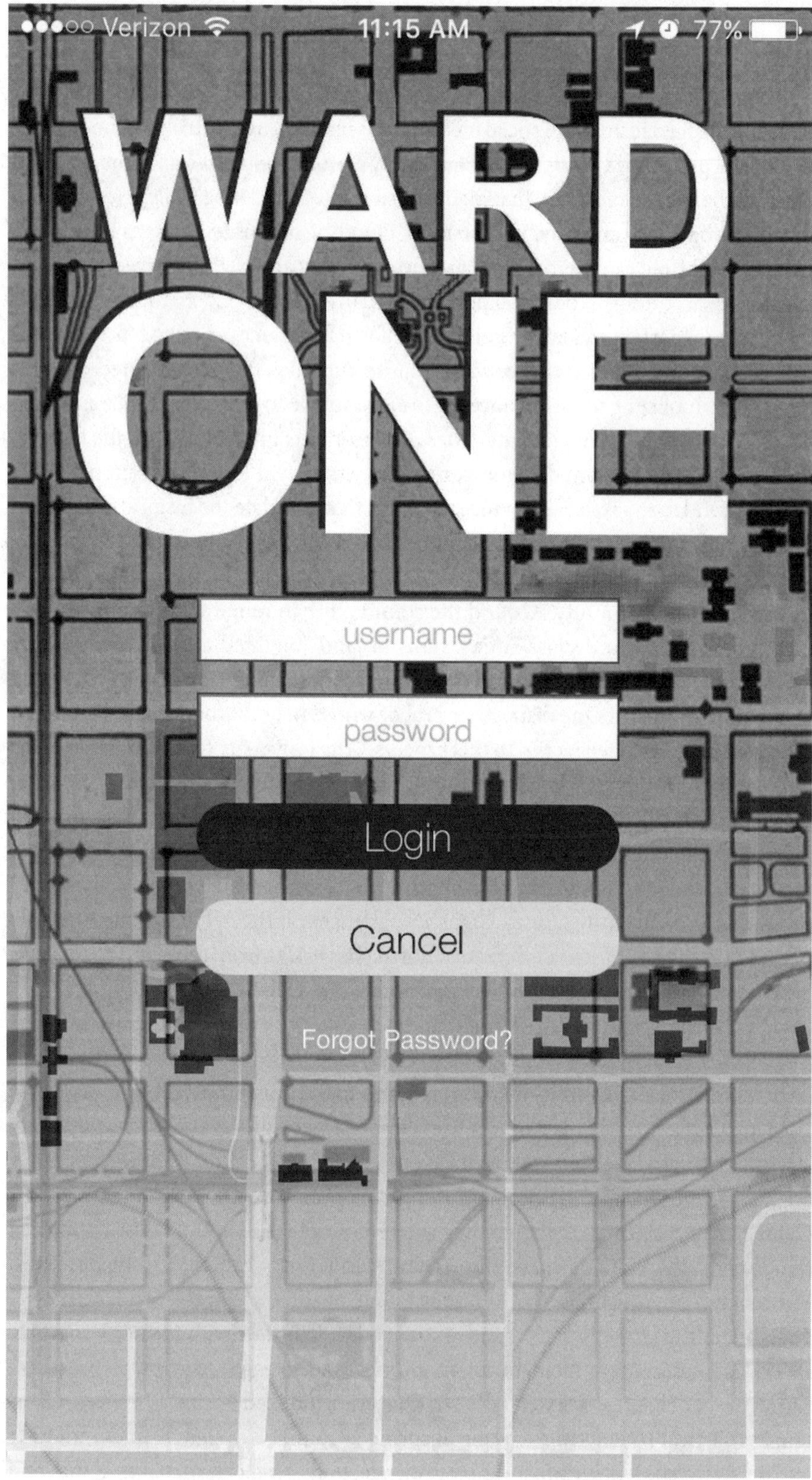


**Figure 33.1.** This screen grab shows *Ward One*'s log-in screen. Creating an account and logging into *Ward One* allows the app to collect data about an individual's interactions with content in order to personalize future experiences. Courtesy of Heidi Rae Cooley and Duncan A. Buell.

Booker T. Washington Auditorium to an audience including members of the Ward One Organization, USC faculty, community members, and friends and family of the students. Dr. Bobby Donaldson, whose eight-year relationship with the Ward One community serves as the point of departure for this project, offered introductory remarks. The spring 2016 class developed Global Positioning System (GPS) functionality and the backend data architecture and conducted oral history interviews with former residents of Ward One.[5]

To present these personal narratives of hardship, perseverance, and accomplishment, as well as the local and national histories with which they are entwined, requires a combination of outreach, research, content development, and software development. Our collaboration conceives these activities to be mutually informing. How the software that "lies beneath" matters to this manifold effort, we discuss below.[6] We address three aspects of the backend that make the app an operationally and nontrivially critical interactive: the structural logic of the Content Management System (CMS)[7] and the micro-processes that "push" (not "pull") content to the touchscreen interface, how tracking location histories and dwell time affords personalization of experience at the machine level, and preference and "like" features that allow interactors to tailor their own experiences. We also discuss how guided and unguided learning software extracts particular features to create individualized experiences. Following Paul Dourish and Genevieve Bell (2011), we ultimately show how everyday technological processes that run unnoticed in the background, tracking and keeping track of us, might very well produce the conditions for meaningful sociocultural change in the present. Specifically, we point to how the affordances of mobile networked technologies might undo longstanding practices of historical erasure whereby newly erected structures serve as evidence of development, expansion, and progress, rather than social injustice and discrimination based on race.

### *Not a Pre-scripted Tour: Pushing Content and Dynamically Assembling Experiences of Place*

Curating and publishing location-based content are increasingly prevalent in public history projects. Historypin and Curatescape provide typical examples in that both serve pre-scripted content. These applications afford few ways to navigate information because the data is fixed in relation to single points of interest. A guided tour, for example, displays a bouncing blue dot for the user's current GPS coordinates, and site pins on a map indicate the location of content points. As with the "canned" audio tours supplementing museum exhibitions, identical content is revealed to every user who opens the site pin's link. Such apps make the user responsible for "finding" the location and choosing to access its content, which may or may not succeed in anticipating their interest.

As we plan it, *Ward One* avoids "canned" information. Instead of merely presenting containers of static, non-relational content, it uses GPS functionality to "push" context-rich content to the networked touchscreen device in real time and according to "smart" processes (i.e., analytics, or the mathematical interpretations of how content is related in a particular instance) based on previous individual and collective transactions.[8] *Ward One* (see Figure 33.2) knows that an interactor is near a point of interest as indicated on screen by a pulsing navigation bead drawing closer to a content point icon; in response to her geo-position, it proactively pushes a notification that, when activated, opens onto relevant (e.g., site-specific, theme-oriented, and appropriately filtered) content. This action is a push and not a pull—the app does not wait for the interactor to notice that she happens to be close to a content point and to ask for that content. As an interactor traverses a physical space, the content pushed to the screen becomes part of the experience of that space. New spatially oriented relationships result as code and space become mutually constituted. The software, as Rob Kitchin and Martin Dodge (2011) describe, "modulates how space comes into being" (16); it shapes how space is practiced, how it acquires significance and meaning.[9] At the same time, space and an interactor's passage through (or use of) it give rise to a particular instantiation of software. The one-mile-square area of land once known as Ward One emerges anew and reorients one's relationship to sites she would have simply passed without notice or regard.[10]

For example, an interactor arrives at the corner of Assembly and College Streets. She might have just exited the CVS Pharmacy (northeast corner), she might be driving into the Shell station for gasoline (southeast corner), or she might be headed to class in the music school (southwest corner). Her proximity to the site of a content point, the Koger Center, registers on a touchscreen device: an opaque icon bearing the image of a house appears on *Ward One*'s map interface, before opening onto an informational panel specifying that one is facing the structure now home to the School of Music. The voice of Mae Johnson Jenkins speaks: "I was born [at] 827 Assembly Street. That's where the Koger Center is now." A panorama of Assembly Street fills the screen. As the interactor pivots with a touchscreen device raised and camera facing forward, an archival photograph of a row of houses overlays the contemporary streetscape, and 827 Assembly Street stands insistently—in relation to what has supplanted it. Ms. Jenkins's words, "I was born [at] 827 . . . ," interrupt the everydayness of the street, its patterns of movement, and the rhythmic sounds of traffic. Her voice bridges past and present to confront the interactor with the fact that urban renewal displaced individual people, their families, and their ways of living in Columbia, South Carolina. What the Koger Center means has shifted.

On site, in real time, *Ward One* produces palpable effects in its interactors by pushing content effectively. To do so, several "hard" and "soft" components must collaborate. The software must register an interactor's geolocation and "talk" to the CMS. That system must make the content organizable according to various possible "narrational" paths an interactor might take. In addition to literal walkable paths, these narrational paths are modified by the interactor's preferences and directed by

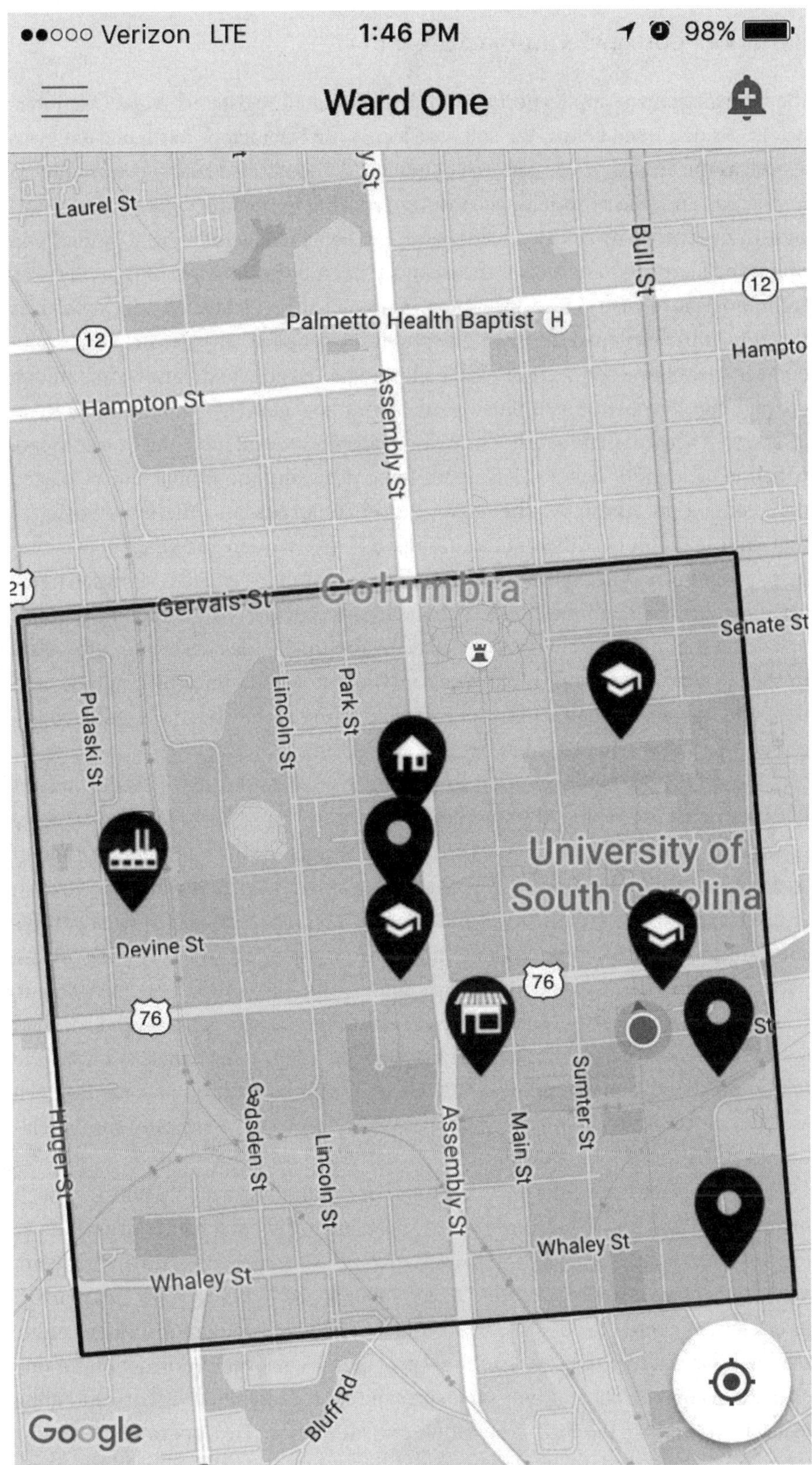


**Figure 33.2.** This screen grab shows *Ward One*'s navigation interface. On Google Maps, a line demarcates the borders of the former Ward One vicinity, and site pins indicate locations where interactors can access site-specific content. Courtesy of Heidi Rae Cooley and Duncan A. Buell.

the information the application accumulates about all registered *Ward One* interactors. As discussed below, the software learns the interactor's particular interests as well as the tendencies or patterns of interest demonstrated by the community of interactors and selects content accordingly, altering in the process its initial ontology. In order for any of this geolocation, content management, and guided and unguided learning to function, the software must be compatible with a physical, technological infrastructure. All components must be conceived and, insofar as this is possible, designed together. The physical layer of a computer network, backend servers, phone connections, GPS coordinate sensing, and bandwidth, among other things, imposes constraints on when and how content can be pushed to an interactor's screen. Bandwidth issues, for example, require judicious use of video, which is bandwidth-heavy; GPS issues force decisions about how closely placed one's content points can be. The software layer comprises computational processes that impose their own different constraints; a clearly written and efficient program helps programmers to begin where previous programmers left off. Logging an interactor's progress, or an image or text commentary provided by interactors, requires balancing the initial local storage of data on the mobile device, sending this data to the backend server in larger blocks, merging new data into the database, and then updating for all interactors—perhaps including those who are simultaneously online—any new articulation of data.

*Ward One* distinguishes itself from similar projects through its development of data structures enabling the complex collection and curation of stories that comprise, in the case of *Ward One,* a community and its history. Crisp imposition of structure on the content is the key to effective and efficient software. As Dourish and Bell explain, the structuring of assets into discrete spaces is part of what permits software processes to proceed along independent paths (98–100). But imposing a particular structure runs the risk of pigeonholing human activity and engagement. Computational processes must then run behind the scenes, often on the backend server, to reconstruct nuances and remove rigidity. What lies beneath the surface of the app, shaping an interactor's experiences, are infrastructures of content as well as database and software processes that assemble content dynamically and in relation to geolocation.

Curating content means organizing and understanding it algorithmically. Such organization and understanding require analyzing the general nature of asset types to specify the character and degree of interrelationships between and across them. *Ward One* takes advantage of the Django open source CMS to store and manage its content. A central table of the main content includes photographs, video, audio, scanned documents, and text. Each row provides the relevant information for one element of content: content type (and size), file type, content name (corresponding to its presentation in the app), description, and file name.[11] Two separate tables register individual persons and important places. The rows in the person table, for example, provide information specific to different individuals. Required fields for each person furnish a basic description (e.g., name and Ward One address, if available). Additional lists of pointers, essentially row numbers in other tables, complete the content for each person. These pointers might link to other persons (e.g., siblings), to photographs of the person or house in which they lived, to audio clips, and so forth. In response to a software query for "this person," the database software chases down the pointers and dynamically assembles the entire record for "this person," and then the app software decides which content to push to the screen in that instance.

Ultimately, the ontological structuring of *Ward One* content resembles a linked open data architecture familiar to semantic web application developers. As with a Resource Description Framework (RDF) approach to metadata, resources (including text, still and moving images, and audio files) are interrelated through a term describing their relation, establishing a network of connections across different topical categories (persons, places, narratives, and events). A "person" is connected to other people (family members and friends) in the "persons" category, to places (home, school, and church) in the "places" category, and so forth. From a person, we can link to places and then to other people connected with that place, creating a network of interrelationships. For example, Mattie Johnson Roberson-Anderson,[12] as one node in the cluster of Ward One community members, links to places, such as 827 Assembly Street (where she and her sisters, Mae and Janessa, were born), the Celia Dial Saxon school (where she went to elementary school), and Booker T. Washington High School (where she graduated). She also has varying degrees of connection to other people, such as her sisters, her aunt, and other members of the Ward One Organization, for which she serves as president. Similarly, each person and place listed in the CMS acquires a relational architecture whose connections map differently to each other and to various content types by degree of relevance (e.g., thematically: education, community, recreation, economics, and gender roles) and proximity (e.g., content similarity and physical location). All content, persons, and places cluster variously to populate content points particular to specific geo-coordinates.

## *Profiles and "Signatures": Designing Complex Interactions with Content*

The initial organization of content (ontology) for *Ward One* provides a foundation for interactor experience. The real power of the underlying software processes comes from the ability to change dynamically the strength of connections linking from one content item to the next. This relation is not to imply sequentiality. Rather, we begin with static local links to nearest neighbors (e.g., Ms. Johnson to sister and Ms. Johnson to school). Additional links branch out from these first connections (e.g., Ms. Johnson's sister to school and Ms. Johnson's sister to Ms. Johnson's sister's friend). Connections and strengths of connection increase according to combinations of content items activated by an interactor's drawing near a content-point location. As an interactor explores the vicinity and acquires a signature (a digital inscription of her interactions with *Ward One*), new valences register across connections and clusters of connections. We can readily assign a connection strength from Mattie Johnson to her house, her siblings, and the schools she attended. Assigning connection strengths from Ms. Johnson to Booker T. Washington High School, then to her sister at the high school, then to her sister's friend at the high school and her sister's friend's narrative of shopping on Main Street, is more difficult. As discussed below, *a priori* connection strengths from the original ontology can be augmented or attenuated by the software depending on an interactor's location history, dwell time on content point sites, duration of interaction with kinds of content (e.g., individual persons, thematic threads, and media type), or explicit preferences and filter selections. The result is an app that adapts to an interactor and anticipates next possible points of interest or content types, doing so according to individual patterns of movement, activity, and access as well as aggregate patterns of the community of interactors.

*Ward One* has the potential to push a vast amount of content to touchscreen devices. Local archives supply photographs, television news footage, newspaper articles, and city council and related official documents to supplement the oral histories, family albums, and personal documents volunteered by Ward One community members. As we gather and add content to the backend database, new connections across content elements will cluster content into ever-evolving interaction vectors. These paths will be both adaptable and adaptive. Interactors may define (and refine) the nature of their experiences by developing a profile, using filters, and tagging and "liking" content—in keeping with social media conventions. For example, an interactor may wish to explore the Ward One vicinity by focusing on churches or schools. *Ward One* will permit the registered interactor to filter her experiences by selecting, for example, "Church" and/or "School," thereby raising the prominence of church- and/or school-related content and increasing the likelihood of having that content pushed to the screen. "Liking" and tagging content likewise affects how the software calculates relevancy of certain kinds of content.

*Ward One* will simultaneously and indirectly construct for each interactor a "signature" based on previous interactions. Similar to the "customers who bought . . . also looked at . . ." model that is common with e-commerce, *Ward One* quantifies an interactor's experience, calculating duration of stay at content point locations, dwell time on types of content, and patterns produced by paths taken through the app. These measures allow the app to adapt to an interactor's interests.[13] Moreover, an interactor can choose to augment or suppress the use of specific features used to make suggestions. An interactor could choose to suppress "School," if she felt she had missed other content by an overemphasis on school or having spent significant time on school content. Global *a priori* assignments of strengths of connection with which all interactors begin are modified by each interactor's expressions of interest indirectly inferred from her actual experience and directly by any changes she makes by updating preferences and/or "likes."

### *Historical Awareness on Site, in Real Time: Countermapping the Contemporary Landscape*

Those of us who regularly consult or rely on our mobile connected devices for constantly refreshed information regarding our whereabouts (e.g., route status and weather updates) may—but probably do not—explicitly consider the micro-processes that work ceaselessly in the background. We simply expect the convenience such processes offer: estimated times of arrival at frequently visited destinations, notifications regarding detours or delays, auto-magically generated lists of nearby restaurants, retail outlets, service providers, and ATMs, along with best and alternate routes to sites likely of interest. As Mark B. N. Hansen (2015) explains, these micro-processes typically "disappear" into their surroundings; they are, as he describes, atmospheric (8, 25).[14] For Hansen, this means that we do not perceive the effects of such processes until after the fact; we do not experience them as having taken place until they have already influenced our relation to our surroundings. In this way, they "seep into the texture of experience . . . directly flavoring" our daily lives (187). They modulate our relationships to people, places, events, information, and more—often to the benefit of corporations and government. And they have the potential to—and frequently do—shape our actions *before* we think to enact them.[15]

*Ward One* initially addresses its interactors precisely at this level of (un)awareness. Sensing an interactor's geolocation coordinates, it pings her with site-specific notifications. If, for example, she is nearing Booker T. Washington Auditorium, a pushed alert prompts her to pause and consider that the brick structure is what remains of the high school that opened in 1916 and served African American students until it was desegregated in 1970. Should she continue to swipe through Page Views, she will encounter archival photographs and local television news footage of the school that invite acknowledgment of structural modifications. Two wings of the former high school no longer stand—what happened? Continued exploration might present her with audio content featuring the voices of Booker T. Washington High School alumni, including the voice of Betty Corbin, who in one particularly impassioned instance states, "I graduated from Booker T. Washington, and I have one thing to say: My heart has never left Ward One." Such moments demonstrate how *Ward One* revises an interactor's encounter with the physical campus in ways that take advantage of the atmospheric attributes of the mobile touchscreen device. The results are not simply a newly materialized understanding of urban space; rather, routinely accepted notions of history and progress are revised, made tangible and palpable.

If, as Wendy Chun (2012) argues, "race . . . was wielded—and is still wielded—as an invaluable mapping tool," then we propose that *Ward One* functions as a countermapping tool (40). With its capacity to map the contemporary landscape in ways that draw attention to (infra)structural absences and changes (e.g., homes, schools, and alleys), it creates opportunities for reconsidering the historical processes that were responsible for not only dislocating Ward One residents but also the subsequent reapportionment of properties comprising Ward One. Here, one faces the fact that racially motivated political decisions were legitimated by federally sanctioned policies, which promoted and supported urban renewal projects across the nation. Taking advantage of the Federal Housing Acts (1937, 1949, 1954), city planners in Columbia, South Carolina, sought to eliminate slums, as did city planners throughout the United States.[16] In the 1950s, Columbia's Urban Rehabilitation Commission adopted the term "blight" in order to broaden the reach of urban redevelopment policy to address instances of physical deterioration (broadly interpreted) as well as examples of offensive or inappropriate use of property and area-specific social problems (corresponding to the supposed lack of personal initiative and/or community responsibility). The focus of these efforts was the downtown district, specifically near where the state house and university stand, and where the university has built and continues to expand its Columbia campus.

Accounts by former Ward One residents complicate not only routine traversals of and interactions with the downtown vicinity and university grounds but also understandings of privilege and poverty. Paul R. Mullins and Lewis C. Jones (2011) have explained an analogous situation in Indianapolis, Indiana, where urban renewal similarly benefited Purdue. According to Mullins and Jones, the narratives shared by individuals who have suffered personal losses as a consequence of urban renewal frame poverty in ways that "reveal [poverty] to be an important but not deterministic backdrop to their lives" (35). While black-and-white photographs of dilapidated houses, which served as visible evidence of unsuitable living conditions, and the use of the term "blight" paint a grim picture, the individual stories underscore the community's strength of spirit in the face of "material scarcity" (35). "This position is less a refutation of poverty," Mullins and Jones argue, "than it is a rejection of ideologically loaded slum caricatures that present urban poverty as a reflection of essential African American attributes or a structural framework that determined the lives of African Americans" (35).

As a counter-mapping tool, *Ward One* challenges interactors to contend with a history that intrudes upon the contemporary landscape. It serves as an active response to the "enforced forgetting" (Nakamura and Chow-White 3) that past discriminatory policies instantiated in the name of civic good. The students, faculty, and community members who are collaborating on the development of *Ward One* belong to a tradition of "intelligence workers," who take up "the very instruments said to be responsible for mass ignorance and distraction" (Kahana 14) in order to trouble habits of thinking.[17] Geolocative functionality, typically put to uncritical uses such as restaurant recommendations and alternate route options, is "[adapted] . . . to socially and culturally productive ends" (15). The result is a software application that aims to intervene in how an interactor understands and subsequently moves through Columbia, South Carolina (see Figure 33.3).

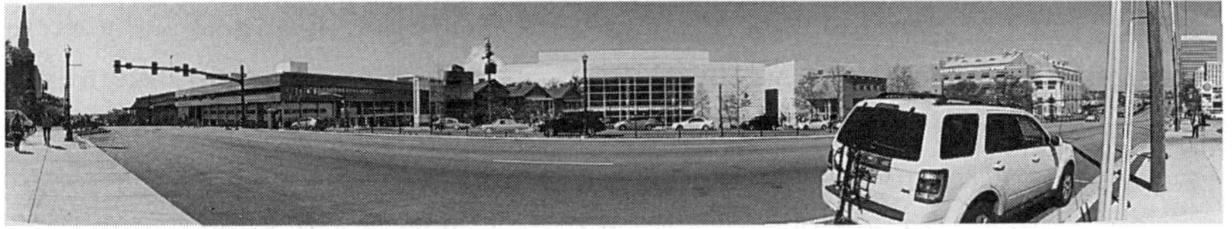

**Figure 33.3.** Visible in this panorama of the 800 block of Assembly Street are the Darla Moore School of Business and the Koger Center, home to the University of South Carolina's music school. When activated, an archival photograph of houses overlays the contemporary streetscape; interactors can see where 827 Assembly Street—Mattie Johnson's birthplace and childhood home—once stood. Panorama photograph by students enrolled in the spring 2015 Critical Interactives course. Archival photograph courtesy of the Joseph E. Winter Photograph Collection, University of South Carolina Libraries. Courtesy of Heidi Rae Cooley and Duncan A. Buell.

In *Designing Culture: The Technological Imagination at Work,* Anne Balsamo (2011) advocates for the development of "critically important cultural technologies" that produce "cultural innovation" because they are designed *for* culture (15). Designers of such projects take culture seriously insofar as they acknowledge the fact that "new technologies, and new media experiences, do significant [cultural] work" (130) that have the potential to shape "[common] 'public culture' in the future" (132). As a consequence, they mobilize new technologies and interfaces to achieve "*active* reproduction of technocultural understandings, mythologies, values, and the circulation of *new* knowledges" (132, our emphasis). In this way, designers and contributors to digital humanities projects take responsibility for their participation in shaping culture.

*Ward One*, like the public interactives of which Balsamo speaks, endeavors to cultivate a new common public culture that acknowledges the past and takes responsibility for how it shapes the present to imagine a more equitable future. By means of geo-functionality and computational processes that dynamically push content to the networked touchscreen device, the app mobilizes the stories of people and the community of which they were a part. The "old Ward One" has been erased from the landscape. The physical neighborhoods are gone, the vacated houses long since bulldozed. Businesses, churches, and schools no longer stand, but memories of the former community remain vivid through not only the stories former residents share but also the Ward One Organization that gathers to remember life as it was—and to celebrate the spirit of community that once was and has not been forgotten. The stories they tell are stories of people, school, church, work, friendship, and congregation. They are stories of life before the civil rights movement changed at least the official rules by which we live in the United States.

Those who interact with *Ward One* are invited to experience these stories in situ, to bear witness to the neighborhood that is no longer present. But they are also invited—or perhaps called upon—to cultivate an awareness of and appreciation for histories that have been suppressed, not just explicitly by institutions and government, but also conveniently by general habits of remembering. Perhaps interactors, in their exploration of the Ward One vicinity via *Ward One*, might be inspired to involve themselves more frequently in community concerns; perhaps they might decide to learn more about how national and local policies continue to shape the local present, including the very grounds upon which they stand. (After all, construction continues in Columbia, South Carolina, on the very grounds that used to be Ward One.) Perhaps they might be inclined to reflect upon the narratives they tell themselves and others about where they are and how place matters. And perhaps they might better understand how their mobile, networked devices participate in placing (and tracking) them, or how those devices might serve ends beyond routine wayfinding and communication. If *Ward One* is about not forgetting, then it is about not forgetting on all these levels—the social, political, institutional, and technological.

## NOTES

1. It is worth mentioning that the university's flagship campus sits in the shadows of the state capitol building.

2. Collaboration, for us, is the first instance of how software matters. Our collaboration transpires across two colleges—the College of Arts and Sciences and the College of Engineering and Computing. We have initiated relationships with local cultural institutions, including Historic Columbia and the Nickelodeon Theater, who assist us with thinking about how best to leverage the potential cultural value of our projects. And we have secured commitments from local and national experts with whom we consult periodically regarding the state and direction of our work. More recently, our collaboration has benefited from the time and contributions of members of the Ward One Organization. This complex and evolving network makes possible the work we do.

3. Initial development of *Ghosts* transpired across two cross-College courses led by us, one taught in fall 2012 and a second taught in spring 2014. Richard L. Walker coded the 1.0 version of the *Ghosts of the Horseshoe* app as part of his dissertation, "*Ghosts of the Horseshoe*: A Mobilization of a Critical Interactive" (PhD diss., University of South Carolina, 2014). The project draws on the scholarship of graduate students enrolled in Dr. Robert Weyeneth's 2011 spring public history seminar, which produced a website (see http://library.sc.edu/digital/slaveryscc).

4. The state capitol is geographically within the boundaries of the Ward One district.

5. The presentation and demonstration of the prototype of *Ward One* took place on April 21, 2016, in Booker T. Washington Auditorium.

6. The phrase "what lies beneath" quotes the title of a chapter in Dourish and Bell's *Divining a Digital Future.*

7. A content management system is a relational database, which functions much like a set of interconnected spreadsheets or tables. Each main table of the database is a separate spreadsheet with a different row for discrete elements. Columns (called fields) in the

spreadsheet then point (as if by row number) into other tables. It is the responsibility of the database software to maintain correctness of these pointers as the database itself has content added or modified. More important, the database software dynamically creates a record instance in response to a query by following all the links on the fly. In this way, the software has the effect of having all the information for all tables stored as if in a combined spreadsheet, but without unnecessary duplication of data.

8. *Ward One* records each interactor's GPS location at timed intervals that will be stored locally on the phone. Periodically, the app pushes that data to the server. When it does so, it builds a message that includes the interactor's unique ID and all of the interactor's GPS locations since the last message sent. Each GPS location includes a latitude, longitude, and timestamp. The app's message is formatted in JSON, which is a simple way to organize data that the server can understand. We thank Steven Dao, Cameron Godbout, and Austin Pauhl for providing us with language for describing these processes.

9. Dourish and Bell make a similar claim: "The embedding of a range of infrastructures into everyday space shapes our experience of that space even as it provides a framework through which our encounters with space take on meaning" (98).

10. While anyone can interact with *Ward One* content as a guest, those who register will experience, for example, increased personalization, including filter preferences and "like" functionality. They will also have access to interaction histories according to which the software will offer suggestions for further exploration, and they will be able to resume interaction and exploration from more than one device, as well as revisit previously accessed content (e.g., oral histories) from remote locations. Registering involves individuals inputting a user ID and password.

11. In keeping with the widely accepted Dublin Core field set, our CMS also includes fields for names of persons and places relevant to or somehow associated with a particular asset. Additional fields document reference citations and links to digital collections, name of the individual responsible for inputting assets, and the date an asset is added. Fields will also exist for specifying relevant themes (e.g., community values, neighborhood life, urban renewal, racial tensions, and institutional expansion).

12. As Mattie Roberson explains, she was Mattie Johnson when she lived in Ward One and prefers to be identified that way for this project.

13. Construction and use of such signatures is a two-step process. First, in the database on the back end, software performs "feature extraction" by means of guided or unguided learning. In the case of guided learning, the software specifically looks for features thought to be of interest (e.g., visits to Celia Dial Saxon School content correlating with visits to the Booker T. Washington High School content). In an unguided process, which is similar to item set mining, the software searches for the most common pairs, triples, or quadruples of content locations, or perhaps for each of the main content locations, and mines the data relevant to those locations to determine the most common other locations. The second phase of filtering involves similarity comparison across the community of interactors, the results of which can be used to recommend to the interactor additional related and/or relevant content and content-point locations.

14. Hansen explains that twenty-first-century media technologies and the networks they articulate operate according to a "feed-forward" structure that "registers the *environmentality* of the world itself, prior to, and without any necessary relation with, human affairs" (8, our emphasis). Computational processes, data-gathering, and passive sensing capacities constitute an "operational present" that proceeds according to a "future anterior time frame" (25).

15. Dourish and Bell offer a complementary account when they identify a mutually recursive relationship between the "infrastructure of experience" and the "experience of infrastructure" (114).

16. See Bouknight; Richey.

17. For Kahana, "intelligence work" characterizes American social documentary. We do not have the space to develop the connection here but find the term appropriate for describing the *Ward One* project.

## BIBLIOGRAPHY

Balsamo, Anne. *Designing Culture: The Technological Imagination at Work*. Durham, N.C.: Duke University Press, 2011.

Bouknight, Ashley. "'Casualty of Progress': The Ward One Community and Urban Renewal, Columbia, South Carolina, 1964–1974." Master's thesis, University of South Carolina, 2010.

Chun, Wendy. "Race and/as Technology, or How to Do Things to Race." *Race after the Internet,* ed. Lisa Nakamura and Peter A. Chow-White, 38–60. New York: Routledge, 2012.

Curatescape. Cleveland: Cleveland State University. https://curatescape.org/.

Dourish, Paul, and Genevieve Bell. *Divining a Digital Future: Mess and Mythology in Ubiquitous Computing.* Cambridge, Mass.: MIT Press, 2011.

Hansen, Mark B. N. *Feed-Forward: On the Future of Twenty-First-Century Media*. Chicago, Ill.: University of Chicago Press, 2015.

Historypin. https://www.historypin.org/.

Kahana, Jonathan. *Intelligence Work: The Politics of American Documentary.* New York: Columbia University Press, 2008.

Kitchin, Rob, and Martin Dodge. *Code/Space: Software and Everyday Life*. Cambridge, Mass.: MIT Press, 2011.

Mullins, Paul R., and Lewis C. Jones. "Archaeologies of Race and Urban Poverty: The Politics of Slumming, Engagement, and the Color Line." *Historical Archaeology* 45, no. 1 (2011): 33–50.

Nakamura, Lisa, and Peter A. Chow-White. "Introduction—Race and Digital Technology: Code, the Color Line, and the Information Society." *Race after the Internet,* ed. Lisa Nakamura and Peter A. Chow-White, 1–18. New York: Routledge, 2012.

Richey, Staci. "Variation on a Theme: Planning for the Elimination of Black Neighborhoods in Downtown Columbia, South Carolina, 1905–1970." Master's thesis, University of South Carolina, 2004.

Thomas Cooper Library. "Slavery at South Carolina College, 1801–1865: The Foundations of the University of South Carolina." Last modified May 2011. http://library.sc.edu/digital/slaveryscc.

Walker, Richard L. "*Ghosts of the Horseshoe:* A Mobilization of a Critical Interactive." Ph.D. dissertation, University of South Carolina, 2014.

*Ward One*. Columbia, S.C.: University of South Carolina. http://calliope.cse.sc.edu/wardone/.

# Placeable: A Social Practice for Place-Based Learning and Co-Design Paradigms

AARON D. KNOCHEL AND AMY PAPAELIAS

As a four-year residential public university located in New Paltz, New York (a small college town in the Hudson Valley), SUNY New Paltz prides itself as a welcoming and inclusive community. With many academic programs rooted in social justice and political activism as well as student organizations committed to promoting cultural diversity, students and faculty openly engage in complex dialogue regarding issues of race, gender, ability, and identity politics. As Art Department faculty, we built curriculum in conversation with intersectional identities and initiated through a design process that augments the campus geography as a social space. We used intersectionality to highlight how sociological systems of oppression are interdependent and create "intersections" representative of multiple forms of discrimination (Knudsen 62). Intersectional constructs of society posit complex navigations of an entangled social and political life. We felt compelled as faculty to engage students in exploring concepts of intersectionality through their art and design work as a strategy to spark dialogue and respect difference within our campus community. In this chapter, we present the construction of a "placeable" curriculum (see Figure 34.1) that explores intersectionality through place-based knowledge and creates dynamic but fleeting social provocations for mobile computing.

Our case study reviews recent curriculum developed through collaborations between the two of us: Knochel, a faculty member in Art Education, and Papaelias, a faculty member in Graphic Design. This case study demonstrates how social practice interfaces with design strategies for interactive media. In this context, social practice is derived from contemporary performative art and design work that is engaged within a community context. We refer to our curricular conception as "placeable," or a place-based approach to education particular to art and design. Place-based education is an extension of eco-humanist traditions of the late twentieth century that sought to align issues of sustainability and civic engagement (Ball and Lai 262). It emphasizes community resources, ecological thinking, and active citizenry (Sobel 2004). Placeable is a derivative curricular approach that focuses on

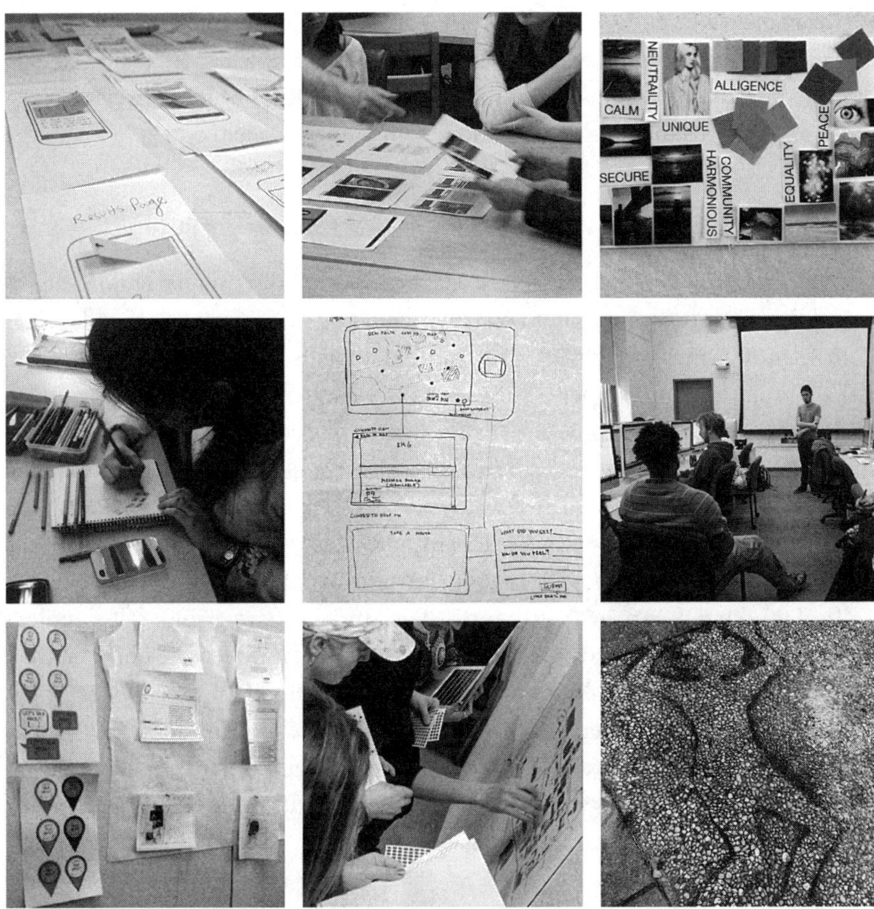


**Figure 34.1.** Representing the placeable curriculum, this grid of images provides a survey of different co-design practices in mobile making, including prototyping, sketching, participatory asset mapping, critiques, and user-feedback sessions. Courtesy of Aaron D. Knochel and Amy Papaelias.

three core constructs: seeking place-based knowledge to incorporate community assets that are relevant to the arts and humanities, using connective mobile making to allow for on-site rich media production, and employing co-design strategies to engage in critical intervention. Placeable activates interaction design, qualitative research methods, and community asset mapping to intersect humanities inquiry with making practices. In this sense, mobile making is less a practice of crafting tactile objects and more a practice of designing experiences through digital materials: design involving geolocation technologies, mobile interfaces, and visual systems, for instance. Our case study is not about digital products. It focuses on a curricular approach to engender critical making as a co-designed social practice. In what follows, we develop a backdrop by reviewing work from 2014, explore placeable's three core constructs as principles of a curricular approach, and then present two examples of student work from 2015. We offer insights into the complexities of social practice and higher education, not in a predetermined curricular structure, but as co-design paradigms within the pedagogical spaces of the university classroom and campus that position art and design in the broader context of making.

## *Finding Our Place:* Let's Talk About . . . *Project from Spring 2014*

In 2013 and 2014, two heinous acts of racist tagging within campus buildings provoked the campus community to respond with a one-day symposium called *Let's Talk About It,* which brought together over 300 students, faculty, and staff (Newman 2013). Inspired by the symposium, in spring 2014 undergraduate students enrolled in Art Education and Graphic Design courses developed a website and digital map that documents historical and current events surrounding race and cultural and social identity on campus.[1] The art education course, Learning in Digital Visual Culture, is a 300-level lecture course that explores the historical, cultural, and social implications of using technologies as both learning opportunities and artistic media. Critical thinking occurs in this context when "students have greater opportunities to discover, interrogate, and analyze the links that exist between the object of their study and the broader social world that informs their object of study" (Taylor 2). The graphic design course, Interaction Design, is a 400-level design studio that focuses on user-centered design practices for screen-based environments through project-based instruction. Over six weeks, two groups of students worked separately, developing content and interfaces in the following activities.

### DEVELOPING CONTENT

Sixteen art education students began collecting data related to the central question, "How can place-based knowledge inspire dialogue on issues of race and identity on the SUNY New Paltz campus?" Our place-based pedagogy engaged students by "teaching the local . . . paying close attention to local students' interests and by examining texts, artifacts, and performances of local cultural production" (Ball and Lai 261–62). As a practice that engages social contexts and politics, art education connects experiences in making art to local cultures and activities (Darts 6–12). As a method to access local cultural production, we examined student organizations as access points to understanding diversity on our campus. While initially focused on race, issues of diversity and identity intersected with issues of sexuality, gender, culture, and social interests. We used a participatory asset mapping methodology[2] to gather information about student organizations via participation in events, member interviews, and photography. In this initial phase, students noticed that our approach occluded historical events from our investigation, and so data gathering expanded to include historical and recent events. Additionally, students proposed a range of art interventions involving public performance and community engagement relating to our central research question. Conducted in small groups, our data gathering was then brought into collaborative mapping sessions where students physically mapped historical, recent, and interventionist events onto a printed map with colored stickers. Once the physical map was created, we charted pins onto a Google map using the multimedia (e.g., digital images, website links, videos, and sound files) that was collected.

## INTERFACE DESIGN PROCESS

Eight students in the Interaction Design course engaged in a user-centered design approach to develop the project's information architecture and visual components through iterative and reflective design processes (Mao et al. 105–9). Students built the information architecture—the underlying structure for how users move through the website—through wireframing, paper prototyping, user personas, and storytelling. Wireframing allows quick iterations on structure and flow to ensure the site is organized and easily navigable. Paper prototyping involves the construction of a paper model of the site to perform quick user testing. Students wrote personas of fictional users and how they might engage with the site. Storytelling and personas keep users at the forefront of the students' processes. Meanwhile, the visual components—the graphical user interface (icons and visual identity as well as color and typography)—inform the content in meaningful ways. Creating an appropriate visual language, one that honors the content and provides an engaging experience, is paramount to the design process (Bringhurst 2012). Students began by developing mood boards: layouts created with images, text, color swatches, and textures that represent an emotion or feeling of the overall visual direction. Mood boards are a common method of exploring early visual approaches within a design, communicating the overall tone and visual direction without focusing on the specifics of information architecture. A semiotic analysis of icon and layout designs examined common symbols used to signify controls (e.g., "play," "exit," or "wifi" icons) as well as how visual trends (e.g., flat versus skeuomorphic design) impact user experience. Digital prototyping combined the visual elements with the site's information architecture to refine a functioning prototype.

User feedback sessions focused on the prototype brought together students, faculty, and staff from Sociology and Black Studies. Participants' anonymous feedback and discussions from the feedback sessions were incorporated into the final functional website. These interactions between students and potential users of the site produced lively conversations about not only the interface and user experience but also the project's use of the term "diversity." Session participants wondered about the potential of the project to affect race relations on campus and lead to greater dialogue. Important considerations were raised, including expanding user contributions, ongoing content moderation, and the challenge of deployment within a mobile context.

In reflecting on this initial project, important modifications needed to be implemented. First, we needed a more concerted logistical effort to create time and space for collaboration. We co-designed the curriculum, but the limited opportunities for our students to work together hampered the overall results. As faculty, we perceive shared dispositions of co-design practice between education and design. These dispositions place a high value on the contributions of users, students, and audiences to the realization of outcomes and the relevance of making. However, art education and design students perceive their contributions from disciplinary positions. Ultimately, then, our goal was to encourage students to experiment within a transdisciplinary environment where no one lays claim to full authorship. Second, conceptualization of the central inquiry needed more input from design teams to propel more nuanced research, methods, and implementation. A more fully realized negotiation of the affordances of mobility and computing may impact how interaction and user experience are conceived and place-based learning is realized within a community. Third, our initial catalyst event focused on dialogues about race, but our project evolved to capture a more diverse array of identity positions reflecting the realities of intersectional discrimination. Our students began with race as an entry point to our community dilemma. However, during our asset mapping activities, issues of gender, sexuality, ability, and socioeconomic status populated our mapping in ways that extended dialogue beyond race as the only marker or identity. In future work we opened our investigations to this full range of intersectional identities to broaden the possibilities of placeable projects.

## *Taking a Position: Three Core Constructs for Placeable Curriculum*

After iterations in 2013 and 2014, we formed three core constructs that guide placeable as both a curricular approach and critical design methodology. They are:

### SEEKING PLACE-BASED LEARNING TO INCORPORATE COMMUNITY ASSETS THAT ARE RELEVANT TO THE ARTS AND HUMANITIES

The potential for accessing local cultural producers and community involvement is important to place-based learning initiatives in the arts and humanities. Our particular interest is in how mobile computing can involve community members in socially engaged exchanges. Mobile computing may also engage learners in research beyond the institutional classroom and create a rich data corpus for co-design practice.

Our approach to the intersection of design education and place-based learning involves currents of critical practice associated with three distinct fields: critical pedagogies in visual culture (Tavin 197–213), critical design (Dunne and Raby), and critical geography (Bauer and Engel-Di Mauro 2008). Historically, antecedents may be found in Guy Debord and the Situationist International's use of psychogeography for a "study of the precise laws and specific effects of the geographical environment, whether consciously organized or not, on the emotions and behavior of individuals" (Debord 23). Moving beyond the Situationist performative practice of navigating an unfolding geography and human psyche, we are intrigued by the layers of virtual and physical embodiment afforded by a range of "volunteered" geographic information (Goodchild 2007). We use mobile computing as an interface with place. It augments and articulates social relation with place to form situated knowledge that is both social and technological (Elwood 2008). Importantly, this interface is significant for design practice, as it values data and visual phenomena. As art and design educators, our orientation is grounded in making visual culture, and through the placeable curriculum this aesthetic practice is layered with power dynamics of the seen and unseen (placed or unplaced). Longitude and latitude are coordinates of finite possibility, but placeable advances a critical reflexivity in the arts and humanities that is mindful of power, place, and community assets.

## MAKING CONNECTIVE MOBILE INTERFACES THAT ALLOW FOR ONSITE RICH MEDIA PRODUCTION

Mobile making may integrate place-based assets into projects and increase student participation and engagement. Examples such as ARIS, an augmented reality gaming platform, demonstrate this growing potential. Whereas ARIS relies on game-based approaches, placeable focuses on cultural phenomena to enhance onsite experiences and invite participation through rich media production. Placeable invests in making mobile interfaces within a specific community context.

Media theorists have been critical of the cultural biases and limitations of programmable objects such as videogames (Bogost 2007) and image editing software (Manovich 2013). We share this critical position with respect to mobile infrastructures. In this context, making requires an ability to navigate larger ecosystems of hardware and software that come with a range of attachments and determinations. Mobile applications especially shape how a specific group may access a project in a particular place. Access depends on the parameters and contextual needs of communities as well as technologies. Within the continuum of art education's role in critically investigating the creation of objects and contexts for those objects, we believe that art students should develop practices of critical digital making (Knochel and Patton 2015) that traverse both the visual culture of mobility and the procedural rhetoric (Bogost 2) of operating systems.

## EMPLOYING CO-DESIGN STRATEGIES TO ENGAGE IN CRITICAL INTERVENTION

Critical interventionist art and design practices that engage with communities through co-design strategies inform our development of environments. Placeable situates mobile technology as a site for investigating and engaging complex social issues.

Interventionist art and design practices activate political and social issues beyond the walls of the gallery or museum. The 2004-05 Massachusetts Museum of Contemporary Art exhibition, *The Interventionists: Art in the Social Sphere*, surveyed the interventionist practices of artists and collectives working in the late-twentieth and early-twenty-first centuries. These artists and collectives distinguished themselves from earlier political art movements through their "relatively lighthearted mixture of subversion and humor and [their] favoring of the dialogic over the declamatory" (Demos 228). We introduced our students to several interventionist collectives and artworks, including Thomas Hirschhorn's *The Gramsci Monument* (2013), Lisa Orta's *Refuge Wear City Interventions* (1993–98), Michael Rakowitz's *paraSITE* (1998), and Natalie Jereminjenko's *Environmental Health Clinic*. These examples inspired them as they brainstormed ways to situate issues of campus culture, intersectional identities, and social dynamics within their projects.

Generally, art and design students are accustomed to working independently toward refined design deliverables or a resolved artwork; they are less familiar with collaborative and co-design strategies. In the context of placeable, co-design strategies:

- provide political and social capital for stakeholders to have a voice in the design process;
- break down barriers of designer/user, creator/audience, maker/thinker, and student/teacher; and
- commit to collaboration as a process of refinement, revision, and reflection.

To this end, the project introduces students to thinking beyond disciplinary boundaries and toward critical making. We subscribe to Ratto's (2011) definition of critical making as "an act of shared construction, joint conversation, and reflection" (253). Placeable and the resulting work are less concerned with building refined, functional solutions than with a collaborative process of research, iterative prototyping, and discussion that functions as "a site for enhancing and extending conceptual understandings of critical sociotechnical issues" (254). We bring together design and art education students to explore these sociotechnical issues.

### *Our Place, Your Space: A Proof of Concept in Mobile Media and Intersectional Identities*

Building upon lessons learned from work in 2014—namely, to give more attention to the affordances of mobile computing, meaningful collaborations, and open inquiry into a wider array of subject positions that constitute intersectional identities—we focused our spring 2015 project, with two entirely new groups of students, on designing a *proof of concept* rather than a functioning application. Considering our time constraints, we committed early on to the ideation of projects over more robust prototyping. During a five-week period, our classes met biweekly for 90 minutes, and we ensured our class meetings overlapped. Divided into small groups, students collaboratively explored issues surrounding mobile media, identity narratives, and critical interventions in place-based learning environments. During class discussions, we presented students with projects, artists, and designers divided into distinct but related categories: Creative Mapping, History and Heritage, Art and Design Tactics, Games and Augmented Realities, Current Events, and Storytelling. These resources helped to cultivate student work. Our exploratory focus generated ideas, provoked investigations of possible platforms or technical capacities, and employed design methodologies such as wireframing, mood boarding, and interface prototyping to make student thinking visible. Students developed a co-design research process by collaboratively devising their central inquiry, gathering data, developing a proposal and prototype, and providing possibilities for implementation. The deliverables of the project included a public presentation about the group's process and research, a visual interface prototype, and a short promotional video or one-page website explaining the purpose and ambitions of the application.

We also asked students to make collaborative structures that would inform their decisions and allow them to share the burden of the unknown. Team roles, including project manager, user experience designer, content producer, and research director, were clearly defined at the beginning of the project, allowing each student to own specific tasks while still being responsible to teammates for all components of the project. By articulating team roles, we tried to formulate collaboration as a learned skill: a set of performances that can be catalyzed, nurtured, and contested within boundaries that build accountability. As Papaelias often remarked in class, "Life is a group project."

In addition to small group collaboration, we established three formats for feedback and development: peer review, mentor critiques, and interdisciplinary faculty critiques. Critiques are long-established pedagogical tools in the art and design making process, and our students are very familiar with them. Peer review happened informally as well as during critiques, with feedback provided on draft presentations and promotional media. Mentor critiques happened in almost every class session, as we spent time meeting with groups, reviewing project progress, and tracking time-management components. These mentoring sessions were vital in challenging students to engage with intersectionality as a critical framework for our focus on place and community. Certain students questioned the efficacy of mobile applications in having an impact on discrimination. The ubiquity of apps provided a rationale for potentially affecting discrimination (Grant 2014), but the question of relevancy was positioned as a design challenge. Interdisciplinary faculty critiques invited faculty and staff from English, Computer Science, Psychology, Instructional Technology, and the Sojourner Truth Library to provide thoughtful suggestions to students on in-progress work. As reflexive actions occurring regularly within the iterative process of making, critiques supported students' work to increase rigor and enable persistence in the refinement of their ideas, the synthesis of data, and the capacity to incorporate important conceptual aspects into the project outcomes. This style of group focus and constructive feedback is common to critiques in the creative process and would benefit making in disciplines beyond the arts. We therefore advocate for its use in the humanities.

In total, eight groups worked on proposals exploring difference through intersectional subjectivity using mobile affordances ranging from specialized social media platforms to mapping social and cultural geographies. The following is a summary of two projects from spring 2015 that balance placeable's three core constructs and capture the breadth of student interests and investigations.

### CASE 1: MOBILITY MAP

Summary: *a campus navigation app intended to help locate accessible routes and identify trouble spots in buildings and walkways*

In Mobility Map, campus terrain is a site for engaging issues of accessibility. Students proposed a mobile application that allows users to identify accessible routes and mark inaccessible spots on the campus map in order to arrive at their destination on time. Users can pinpoint places on campus where they found inaccessible buildings or classrooms and post personal stories and tips to the community. Inspired by previous coursework in disability studies, the group's research process included gathering building attributes related to campus accessibility. The students created a visual survey of main stairways, doors, and building access points, visually documenting situations that present access issues. Students also developed a survey that posed general questions about accessibility on campus. While the survey was not distributed due to time constraints, the process of survey design led the group to communicate with our local disability resource center and begin to learn about the ethical involvement of human subjects in qualitative research. The process also helped the group to produce content for the final proof of concept.

Students used InVision, a digital prototyping tool for rapidly generating functioning prototypes of mobile and web applications. With an interactive digital prototype, the group was able to test basic functionality around campus on mobile devices. This process led them to identify interface design problems that would have been difficult to discover without an interactive prototype. For example, some buttons needed to be resized to accommodate different hand sizes, colors needed to be aligned with recommendations from the Americans with Disabilities Act (ADA), and the legibility of instructions and other text needed to be increased for reading while en route to a destination.

With Mobility Map, students engaged in a co-design practice within the context of a place-based project and leveraged community assets such as campus maps, course schedules, surveys, discussions with the campus disability resource center, and photo-documentation of campus walkways to design a concept for a mobile application that seeks to increase accessibility on campus. Their conceptualization not only facilitated an active community mapping of the campus but also afforded users with opportunities to critically intervene in how community members with a range of mobilities traverse it.[3]

#### CASE 2: TAG IT

Summary: *a social media app that encourages dialogue on street art and vandalism within the local community*

Tag It explores issues regarding public art, acts of vandalism, and community action through critical interventionist art practices. The students began their concept as a way to map and discuss racist acts of vandalism on campus. As their conversations and explorations into interventionist art practices expanded, they became interested in the applications of user-generated media for engaging the local community in place-based discussions about the tenuous position of graffiti and street art. The students were specifically interested in what and who determine whether something is street art or vandalism.

Tag It creates dialogue about public art and the subjective nature of labels such as "street art," "vandalism," and "graffiti." When users are in the local community and encounter a public work they want to share or discuss, they can "tag" it with geospatial and descriptive metadata (a geotag and hashtag, respectively). When another user comes upon a tag, they will receive a mobile device notification allowing them to view and comment on the public work. Tag It creates a geo-cached dialogue that is activated in context and expands conversation about the visual culture that fills our shared environment. Critical interventionist practices that rely on public discourse informed the group's development process. User testing uncovered how gray areas surround dichotomies of art and vandalism in public spaces. As the group further refined their concept, the interface design needed to reflect the complexity of these polarizing definitions and incorporate a place for debate about these topics.

### *Place Making: Speculative Design and Mobility*

Placeable exists on a continuum between ideas and designed interactive spaces. In some instances, the process is akin to speculative design: using a design process to imagine the interface of objects, environments, and social entities (DiSalvo 2012). In spring 2015, we strategically underemphasized technical implementation to focus on engaging inquiry: enhancing concepts around critical intervention and mobility over a functioning project. We learned that speculative design is powerful even when it stops short of a working product. Within the constraints of undergraduate education, not worrying about whether a prototype works allows for a stronger emphasis on inquiry, co-design frameworks, and community-based design. Implementation may come later.

And implementation may never end. Since these projects were completed, the tumultuous discourse of intersectional identities that populate university campuses has only become more prevalent. As placeable projects find new expressions in curriculum and proof of concept explorations, we continue to locate tensions for critical practice in art and design learning. Intersectionality, interaction design processes, and interventionist art practices inform our collaborative pedagogy. Under the three core constructs—seeking place, making mobile interfaces, and employing co-design—our recommendations may transfer to a broader set of disciplines that explore the performances of mobile computing as they relate to conceptions of space and politics. Co-design is part of making a curriculum, interface, or archive of historical documents. Well-developed hierarchies of teacher/student and designer/user persist within our home disciplines of art education and graphic design. Questioning these power structures could have broader implications for design and making. As a practice across disciplines, placeable offers evidence of how approaches to social understanding in the arts and design can benefit collaborative strategies in the humanities and beyond.

## NOTES

1. See http://www.placeable.org/letstalkabout.
2. See Burns, Paul, and Paz.
3. Mobility Map became the senior project for one of the group's graphic design students, who further pursued the design and development of a functioning application.

## BIBLIOGRAPHY

ARIS. http://arisgames.org.

Ball, Eric L., and Alice Lai. "Place-based Pedagogy for the Arts and Humanities." *Pedagogy* 6, no. 3 (2006): 261–87.

Bauer, Harald, and Salvatore Engel-Di Mauro. *Critical Geographies: A Collection of Readings*. Kelowna, Canada: Praxis, 2008.

Bogost, Ian. *Persuasive Games: The Expressive Power of Videogames*. Cambridge, Mass.: MIT Press, 2007.

Bringhurst, Robert. *The Elements of Typographic Style*. Seattle, Wash.: Hartley & Marks, 2012.

Burns, Janice C., Dagmar Pudrzynska Paul, and Silvia R. Paz. *Participatory Asset Mapping: A Community Research Lab Toolkit*. Los Angeles: Advancement Project and Healthy City, 2011. http://communityscience.com/knowledge4equity/AssetMappingToolkit.pdf.

Darts, David. "Art Education for a Change: Contemporary Issues and the Visual Arts." *Art Education* 59, no. 5 (2006): 6–12.

Debord, Guy. "Introduction to a Critique of Urban Geography." In *Critical Geographies: A Collection of Readings,* ed. Harald Bauer and Salvatore Engel-Di Mauro, 23–28. Kelowna, Canada: Praxis, 2008. Originally published in *Situationist International Anthology,* translated by Ken Knabb. Berkeley, Calif.: Bureau of Public Secrets, 2006.

Demos, T. J. "'The Interventionists: Art in the Social Sphere'; Mass MOCA." *Artforum International* 43, no. 3 (2004): 228.

DiSalvo, Carl. "Spectacles and Tropes: Speculative Design and Contemporary Food Cultures." *The Fibreculture Journal* 20 (2012): 109–22.

Dunne, Anthony, and Fiona Raby. "Critical Design FAQ." www.dunneandraby.co.uk /content/bydandr/13/0.

Elwood, Sarah. "Volunteered Geographic Information: Future Research Directions Motivated by Critical, Participatory, and Feminist GIS." *GeoJournal* 72 (2008): 173–83.

Goodchild, Michael F. "Citizens as Sensors: The World of Volunteered Geography." *GeoJournal* 69, no. 4 (2007): 211–21.

Grant, Nichole. "The Anitracism App: Methodological Reflections for Theory and Practice." *Critical Literacy: Theories and Practices* 8, no. 1 (2014): 20–32.

Hirschhorn, Thomas. *The Gramsci Monument.* Bronx, N.Y.: Forest Houses, 2013.

*The Interventionists: Art in the Social Sphere.* North Adams, Mass.: Massachusetts Museum of Contemporary Art, 2004–05.

Jereminjenko, Natalie. *Environmental Health Clinic.* New York: New York University. http://www.environmentalhealthclinic.net/.

Knochel, Aaron D., and Amy Papaelias. Placeable. http://www.placeable.org/.

Knochel, Aaron D., and Ryan Patton. "*If* Art Education *Then* Critical Digital Making: Computational Thinking and Creative Code." *Studies in Art Education* 57, no. 1 (2015): 21–38.

Knudsen, Susanne V. "Intersectionality: A Theoretical Inspiration in the Analysis of Minority Cultures and Identities in Textbooks." In *Caught in the Web or Lost in the Textbook?* ed. Eric Bruillard, Bente Aamotsbakken, Susanne V. Knudsen, and Mike Horsley, 61–76. Caen, France: IARTEM, 2006.

Manovich, Lev. *Software Takes Command.* New York: Bloomsbury, 2013.

Mao, Ji-Ye, Karel Vrendenburg, Paul W. Smith, and Tom Carey. "The State of User-Centered Design Practice," *Communications of the ACM* 48, no. 3 (2005): 105–9.

Newman, Jennifer. "'Let's Talk About It' Event Addresses Campus Issues." *The New Paltz Oracle.* November 21, 2013. http://oracle.newpaltz.edu/lets-talk-about-it-event -addresses-campus-issues.

Orta, Lisa. *Refuge Wear City Interventions.* 1993–98. https://www.studio-orta.com/en /artworks/serie/1/Refuge-Wear.

Rakowitz, Michael. *paraSITE.* 1998. http://www.michaelrakowitz.com/parasite/.

Ratto, Matt. "Critical Making: Conceptual and Material Studies in Technology and Social Life." *The Information Society* 27, no. 4 (2011): 252–60.

Ridge, Mia, Don Lafreniere, and Scott Nesbit. "Creating Deep Maps and Spatial Narratives through Design." *International Journal of Humanities and Arts Computing* 7, no. 1–2 (2013): 176–89.

Sobel, David. *Place-based Education: Connecting Classrooms and Communities.* Great Barrington, Mass.: Orion Society, 2004.

Tavin, Kevin. "Wrestling with Angels, Searching for Ghosts: Towards a Critical Pedagogy of Visual Culture." *Studies in Art Education* 44, no. 3 (2003): 197–213.

Taylor, Pamela. "Critical Thinking in and through Interactive Computer Hypertext and Art Education." *Innovate: Journal of Online Education* 2, no. 3 (2006): 1–7.

# Making the Model: Scholarship and Rhetoric in 3-D Historical Reconstructions

ELAINE SULLIVAN, ANGEL DAVID NIEVES, AND LISA M. SNYDER

The workflow for traditional humanistic scholarship might be loosely described as follows: (1) identify a research question, (2) gather and critically analyze the materials (primary and secondary) that inform said question, and (3) write an interpretive analysis using selected elements from your materials to support and communicate an argument.[1] In evaluating the resulting scholarship, reviewers are asked to gauge the work and its potential impact on their field. Is the research question important? Did the author use the appropriate source materials (in terms of both quantity and quality)? Were the source materials harnessed to make a convincing argument? Did the author approach the question in a unique or interesting way?

In this chapter, we argue that the creation of three-dimensional (3-D) virtual reconstruction models of historic sites is a new form of knowledge production equivalent to traditional textual analysis. The process of making a computer model asks scholars to perform the steps described above; however, the final product is an interactive environment and not the written word. To design a research project focused on reconstructing now-disappeared (or altered) historic places, the scholar must identify a question that is best (or sometimes can only be) answered when considering space and spatial relationships in three dimensions. In each step of building the model, the researcher must select and discard information, weighing its validity and pertinence to the research being addressed. The resulting model is not a neutral representation of "the past," but the scholar's interpretation of *specific* aspects of a place at a certain time—an interpretation that can be challenged, revised, or rejected by others. 3-D reconstruction models are thus not illustrations or simple representations of an incontestable past; they are a form of rhetoric (here in visual form) akin to the traditional scholarly argument.

Building such models and using them as tools of analysis creates a wealth of new research opportunities. Models can offer new techniques to investigate questions of how gender, ethnicity, and power are conceptualized by a society and inscribed into the very space that structures such relationships. The process of modeling helps us to confront and define our own gaps in the historical record, challenging our ability to recover and comprehend the past. The use of 3-D reconstruction models offers methods for virtually exploring issues of human experience, such as how visibility and movement influenced actions or meaning in a place, that are otherwise impossible (due to the degradation or disappearance of sites). The process of navigating through 3-D models constructed for pedestrian-level, real-time interaction also allows us to ask questions about scale, adjacency, design, and experience. Finally, these models move beyond strictly subject-specialist questions, contributing to broader debates about learning (such as visual literacy) and human-computer interaction.

This chapter identifies two major foci where 3-D models impact historical research. First, we posit that historical argumentation can be made through the very process of modeling spaces in three dimensions. If modeling is a form of rhetoric, then both the development of the 3-D reconstruction and the selection and evaluation of source materials constitute interpretive processes. In untraditional ways, the scholar interrogates source materials at vastly different levels of resolution and uncertainty, at each point formulating and revising hypotheses. Second, the completed reconstruction model functions as a locus for dialogue. It offers fresh points of entry into the examination of lived spaces, placing research questions into a spatial framework for new types of analysis. We see models as specifically relevant to not only understanding complex spatial change over time but also addressing how power manifests spatially through aspects of human experience and movement in past places.

We use three examples of scholarly historical reconstruction models as case studies to support these suppositions. Intentionally, these projects cover vastly different historical times and places and were designed with different research goals. The Digital Karnak model is a diachronic model, visualizing 30 separate reconstruction phases of the ancient Egyptian temple of Karnak, starting in approximately 2000 B.C.E.[2] The model of the World's Columbian Exposition held in Chicago in 1893 was initiated as a testbed for research on educational applications for interactive computer models of historic urban environments. The twentieth-century South African township of Soweto model considers how historical reconstructions of the recent past could be used to document resistance and help to gather victim testimony of crimes committed by the apartheid state.[3] What these projects hold in common is their attempt to visually (and virtually) reconstruct important historic places in order to investigate how space influenced human experience.

## *The Model as Rhetoric: "Building" an(d) Argument*

In *A Companion to Digital Humanities,* Willard McCarty (2004) defines models as "a representation of something for purposes of study," and the act of modeling as "the heuristic process of constructing and manipulating models" (26). The physicist Freeman Dyson (1999) similarly describes models as "a construction that describes a much simpler universe, [by] including some features of the actual universe and neglecting others" (xiv). What is vital here is the emphasis on the process of construction and interpretation as a means of gaining knowledge. Reconstruction models differ from "reality-based" models (produced through techniques such as laser scanning and photogrammetry) that capture the state of an object or site in the present and are used frequently for archaeological or cultural heritage recording, study, and conservation.[4] Virtual reconstruction models attempt instead to harness many types of information (both what exists in the present and through documentation/supposition of what is lost) to investigate what is *not* present.[5] Frequently, the original structure or site has been destroyed or altered so dramatically that capturing a "reality-based" model is impossible. Degradation can occur because of the age of the structure and ancient modification (e.g., Karnak's buildings are now between two and four thousand years old and were frequently modified in ancient times), purposeful disassembling of a site at the end of its use-life (e.g., the Columbian Exposition was an ephemeral event, only open to the public for six months), or environmental change, looting, or intentional modern destruction. Some sites (such as Soweto) remain in use, and tens or hundreds of years of human occupation have altered them in ways that obscure their earliest history. Reconstruction models therefore often combine information from existing structures, archaeology, photographs, ground plans, or observer descriptions. The reconstruction process uses existing evidence to interrogate that which remains unknown. It is thus always biased, selective, and interpretive. Models can never fully re-create a real "lived" moment in the past. Instead, reconstruction modeling centers on the production of "potential pasts" (Forte 7–18), hypothetical slices of what may have been that offer new potential for studying past environments (Favro 276).

The following section focuses on how scholars use modeling to acquire new knowledge about past places. This knowledge includes the modeling process as a form of scholarly discovery, where information on the architectural and social history under examination can be considered variously, testing out conflicting narratives and inconsistent sources within a defined space as well as integrating and reconciling data at different resolutions, scales, and levels of detail. Data incompatibilities are often left (silently) unresolved in traditional scholarship but are glaringly obvious in visual models. Both processes ask scholars to grapple with the historical record and make conclusions based on the strength of existing evidence.

## RECONSTRUCTION AND CONFLICTING DATA

Historical writing can be described as a type of "verbal model"—a series of abstractions about the past woven together to create meaning (Staley 58–59). Like traditional written scholarship, the 3-D modeling process asks scholars to collect and weigh primary and secondary sources and to build a visual and/or spatial argument that interprets the past. In both cases, the scholar "constructs" understanding from a selection of materials, choosing what is important to the argument and omitting the irrelevant. The modeled outcome, like a written article, is the culmination of choices made by the author that must be cited and supported.[6] Some sources are familiar to most humanities scholars: the archive, archaeological materials, artistic representations, literature, and historic maps. Some perhaps less common sources include satellite imagery, aerial photographs, "reality-based" models, and geographic information systems (GIS) data. While the source materials used to build a historical reconstruction model may differ widely from project to project, all such scholarly models have the same goal: to interpret past material culture through the combination and consideration of multimodal forms of historical evidence.

Each model is unique, as each reflects the specific research goals of the author as well as the source materials harnessed. Some models attempt to replicate the appearance of historic sites with photo-realistic visualizations, reconstructing colors, patterns, artwork, brickwork, landscape features, and other details.[7] Other models are concerned with reconstructing the ephemeral: human movement, sound, or one-time events such as ritual spectacles (Johanson 403–418). Visual hyperrealism may be quite unnecessary for such models, and instead they can be designed to seem almost schematic.[8] Authors interested in visualizing entire historic cities or large numbers of structures for which only basic information is important can use "procedural" modeling, which rapidly generates shapes based on geometric rules articulated in computer scripts (Saldana and Johanson 205–210; Haegler, Müller, and Van Gool 1–11). Here again, the goal of scholarly models is not to fully replicate past places, but to selectively examine and interpret certain aspects of historic sites, leaving other elements unstudied. In each case, the author chooses how best to structure the model to address the question at hand: What was the potential viewing experience of a person inside this lavishly painted room? Could the oration at a funeral spectacle be heard standing in a particular place? What form might an entire ancient city take at a specific moment in time, and how might that form have changed one hundred years later? As David Staley (2003) usefully reiterates, the point of historical scholarship is not to reduplicate the past. "It is the inquiry that matters most, the questions and answers and the benefits therein that historians seek" (Staley 59).

Scholars producing digital reconstruction models necessarily grapple with issues of incomplete information that also face traditional historical scholarship. The vagaries of the archaeological record, missing data in the archive, and incomplete information mean that models are never a simple reassembly of an existing whole. In creating a historic reconstruction, the author is interpreting information that is always ambiguous. One of the largest challenges to reconstruction work is also one of the major strengths of 3-D visualization: making gaps and suppositions inherent in each model. At every point, the researcher is confronted with shifting levels of certainty and missing/conflicting information that result in a literal hole in their model. They are forced to grapple with the impact of each interpretive choice on the larger meaning of the modeled space and to imagine the result of their choices for the viewer. The following three examples illustrate different challenges and opportunities emerging from the reconstruction process.

## MODELING CONFLICTED SPACES

Generally, the physical reimaginings of a conflicted space—the fact-finding involved in the reconstruction of a historical model—pose a unique set of problems. In the case of recent histories, a scholar must remember that some constituencies may be actively contesting disputed documentation. In other instances, some groups may have privileged existing documentation from the site of the model and events related to it, and any surviving accounts that take exception to the dominant narrative may be in short supply. For example, did a so-called "Fourth Estate" or neutral press corps document breaking news in the townships of Johannesburg during the resistance against apartheid regimes of the twentieth century? In the case of South Africa, at best one journalist from the mainstream press may have written dispatches at a certain flashpoint, but the official reports from the dominant apartheid regime most likely stuff the ministries' filing cabinets.

Scholarly inquiry into how historical reconstruction models might incorporate conflicting narratives about real-life victims living at a particular time and place informs Nieves's analysis of the Student Uprisings. In particular, Nieves's research in South Africa focuses on Soweto, a so-called "model native township" comprised of systematically planned, would-be South African garden cities designed to reinforce the state system of apartheid. (Physical spaces such as Soweto and other townships built under the apartheid system have provided the social, political, and economic context for black urban life since the founding of Johannesburg in 1886.) Nieves's unique work of historical recovery is grounded in the inter- and multi-disciplinary field of African American studies and the African diaspora. His research into spatial reform and resistance in conflicted spaces also incorporates landscape studies, architectural history, historic preservation, women's studies, and cultural studies.

Nieves offers this example of how 3-D spatial analysis contributes to the study of place-based history: on the watershed morning of June 16, 1976, in Soweto, members of the South African police and security forces gunned down black African students who marched to protest the use of Afrikaans as the primary language of school instruction. The subsequent worldwide distribution and dissemination of Sam Nzima's iconic photograph depicting the shocking death of Hector Pieterson—a child who was a casualty of the protests that day—coupled with the deaths of tens of other school children, catalyzed the student uprisings and sparked the global anti-apartheid movement. To this day, the various accounts of both Pieterson's death and the site of the shooting are subject to dispute. Nieves's model of Soweto (see Figure 35.1) combines 3-D reconstructions of structures and landscapes with the

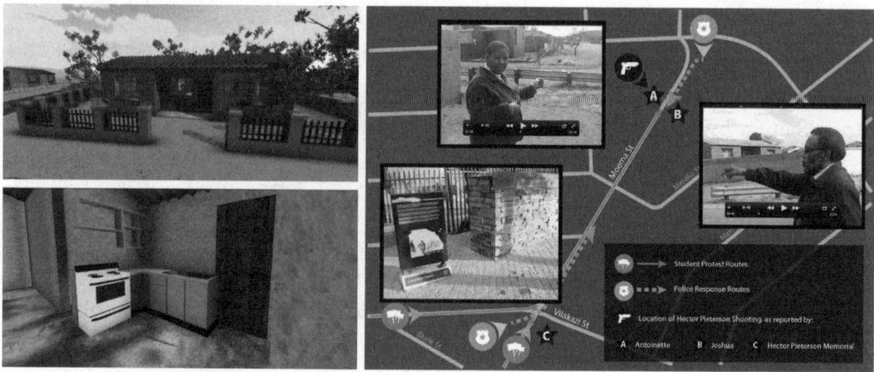


**Figure 35.1.** (top left, bottom left) Soweto virtual heritage environment model, 2015. Image courtesy of Greg Lord and Angel David Nieves; (right) Antoinette Sithole provides testimony of Hector Pieterson's death; it conflicts with other accounts of events on June 16, 1976. Courtesy of Greg Lord and Angel David Nieves.

use of avatars as virtual persons inhabiting the site at the time in question. This use of avatars allows people to act out and study contested scenarios from the Student Uprisings.

## CONTEXT AND LOST ENVIRONMENTS

Environmental information is vital to contextualizing the temple of Karnak within the larger landscape of the ancient city of Thebes. However, during the two thousand years of the temple's use, the contemporary position of the Nile river (the state's most important conduit for commerce and communication) is only (vaguely) known in a handful of moments because it gradually shifted westward. Nevertheless, its interpreted position is included in all 30 phases of the Digital Karnak model, placed appropriately within the known parameters of all existing information (see Figure 35.2). The modeled location of the river at any given moment is based on Sullivan's interpretation of source material that includes the dates of quays found through archaeological excavations, an image of the temple on a tomb painting in Thebes's Tombs of the Nobles, and geomorphological studies in modern Luxor (Sullivan). The expansion of the temple structure at key moments was directly linked to the movement of the Nile, as the river's drift opened up new land for expansion but also threatened to leave the temple without riverfront access. While the river's location in the model lies on a spectrum of uncertainty, without its inclusion the direct relationship between the position of the Nile and the westward expansion of the temple is obscured. At every stage of the construction, inclusion of the river in the model forced Sullivan and the project team to question the correlation between the two entities as well as how gaps in that information impact our general understanding of the temple's form and the larger landscape of Thebes at that time.

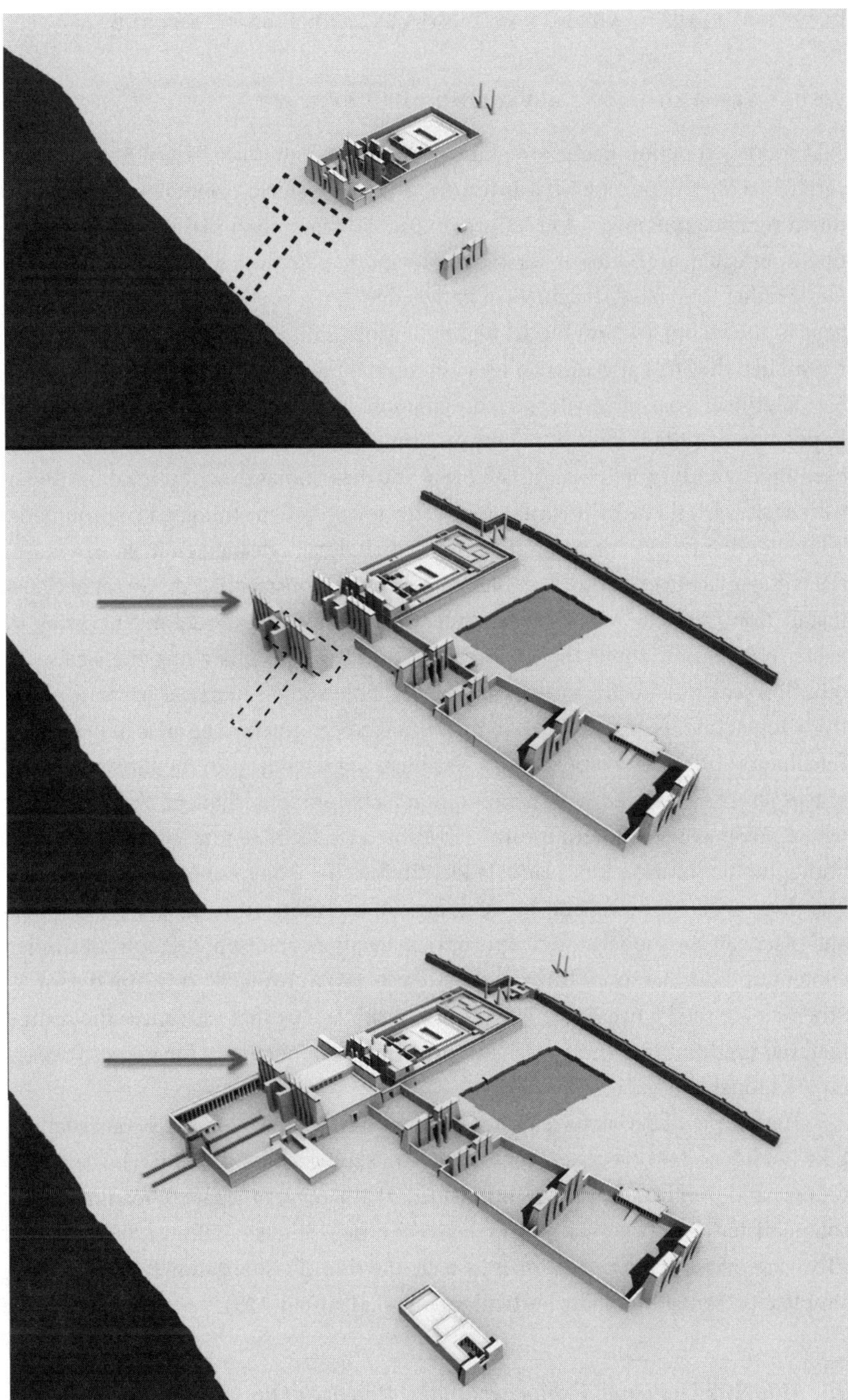

**Figure 35.2.** A rendering of Karnak temple in the early 18th Dynasty (1473–1458 B.C.E.), the late 18th Dynasty (1316–1302 B.C.E.), and Dynasty 22 (962–941 B.C.E.), with hypothetical location of the river for each period. A T-shaped basin (dotted lines) that possibly linked the river to the temple to the east was later filled in, and a new pylon was constructed in the area (arrow), allowing the temple to be further expanded westward, chasing the moving river. Image courtesy of UC Regents.

### VISUAL STRATEGIES FOR REVEALING THE UNKNOWN

3-D models function usefully as knowledge representations (Favro 326–27); the careful reconstruction of what is known about a historic place makes clear how much remains *unknown*. As McCarty explains, "Computational models, however finely perfected, are better understood as *temporary states in a process of coming to know* rather than fixed structures of knowledge" (257, emphasis in original). While gaps in the reconstruction model highlight aspects of place undertheorized by the researcher, they can also distract users in negative ways.

A critical goal of Snyder's reconstruction model of the World's Columbian Exposition of 1893 is to explore how real-time interaction with the model impacts user understanding of this landmark event and determines the circumstances under which users would be intrinsically motivated to explore the modeled environment. To that end, incorporating into the model small details gleaned from source material is essential but oftentimes problematic. When reconstructing the Street of Cairo installation from the Midway Plaisance, for example, the model must convey to users information about the various shops and restaurants along the street. At question was how to fill in the gaps of available source material without negatively impacting user experience in the virtual environment. The atlas in Daniel H. Burnham's (1989) final report on the fair included references to the function of the spaces, cross-referenced with contemporary photographs. Signage was replicated where possible, with "lorem ipsum" substituted for illegible text. In the absence of photographic information, placards identifying the shops' contents were created. The three available black-and-white images of the shops from 1893 were cropped and placed in the model at their appropriate location; color photographs of similar content-appropriate shops from modern-day Cairo were placed in the model for all other shops (see Figure 35.3). The result is a subtle clue that references the source material used to build the model and provides an opportunity for users to reflect on the model as a site of interpretation.

These types of decisions reinforce the interpretive nature of model construction. Like books, no two models (even of the same subject) are the same, because the process and the final output are influenced by the content creator's reading of the source material and over-arching objective for the work. As Gaffney (2008) asserts, "The experience of interpretation is . . . a central role of visualization rather than the simple representation of any particular reality" (Gaffney 129).

## *The Model as Dialogue: Exploring Spatial Research Questions*

Through its formulation, each historical reconstruction model represents a scholar's argument about a potential past. Embedded within and extending out from this construction are complementary humanistic research issues. We identify three major areas where modeling offers unique contributions to ongoing scholarly dialogue.

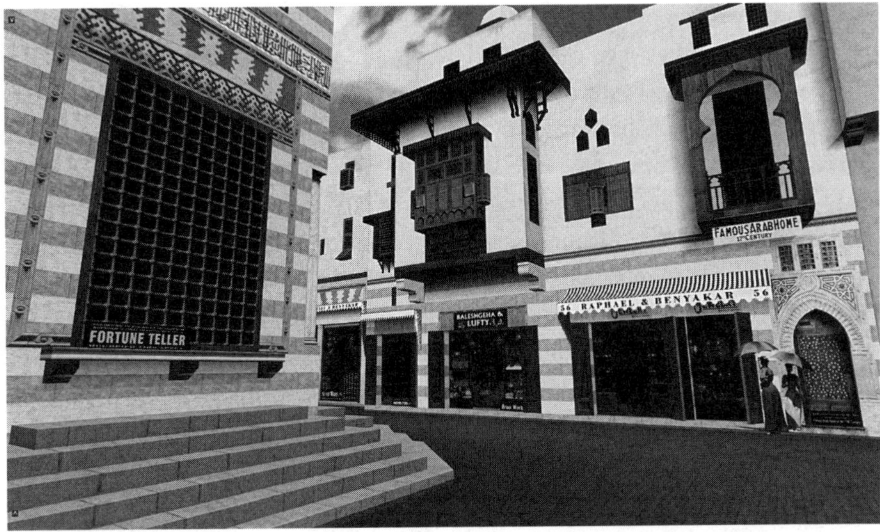


**Figure 35.3.** In the foreground of this screenshot of the Street of Cairo installation at the World's Columbian Exposition, a sign tells users that Burnham's final report on the fair lists a fortune-teller at that location. Across the street, color images from modern-day Cairo suggest the wares offered by a jewelry store; a black-and-white image from 1893 is shown in the adjacent brassworks shop. Image courtesy of UC Regents.

First, questions about how race, gender, sexuality, and power were inscribed into built spaces and then renegotiated by those inhabiting the spaces can be an integral part of the modeling and post-modeling process. A second powerful aspect of modeling (in contrast to textual description) is the attention it draws to our *lack* of complete knowledge about past places and their historical meaning and function. The reconstruction process forces us to engage with uncertainty at every level, in ways often ignored when we do not directly confront the lived realities of the three-dimensional world.[9] Finally, the creation of diachronic models—models that trace change across time in a historic space—generates other points of analysis. To produce each phase of a model, the author must grapple with temporal uncertainty, how earlier stages influenced or impacted later forms, and how people's perception of places changed as they did. In all three of these instances, modeling offers a new technique to answer complex research questions about the relationship between human action and space in the past.

## INVESTIGATING POWER AND SPACE

In the past 30 years, archaeologists and historians have persuasively demonstrated how space is socially constructed; human actions and relationships shape and are shaped by the natural and built world in which people live.[10] More recent scholarship goes further, suggesting that space should be understood "as the relational arrangement of objects and humans in a place . . . permanently constituted as well as changed by social practice" (Meier 507). Space is thus directly constituted by the social interactions between people and things, the same interactions that are laden with power dynamics based on gender, race, ethnicity, and sexuality. A scholar can study past manifestations of these dynamics through 3-D spatial analysis.

Nieves's model of Soweto offers one example. As Edward Gonzalez-Tennant (2013) argues, the "uncritical" use of digital technologies and new media methodologies at sites of "dark" history have resulted in the de-politicization of inequality in those places (Gonzalez-Tennant 64). Modeling provides a means to explore how the very fabric of sites such as Soweto was designed for control and repression, re-situating ostensibly innocuous spaces directly within the ideological context of apartheid. It also affords opportunities to examine how such seemingly homogenous urban fabrics can reveal social and political strategies of resistance, such as the re-appropriation and modification of space by inhabitants of Soweto who resisted apartheid policies. The spatial *is* political, and the Soweto model is used to consider how particular strategies signaled political and social resistance to the internal community.

Much like other models in this chapter, Soweto was not built only from primary source materials found in the archive. As with any humanities project, it suggests and even encourages reinterpretations of existing historiographies. As such, the Soweto model permits interrogations beyond the research of previous scholars. Specifically, its 3-D model-making process intervenes in and corrects state-sponsored narratives that have erased the everyday lived experiences of those involved in the liberation struggle. These interventions and corrections are important because the South African apartheid security state actually produced its own documentation to facilitate diachronic model-making of Soweto's dark history. For instance, a cache of aerial images taken of Soweto over several decades was unearthed recently in the offices of the Chief Directorate: Spatial Development Planning Archives in Cape Town. Although it is now difficult to determine exactly why these aerial images were taken over a fifty-plus-year period, the white-minority government's paranoia over black-majority rule may have meant that surveillance of this magnitude was deemed critical to political and social control.

Additionally, some hypotheses about the influence of the Garden City urban planning movement on Soweto suggest that the densities resulting from planned interventions might have encouraged empowerment among its residents. The indigenous black population (specifically in Johannesburg), which was widely dispersed and even landless before arriving in the emerging megacity, could organize politically and culturally in Soweto to resist the National Party and its apartheid policies. By 1950, well over 40 acts and amendments were passed to secure the Nationalist Party's formal control over the urban landscape and its growing urban population in townships such as Soweto. However, these acts also insured that, over the course of several generations, the majority of the black population would develop longstanding ties to—and a rich cultural heritage within—their respective townships as they waged a struggle against apartheid. Nieves's 3-D reconstructions of Soweto examine the micro-geography of resistance as well as the layering of meaning and action between the apartheid state and township residents in the low brick bungalows and city blocks characteristic of the township. For example, the reconstruction of Hector Pieterson's slaying—in a circumscribed, micro-geography of an imagined Soweto (i.e., a handful of dense blocks within the township) from 1976—is just one part of scholarly inquiry into the conflicting narratives of other various, real-life victims and sites of the Uprisings. Such reconstructions restore suppressed material evidence of this traumascape.

## ACKNOWLEDGING AND INTERROGATING THE UNKNOWN

While the level of architectural reconstruction in each model may vary widely, even a complete record of a past place cannot lead to a model that inherently "reveals" the cultural relationships enacted there. Researchers must investigate and hypothesize the myriad ways such spaces could be used and understood, and also admit that different people's perspectives significantly influence such understandings. Building the model is thus in many ways an *attempt* at recovery: of spaces as well as real embodied human movement, actions, and feelings. Modeling asks us to lay out in detail the possible forms that contributed to human experiences, while acknowledging that some elements will always remain unknown.

Many visitors to the Columbian Exposition traveled, for example, by boat to Jackson Park from downtown Chicago, landing on an immense wooden pier jutting into Lake Michigan. Where guidebooks like Rand McNally's *Handbook of the World's Columbian Exposition* and *A Week at the Fair* provide great detail about transportation options for getting to the fair and suggested routes for adventures once there, they are silent on the specifics of how visitors might transition from the pier to the grounds. When considered on a 2-D plan, their most direct route into the Court of Honor, the formal core of the fair, appears to be through the Peristyle, a screen of monumental columns representing the original states of the union. In navigating through the computer model, it quickly becomes apparent that movement along the southern edge of the pier was more likely the dominant route. From this promenade, fairgoers' first impression of the exposition would have been of the primary artifacts and relics related to Christopher Columbus, the namesake of the fair, which was held in honor of the four hundredth anniversary of his journey to the New World. On a promontory to the south stood a replica of the complex—the Convent of La Rabida—where he began planning his expedition and which was filled with Columbiana; straight ahead were replicas of his fleet: the *Niña,* the *Pinta,* and the *Santa Maria*. Reinforcing the importance of reconstruction models as research outputs, the ability to interact with the 3-D computer model generates new arguments for movement through the exposition and reveals new interpretations that suggest a logical sequencing of visitor experience that established the country's historical foundations before revealing the wonders of the great exhibition halls.

### DIACHRONIC MODELING

Diachronic (or temporal) models offer new tools to the humanist to investigate how the meaning and function of places change over time. At complex historic sites, it is often difficult to reimagine how the meaning of a space shifted through a series of renovations, all but the last of which are usually inaccessible in the present. Perhaps most instructive is the opportunity with each model phase to challenge the inevitability of the latest phase and to examine intentionality with each addition or subtraction. Even more challenging is mentally reconstructing the experiential aspects of a person inhabiting those now-gone spaces. In modeling multiple phases of a historic place, the researcher is confronted with each small and large modification. Why this particular change? What does it tell us about how people lived? Why did their priorities or actions change at this time? How is this change related to the previous phase or the one before it? The model itself can then be used to answer a second layer of questions concerning human experience in those spaces, including questions of changing visibility, aurality, access, paths of movement, or chiaroscuro.

The Digital Karnak model clearly demonstrates the opportunities emerging from temporal modeling. One of the main functions of the temple was to provide a sort of stage for the performance of ritual events. On these occasions, the statue of the god Amun left his shrine to visit important cult sites or specific areas of the temple in an elaborate parade. The routes of these processions, some of which can be traced following textual and artistic depictions, changed over time according to religious and political priorities of the king. At Karnak, even over very short periods of time, spaces that would have been important parts of these religious events were radically modified. For example, the Wadjet Hall, which texts tell us served as the place where special ceremonies related to kingship were conducted, was built and significantly remodeled in five major phases in the reign of four kings, covering only 80 years.[11] Sullivan and the project team modeled this rapid reconceptualization of the space; the resulting reconstruction leads to a number of questions concerning how rituals and religion at the temple functioned. During the first two stages, the edges of the open-air hall were lined with peristyle; the next phase substituted the peristyle for a wooden roof supported by papyrus-form posts on two sides of the hall, and a pair of monumental obelisks was erected in the center of the court. The fourth phase saw the bricking-in of the obelisks by a large gateway; the final renovation replaced the wooden roof and posts with monumental stone papyrus columns and a matching roof. Thus, the original light-filled open space was darkened, visibility across sides of the hall was blocked, and the scale of construction continually increased. While the central axis of the temple (running through the middle of the hall) was respected, movement within the hall at each later stage was constricted and redefined, and the interior space filled in, significantly reducing the number of people who could have stood within it.

In studying the physical manifestation of the rituals that occurred in this space, it is clear that they could not have remained the same after such drastic modification.[12] Did aspects of the rituals move to other areas of the temple, or were the forms of the rituals adapted to the new space? Should we interpret these rapid alterations of key cult spaces as evidence of intense development of new religious ideas at the time—ideas that needed new architectural expression? The diachronic Karnak model shows that the temple and its rituals were not fossilized timeless forms but rather dynamic expressions of shifting royal priorities. Scholars are asked to address each moment at the temple, not to collapse and simplify complex religious changes that impacted the performance of ritual within it.

We argue that the creation, publication, and use of 3-D models for research and education form new types of interdisciplinary scholarship that integrate design, technology, archives, and historical information in ways that test the boundaries of current academic production. The act of modeling—of making—is a complex, iterative form of experimental research analogous to more traditional forms of scholarship. In this interpretive space between archival research and construction, scholars have the opportunity for new discoveries and experimental interactions. Each new piece of source material adds to the fabric of the computer model, slowly building toward a cohesive whole.

Beyond discipline-specific research questions, the process of modeling and the potential for dissemination to the broader academic community demand new forms of interdisciplinary scholarship, technology, and learning. Critical areas of related future research include the teaching and learning affordances of interactive computer technology, the thresholds for user engagement with academically generated reconstruction models, the design of instructional technologies and interfaces for educational use of cultural heritage reconstructions, the requirements for peer review of 3-D scholarship, the use of 3-D content as a boundary object of knowledge production, and long-term sustainability for this form of academic production and argumentation.

Reconstruction models and 3-D spatial analysis are rapidly increasing the relevance of historical research because improvements in personal computer memory and content sharing platforms make possible broad dissemination. 3-D materials will get bigger, faster, and easier to access. Most important, however, is the potential of 3-D content for scholarly innovation. Humanistic inquiry hinges on the idea that there is no single way to read a source, research a question, or interpret an argument. We reassess and revisit past people, places, and texts in order to examine them from fresh perspectives and see them in new ways. As historians, we consider 3-D modeling to be an exciting method to open up new viewpoints on the past—viewpoints that ask us to look again at places we *thought* we knew, approaching embodied human experience, time, and the unknown through a different lens.

## NOTES

1. This list is an abbreviated version of the process, as opposed to the methods described in Unsworth's list of scholarly primitives.

2. The model was developed in 2007/2008 at UCLA under the direction of Diane Favro and Willeke Wendrich. For resources related to the model, see the project website: http://dlib.etc.ucla.edu/projects/Karnak.

3. A wide range of tools and digital scholarship on aspects of Soweto's history can be found at http://www.apartheidheritages.com.

4. A brief discussion of image-based modeling can be found in Sauerbier.

5. In Frischer and Dakouri-Hild's *Beyond Illustration,* Maurizio Forte describes the distinction between "reality-based" 3-D models and reconstruction models in archaeology as "observed antiquity" versus "virtual antiquity." A definition of "virtual reconstruction" models for the field of archaeology is given in the *Seville International Principles on Virtual Archaeology* as "using a virtual model to visually recover a building or object made by humans at a given moment in the past from available physical evidence of these buildings or objects, scientifically-reasonable comparative inferences and in general all studies carried out by archaeologists and other experts in relation to archaeological and historical science": http://www.arqueologiavirtual.com/seav. Our discussion here does not limit such models to the field of archaeology.

6. Staley suggests we think of models as "visual secondary sources," as opposed to written secondary sources, the predominant form of discourse in the field of history (60).

7. An example would be the historical reconstruction model of the Villa of Poppaea at Oplontis that focuses on reconstructing the original appearance of ancient interiors and wall paintings at a Roman villa destroyed by the eruption of Vesuvius: http://www.oplontisproject.org.

8. Photorealism is not the goal of all reconstruction models, and the "authenticity" of a model based on this criteria is problematic. A good discussion of the problem with photorealism as a standard is found in Goodrick and Gillings (44–45). Research on the use of "non-photorealism" in virtual heritage is briefly reviewed in de Boer, et al. (189).

9. Diane Favro argues, "A comprehensive historical digital reconstruction model requires the same amount of information as a new building, compelling scholar modelers to study every single aspect, not solely a parsed segment" ("Se Non È Vero, È Ben Trovato" 273).

10. For landscape, see Tilley. For gendered space, see Sørensen, Chapter 8.

11. This space was excavated and the suggested chronology for the changes published by a team of French scholars (Carlotti and Gabolde).

12. A detailed study of these changes and how they impacted the size of the portable bark carrying the statue of the god is available in Sullivan, "Visualizing."

**BIBLIOGRAPHY**

Burnham, Daniel H. *The Final Official Report of the Director of Works of the World's Columbian Exposition*. New York: Garland Books, 1989.

Carlotti, Jean-François, and Luc Gabolde. "Nouvelles Données Sur La Ouadjyt." In *Cahiers de Karnak* XI (2003): 255–338.

de Boer, Arnoud, Leen Breure, Sandor Spruit, and Hans Voorbij. "Virtual Historical Landscapes." In *Exploring the Visual Landscape: Advances in Physiognomic Landscape Research in the Netherlands*, 185–204. Amsterdam: IOS Press, 2011.

Dyson, Freeman. *The Sun, the Genome, and the Internet: Tools of Scientific Revolutions*. Oxford: Oxford University Press, 1999.

Favro, Diane. "In the Eyes of the Beholder: Virtual Reality Re-Creations and Academia." In *Imaging Ancient Rome: Documentation, Visualization, Imagination: Proceedings of the Third Williams Symposium on Classical Architecture, Held at the American Academy in Rome, the British School at Rome, and the Deutsches Archäologisches Institut, Rome, on May 20–23, 2004*, ed. Lothar Haselberger, J. Humphrey and D. Abernathy, 321–34. Portsmouth, R.I: Journal of Roman Archaeology, Supplementary Series, 2006.

———. "Se Non È Vero, È Ben Trovato (If Not True, It Is Well Conceived): Digital Immersive Reconstructions of Historical Environments." *Journal of the Society of Architectural Historians* 71, no 3 (2012): 273–77.

Favro, Diane, and Willeke Wendrich. "Digital Karnak." University of California, 2007–08. http://wayback.archive-it.org/7877/20160919152116/dlib.etc.ucla.edu/projects/Karnak.

Forte, Maurizio. "Cyber-Archaeology: Notes on the Simulation of the Past." *Virtual Archaeology Review* 2 (2011): 7–18.

———. "Virtual Archaeology: Communication in 3D and Ecological Thinking." In *Beyond Illustration: 2D and 3D Digital Technologies as Tools for Discovery in Archaeology, Bar International Series*, ed. Bernard Frischer and Anastasia Dakouri-Hild, 75–119. Oxford: Archaeopress, 2008.

Gaffney, Vincent. "In the Kingdom of the Blind: Visualization and E-Science in Archaeology, the Arts and Humanities." In *The Virtual Representation of the Past*, ed. Mark Greengrass and Lorna Hughes, 125–34. Farnham, U.K.: Ashgate, 2008.

Gonzalez-Tennant, Edward. "New Heritage and Dark Tourism: A Mixed Methods Approach to Social Justice in America." *Heritage and Society* 6, no.1. (2013): 62–88.

Goodrick, Glyn Thomas, and Mark Gillings. "Constructs, Simulations and Hyperreal Worlds: The Role of Virtual Reality (VR) in Archaeological Research." In *On the Theory and Practice of Archaeological Computing*, ed. G. R. Lock and K. Smith, 41–59. Oxford: Oxbow, 2000.

Haegler, Simon, Pascal Müller, and Luc Van Gool. "Procedural Modeling for Digital Cultural Heritage." *EURASIP Journal on Image and Video Processing* (2009): 1–11.

Johanson, Christopher. "Visualizing History: Modeling in the Eternal City." *Visual Resources* 25 (2009): 403–18.

McCarty, Willard. "Modeling: A Study in Words and Meanings." In *A Companion to Digital Humanities,* ed. Susan Schreibman, Raymond George Siemens, and John Unsworth, 254–72. Oxford: Blackwell, 2004. http://www.digitalhumanities.org/companion.

McNally, Rand, and Company. *A Week at the Fair: Illustrating Exhibits and Wonders of the World's Columbian and Handbook of the World's Columbian Exposition*. Chicago, Ill.: Rand, McNally & Company, 1893.

Meier, Thomas. "'Landscape', 'Environment' and a Vision of Interdisciplinarity." In *Landscape Archaeology Between Art and Science: From a Multi- to an Interdisciplinary Approach,* ed. Sjoerd J. Kluiving and E. B. Guttmann-Bond, 503–14. Amsterdam: Amsterdam University Press, 2012.

Nieves, Angel David, and Gregory Lord. "Soweto '76 3D." *Apartheid Heritages: A Spatial History of South Africa's Townships*. Clinton, N.Y.: Hamilton College, 2007-08. http://apartheidheritages.org/projects/soweto-76-3d/.

Saldana, Marie, and Chris Johanson. "Procedural Modeling for Rapid-Prototyping of Multiple Building Phases." *International Archives of the Photogrammetry, Remote Sensing and Spatial Information Sciences* XL-5/W1 (2013): 205–10.

Sauerbier, Martin. "Image-Based Techniques in Cultural Heritage Modeling." In *Scientific Computing and Cultural Heritage,* ed. H. G. Bock, Willi Jager, and Michael Winckler, 61–70. Berlin: Springer-Verlag, 2013.

*Seville International Principles on Virtual Archaeology.* Sociedad Española de Arqueologia Virtual, 2013. http://www.arqueologiavirtual.com/seav.

Snyder, Lisa M. "The World's Columbian Exposition of 1893." *Urban Simulation Team.* Los Angeles: University of California, Los Angeles. https://idre.ucla.edu/research/wce.

Sørensen, Marie Louise Stig. *Gender Archaeology*. Cambridge: Polity, 2000.

Staley, David. *Computers, Visualization and History: How New Technology Will Transform Our Understanding of the Past*. Armonk, N.Y.: Sharpe, 2003.

Sullivan, Elaine. "Karnak: Development of the Temple of Amun-Ra." In *UCLA Encyclopedia of Egyptology,* ed. W. Z. Wendrich. Los Angeles, Calif.: 2010. http://escholarship.org/uc/item/1f28q08h.

———. "Visualizing the Size and Movement of the Portable Festival Bark at Karnak Temple." *British Museum Studies in Ancient Egypt and Sudan* 19 (2012). http://www.britishmuseum.org/research/publications/online_journals/bmsaes.aspx.

Tilley, Christopher. *A Phenomenology of Landscape: Places, Paths, and Monuments, Explorations in Anthropology*. Oxford: Berg, 1994.

Unsworth, John. "Scholarly Primitives: What Methods Do Humanities Researchers Have in Common, and How Might Our Tools Reflect This?" Part of a symposium on "Humanities Computing: Formal Methods, Experimental Practice" sponsored by King's College, London, May 13, 2000. http://people.brandeis.edu/~unsworth/Kings.5–00/primitives.html.

# PART V

# MAKING, JUSTICE, ETHICS

# Beyond Making

DEBBIE CHACHRA

Every once in a while, I am asked to describe what I "make." The question was part of an application for a technology conference a few years ago; when I saw it, I closed the browser tab, and I only applied later (and eventually attended) because of the enthusiastic encouragement of friends. I am always uncomfortable identifying myself as a maker. I am uncomfortable with any culture that encourages taking on an entire identity rather than expressing a facet of my own identity ("maker" rather than "someone who makes things"). This is not to say that I am opposed to "making" itself. I am a professor at a small engineering college that places a strong emphasis on design and hands-on experiences, and I have been making things my entire life. But, especially in technology culture, there is a pervasive sense that "making" is the most, or indeed the only, worthwhile way to spend one's time. And this assumption has a long history.

Walk through a museum. Look around a city. Almost all the artifacts that we value as a society were made by or at the order of men. But behind every one is an invisible infrastructure of labor—primarily caregiving, in its various aspects—that is performed mostly by women. As a teenager, I read Ayn Rand on how any work that needed to be done day after day was meaningless, and that the only worthwhile endeavor was creating new things. To the distress of my mother, my response was to stop making my bed every day. (While I admit the possibility of misinterpretation, as I have not read Rand's writing since I was so young my mother oversaw my housekeeping, I have no plans to revisit Rand anytime soon.) The cultural primacy of making, particularly in tech culture—that it is intrinsically superior to not-making, repair, analysis, and especially caregiving—is informed by the gendered history of who is credited with making things and, in particular, who made things that were shared with the world, not merely for hearth and home.

Making is not a rebel movement of scrappy individuals going up against the system. While the shift might be from corporations to individuals (a shift that is supported by a different set of companies selling things), and from what Ursula Franklin

(1999) described as "prescriptive technologies" to ones that are more holistic (10–18), it mostly reinscribes familiar values in a slightly different form: that artifacts are important, and people are not.

In light of this history, it is unsurprising that coding has been folded into "making." Consider the instant gratification of seeing "hello, world" on the screen. Coding is nearly the easiest possible way to "make" things and certainly one where failure has a very low cost (Boyer 2011). Code is "making" because we have figured out how to package it into discrete units and sell it, and because it is widely perceived to be done by men. But you can also think about coding as eliciting a specific set of desired behaviors from computing devices. It is the Searle's-Chinese-room take on the deeper, richer, messier, less reproducible, immeasurably more difficult version of what we do with people—change their cognition, abilities, and behaviors. We call the latter "education," and it is mostly done by underpaid, undervalued women.

When new products are introduced, we hear about the exciting technological innovations behind them that are ostensibly worth paying (more) for. In contrast, policy and public discourse around caregiving—besides education, healthcare comes immediately to mind—are rarely about paying more to do *better* and are instead mostly about how to lower costs. Consider the economics term, "Baumol's cost disease": it suggests that it is somehow pathological that the time and energy—and therefore the cost—a string quartet takes to prepare for a performance has not fallen in the same way as goods, as if people and what they do should become less valuable with time. (To be fair, given the trajectory of wages in the United States over the last few years, this decrease seems to be exactly what is happening.[1])

It is not, of course, that there is anything wrong with making (although it is not all that clear that the world needs more stuff). It is that the alternative to making is usually not doing *nothing*—it is nearly always doing things for and with other *people*, from the barista to Facebook community moderators (Chen 2014) to the social worker to the surgeon. Describing oneself as a maker—regardless of what one actually or mostly does—is a way to accrue the gendered capitalist benefits of being a person who makes products.

I am not a maker. In a value system that is about creating artifacts, specifically ones you can sell, I am a less valuable human. As an educator, the work I do is, at least superficially, the same year after year. That is because all of the actual change is at the interface between me, my students, and the learning experiences I design for them. People have happily informed me that I am a maker because I use phrases like "design learning experiences." These comments mistake what I do for what I am actually trying to elicit and support from students. The appropriate metaphor for education, as Ursula Franklin has pointed out, is a garden, not the production line (Franklin 22–23).

I educate. I analyze. I characterize. I critique. Almost everything I do these days is about communicating with others. To characterize what I do as "making" is either to mistake the methods—the research, the editorials, the workshops, the courses—for the purpose or, worse, to describe what I do as "making" other people, diminishing their own agency and role in sensemaking, as if their learning is something I impose on them.

Making in education can be tremendously valuable, particularly when it gives students from disadvantaged groups access to the types of hands-on education and opportunities they would not otherwise receive. Because students are frequently allowed to choose or design their own projects, making is a useful proof of concept for how autonomy and meaningful work also foster motivation (Deci and Flaste 1996) and positive learning outcomes. These approaches can and should be extended across the curriculum. But at the same time, as we broaden access to making, we should celebrate and foster education, maintenance, analysis, critique, and, above all, caregiving—all of the undervalued, underappreciated, ongoing work of making other people's lives better.

## NOTES

This chapter is a revised and edited version of an essay originally published online at https://tinyletter.com/metafoundry/letters/metafoundry-15-scribbled-leatherjackets on November 23, 2014, as "Homo Fabber."

1. See Gould.

## BIBLIOGRAPHY

Boyer, Bryan. "Matter Battle!" January 24, 2011. http://matterbattle.com.

Chen, Adrian. "The Laborers Who Keep Dick Pics and Beheadings Out of Your Facebook Feed." *Wired,* October 23, 2014. http://www.wired.com/2014/10/content-moderation.

Deci, Edward, and Richard Flaste. *Why We Do What We Do: Understanding Self-Motivation.* London: Penguin, 1996.

Franklin, Ursula M. *The Real World of Technology (CBC Massey Lectures),* rev. ed. Toronto, Ont.: House of Anansi Press, 1999.

Gould, Elise. "Why America's Workers Need Faster Wage Growth—and What We Can Do about It." Economic Policy Institute Briefing Paper #382, August 27, 2014. http://www.epi.org/files/2014/why-americas-workers-need-faster-wage-growth-final.pdf.

Searle, John R. "Minds, Brains, and Programs." *The Behavioral and Brain Sciences* 3, no. 3 (1980): 417–57.

# Making It Matter

JEREMY BOGGS, JENNIFER REED, AND J. K. PURDOM LINDBLAD

In the 2014 documentary *Tales of the Grim Sleeper,* Nick Broomfield investigates how Lonnie Franklin Jr. killed between ten and 180 working-class black women across three decades without being apprehended. The exact number of murders is unknown partly because some Los Angeles police officers used the code NHI, or "No Humans Involved," when reporting on the crimes. Of course humans were involved, but the officers decided not to count murdered black women as humans. Following Saidiya Hartman (1997), such instances of institutional racism and oppression prompt "us to question whether the rights of man and citizen are realizable or whether the appellation 'human' can be borne equally by all" (6). All too often, we conflate *humane* with *just* or *justice.* Yet examples like NHI, where prejudice and discrimination establish a scale of humanness, illustrate why relying on "humane" to convey justice and empathy can be problematic.

Deb Chachra (2015) criticizes a pervasive tenet of the maker movement: "artifacts are important, people are not." She resists the imperative to label people as "makers" because the label carries with it a gendered history that values objects to be produced and sold at the expense of the people who make them and, more detrimentally, the people whose labor—repairing, thinking, caretaking—is not considered to be making. In this chapter, we confront biases that some people, practices, and places are more valuable than others, and what those biases mean in terms of making. How do we build considerations of bias into the process and products of making? For instance, how do we construct platforms that not only confront biases but also create spaces for people who are unheard, dismissed, or oppressed? What does it mean to make things in humane, empathetic, and just ways? And how do we encourage the humanities to engage in this kind of reflective, aspirational making?

For making to matter in the humanities, we need to show how humans and labor are involved in using and maintaining as well as making. We must focus making in ways that attend to, and advocate for, varieties of human experience and interactions with the world. Whether the act of making is one of production, praxis, theory, or a combination of the three, thoughtful making in the humanities should seek a better understanding of activities and impacts.

Here, we build on work in the Scholars' Lab at the University of Virginia Library—including the Lab's charter, Praxis Program, and Makerspace—to argue that making alters the nature of individual and collective agency. Making things can and should help us to empathize with and advocate for just engagement across local and global scales. We elaborate on three interrelated areas of making:

- A *theory* of making that is driven by a holistic concern for social justice and also positions making as a mode of advocacy,
- A *praxis* of making that establishes spaces for experimentation and is anchored in empathy for the people involved, and
- A *product* of making that relies on reflexivity and polyvocality in design.

Our work in the Scholars' Lab privileges iterative practices toward inclusiveness, transparency, and accountability (Sadler and Bourg 2015; Caswell 2014; Olson 2002). These practices are not destinations because they are never finished. We return to them again and again in our daily work. Attention to these values encourages conversations about how to best incorporate compassion and advocacy into our projects. In this chapter, we share examples of how we have approached issues of representation and responsibility in Scholars' Lab projects. The following definitions ground our evaluations of inclusiveness, transparency, and accountability:

- *Inclusiveness:* Cultural bias and a single perspective can be, intentionally or not, enforced in the things we make. We strive to include many perspectives, voices, and modes in our projects.
- *Transparency:* We seek clarity and justification in design, development, and ethos. We document our choices, the things we have tried and abandoned, and moments when something is unclear and why.
- *Accountability:* We develop awareness of how what we make can and should impact others, and how that influence should be considered and measured.

These three broader concerns are then translated into specific approaches to project design, documentation, and use. For example, transparency and accountability are realized through *Take Back the Archive*'s publicly available notes, which detail collection decisions, provide a history of iteration and design choices, list names of collaborators, and articulate the archive's intent. Likewise, the Makerspace aims for inclusiveness by fostering a space where it is safe to tinker, learn, and experiment. Similarly, the Thistlewood project attends to respectful and just ways of representing people through archival interfaces.

Together, the Scholar's Lab's Makerspace, *Take Back the Archive,* and Thistlewood projects demonstrate how we put inclusiveness, transparency, and accountability into practice. However, our approach is not prescriptive and does not claim to offer the best solution for combining making and social justice. Rather, we offer documentation for the recent work we have done and a guide for the work we hope to do.

### MAKERSPACE

The Makerspace in the Scholars' Lab advocates for people as learners, thinkers, and explorers. It takes *accessibility* as its starting mantra and builds on the concept of the *Imagination Playground* (Jost 2010). Instead of providing rigid, locked-down structures for play, the *Imagination Playground* emphasizes loose parts and lets children construct the playspace themselves. The playground makes a clear statement: loose parts afford children agency, allow them to use the playground imaginatively, and encourage them to confront the responsibilities of freedom and choice. Children can decide how to play, and in doing so they can develop interesting ways of playing. Of course, children already do this, but—by eschewing stationary equipment for loose parts—*Imagination Playground* critiques how decisions about playspaces are made and how our environments shape play. Children come to terms with independence, freedom, and choice on their own. Of course, the ability to choose between loose parts and prefabricated systems is a privileged one. One goal of the Makerspace is to critique those pre-built systems, but also consciously reflect on how making changes our perspectives. The aim, then, is not tinkering for tinkering's sake. A "hermeneutics of screwing around" can be revealing, but inclusiveness, transparency, and accountability require deliberate attention to that hermeneutics, its biases, and how making *shapes* our thinking (Ramsay 2014; Thomas and Brown 2011; Elliott et al. 2012; Grayburn 2016).

Devon Elliott et al. demonstrate how making in the context of historical research requires space and support to conduct *experiments,* which "imaginatively remake past technological artifacts" (123). Their work explores turn-of-the-last-century magic, using 3-D modeling and printing to re-create magic tricks, with historical documents describing and illustrating particular tricks. Their goal is to neither re-create the past nor create exact replicas of artifacts. Rather, they illustrate the affordances of play and experimentation with things as ways to provoke new questions about history and historical research. Meanwhile, Jennifer Grayburn, a technologist in the Scholars' Lab's Makerspace and a Ph.D. candidate in architectural history, conducts research and teaches using models and fabrications of historical artifacts. Grayburn notes the affordances of desktop fabrication and fab labs, particularly when studying cultural heritage artifacts that are being systematically destroyed. For a class assignment, she has students consider how modeling and fabrication—actually making an artifact—affect their understanding of that artifact. In addition to using fabrication to ask new questions about historical materials, Grayburn notes its relevance to not only observing but also remembering artifacts and, more important, the people who made and used them:

> Obviously our priorities today must fall firmly on the living people who are suffering the deprivations of warfare and occupation; but it's important, too, to remember that the value of these sites and objects doesn't really lie in their physical remains. It lies in the fact that this is all we have to remember the dead, to remember the acts of past peoples—workers and kings, everyday families, mothers and children, farmers, travelers and priests—real human beings whose lives are commemorated only by the tactile remains they crafted.

Grayburn's iterative approach and corresponding documentation embody a transparency and accountability that benefits her as well as the faculty and students who visit the Makerspace.

We present the Makerspace to humanities scholars as an intellectual space, where they are free to explore questions in experimental ways. Learning how to make things not only fosters a community of practice but also helps people to strive for a conscious and deliberate sense of responsibility for making *and* the ability and freedom to make. To achieve these aims, the space itself, its resources, and its staff all have to contribute to inclusiveness, transparency, and accountability.

### *TAKE BACK THE ARCHIVE*

Created by University of Virginia faculty, students, librarians, and archivists, *Take Back the Archive* is a public history project to preserve, visualize, and contextualize the history of rape and sexual violence at the University of Virginia, while honoring individual stories and documenting systemic issues and trends. All aspects of the project—design, access, labels, interface, content—advocate for victims and survivors of sexual violence and for the people who encounter their stories.

Imperative to the project's success is the need to attend to the collection and presentation of materials in ways that advocate for rape survivors and challenge a community of complacency and ignorance. For instance, Hope Olson (2007) critiques traditional subject hierarchies rooted in Aristotelian logic and prescribes a feminist approach that rejects universality and treats traditional information hierarchies as some among many possible structures to use (509–10). Especially relevant to an archive that includes rape survivors, Michelle Caswell (2014) argues for an archiving practice that embodies community-centric values and respects the need for survivors to maintain decision-making power in how materials are presented and shared (309). Going further, Bess Sadler and Chris Bourg (2015) argue for feminist interfaces and computer interactions that encourage advocacy and pluralism: "A feminist rhetoric and agenda for the future of library discovery would leverage technology to promote the feminist values of plurality, self-disclosure, participation, ecology, advocacy, and embodiment." Several of these principles shape *Take Back the Archive,* including: *activism,* by deliberately positioning the archive not as an objective study of sexual violence, but as a clear advocate for its end; *stewardship,* by acknowledging we are caretakers of content, not owners or custodians who exert rights on archival materials; and *pluralism,* by eschewing design and presentation that universalize archive contents.

Attention to advocacy requires developers to understand, critique, and modify the tools and methods they use. *Take Back the Archive* is built on Omeka, an open-source collections management system developed by the Roy Rosenzweig Center for History and New Media at George Mason University. Omeka is a web application platform that is designed to give archives, museums, and individual scholars the means to publish an online database and use that data for interpretation. Omeka relies on open-source tools, and it is designed and developed for easy installation on most web servers.[1] It does not attempt to be everything to everyone. Instead, it provides the mechanisms whereby users can more easily alter that functionality to suit their own needs.

The default labels and presentations in many content management systems and metadata standards are decidedly agnostic; they attempt to be as neutral as possible to make repurposing or exporting data more fluid. (By default, Omeka provides Dublin Core for describing collections and items, as well as a number of public-facing views for users to browse, search, and sort a given collection.) But in doing so, those systems tend to make our collections data friendlier for computers than for users of our resources or, more detrimentally, for the people whom our collections represent. Therefore, project developers must attend to the responsibility of tailoring the labeling and presentation of data to goals specific to their project, subject matter, and audiences.

With records described and saved to the database, we have developed interfaces that encourage discovery and exploration and advocate for users and the people represented in our collections. Rich-prospect browsing helps us to accomplish these aims, and it contributes to several of our guiding principles for the *Take Back* project. Developed by Stan Ruecker, Milena Radzikowska, and Stéfan Sinclair (2011), rich-prospect browsing focuses on building meaningful browsing interfaces for an entire collection, instead of developing search-first interfaces that often obscure the contents of a collection. It relies on two related concepts: prospect and affordance. *Prospects* are the allowances and restrictions that a given environment or situation presents. Similarly, *affordances* are the opportunities for action perceived by someone in a given environment. From these, rich-prospect browsing offers a set of principles that can help to guide design decisions for discovery interfaces:

- Present every record in the collection in some meaningful way;
- Provide obvious, intuitive methods for organizing and adjusting the presentation of records;
- Provide prospects for sorting and faceting the presentation of records and for getting more data for each record;

- Provide item metadata that inform the kinds of interfaces used;
- Present options for how to represent the item in the interface; and
- Allow researchers to mark items for tracking and revisiting.

The principles of rich-prospect browsing fit perfectly with the goals of feminist discovery interfaces discussed by Sadler and Bourg, in terms of people represented in a collection as well as those who would use it. Rich-prospect browsing inherently shares a set of values with feminist interface design, centered primarily around empowering users and valuing a polyvocal representation of a collection. It also corresponds with our investments in inclusiveness, transparency, and accountability. By presenting users with the entire collection, it gives equal importance to all records. At the very least, researchers become more aware of the many voices in a collection and the perspectives they have seen and not seen in any given research session. This awareness is especially important for archives and collections with materials about people who are victims and survivors of traumatic events. More than simply collecting and sharing this material, we plan to ensure that practices of collection and presentation used across the project help contributors and users to dismantle passive acceptance of rape culture.

### THISTLEWOOD

The Thistlewood project explores how sympathy is mapped cognitively and culturally in the eighteenth century. As a case study, it uses Breadnut Island Pen, a Jamaican plantation owned by Thomas Thistlewood. Thistlewood lived on Breadnut Island Pen from September 1767 until his death in November 1786. In that time he committed 1,584 acts of rape on women he owned, as documented in his detailed diaries. The Thistlewood project maps the plantation to show where Thistlewood's individual acts of brutality, stigmatization, and caretaking took place.

Louis Nelson (2013) points out that "sites of terror," such as whipping posts and scenes of rape, neither survive physically nor appear on plantation plans. Moreover, the people who suffered at these sites rarely leave records of their own. As Barry Higman (2001) observes, "The people who did the hard work of the plantations remain essentially voiceless in the narrative, reduced to the tools of capital and themselves literally to human capital" (xiii). The Thistlewood project seeks to represent these people, if not their voices. As a result, it has provoked serious consideration about what constitutes an ethical representation of violence and what kinds of ethical representations the digital permits. Hartman asks, "How does one give expression to these outrages without exacerbating the indifference to suffering that is the consequence of the benumbing spectacle or contend with the narcissistic identification that obliterates the other or the prurience that too often is the response to such displays?" (4). The Thistlewood project responds to that difficult question, and it uses maps and illustrations to represent slave experiences along a fine line between "the benumbing spectacle" and "the narcissistic identification." These representational practices demand transparency and accountability in design.

The rapes that took place on Breadnut Island Pen are mappable because Thistlewood kept very detailed, even obsessive accounts of exactly where on the Pen he raped women. Thistlewood documented his rapes of 33 women in total. The project represents each of these women. When representing violence, the major challenge in this project is to preserve the humanity of the rape victims while having very limited historical material about their experiences. There are no existing narratives or documents produced by the slaves who lived on Breadnut Island Pen; the only voice available is that of their oppressor and serial rapist, Thistlewood. In an attempt to reject the domination of Thistlewood's voice and to articulate a polyvocal narrative, the project dedicates a map to each victim of sexual violence on Breadnut Island Pen and then examines Thistlewood's diaries for every reference to each victim.

The map is obviously limited in representing hundreds of rape events. Instead of creating a visual marker for each rape, the interface shows the large number of rapes that took place in multiple locations across the plantation. On one map, we use a differently shaped marker for each woman who was raped, and we place it on the locations of the rapes. From a design and social justice perspective, it was important to differentiate each woman as much as possible and mark her experience on the land. In addition, we include, where possible, a scan of Thistlewood's diary as it relates to the rape. This gesture is intended not to increase Thistlewood's presence but rather to present evidence of rape—to make the woman's experience more material and lessen its distance from the viewer. The hand that wrote the diary entry is also the hand that oppressed these women.

## *Toward a Working Model of Making*

The act of making is not neutral, because we—the makers, the consumers—are not neutral. Thus our goal is not neutrality. Instead, we strive to incorporate reflection on the process of making. Such reflection can lead to self-disclosure and transparency around the choices informing the made object, toward clear, more deliberate choices that advocate for social justice. The process of making has significant potential to not only render visible the bias of a single reflection and experience but also expose adjacent possibilities. While making neither immediately scaffolds a reflective practice nor automatically confronts social issues, it affords opportunities to do both through iteration.

### NOTES

1. Omeka employs PHP (Hypertext Preprocessor) as its main scripting language and MySQL as its database management system. Templates in Omeka are written primarily

in Hypertext Markup Language (HTML) and styled using Cascading Style Sheets (CSS). Omeka also features an Application Programming Interface (API) for writing plug-ins that allows developers to extend the functionality of Omeka in any way programmatically possible.

## BIBLIOGRAPHY

Broomfield, Nick, dir. *Tales of the Grim Sleeper*. HBO Documentary Films, 2014.

Caswell, Michelle. "Toward a Survivor-Centered Approach to Records Documenting Human Rights Abuse: Lessons from Community Archives." *Archival Science* 14, no. 3/4 (2014): 307–22.

Chachra, Debbie. "Why I Am Not a Maker." *The Atlantic,* January 23, 2015. www.theatlantic.com/technology/archive/2015/01/why-i-am-not-a-maker/384767.

Elliott, Devon, Robert MacDougall, and William J. Turkel. "New Old Things: Fabrication, Physical Computing, and Experiment in Historical Practice." *Canadian Journal of Communication* 37, no. 1 (2012): 121–28. www.cjc-online.ca/index.php/journal/article/view/2506/2773.

Gerhard, Kristin H., Mila C. Su, and Charlotte C. Rubens. "An Empirical Examination of Subject Headings for Women's Studies Core Materials." *College and Research Libraries* 59, no. 2 (1998): 129–37.

Goffman, Erving. *Stigma: Notes on the Management of Spoiled Identity*. New York: Touchstone, 1986.

Grayburn, Jennifer. "3D Printing in the Classroom: Course Assignments and the Makerspace." *Scholars' Lab*, February 22, 2016. http://scholarslab.org/uncategorized/3d-printing-in-the-classroom-course-assignments-and-the-makerspace.

Harris, Verne. "Antonyms of Our Remembering." *Archival Science* 14, no. 3/4 (2014): 215–29.

Hartman, Saidiya. *Scenes of Subjection: Terror, Slavery, and Self-Making in Nineteenth Century America.* Cambridge: Oxford University Press, 1997.

Hertz, Garnet, ed. *Critical Making*. Hollywood, Calif.: Telharmonium Press, 2012.

Higman, Barry W. *Jamaica Surveyed: Plantation Maps and Plans of the Eighteenth and Nineteenth Centuries*. Jamaica, West Indies: University of the West Indies Press, 2001.

Jost, Daniel. "New York Loosens Up." *Landscape Architecture.* November 2010, 80–94.

Knowlton, Steven A. "Three Decades Since *Prejudice and Antipathies*: A Study of Changes in the Library of Congress Subject Headings." *Cataloging & Classification Quarterly* 40, no. 2 (2005): 123–45.

Makerspace. University of Virginia. http://scholarslab.org/makerspace/.

Mason, Karen M., and Tanya Zanish-Belcher. "Raising the Archival Consciousness: How Women's Archives Challenge Traditional Approaches to Collecting and Use, Or, What's in a Name?" *Library Trends* 56, no. 2 (2007): 344–59.

Nelson, Louis. "The Jamaican Plantation: Industry, Empire, and Resistance." *The Eighteenth Centuries: An Interdisciplinary Symposium*. Montalto, Virginia. March 2, 2013. Unpublished conference paper.

Nowviskie, Bethany. "Evaluating Collaborative Digital Scholarship (or, Where Credit is Due)." *Journal of Digital Humanities* 1, no. 4 (2012). http://journalofdigitalhumanities.org/1-4/evaluating-collaborative-digital-scholarship-by-bethany-nowviskie.

Nowviskie, Bethany, Jeremy Boggs, and J. K. Purdom Lindblad. "Praxis." *Digital Pedagogy in the Humanities: Concepts, Models and Experiments.* https://digitalpedagogy.commons.mla.org/keywords/praxis.

Olson, Hope A. "How We Construct Subjects: A Feminist Analysis." *Library Trends* 56, no. 2 (2007): 509–41.

———. *The Power to Name: Locating the Limits of Subject Representation in Libraries.* New York: Springer, 2002.

Omeka. Roy Rosenzweig Center for History and New Media, George Mason University. http://omeka.org.

Ramsay, Stephen. "The Hermeneutics of Screwing Around; or, What You Do with a Million Books." *Pastplay: Teaching and Learning History with Technology.* Ann Arbor, Mich.: University of Michigan Press, 2014.

Ruecker, Stan, and Milena Radzikowska. "The Iterative Design of a Project Charter for Interdisciplinary Research." *Proceedings of the 7th ACM conference on Designing interactive systems,* 2008.

Ruecker, Stan, Stéfan Sinclair, and Milena Radzikowska. *Visual Interface Design for Digital Cultural Heritage: A Guide to Rich-Prospect Browsing.* Farnham, U.K.: Ashgate, 2011.

Sadler, Bess, and Chris Bourg. "Feminism and the Future of Library Discovery." *The Code4Lib Journal* 28 (2015). http://journal.code4lib.org/articles/10425.

Siemens, Lynne, Ray Siemens, Richard Cunningham, Teresa Dobson, Alan Galey, Stan Ruecker, and Claire Warwick. "INKE Administrative Structure, Omnibus Document." *New Knowledge Environments* 1, no. 1 (2009): http://journals.uvic.ca/index.php/INKE/article/view/546.

*Take Back the Archive.* University of Virginia. http://takeback.scholarslab.org/.

Thomas, Douglas, and John Seeley Brown. *A New Culture of Learning: Cultivating the Imagination for a World of Constant Change.* Seattle, Wash.: CreateSpace Independent Publishing Platform, 2011.

Unsworth, John. "The Library as Laboratory." Presentation at the Annual Meeting of the American Library Association, 1999. www3.isrl.illinois.edu/~unsworth/ala99.htm.

# Ethics in the Making

ERIN R. ANDERSON AND TRISHA N. CAMPBELL

In her 2012 polemic, "This Digital Humanities Which Is Not One," Jamie "Skye" Bianco challenges a trend toward unreflective tool building in digital humanities, with its emphasis on the aggregation, mining, and visualization of texts-as-data-for-data's-sake. Urging us to consider the question, "What do we *do* with the data?" (Bianco 99), she proposes a theoretically informed alternative of "creative critique," which uses digital media and methods to not only break down, interpret, and reconstitute texts-as-data, but also invent new texts and new sensory experiences of textual remains or ruins (102). Importantly, this move toward performative, affective, and generative modes of digital practice is not simply a methodological one; it is profoundly ethical, with potentially far-reaching consequences on how we relate with one another and the broader material world. In other words, if we want to proceed under the assumption that *making things* in digital humanities might be one way of *making humanities matter,* then we must take seriously the relationship between making and ethics—indeed the possibility for making *as* ethics—through relational and material practice.

We find promise in the work of digital rhetoric scholar Anne Frances Wysocki (2010), who explores the rhetorical intersection of ethics and aesthetics in digital art and media. Starting from the premise that "our senses are persuadable," she pushes us to think beyond purely rational and discursive notions of rhetoric to consider the role of bodily perception and aesthetic experience in our social formation as ethical agents (110). In this chapter, we take up Wysocki's definition of ethics as not only a matter of right and wrong. Following her, we see ethics as a richly embodied, sensual orientation to the world that begins from the ways we inhabit our experiences. The many multimodal texts that we routinely produce, consume, and interact with in digital environments have the palpable potential to "shape our senses of selves by shaping our senses themselves" (95), providing a platform through which we might come to experience our bodies in new relationships and configurations. As Wysocki suggests, "By highlighting current aesthetic possibilities of our texts—digital as well as nondigital—we might practice having bodies that can alertly convert sensuous experience into ethical practice" (95).

Work by scholar-artists such as Bianco and Wysocki opens important inroads toward an "ethical turn" in digital humanities by taking seriously the relational encounter between a multisensory work or text and its audience (Bianco 97). If it is true, as Wysocki puts it, that "any text we compose engages us aesthetically" (110), then perhaps we, as digital artists and makers, must also attune ourselves to the ethical potential of our own encounters with the media and materials of our practice. In this chapter, we push the conversation about the ethics of making in digital humanities to consider not only the objects or experiences made (as they affect audiences) but also the act of making itself (as it affects a maker). What we hope to contribute is a close consideration of the relationship between digital artists or makers and the rich constellation of sensory and material, human and nonhuman actors that constitute the "data" with which they work. Grounding this discussion in our own experiences with creative-critical methods, we offer accounts of two digital audio projects that use performance as an attempt to make, speak, and feel *with* the recorded voices of others—the voices of convicted murderers (Campbell) and the voices of the dead (Anderson). By considering our durational, affective, and responsive encounters with the sighs, breaths, and vibrations of these voices, we explore the prospects for practicing new and important forms of empathy across human and nonhuman, social and material boundaries. We respond to Bianco's provocation, "What do we *do* with the data?" by turning the tables and asking instead, *What does the data do with us?*

## *"Call Me a Murderer" (2015, 10 min., Digital Video)*

**TRISHA N. CAMPBELL**

"Call Me A Murderer" is a born-digital performative and conceptual art piece that I made in concert with James,[1] age 21—a convicted murderer, sentenced to death for killing two men in a robbery—and his niece, age 14. It plays out over a three-part, multi-layered monologue, where James recounts why he committed murder, I recount *with* James, and his niece recounts her time with her uncle. Our three voices are layered, echoed, and intertwined as we each variously compete and harmonize our speech and breaths. Using Adobe After Effects, I matched each of our voices to their correlated waveforms—James's dipping at deeper valleys than mine, his niece's subtly pulsating in the background, and my own tenuously vying and aligning at various moments throughout the piece.

The voice recordings are part of a larger project, *The Murder Networks,* which is an archive of collected audio interviews, stories, newspaper articles, and social networks surrounding inner-city murder. I created the project to postpone blame and listen to the web of agential capacities[2] involved in any act of murder. James's recording is one such story. "It was a regular day," as he says, when he and a friend thought they might try to get a little money. It ended in an unforeseen double-homicide. What makes his story even more complicated is that a local news source first collected his confession, archived it, and then released it to the public online, where it garnered an outcry of hateful comments about his immorality and depravity. James was, quite plainly, without a public display of empathy. I was struck by how he was cast as a misfire in an otherwise smoothly operating system, and I was drawn to and disquieted by the lack of empathy in part because it represented an invitation to respond *differently.* What we need, murder historian Karen Halttunen (1998) suggests, is an approach to murder as inseparable from culture, and not as a sociological, pathological, or criminological problem to be analyzed at some distance (Black 781). In this project, I was invested in the potential of digital art and experimentation to invite or imagine another response to James that departed from the popular narrative.

The process began slowly through a careful act of listening. As I sat for hours hearing James's voice, I listened as he repeated, again and again, his story of the day of the murder. I listened to his anger; I listened as his voice broke; I listened as he sighed; and I listened, still, as he sat in moments of silence. I listened for so long that, as I closed my eyes late that first night, I could hear his voice repeating, "Tell my mama I love her, will you?" The meticulous nature of audio editing required long hours spent with James's vocalizations, allowing careful focus on his peaked waveforms and offering repeated listening of his barely audible sighs. After a few days of this active listening, I found myself anticipating his words, voicing with him, and even taking in breath as he did. I began, then, to record and re-record myself *with* his voice, not in an exact imitation, but in an attempt to performatively *reprocess*[3] his voice through my own body and recorded voice, to hear what I sounded like when I said his words or made his noises. I voiced with him in my own voice; I sighed with him in my own sighs. I used performance to enlist my own body in the production of confession. Because of how long I spent with the voice recordings, I can still tell the moment his voice begins to break, a moment that was not perceptible to me upon even the third passive listening, but is now undeniable because I voiced it with him. What followed from this process was an immersion in and among James's obstinacies and rhythms—his "refusals as much as his invitations" (Greg and Seigworth 1). Even now, months later, as I sit quietly reading or attempting sleep, I hear James's rhythm and intonation in my head and notice my own voice inflected with his during my less conscious moments of speaking.

Of course, I am not James. James is a young black man, born into poverty and violence. I am white and privileged. I live in a world where murder and violence are not part of my immediate reality, and in no way do I want to equate my own experience as a stand-in for James's experience. There is an obvious limit to this work's ability to address the deep social and racial injustices that have produced the material conditions in which James lived. What the work does invite is the affective confrontation of those differences. It is a radical attempt to imagine how we respond to the experience of another by trying to *feel with* them. While the heightened moral stakes of murder make it a particularly painful and complex boundary to confront, I am interested in how this practice can help us forge new lines of relations across vast social, cultural, and material divisions while also recognizing, addressing, and negotiating them.

Ultimately, this practice has affected, changed, and implicated me. Speaking very personally, James's family was touched by my project and interest; however, the project did not help James in any practical sense, nor did it change him or his circumstances. Instead, it prompted a particular kind of listening and an altogether different response to suffering and violence. While the digital rendering of "Call Me a Murderer" took 23 total recordings—23 times of listening and recording my own voice with James's—it is not the final rendering that so impinges, but the active practice of making the piece, the long hours and the repetition, the time spent with James's voice. It was only in the practice of working with and between our voices that I began to feel my relationship to James change and my own inquiry expand through the tiny divestments between making and thinking.

## TOWARD A POSTHUMAN EMPATHY

*Empathy* strikes us as a powerful framework for considering these forms of relational, affective encounters that we have come to experience through this project and the one that follows. As we work with the recorded voices of others, we confront our own experience of negotiating distance—the temporal distance between us and them, but also the cultural and material distance between our bodies. These lines can be difficult and even impossible to cross. Empathy as a practice allows us to discern the experiences of others—"experiences that might otherwise go unrecognized" (Halpern 94). Empathy must be applied and practiced, Jodi Halpern (2001) urges, in non-analogous contexts, where affective states, discourses, and experiences are dissimilar. It requires an "imaginative leap" (ix) or imaginative inquiry into the individuality and particularity of another, an act of imagination on affective and cognitive levels. And it bespeaks a long and difficult process, which begins by feeling *with* and thinking *with* another "whose circumstances lie far outside of our own" (Landsberg, "Memory" 223). Importantly, this move has implications that stretch beyond the relations between individual co-participants in our work to suggest social and political possibilities.[4]

In addition to the humans behind the voices in these projects, a complex constellation of "other-than-human" (Barad 392) actors and entities impinge upon us and our relations. As we work with our materials, we begin to actually feel with them, too. To understand how our practice of empathy is intertwined with these myriad temporal, technological, and material phenomena, we find it productive to turn to Karen Barad's (2007) notion of "posthuman ethics" (392). In a world of ubiquitous mediation, Barad argues, a "humanistic ethics can no longer suffice" (392). She revises Emmanuel Levinas's (1981) ethical philosophy[5] to include the "other than human" as well as the "human" (392). For her, to "have-the-other-in-one's-skin," as Levinas's ethics suggests, means we cannot ignore the full set of possibilities that this encounter allows. What happens when the person who is looking back at me cannot see me or is mediated through an audio recording? What happens if my voice has no living referent? If ethical relations extend to the other-than-human, then our ethical responsibility cannot be limited to body-to-body, face-to-face, or human-to-human encounters, because the "very boundaries of the human are continually being reconfigured" (Barad 392), and it is precisely these new configurations to which we must attend. In these projects, we have come to understand ethics—and, by extension, empathy—as our ability to *respond* through and with these new entanglements and to do so through intentional digital practice.

While we are ultimately interested in how this model of practice-based ethics might function across a broad spectrum of compositional methods and materials, our two projects focus particularly on digital audio and, more specifically, the recorded human voice. Partly due to its unique relational quality, the voice offers a powerful inroad to the question of ethics. For philosopher Adriana Cavarero (2005), the voice possesses a capacity to bring us together in a special kind of reciprocal sensory encounter, where we are immersed in the vibrations of others while experiencing their "corporeal uniqueness" as a lived reality (207). On one hand, in its most common manifestation as speech, the voice is always directed outward, "destined for the ear of another" (7). On the other hand, because we hear not just *any*body but a particular *some*body who is "unique" and "unrepeatable" (9), the voice enables us to recognize and engage another as an "incarnate singularity" (7)—a body-like-me-but-not-me. In this sense, the voice serves a dual purpose, as that which unites us *and* sets us apart, inviting precisely the interplay between identification and alterity that empathy requires. In what follows, we discuss a second project that seeks to further extend Cavarero's "vocal phenomenology of uniqueness" (7) beyond the idealized face-to-face encounter and into the realm of digital practice. We are interested in how our experiences with the recorded voices of others might offer a route to a new kind of posthuman ethical personhood, where "personhood is always collaborative, cutting across clear distinctions of materiality/discourse, technology/organicity, and bounded lifetimes/eternal deaths" (Stanyek and Piekut 18).

## Our Time Is Up *(2014, 45 min., Stereo Audio)*

**ERIN R. ANDERSON**

*Our Time Is Up* is an experimental audio drama, which tells the story of Jake and Helen McCleary, an elderly couple struggling to save their troubled marriage. The drama unfolds across a series of weekly therapy sessions, in which Jake and Helen sort through the messy details of their failing relationship—his infidelity, her degenerative blindness, and the everyday struggle to listen, be heard, and be loved. At the end, the couple confronts the decision of whether to end their marriage. In terms of narrative, the drama is fairly conventional, at times even predictable. But conceptually and materially, there is more to it than first meets the ear. Unlike a traditional audio drama, which is pre-scripted and then performed by the voices of live actors, this drama is composed from the archives of oral history and performed by the voices of the dead. The voices of the two main characters are constructed from audio recordings of oral history interviews with my late grandfather, Josiah Patton (1919–2009), and Juanita Bowman (1900–2000), a woman whom neither of us met. With the exception of my own role as the couple's therapist, this drama is made entirely of words actually spoken by Josiah and Juanita—in their own voices, about their own lives, for the purpose of historical preservation. But, in this project, these words and voices have been deliberately disarticulated, recombined, and reanimated, so that they no longer represent, or even *aspire to* represent, the stories or intentions of their now-deceased speakers. Instead, they come together to create a new, shared story and an uncanny dramatic encounter between the living and the dead.[6]

This project first emerged as an ethical provocation; it was a project I took on precisely because of the degree of discomfort it evoked. Inspired by musicologists Jason Stanyek and Benjamin Piekut's work (2010) on the posthumous duet, I set out to explore the limits of prevailing ethical proscriptions against interfering with the voices of the dead. Through a case study of "Unforgettable"—a 1991 collaboration between Natalie Cole and her father, Nat "King" Cole, produced 25 years after his death—Stanyek and Piekut use Barad's new materialist theory to argue that this duet is, in fact, a *collaboration* between the living and the dead (Stanyek and Piekut 18). By taking seriously the capacity of the dead to act and affect in their own right, through the vibrant "effectivity" of their recorded voices, these authors allow us to move away from familiar frameworks of representational ethics to imagine the possibility for a positive, generative "ethics of effects" (34).

At first, I will admit, I saw the possibility of collaboration with the dead as fascinating but a bit far-fetched for my taste. I was well aware of the ethical vulnerabilities of my project—and of the nonliving participants whose voices helped to bring it into being. Initially, I saw in Stanyek and Piekut's approach a theoretical framework that I might apply to my practice at a certain level of remove in order to justify my ethical intervention to my audience, if not also myself. However, I did not expect to actually experience this collaboration at the level of embodied, perceptual practice. In fact, as I edited and imagined the drama, I not only became convinced of the "mutual effectivity" (34) that Josiah's and Juanita's voices contributed to the process; I actually began to feel myself forming complex attachments and relationships with my collaborators across the threshold of death.

In preparation for this project, I selected Juanita's recording from dozens of recorded voices of the dead that I found in online oral history archives and assembled into a randomized playlist to keep me company on a solo cross-country drive. As I moved alone across the landscape over those four days, I felt strangely *accompanied,* as if each voice were somehow a warm body, sitting next to me and telling me stories. Of course, the voices did tell stories, and those stories were most certainly part of the connection that I felt. They also sang songs and spoke of distant wars in languages I could not understand. And others only wailed faintly and indistinctly from beneath the static of decades of tape decay. Yet, I still felt a certain closeness, a certain intimacy—not the deep, slow kind that develops over years of committed friendship, but the intense, fleeting kind that comes with the isolation and forced proximity of sharing a ride across the sprawling Montana Rockies. Certainly, from an ontological perspective, any notion of metaphysical "presence" here is deeply problematic.[7] But, as Norie Neumark (2010) argues, we cannot help but feel some presence of a person behind the recorded voice of another. Voices afford an "authenticity effect" (95).

Of all the voices in the archive, I felt most connected with the voice of Juanita Bowman, whose energy and intensity would bring Helen's character to life in *Our Time Is Up*. Over the weeks and months of the drama's production, I listened to Juanita as no one had likely listened to her in decades, if ever—and certainly not since her death 15 years ago. Engrossed in the sound of every breath, every cough, every subtle shift in intonation, I listened to her in a way that I had never listened to anyone, *ever*. And, for someone I have never met, someone I never *will* meet, someone who died quietly when I was still a teenager in a suburb hundreds of miles away, I cannot help but feel as if I know her all the same.

Unlike Juanita, I did know Josiah during his lifetime, and I loved him for the lively, living, breathing, laughing, sobbing, sensitive, stubborn, proud, vulnerable person he was. But while I may have started this project believing that I knew my grandfather, in the end I was surprised to come to know him quite differently. Indeed, somewhere along the line, as I immersed myself in the painstaking listening and re-listening and editing and re-voicing that went into this drama, I actually started to *feel* like Jake and Helen's therapist. As I sat and listened to the weighty heaves of Jake's sobs or the sad notes of resignation behind Helen's all-too-curt responses, I began to feel them as if they were my own. That is, I began to feel my own investment in their process: in my desire to comfort or heal, my impulse to reach out and put my hand on a slumped shoulder that was not there or, admittedly, to reach out and smack some sense into both of them. Then I would wake up to the sudden realization that I was, in fact, sitting alone in my apartment, or worse, in the middle of a busy café, wincing awkwardly or laughing under my breath or fighting back the tears that I felt, inexplicably, for two people who I knew were not "present" in any sense of the term, but whom I had somehow come to experience as if they were. Indeed, this was the most surprising, and most satisfying, outcome of my experiment—not the extent to which I was able to change these voices into something new, but the extent to which, in doing so, these voices changed me.

## ON LIVING WELL TOGETHER

"What can we do, perceptually, to live well together?" (Wysocki 109). This, we believe, is the crux of the matter at hand. While our two projects differ in their impetus and methods, both of us came to experience a kind of closeness—or what Levinas (1987) might call "the ethical invitation to proximity" (*Time* 109)—through the practice of digital making. Here, we reimagine proximity as not just felt or even observed, but *enacted* via the constellation of machine and human, voice and vibration. Importantly, the invitation to proximity is not about talking to strangers, or being in the same room as another. It is not a physical proximity. It is about risking "contamination" (109) or implication through the blurred lines of us, them, me, her, our voices, and their voices. As Barad puts it, "Not only subjects, but also objects are permeated through and through with their entangled kin; the other is not just in one's skin, but in one's bones, in one's belly, in one's heart, in one's nucleus, in one's past and future" (393). In this sense, we are not responsible to know the other, but we are responsible to know and experience our entanglements. Such a proximal transformation is certainly possible through the act of reception,[8] and we are invested in using our practice to move audiences toward such sensual experiences, reimagined lines of relations, and new forms of attachment. However, our primary interest lies in the extent to which our own experience composing with voices—and being composed by them—represents a particularly "intensified" or "heightened" (Wysocki 109) form of affective encounter, which may outstretch the experience available to an outside audience.

One of the fundamental differences between our own experience of these projects and the experience of a potential audience relates to the temporality of the encounter. A typical listener who approaches our work from the outside is unlikely to spend more time with these voices than the total running time of the pieces themselves and, given the present economy of attention, likely far less than that. Perhaps the most eager audience will return for a second listen. Yet, for the most part, the experience that such projects invite is brief, delimited, and singular. In comparison to the hours and weeks and months we spent with the voices that make up these projects—well, there is no comparison. This is not to say that an audience will not experience some form of intense, fleeting intimacy with the voices of James and Josiah and Juanita. However, there is a palpable difference between the kind of bond that develops over short, singular encounters between speakers and audiences and the kind that grows from more substantial investments of time, energy, and collective labor.

We do not mean to suggest that the connection between ethics and perception boils down to a simple question of duration: listen to someone's voice for long enough and you will feel your connection to them. Rather, as Wysocki argues, "our senses are trained through repetition" (104). With this repetition in mind, perhaps there is something in not only the time we spent listening to these voices but also the way that listening unfolded—namely, the highly repetitious practice of listening and re-listening required by the compositional process. Perhaps such repetition enabled us to listen to these voices beyond the depth of the words and meanings they conveyed, to more closely attune ourselves to the surface-level vibrations of the voices themselves—vibrations that are, in the end, *not* people at all but rather paradoxical performances of personhood that bring together a fuller range of relations between human and machine, past and present, living and dead. And if we are ultimately seeking to open empathy to complex interrelationships with the many "other-than-human" entities that comprise Barad's posthuman ethics, then perhaps our creative engagement with these materials offers a means to experience those interrelationships through conditioned sensory practice.

Furthermore, in making these projects, we were called to not simply listen to these voices through repeated, durational practice, but also respond in an act of "reciprocal invocation" (Cavarero 208). While the audience is invited to experience the "intimacy and intensity" (Neumark 95) of these voices, the works themselves do not, in any explicit way, prompt them to enter into the conversation. Of course, one might reasonably argue that such a reply would be inconsequential, since there is no conscious being on the other end to receive their response. At the same time, if we take seriously Wysocki's argument that we must "learn to be bodies that somehow perceive not alone but socially" (107), then perhaps this act of reciprocal sociality—this act of response—*does* matter, in every sense of the term. Built into the methods of our practice is a requirement that we not only listen but also speak back—figuratively, but also materially and performatively, as we work to reprocess the voices of others through our own bodies and enter into mutual conversation with the voices of the living and the dead. This auto-affective sensation of feeling ourselves listen, and then feeling ourselves respond, suggests a powerful perceptual anchor for the kinds of empathic relations our practice enables. And while such ethical-aesthetic encounters do not require vocal performance, we are interested in further considering this embodied responsivity and its role in creative-critical practice. In the end, voice is only one of the many possible materials with which we might undertake this work. Ultimately, we are interested in how digital media—in their complex material entanglements with humans and machines, with selves and others, with "the living, dead, and not-yet-born" (Stanyek and Piekut 34)—might provide us with a powerful opportunity to both ground and expand our sense of "we" to account for a fuller range of ethical relations.

This challenge is, or should be, at the heart of our work as digital humanists. Yet it is not a challenge that we are likely to address by standing back and looking at the world from a distance. Rather, it calls us to surrender our incessant drive for meaning, mastery, and control. Most important, it asks us to slow down, to lean in, to attune ourselves to our interconnectedness with others and with the felt—and even the not-yet-felt—material world. This is where we end. And where we begin.

## NOTES

1. A note on human subject methodology: James, his real name, gave a recorded and public confession to his murders. With permission from him and his family, I edited and experimented with that confession. I also sought out James's niece for an interview. I have omitted last names to retain the privacy of the family. While Institutional Review Board (IRB) approval was obtained for my larger project, and family permission was obtained for this experimental piece, I do not circulate the project here or anywhere because of my own ethical quandaries about using James's voice or his niece's as an object. However, I think the piece, the experiments within it, and the ethics around it are all productive for our own digital humanities practices.

2. For more on distributed agency and the question of blame, see Bennett.

3. See Miller. Digital production is "all about reprocessing the world around you" (29).

4. See Daniel, "Is it art or is it social work?" (177). For Daniel, the answer is always "both."

5. See Levinas, *Otherwise*: "Proximity, difference which is non-indifference, is responsibility" (139).

6. See Anderson, where I have written about the ethics of this project in greater detail, reconsidering notions of cultural appropriation from a new materialist perspective.

7. For Jacques Derrida's seminal critique of phonocentrism and vocal metaphysics, see *Speech and Phenomena*.

8. Conventional thinking on empathy suggests that it can be felt through transference from film to viewer, writer to reader. See Landsberg, *Prosthetic Memory*, for more on this.

## BIBLIOGRAPHY

Anderson, Erin R. *Our Time Is Up*. https://soundcloud.com/the-sarah-awards/our-time-is-up-by-erin-anderson.

———. "Reanimating the Archive: Collaboration and Performance with the Voices of the Dead." *Reconstruction: Studies in Contemporary Culture* 16, no. 1 (2016).

Barad, Karen. *Meeting the Universe Halfway*. Durham, N.C.: Duke University Press, 2007.

Bennett, Jane. "The Agency of Assemblages and the North American Blackout." *Public Culture* 17, no. 3, (2005): 445–66.

Bianco, Jamie "Skye." "This Digital Humanities Which Is Not One." In *Debates in the Digital Humanities*, ed. Matthew K. Gold, 96–112. Minneapolis: University of Minnesota Press, 2012.

Black, Joel. "Murder: The State of the Art." *American Literary History* 12, no. 4, (2000): 780–93.

Campbell, Trisha N. *The Murder Networks.* http://www.digitaltrishacampbell.com/josephinemiles.html.

Cavarero, Adriana. *For More Than One Voice: Toward a Philosophy of Vocal Expression.* Stanford, Calif.: Stanford University Press, 2005.

Cole, Natalie. "Unforgettable (duet with Nat King Cole)." On *Unforgettable . . . with Love.* Elektra Records, 1991.

Daniel, Sharon. "The Database: An Aesthetics of Dignity." In *Database Aesthetics: Art in the Age of Information Overflow,* ed. Victoria Vesna, 142–82. Minneapolis: University of Minnesota Press, 2007.

Derrida, Jacques. *Speech and Phenomena, and Other Essays on Husserl's Theory of Signs.* Translated by David B. Allison. Evanston, Ill.: Northwestern University Press, 1973.

Greg, Melissa, and Gregory J. Seigworth. "An Inventory of Shimmers." In *The Affect Theory Reader,* ed. Melissa Gregg and Gregory J. Seigworth, 1–25. Durham, N.C.: Duke University Press, 2010.

Halpern, Jodi. *From Detached Concern to Empathy: Humanizing Medical Practice.* Oxford: Oxford University Press, 2001.

Halttunen, Karen. *Murder Most Foul: The Killer and the American Gothic Imagination.* Cambridge, Mass.: Harvard University Press, 1998.

Landsberg, Alison. "Memory, Empathy, and the Politics of Identification." *International Journal of Politics, Culture, and Society* 22, no. 2 (June 2009): 221–29.

———. *Prosthetic Memory.* New York: Columbia University Press, 2004.

Latour, Bruno. "An Attempt at a 'Compositionist Manifesto.'" *New Literary History* 41 (2010): 471–90.

Levinas, Emmanuel. *Otherwise than Being or Beyond Essence.* Translated by Alphonso Lingis. Boston, Mass.: Martinus Nijhoff Publishers, 1981.

———. *Time and the Other.* Translated by Richard A. Cohen. Pittsburgh, Pa.: Duquesne University Press, 1987.

Miller, Paul D. *Rhythm Science.* Cambridge, Mass.: MIT Press, 2004.

Neumark, Norie. "Doing Things with Voice: Performativity and Voice." In *Voice: Vocal Aesthetics in Digital Arts and Media,* ed. Norie Neumark, Ross Gibson, and Theo van Leeuwen, 95–118. Cambridge, Mass.: MIT Press, 2010.

Stanyek, Jason, and Benjamin Piekut. "Deadness: Technologies of the Intermundane." *The Drama Review* 54, no. 1 (2010): 14–38.

Wysocki, Anne Frances. "Unfitting Beauties of Transducing Bodies." In *Rhetorics and Technologies: New Directions in Writing and Communication,* ed. Stuart A. Selber, 94–112. Columbia: University of South Carolina Press, 2010.

# *Acknowledgments*

As editor of this volume, I acknowledge with respect that I live and work on the traditional territories of the Songhees, Esquimalt, and WSÁNEĆ peoples, whose historical relationships with the land continue to this day.

Thanks and love to Brooken, Beckett, and Willem for all of the hugs and support along the way. Thanks as well to each of the volume's contributors, who were a positive force and also very patient with me.

Nadia Timperio (research assistant with the MLab at UVic) worked with me to prepare this volume and facilitate peer-to-peer review in 2015–16. David Goehring copyedited the volume in 2017, and Allison Murphy (research assistant with the Department of English at UVic) proofread it with me. Alex Gil, Matthew K. Gold, and Lauren F. Klein gave valuable feedback on the proposal and manuscript, and all of the contributors went above and beyond during review and revision. Initial research for this volume was supported by the Social Sciences and Humanities Research Council of Canada (SSHRC) and the Canada Foundation for Innovation (CFI) as well as the Departments of English and Visual Arts at UVic. Eternal thanks to Kari Kraus, William J. Turkel, and Kathy Woodward for their advice early on, and to Carrie Bodle, Axel Roesler, and Phillip Thurtle for teaching with me during the University of Washington's 2008 Summer Institute in the Arts and Humanities, which inspired this volume. Of course, *Making Things and Drawing Boundaries* would not have been possible without two amazing teams: Douglas Armato, Anne Carter, Danielle M. Kasprzak, Daniel Ochsner, Kenneth Wee, and everyone at the University of Minnesota Press; and Susan Baker, Melody Negron, Maura Neville, and the crew at Westchester Publishing Services.

## *Contributors*

**ERIN R. ANDERSON** is assistant professor in the writing program at the University of Pittsburgh.

**JOANNE BERNARDI** is professor of Japanese and film and media studies at the University of Rochester.

**YANA BOEVA** is a PhD candidate in science and technology studies at York University.

**JEREMY BOGGS** is design architect for the Scholars' Lab at the University of Virginia Library.

**DUNCAN A. BUELL** is professor and holder of the NCR Chair in the Department of Computer Science and Engineering at the University of South Carolina.

**AMY BUREK** is a scientist and artist based in the San Francisco Bay Area.

**TRISHA N. CAMPBELL** is assistant professor in the writing and rhetoric track at Salisbury University.

**DEBBIE CHACHRA** is professor of engineering at Olin College of Engineering.

**BETH COMPTON** is a PhD student at the University of Western Ontario.

**HEIDI RAE COOLEY** is associate professor of media arts in the School of Visual Art and Design and Film and Media Studies Program at the University of South Carolina.

**NORA DIMMOCK** is associate university librarian for digital technologies at Brown University Library.

**DEVON ELLIOTT** is a PhD student in history at the University of Western Ontario.

**BILL ENDRES** is assistant professor of English and rhetoric at the University of Oklahoma.

**KATHERINE FAULL** is professor of German and humanities at Bucknell University.

**ALEXANDER FLAMENCO** teaches literature in Quebec's Cegep system.

**EMILY ALDEN FOSTER** is an artist and librarian in Oakland, California.

**SARAH FOX** is a PhD candidate in the Department of Human Centered Design and Engineering at the University of Washington.

**CHELSEA A. M. GARDNER** is a PhD candidate in classical archaeology at the University of British Columbia and a project manager for *From Stone to Screen*.

**SUSAN GARFINKEL** is a research specialist at the Library of Congress.

**LEE HANNIGAN** is a PhD student in English and film studies at the University of Alberta.

**SARA HENDREN** is assistant professor of design and director of the Adaptation + Ability Group at Olin College.

RYAN HUNT is an education coordinator at the London Heritage Council.

JOHN HUNTER is associate professor of comparative humanities at Bucknell University.

DIANE JAKACKI is digital scholarship coordinator and faculty teaching associate in comparative humanities at Bucknell University.

JANELLE JENSTAD is associate professor of English at the University of Victoria, director of *The Map of Early Modern London*, and associate coordinating editor of the *Internet Shakespeare Editions*.

EDWARD JONES-IMHOTEP is associate professor of the history of technology at York University.

JULIE THOMPSON KLEIN is professor of humanities emerita in the English department and former Faculty Fellow for Interdisciplinary Development in the Division of Research at Wayne State University.

AARON D. KNOCHEL is assistant professor of art education and embedded researcher in the Art & Design Research Incubator at the Pennsylvania State University.

J. K. PURDOM LINDBLAD is assistant director of innovation and learning at the Maryland Institute for Technology in the Humanities.

KIM MARTIN is a Ridley Postdoctoral Fellow in Digital Humanities at the University of Guelph.

GWYNAETH MCINTYRE is a lecturer at the University of Otago and was formerly a faculty advisor for *From Stone to Screen*.

AURELIO MEZA is a PhD student in humanities at Concordia University in Montreal and a member of the Laboratory of Expanded Literature and Other Materialities in Mexico City.

SHEZAN MUHAMMEDI is a PhD student at the University of Western Ontario.

ANGEL DAVID NIEVES is associate professor and codirector of the Digital Humanities Initiative (DHi) at Hamilton College.

MARCEL O'GORMAN is professor of English and founding director of Critical Media Lab at the University of Waterloo.

AMY PAPAELIAS is assistant professor of graphic design at the State University of New York at New Paltz.

MATT RATTO is associate professor of information at the University of Toronto.

ISAAC RECORD is assistant professor of practice in Lyman Briggs College at Michigan State University.

JENNIFER REED is the Florence Levy Kay Fellow in Eighteenth-Century Studies at Brandeis University.

GABBY RESCH is a PhD candidate in information at the University of Toronto.

JENNIFER ROBERTS-SMITH is associate professor in theatre and performance at the University of Waterloo.

MELISSA ROGERS is a doctoral candidate in women's studies at the University of Maryland and a teaching artist in the MAKESHOP at the Children's Museum of Pittsburgh.

**DANIELA K. ROSNER** is assistant professor in the Department of Human Centered Design and Engineering at the University of Washington.

**STAN RUECKER** is Anthony Petullo Professor of Design at the University of Illinois Urbana-Champaign.

**JENTERY SAYERS** is associate professor of English at the University of Victoria.

**ROXANNE SHIRAZI** is assistant professor and dissertation research librarian at the Graduate Center, CUNY, and a founding coeditor of *dh+lib*.

**JAMES SMITHIES** is director of King's Digital Lab, King's College London.

**P. P. SNEHA** is a researcher with the Centre for Internet and Society, Bangalore, India.

**LISA M. SNYDER** is a research scholar with UCLA's Office of Information Technology and the Institute for Digital Research and Education.

**KAITLYN SOLBERG** is the media and communications director for *From Stone to Screen.*

**DAN SOUTHWICK** is a PhD candidate in information at the University of Toronto.

**DAVID STALEY** is associate professor of history and adjunct associate professor in the departments of design and educational studies at the Ohio State University.

**ELAINE SULLIVAN** is assistant professor of history at the University of California, Santa Cruz.

**JOSEPH TAKEDA** is an MA student in the Department of English at the University of British Columbia and was junior programmer for *The Map of Early Modern London.*

**EZRA TEBOUL** is a candidate for a PhD in electronic arts at Rensselaer Polytechnic Institute.

**WILLIAM J. TURKEL** is professor of history at the University of Western Ontario.

**LISA TWETEN** is a project manager for *From Stone to Screen.*